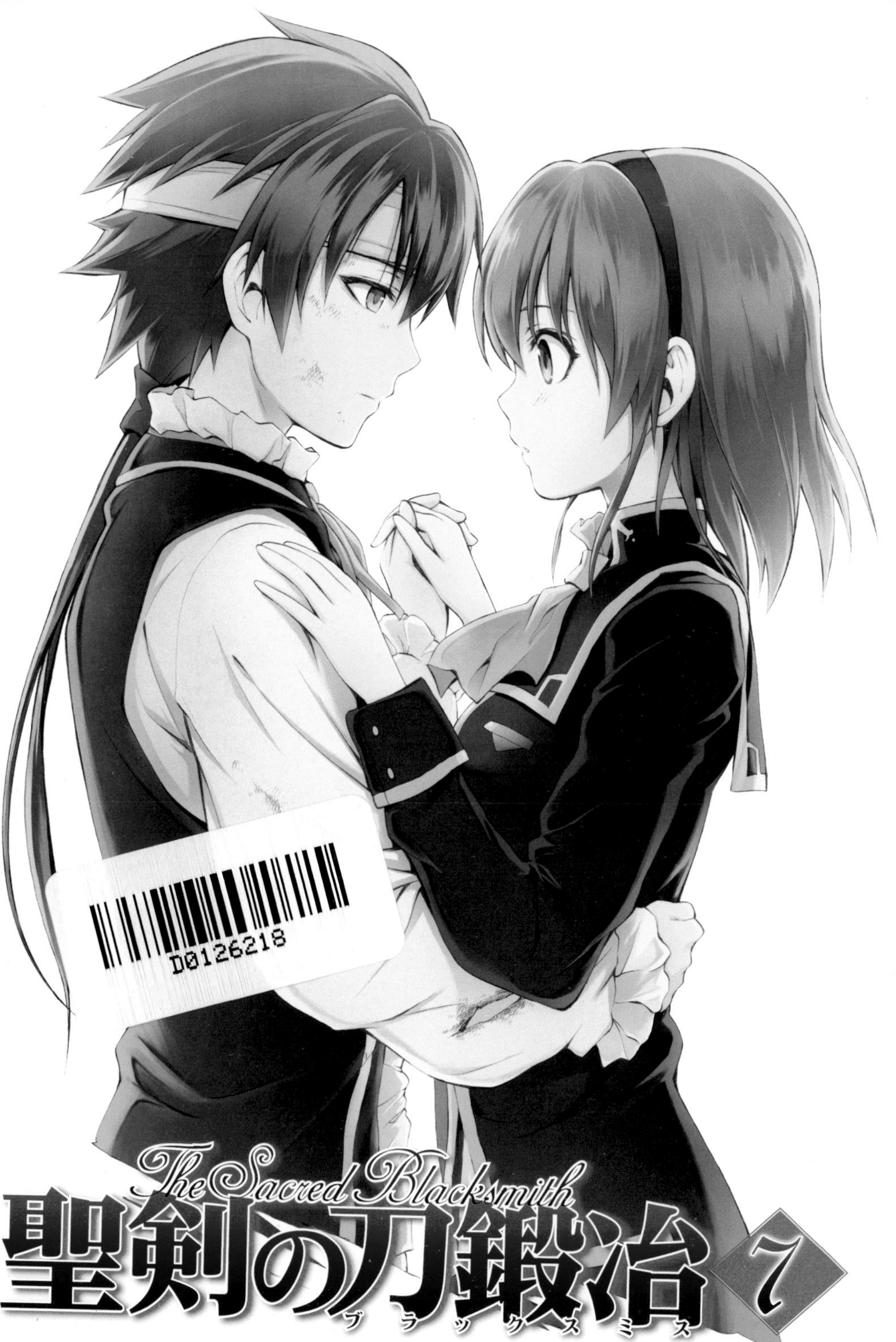

The Sacred Blacksmith
聖剣の刀鍛冶(ブラックスミス) 7

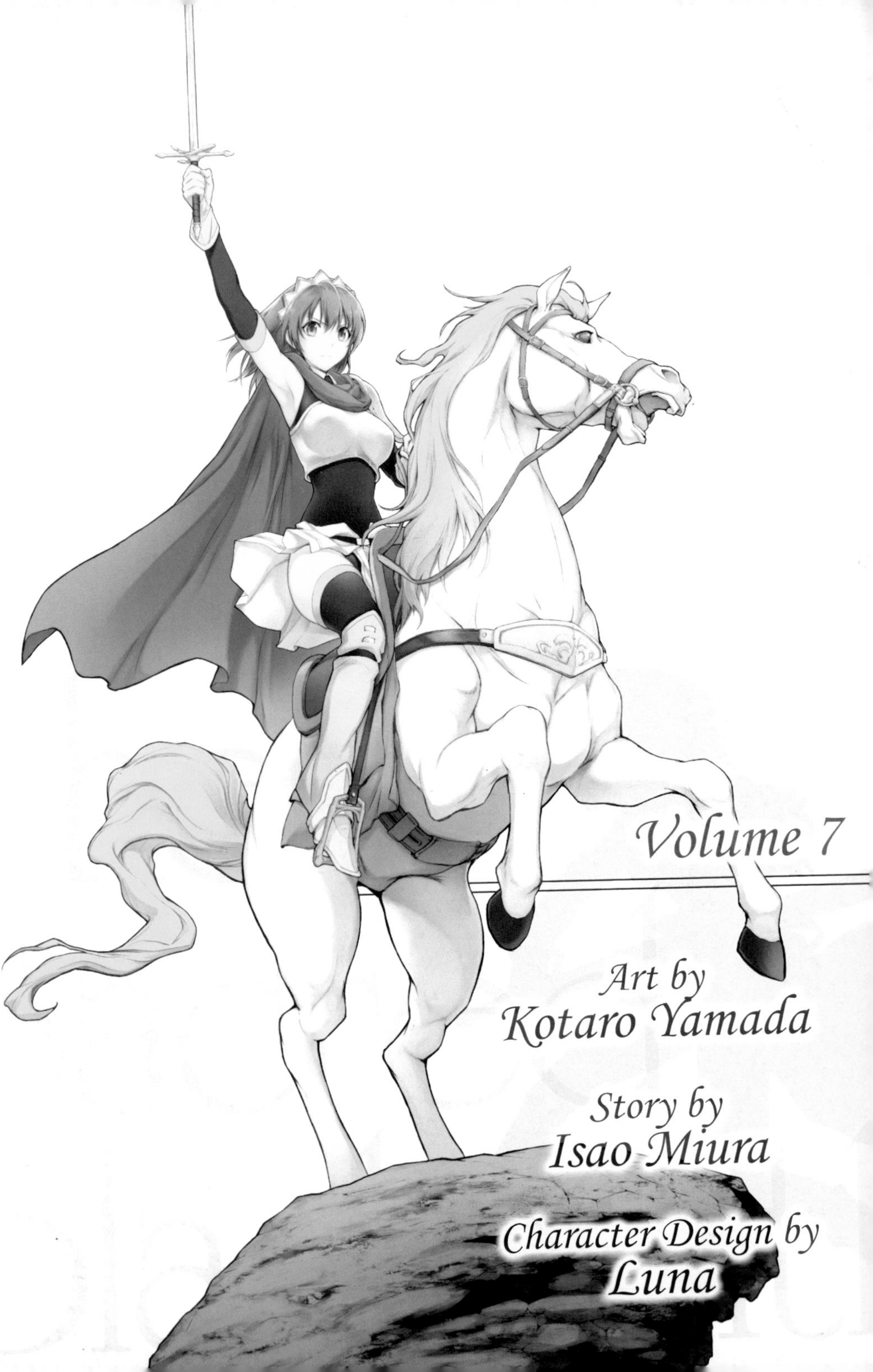

Volume 7

Art by
Kotaro Yamada

Story by
Isao Miura

Character Design by
Luna

登場人物紹介 Character

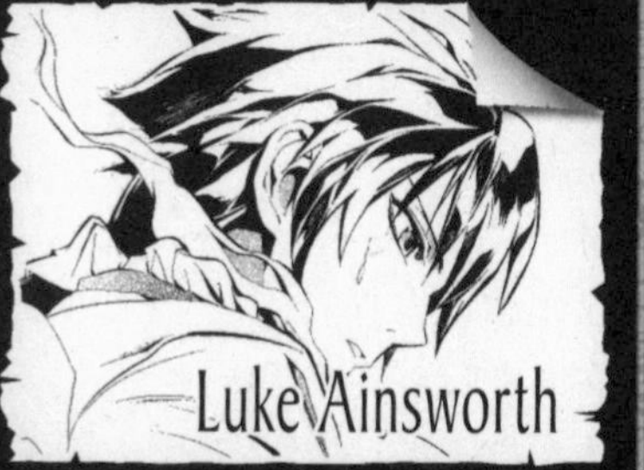

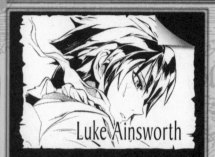

Luke Ainsworth

A proficient swordsman who uses an unusual blade called a "katana." Pessimistic and world-weary, he runs his own smithy.

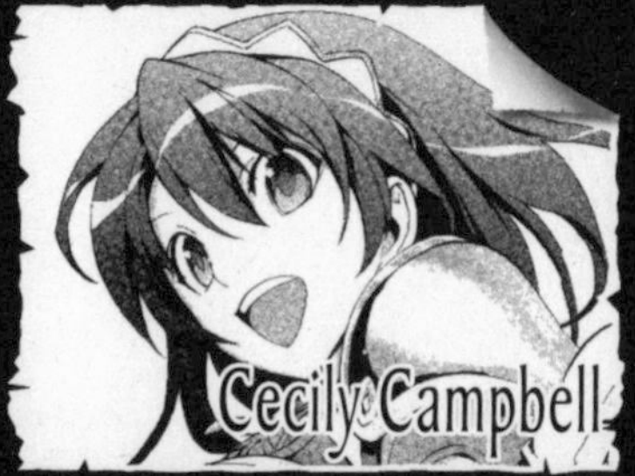

Cecily Campbell

A young lady knight who is part of the Knight Guard, charged with defending the independent trade city of Housman. Ex-nobility, she has a strong sense of justice.

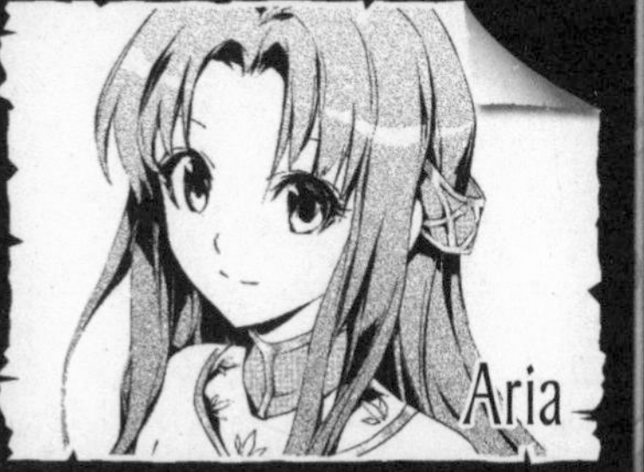

Aria

The "Demon Blade" of wind. A demon "born" at the end of the Valbanill War, she normally walks about as a human woman. However, she can turn into a rapier at will.

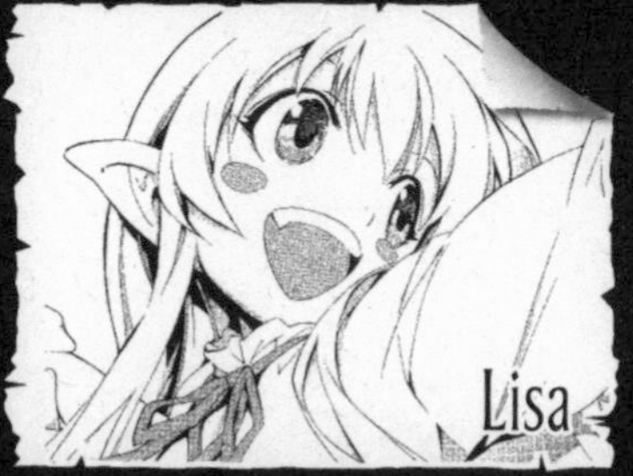

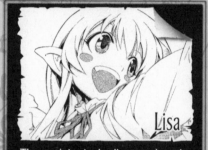

Lisa

The assistant who lives and works at Luke's smithy. Innocent and carefree, she loves talking with everyone. She says she is only three years old.

Other Characters

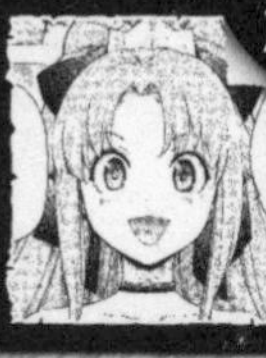

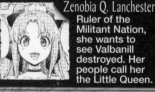

Zenobia Q. Lanchester

Ruler of the Militant Nation, she wants to see Valbanill destroyed. Her people call her the Little Queen.

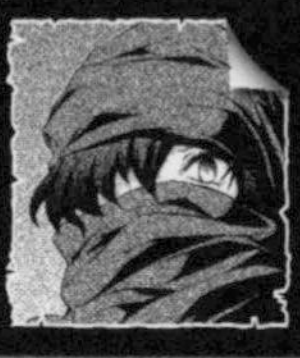

???

An assassin from the Crowd Powers, she tried and failed to kill Cecily. Cecily asked for her release.

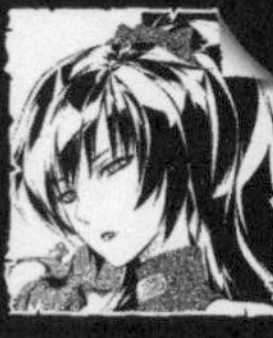

Evadne

A Demon Blade who can create black flame and turn into a flamberge. Belongs to Siegfried.

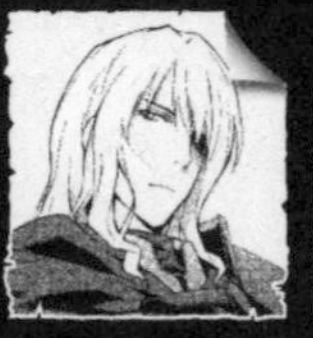

Siegfried

Knight Captain of the Empire. He uses Demon Pacts and keeps inhumans as pets.

Decades ago, a great war raged across the continent. Called the "Valbanill War," it saw the widespread use of powerful Demon Pacts. Forty-four years later, a young lady knight named Cecily Campbell meets a mysterious blacksmith named Luke Ainsworth, and asks him to forge for her a sword.

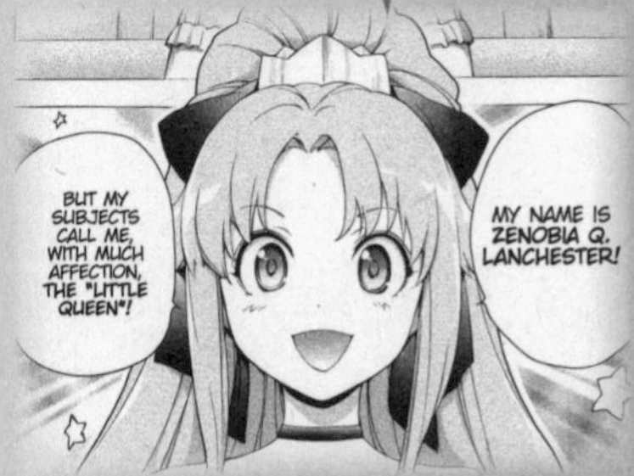
MY NAME IS ZENOBIA Q. LANCHESTER!
BUT MY SUBJECTS CALL ME, WITH MUCH AFFECTION, THE "LITTLE QUEEN"!

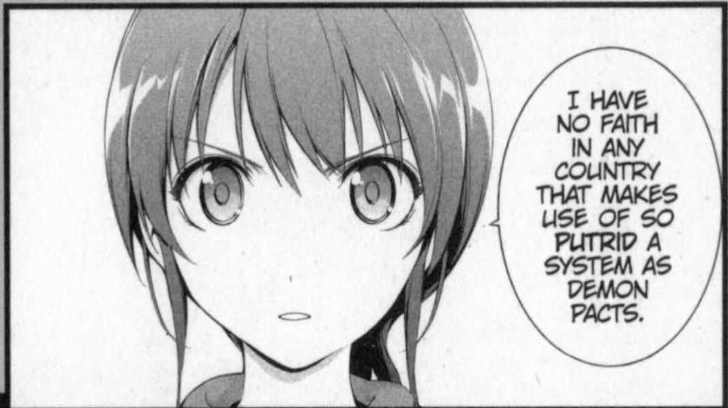
I HAVE NO FAITH IN ANY COUNTRY THAT MAKES USE OF SO PUTRID A SYSTEM AS DEMON PACTS.

In hope of perfecting the Sacred Blade, Cecily and the others traveled to the Militant Nation for an exchange of crafting techniques. During their journey, Cecily was attacked by an assassin from the Crowd Powers. Luke saved her in time, but the incident drove home to Cecily how much stronger she must become.

After arriving at the Militant Nation's capital, Cecily and Luke split up. Cecily found a warm reception from the "Little Queen" Zenobia, while Luke faced cold rejection from the master smith and his team. To make matters worse, Luke revealed to Lisa that he is steadily losing the sight in his one remaining eye, thanks to using Lisa's demon powers. But Luke refused to give up, and in the face of both Luke and Lisa's passionate pleas, the master smith relented and agreed to help Luke.

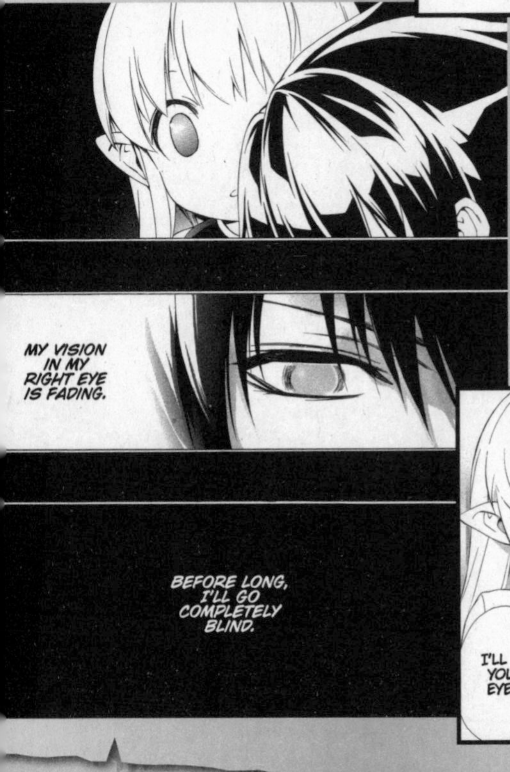
MY VISION IN MY RIGHT EYE IS FADING.
BEFORE LONG, I'LL GO COMPLETELY BLIND.

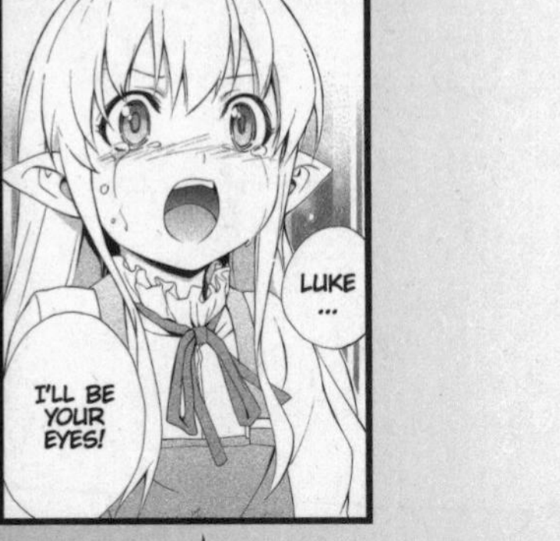
LUKE ...
I'LL BE YOUR EYES!

あらすじ Story

Talks between the two nations were proceeding smoothly until a messenger from the Empire suddenly arrived, declaring that the Empire and the Crowd Powers had merged. The resulting Imperial Crowd Power now controls over two-thirds of the continent. The messenger then proposed a minor "skirmish" to determine which nation would hold the rights to profit from the destruction of Valbanill.

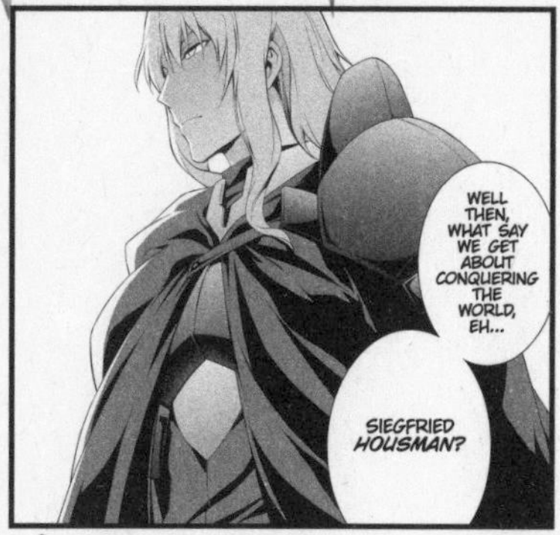

WELL THEN, WHAT SAY WE GET ABOUT CONQUERING THE WORLD, EH...
SIEGFRIED HOUSMAN?

The "skirmish" pitted the Militant Nation's elite anti-Valbanill units against Siegfried's inhuman weapons--and it was no contest. The inhumans tore through the Militant Nation's soldiers like a whirlwind, killing everyone they touched. However, Cecily and Aria--along with Luke wielding his latest Sacred Blade prototype--stepped in and turned the bloody battle into a stalemate.

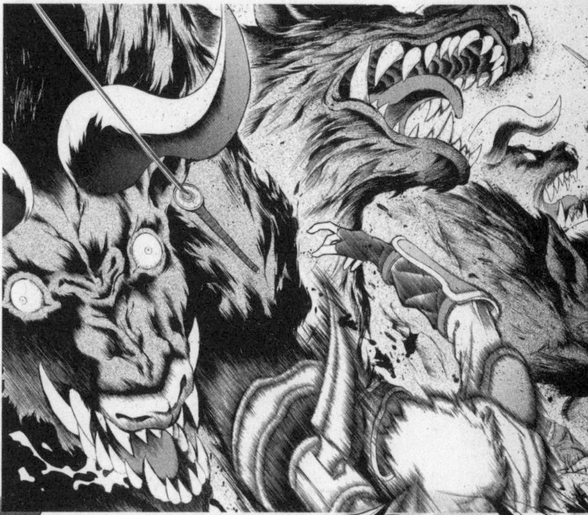

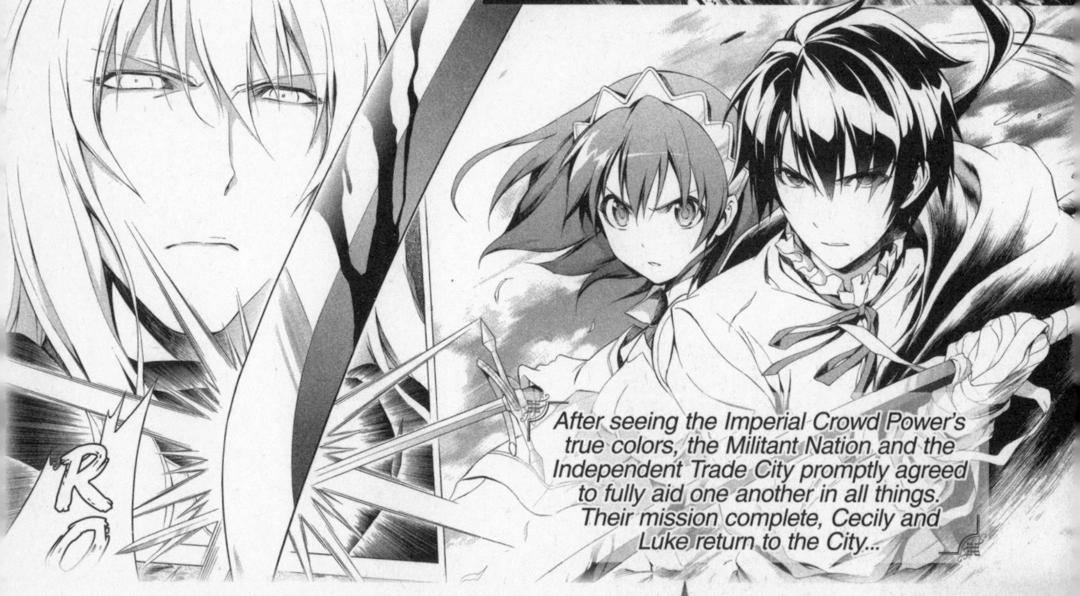

R
O

After seeing the Imperial Crowd Power's true colors, the Militant Nation and the Independent Trade City promptly agreed to fully aid one another in all things. Their mission complete, Cecily and Luke return to the City...

The Sacred Blacksmith

聖剣の刀鍛冶

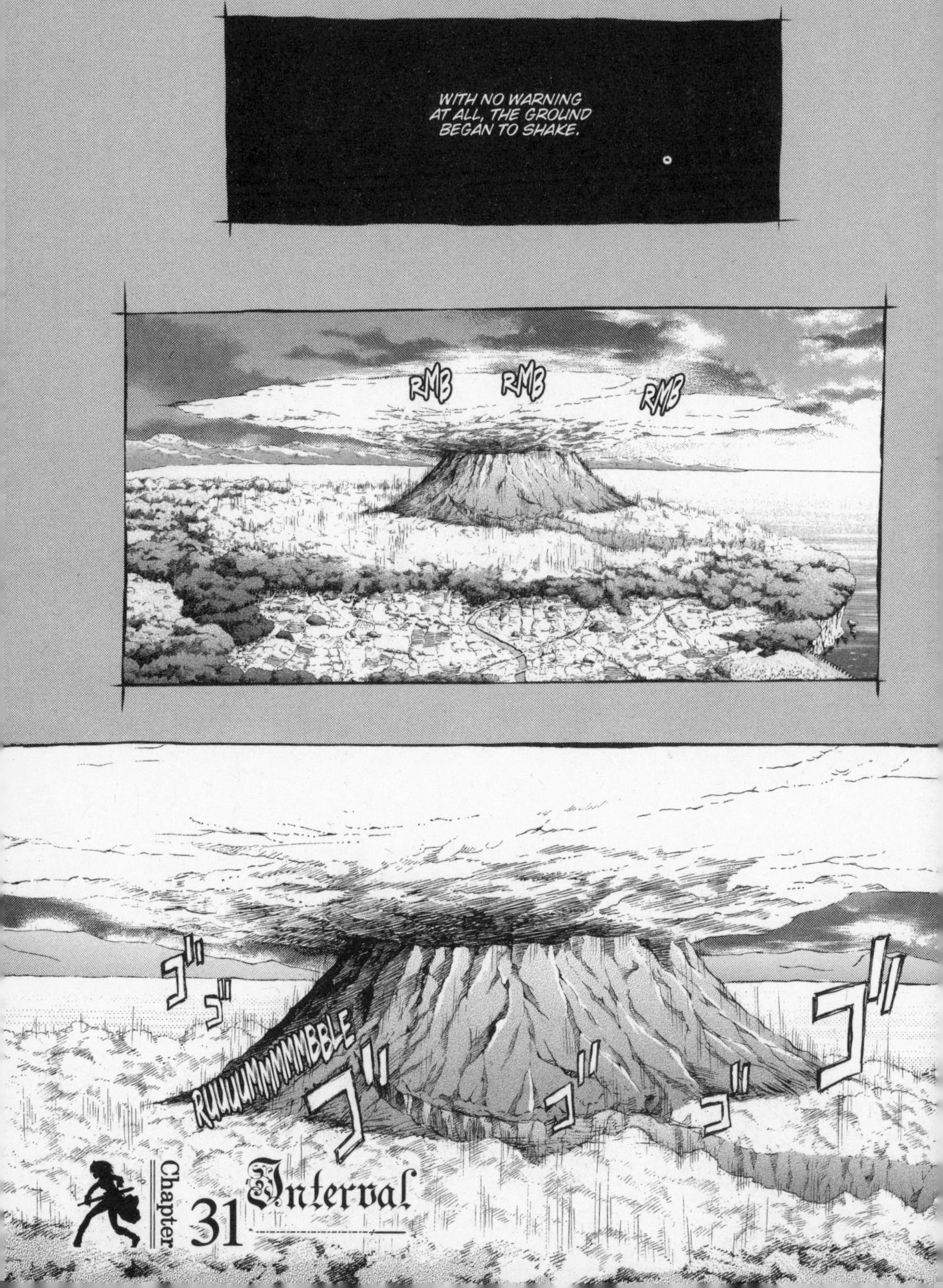
WITH NO WARNING AT ALL, THE GROUND BEGAN TO SHAKE.
RMB
RMB
RMB
ゴゴ
RUUUUMMMMMBBLE
ゴゴ
ゴゴ

Chapter 31 Interval

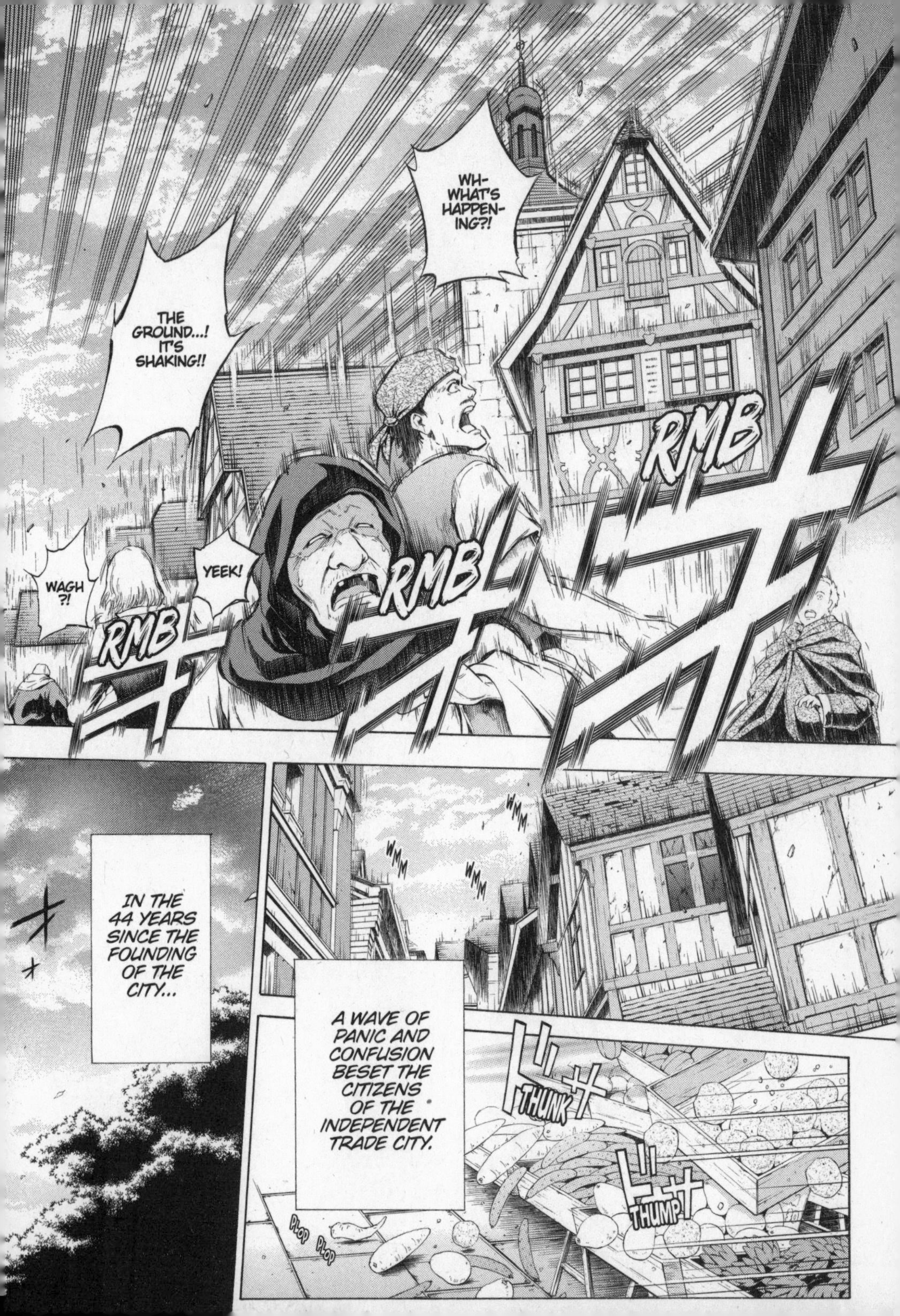
WH- WHAT'S HAPPEN- ING?!
RMB
THE GROUND...! IT'S SHAKING!!
RMB
YEEK!
WAGH ?!
RMB
WMM
WMM
WMM
IN THE 44 YEARS SINCE THE FOUNDING OF THE CITY...
A WAVE OF PANIC AND CONFUSION BESET THE CITIZENS OF THE INDEPENDENT TRADE CITY.
THUNK
THUMP
PLOP PLOP

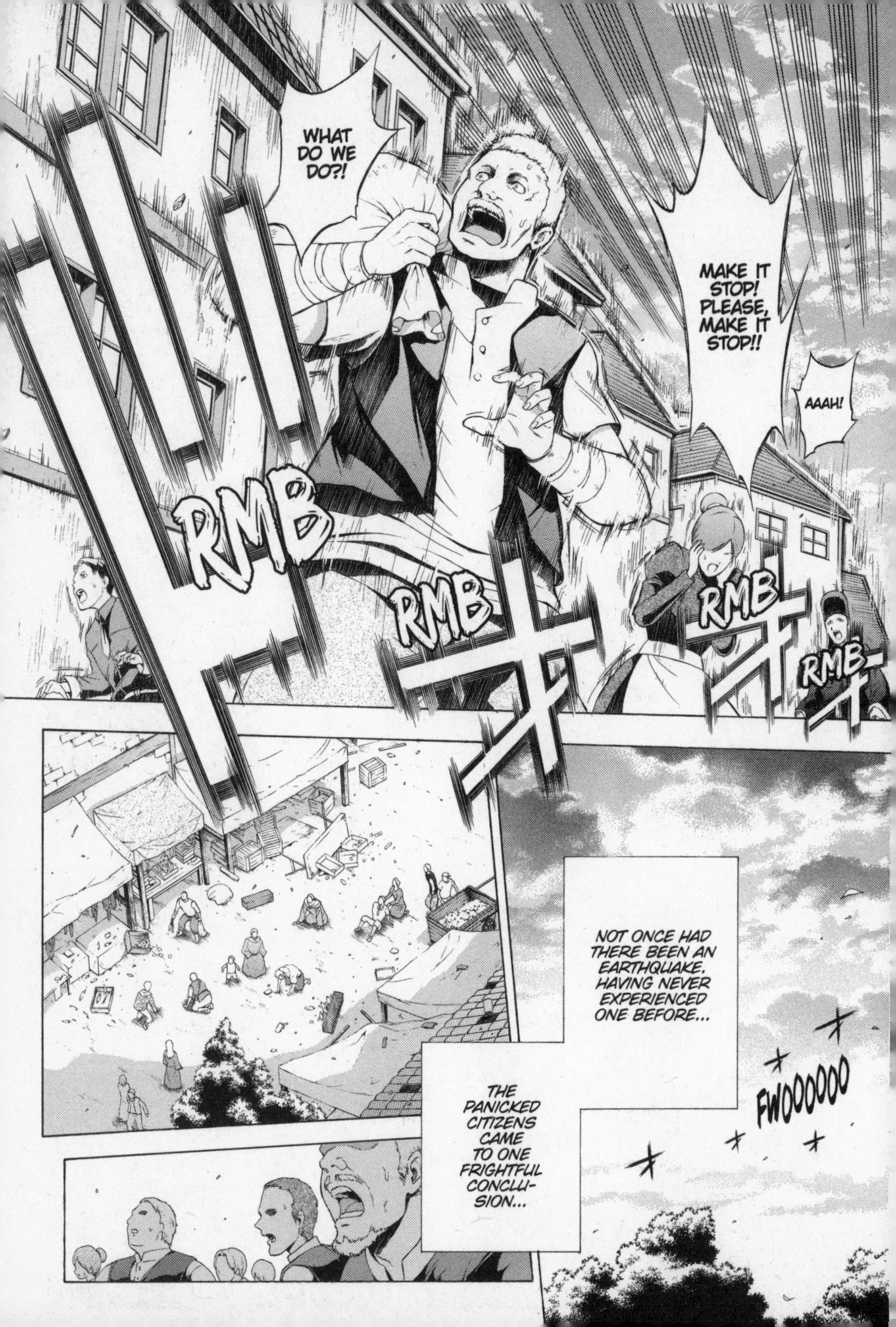
AAAH!
MAKE IT STOP! PLEASE, MAKE IT STOP!!
WHAT DO WE DO?!
RMB
RMB
RMB
RMB
NOT ONCE HAD THERE BEEN AN EARTHQUAKE. HAVING NEVER EXPERIENCED ONE BEFORE...
FWOOOOOO
THE PANICKED CITIZENS CAME TO ONE FRIGHTFUL CONCLUSION...

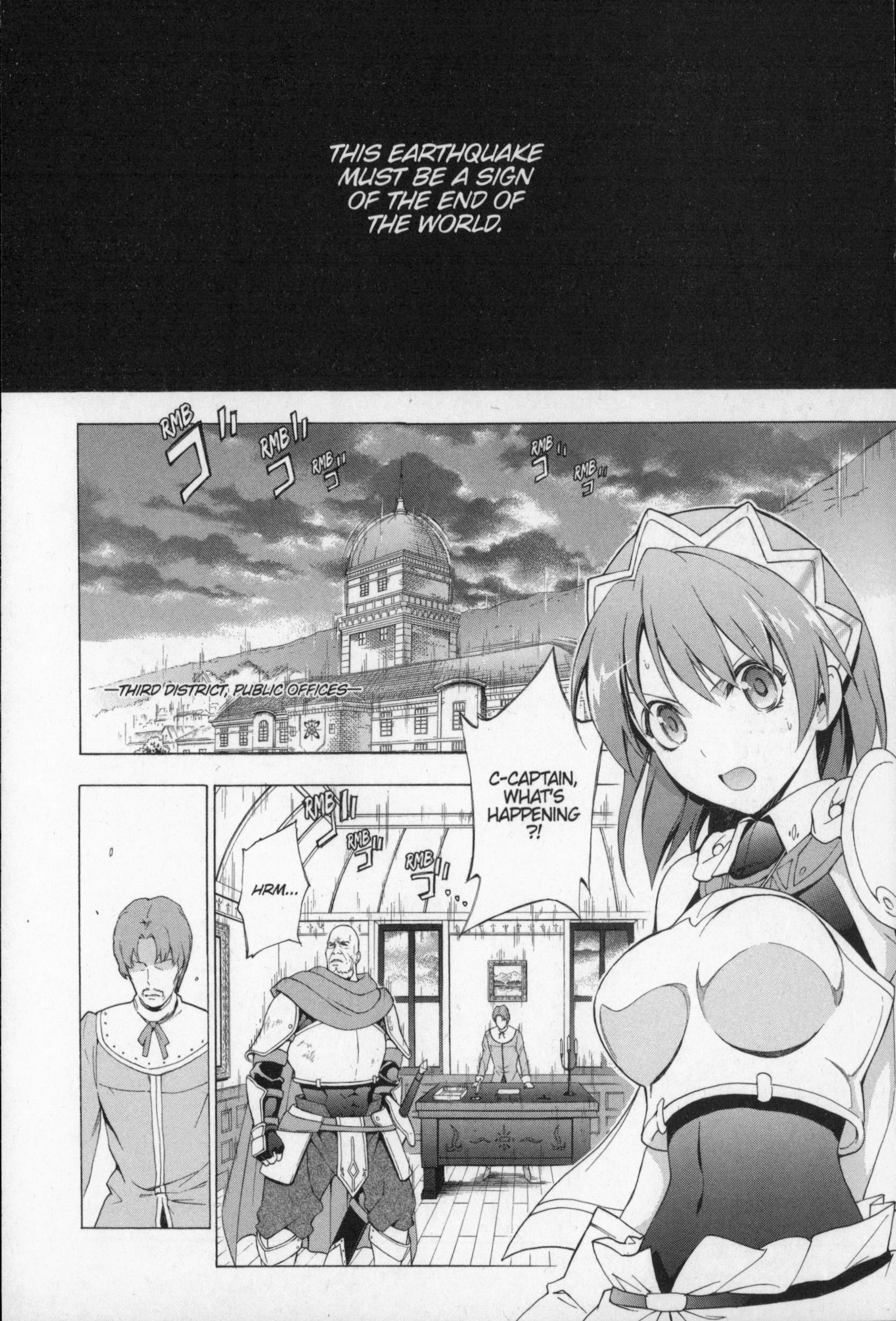
THIS EARTHQUAKE MUST BE A SIGN OF THE END OF THE WORLD.
RMB
RMB
RMB
RMB
RMB
—THIRD DISTRICT, PUBLIC OFFICES—
C-CAPTAIN, WHAT'S HAPPENING?!
RMB
RMB
RMB
HRM...

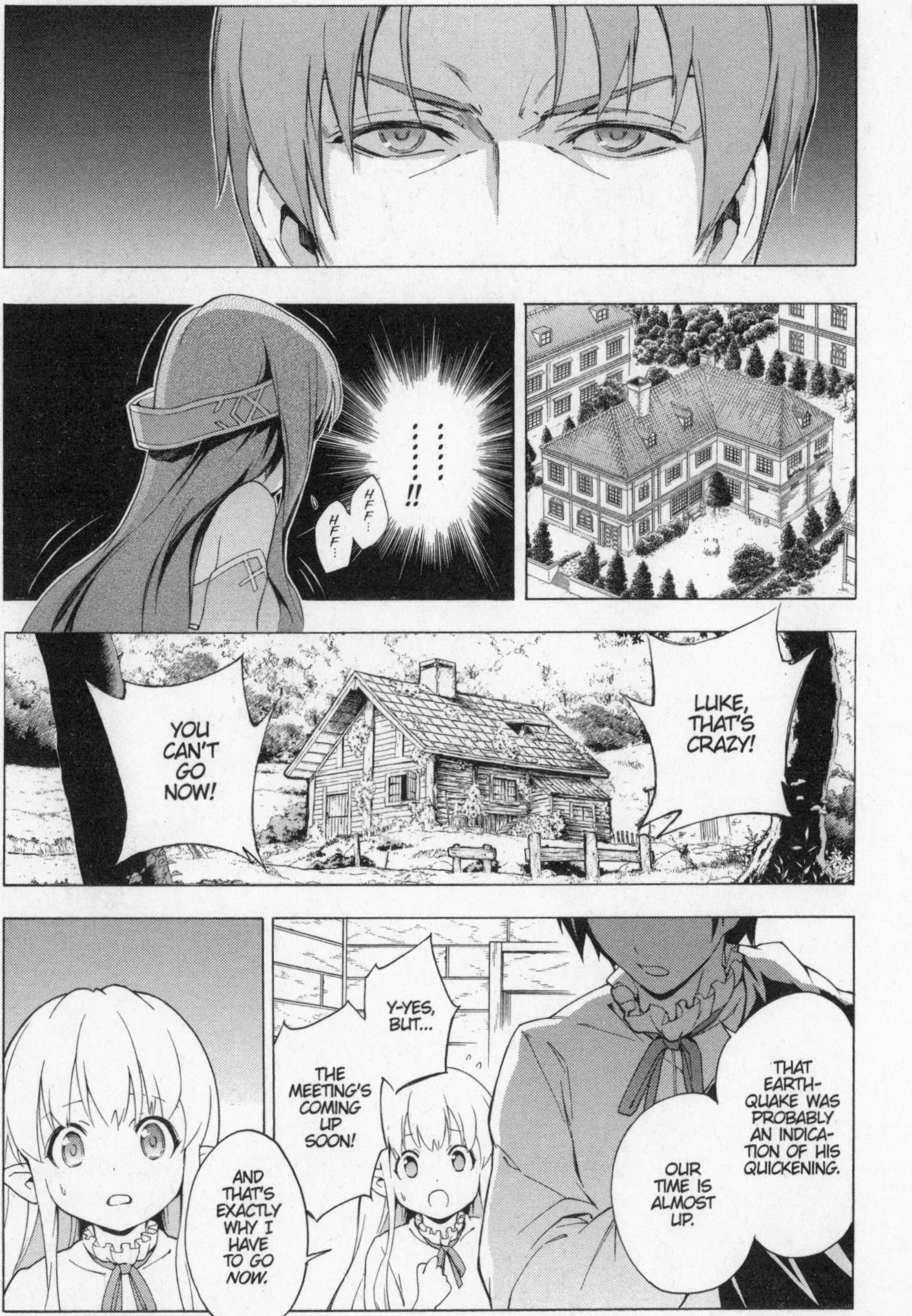
......!!
HFF... HFF...
LUKE, THAT'S CRAZY!
YOU CAN'T GO NOW!
THAT EARTH-QUAKE WAS PROBABLY AN INDICA-TION OF HIS QUICKENING.
OUR TIME IS ALMOST UP.
Y-YES, BUT...
THE MEETING'S COMING UP SOON!
AND THAT'S EXACTLY WHY I HAVE TO GO NOW.

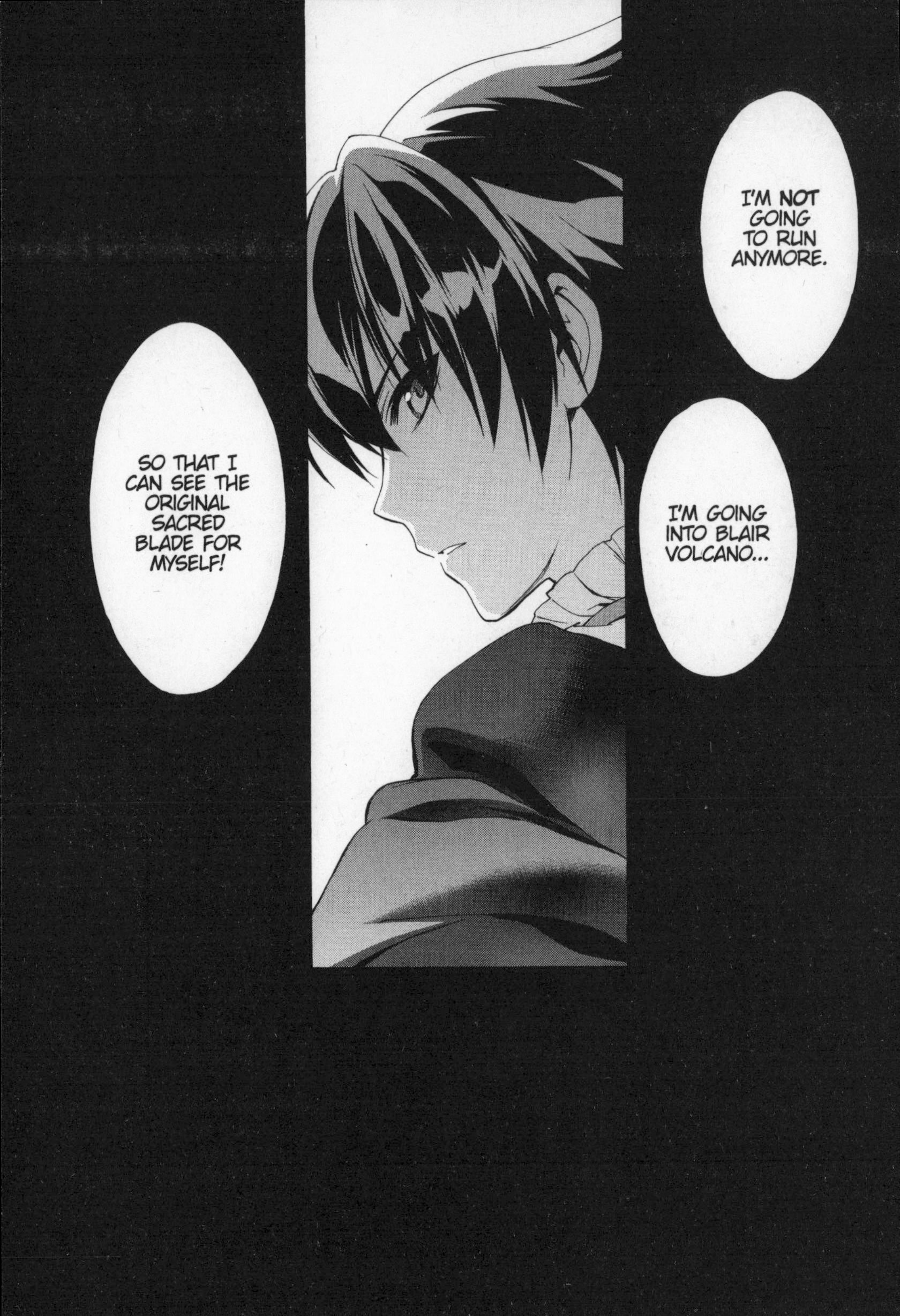
I'M NOT GOING TO RUN ANYMORE.
I'M GOING INTO BLAIR VOLCANO...
SO THAT I CAN SEE THE ORIGINAL SACRED BLADE FOR MYSELF!

Chapter 32 Sacrifice

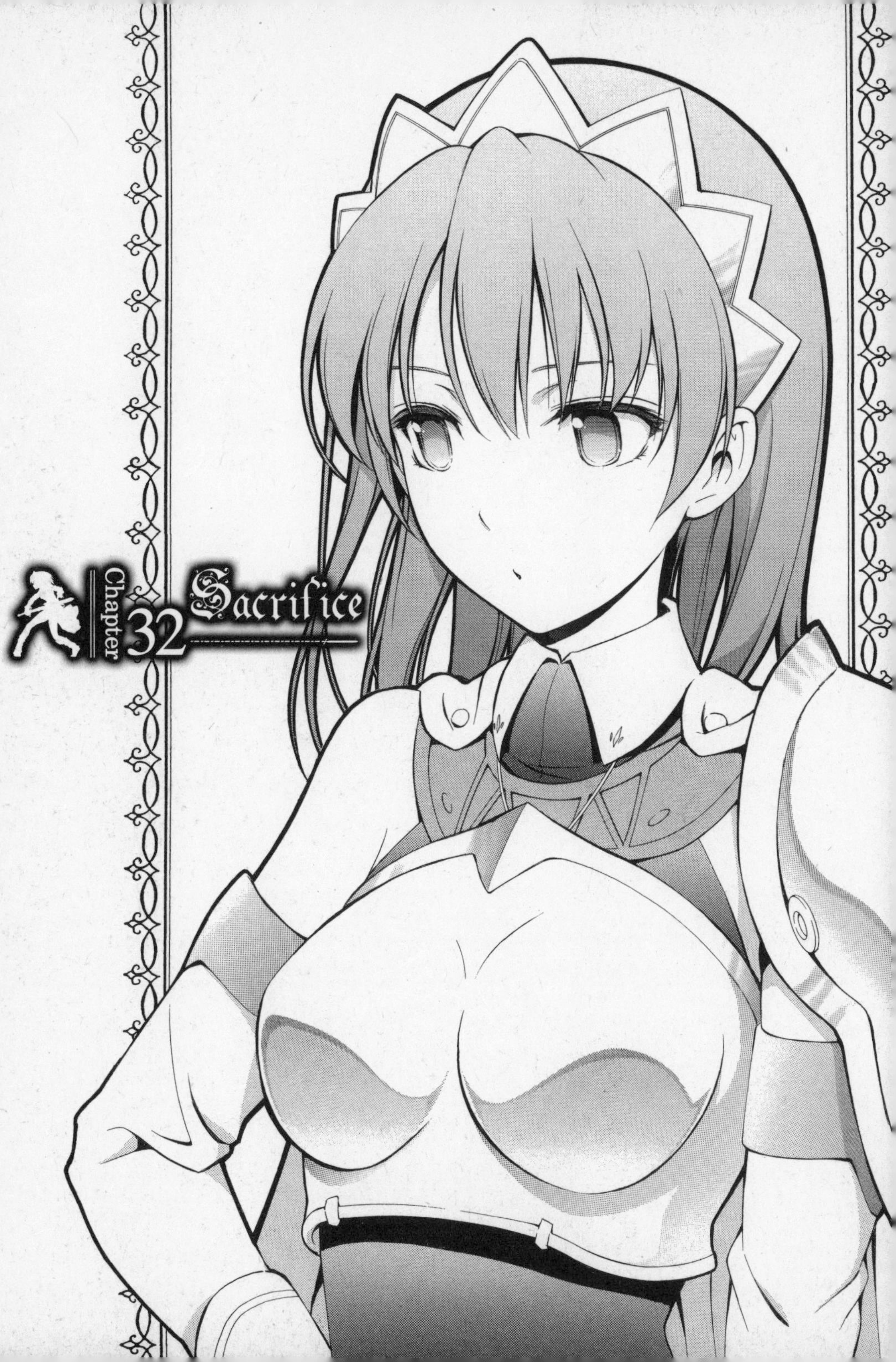

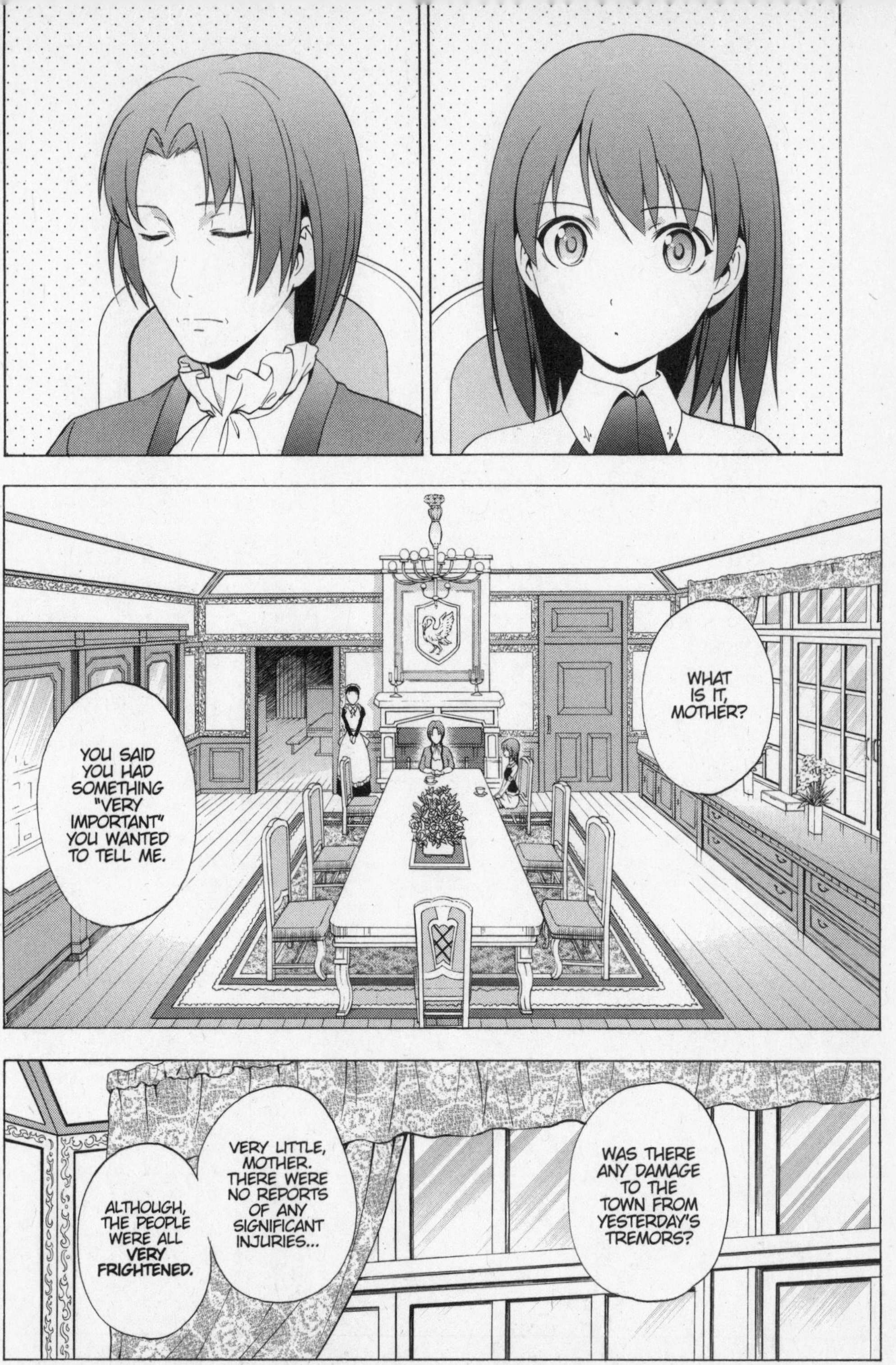
WHAT IS IT, MOTHER?
YOU SAID YOU HAD SOMETHING "VERY IMPORTANT" YOU WANTED TO TELL ME.
WAS THERE ANY DAMAGE TO THE TOWN FROM YESTERDAY'S TREMORS?
VERY LITTLE, MOTHER. THERE WERE NO REPORTS OF ANY SIGNIFICANT INJURIES...
ALTHOUGH, THE PEOPLE WERE ALL VERY FRIGHTENED.

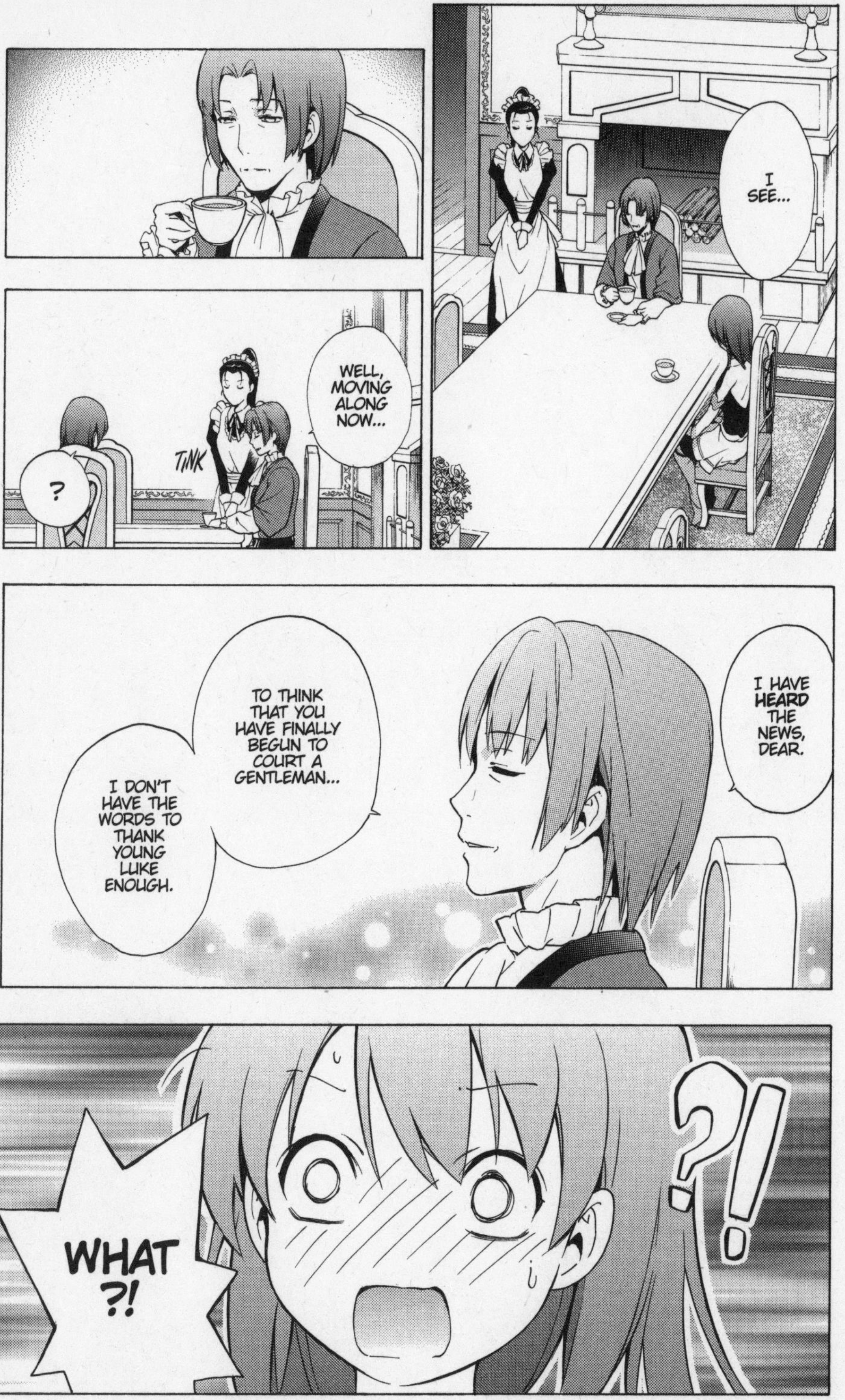
I SEE...
WELL, MOVING ALONG NOW...
TINK
?
I HAVE HEARD THE NEWS, DEAR.
TO THINK THAT YOU HAVE FINALLY BEGUN TO COURT A GENTLEMAN...
I DON'T HAVE THE WORDS TO THANK YOUNG LUKE ENOUGH.
?!
WHAT ?!

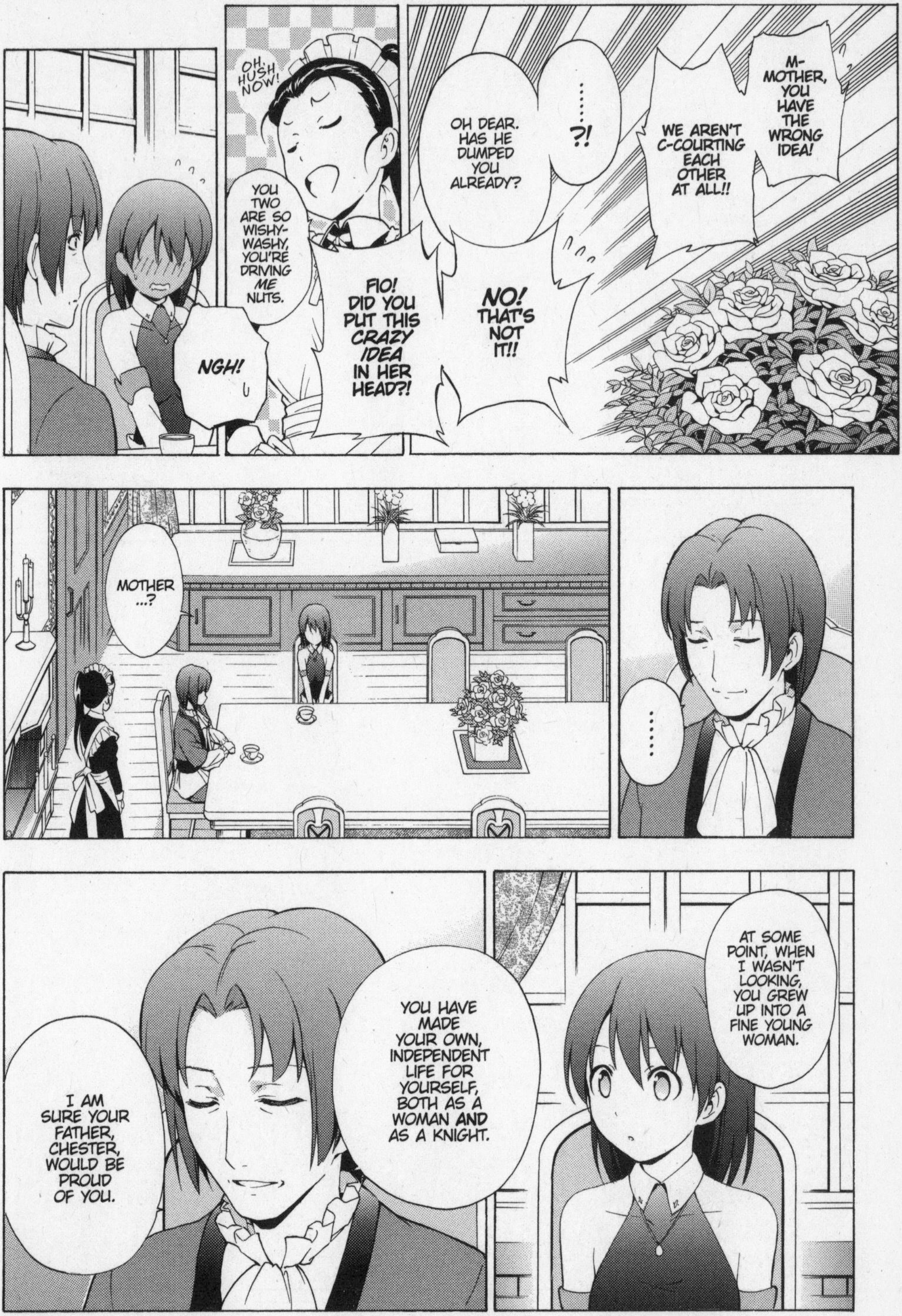
M-MOTHER, YOU HAVE THE WRONG IDEA!
WE AREN'T C-COURTING EACH OTHER AT ALL!!
......?!
OH DEAR. HAS HE DUMPED YOU ALREADY?
OH, HUSH NOW!
YOU TWO ARE SO WISHY-WASHY, YOU'RE DRIVING *ME* NUTS.
NO! THAT'S NOT IT!!
FIO! DID YOU PUT THIS ***CRAZY IDEA*** IN HER HEAD?!
NGH!
......
MOTHER ...?
AT SOME POINT, WHEN I WASN'T LOOKING, YOU GREW UP INTO A FINE YOUNG WOMAN.
YOU HAVE MADE YOUR OWN, INDEPENDENT LIFE FOR YOURSELF, BOTH AS A WOMAN **AND** AS A KNIGHT.
I AM SURE YOUR FATHER, CHESTER, WOULD BE PROUD OF YOU.

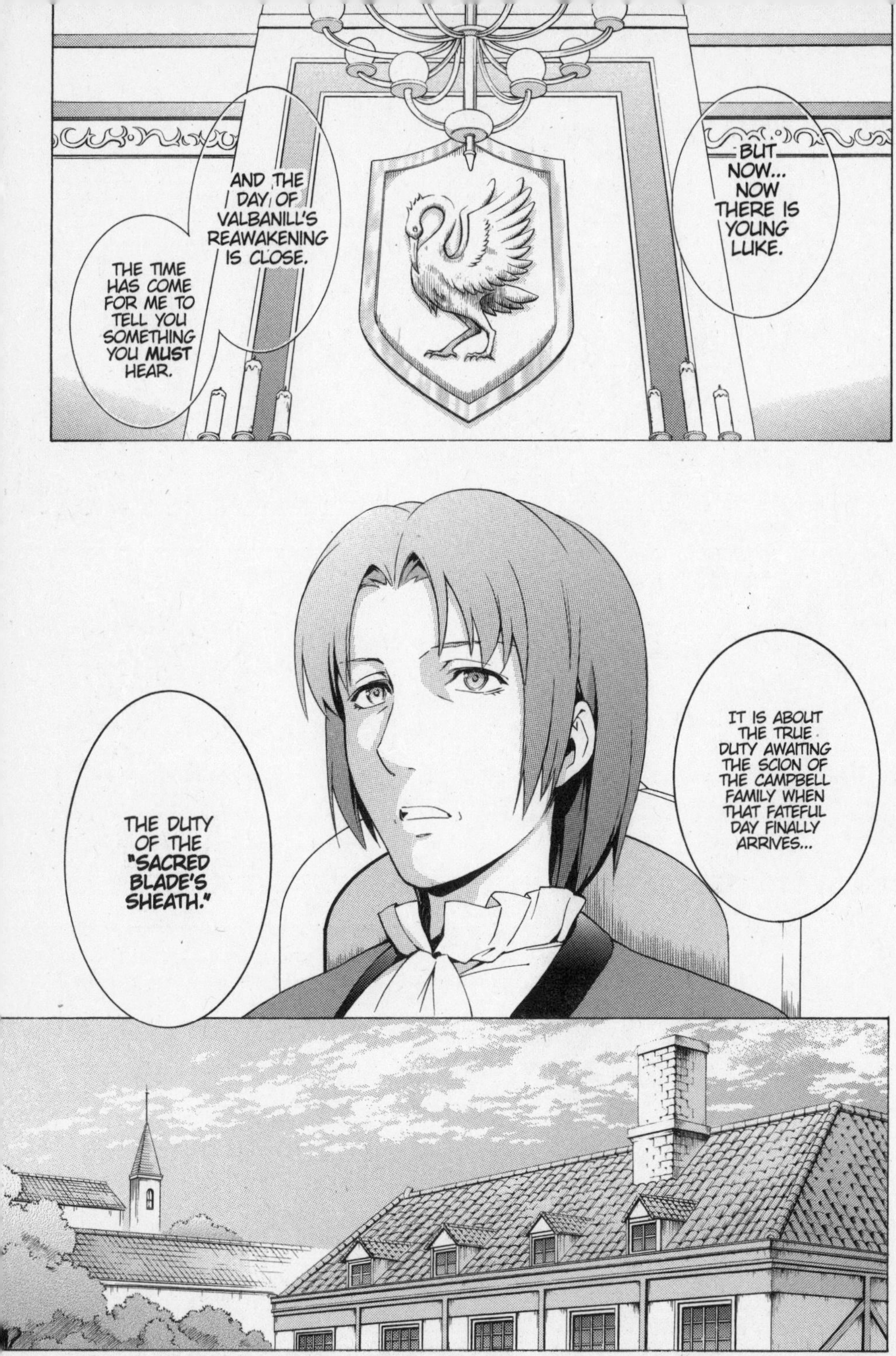
BUT NOW... NOW THERE IS YOUNG LUKE.
AND THE DAY OF VALBANILL'S REAWAKENING IS CLOSE.
THE TIME HAS COME FOR ME TO TELL YOU SOMETHING YOU **MUST** HEAR.
IT IS ABOUT THE TRUE DUTY AWAITING THE SCION OF THE CAMPBELL FAMILY WHEN THAT FATEFUL DAY FINALLY ARRIVES...
THE DUTY OF THE **"SACRED BLADE'S SHEATH."**

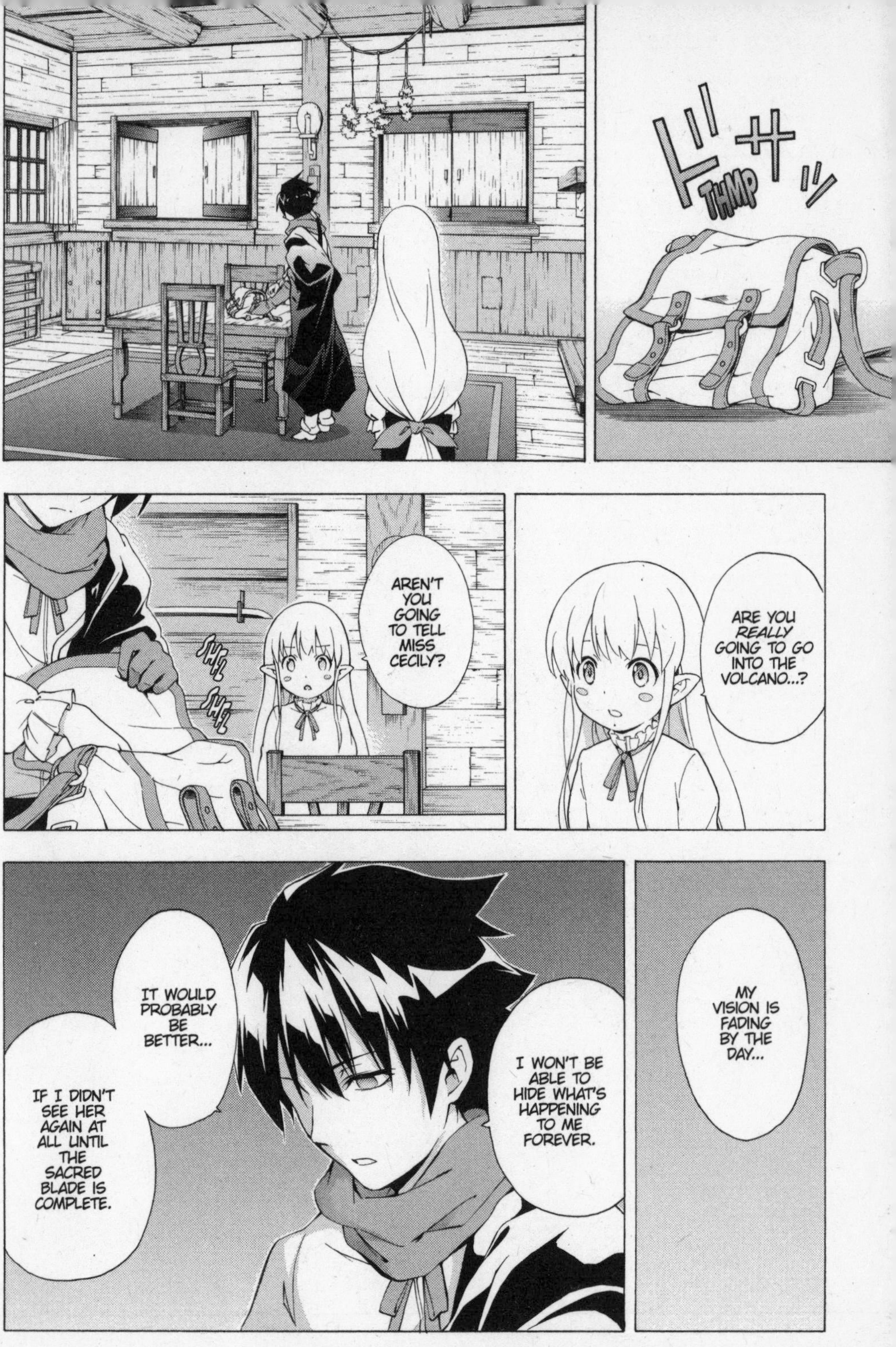
ドサッ
THMP
ARE YOU *REALLY* GOING TO GO INTO THE VOLCANO...?
SHF SHF
AREN'T YOU GOING TO TELL MISS CECILY?
MY VISION IS FADING BY THE DAY...
I WON'T BE ABLE TO HIDE WHAT'S HAPPENING TO ME FOREVER.
IT WOULD PROBABLY BE BETTER...
IF I DIDN'T SEE HER AGAIN AT ALL UNTIL THE SACRED BLADE IS COMPLETE.

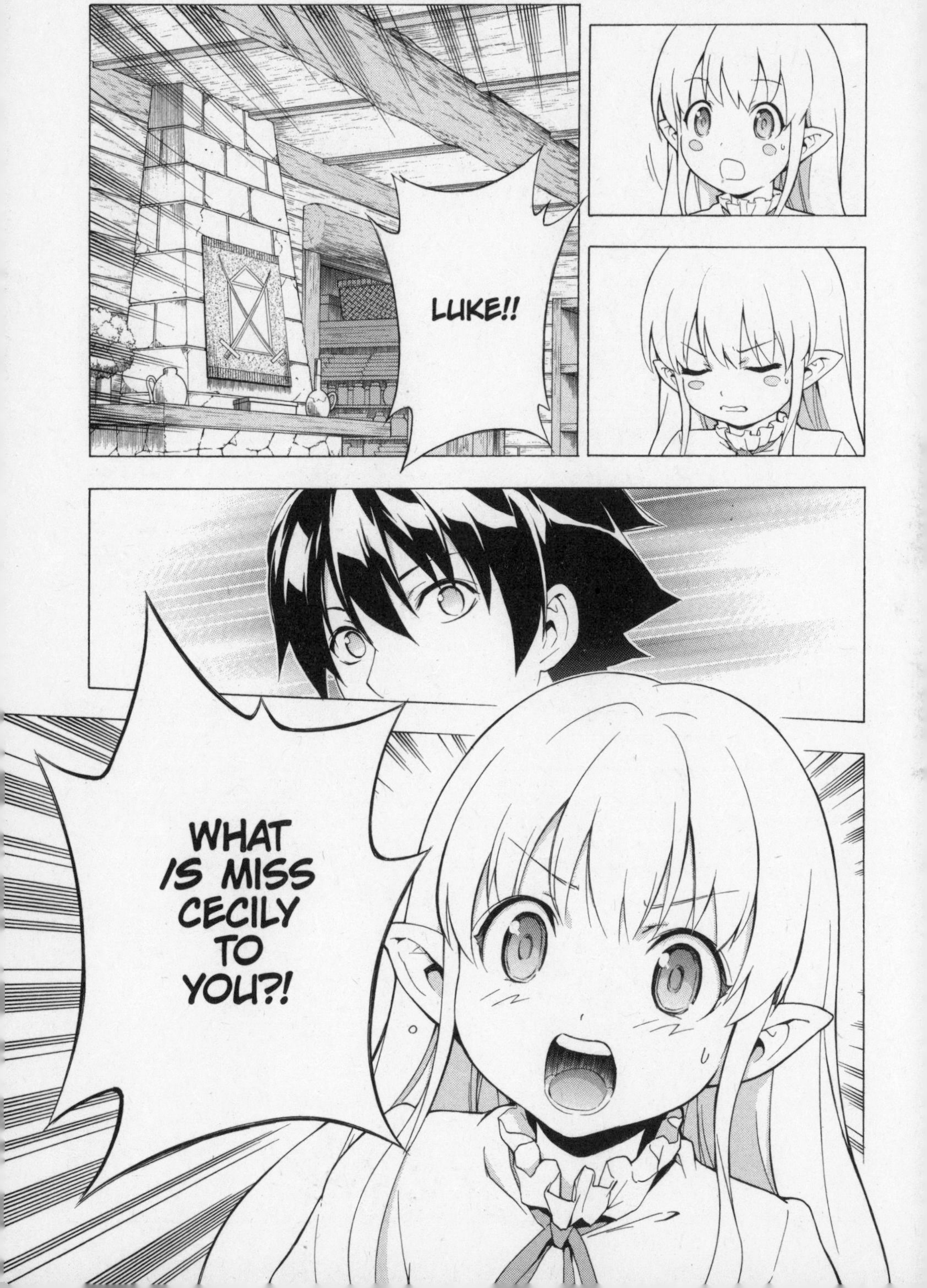
LUKE!!
WHAT IS MISS CECILY TO YOU?!

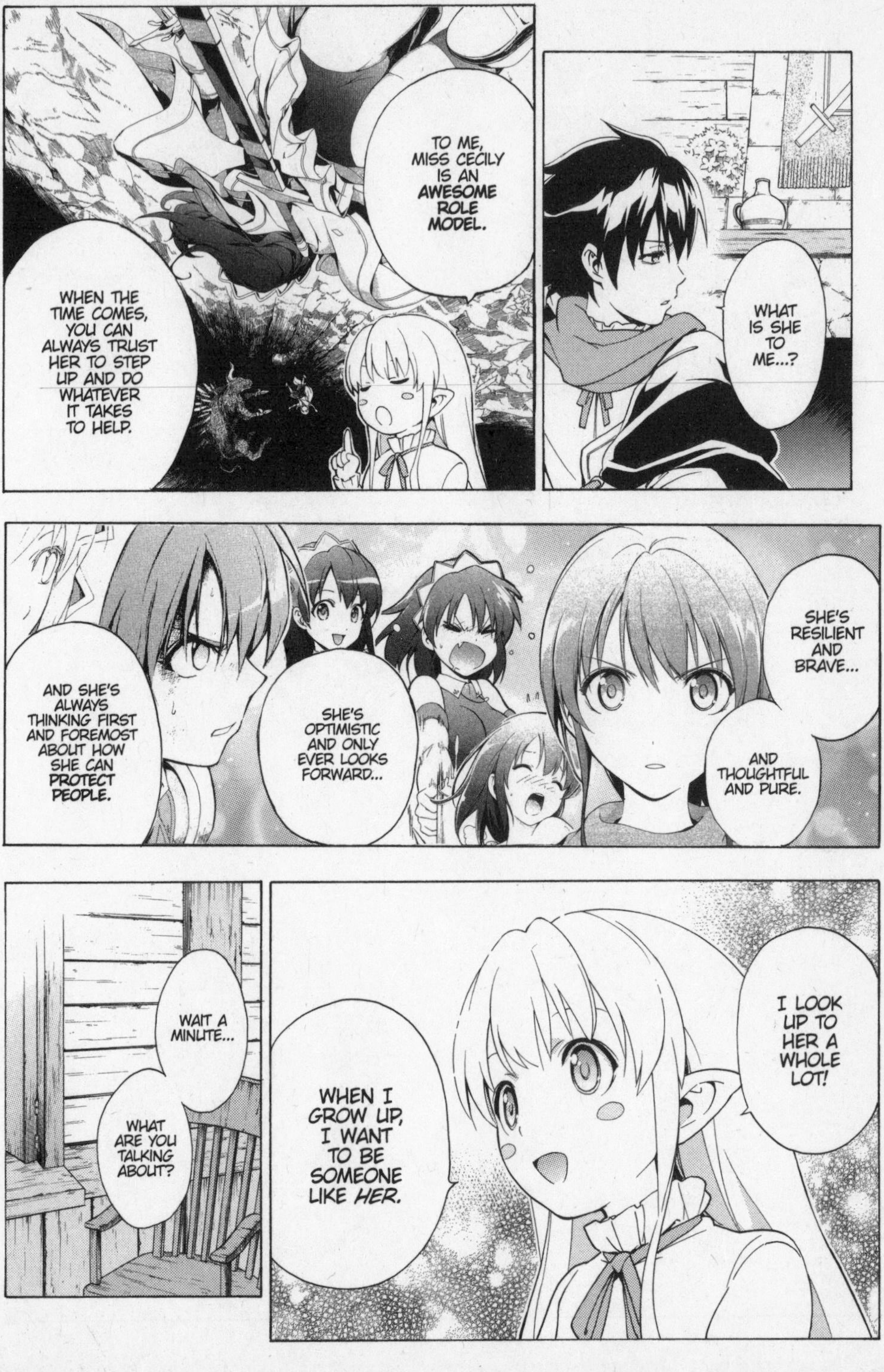
WHAT IS SHE TO ME...?
TO ME, MISS CECILY IS AN **AWESOME ROLE MODEL.**
WHEN THE TIME COMES, YOU CAN ALWAYS TRUST HER TO STEP UP AND DO WHATEVER IT TAKES TO HELP.
SHE'S RESILIENT AND BRAVE...
AND THOUGHTFUL AND PURE.
SHE'S OPTIMISTIC AND ONLY EVER LOOKS FORWARD...
AND SHE'S ALWAYS THINKING FIRST AND FOREMOST ABOUT HOW SHE CAN **PROTECT PEOPLE.**
I LOOK UP TO HER A WHOLE LOT!
WHEN I GROW UP, I WANT TO BE SOMEONE LIKE ***HER.***
WAIT A MINUTE...
WHAT ARE YOU TALKING ABOUT?

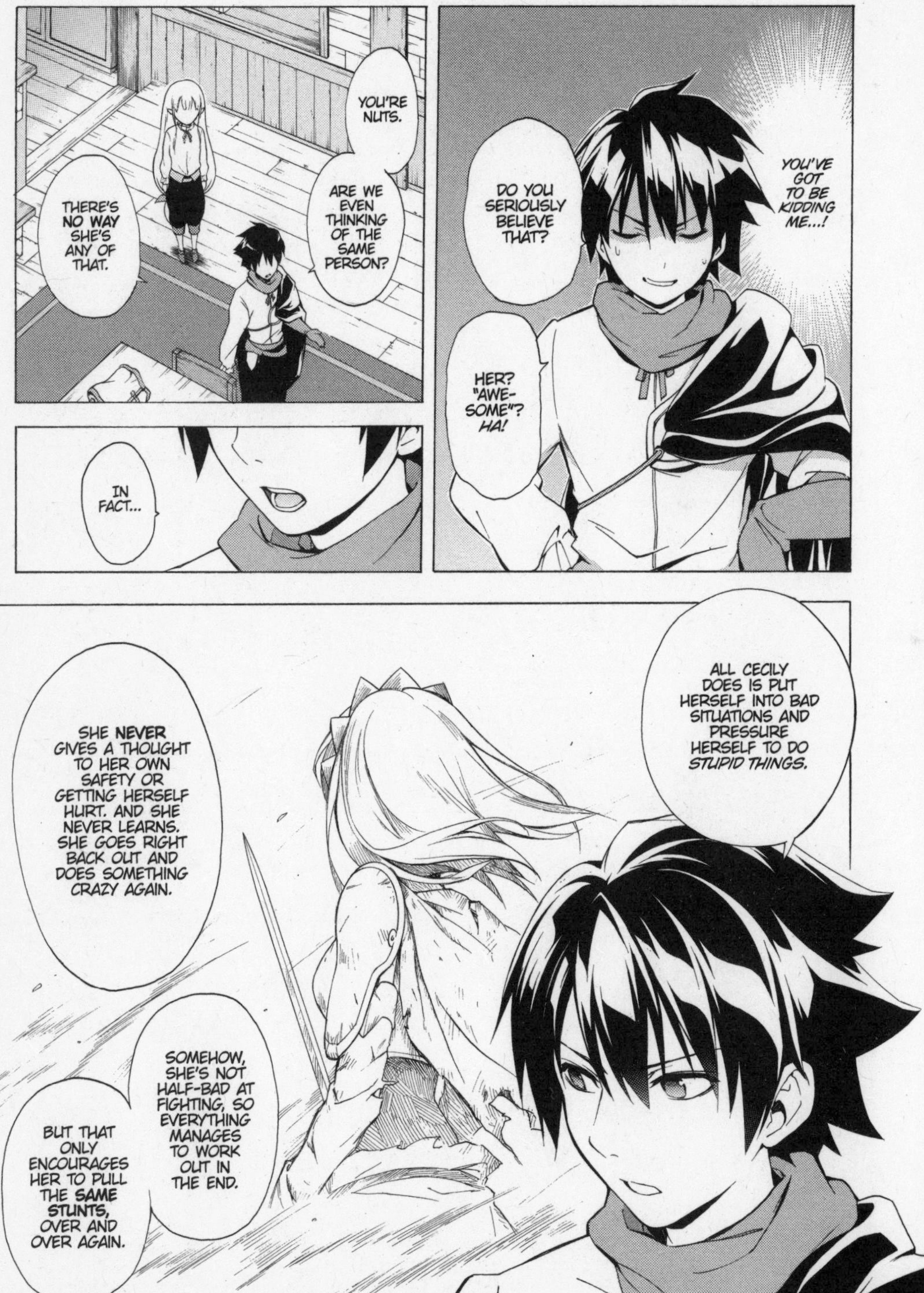
YOU'VE GOT TO BE KIDDING ME...!
DO YOU SERIOUSLY BELIEVE THAT?
HER? "AWE-SOME"? HA!
YOU'RE NUTS.
ARE WE EVEN THINKING OF THE SAME PERSON?
THERE'S NO WAY SHE'S ANY OF THAT.
IN FACT...
ALL CECILY DOES IS PUT HERSELF INTO BAD SITUATIONS AND PRESSURE HERSELF TO DO *STUPID THINGS.*
SHE **NEVER** GIVES A THOUGHT TO HER OWN SAFETY OR GETTING HERSELF HURT. AND SHE NEVER LEARNS. SHE GOES RIGHT BACK OUT AND DOES SOMETHING CRAZY AGAIN.
SOMEHOW, SHE'S NOT HALF-BAD AT FIGHTING, SO EVERYTHING MANAGES TO WORK OUT IN THE END.
BUT THAT ONLY ENCOURAGES HER TO PULL THE **SAME STUNTS,** OVER AND OVER AGAIN.

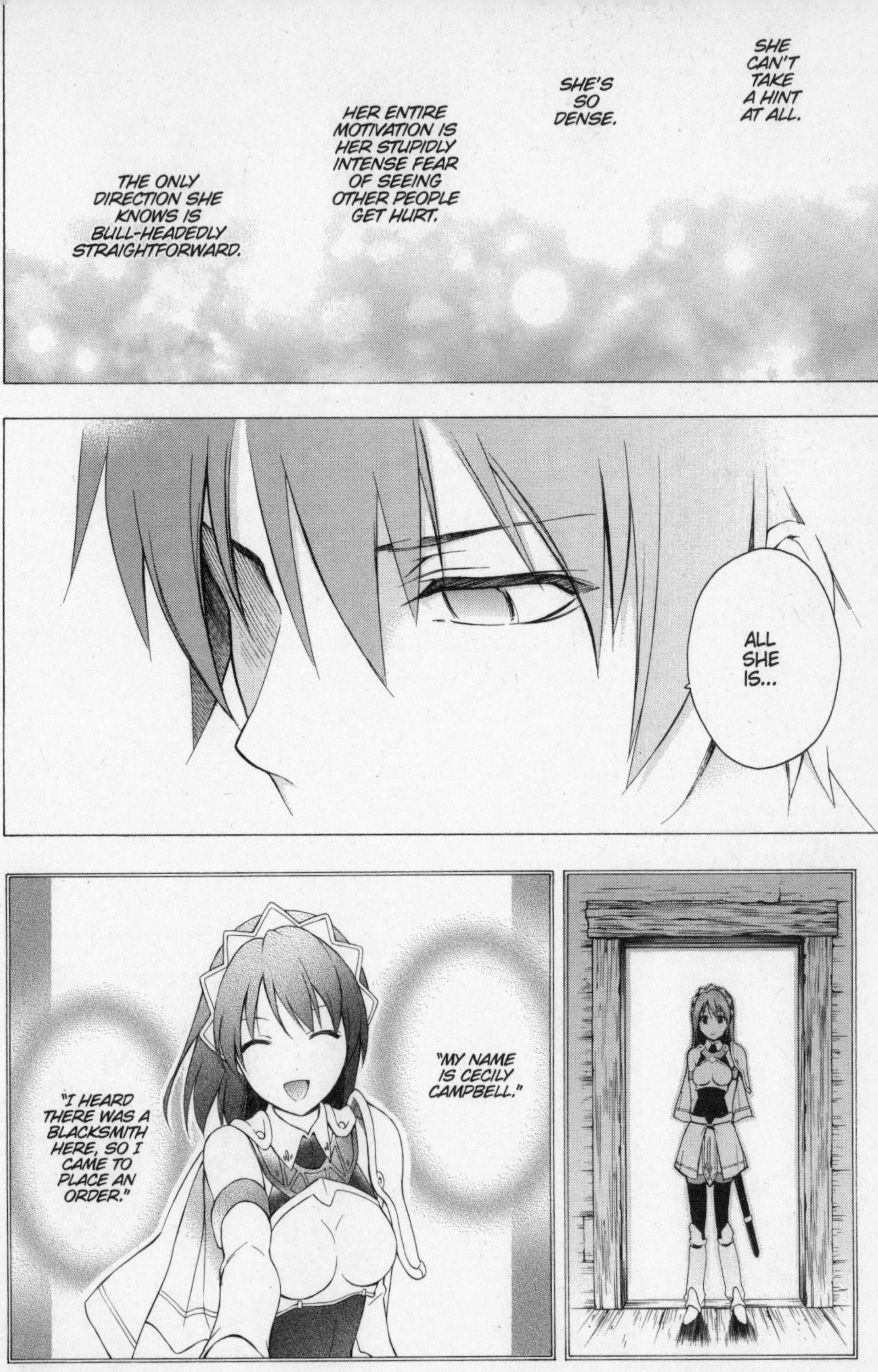
SHE CAN'T TAKE A HINT AT ALL.
SHE'S SO DENSE.
HER ENTIRE MOTIVATION IS HER STUPIDLY INTENSE FEAR OF SEEING OTHER PEOPLE GET HURT.
THE ONLY DIRECTION SHE KNOWS IS BULL-HEADEDLY STRAIGHTFORWARD.
ALL SHE IS...
"MY NAME IS CECILY CAMPBELL."
"I HEARD THERE WAS A BLACKSMITH HERE, SO I CAME TO PLACE AN ORDER."

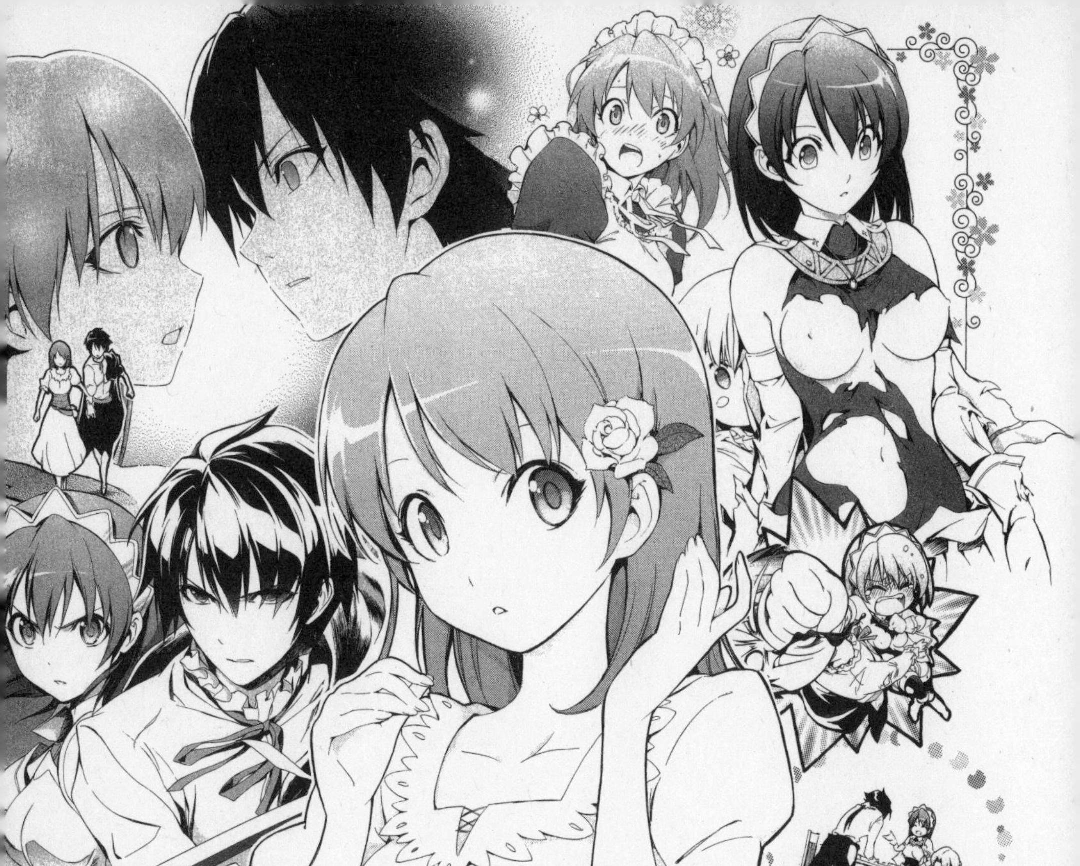

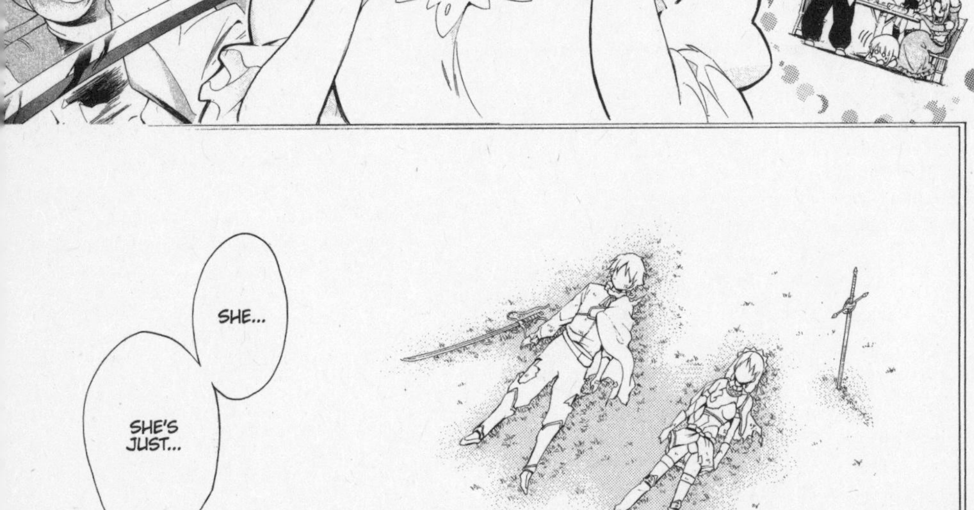
SHE...
SHE'S JUST...

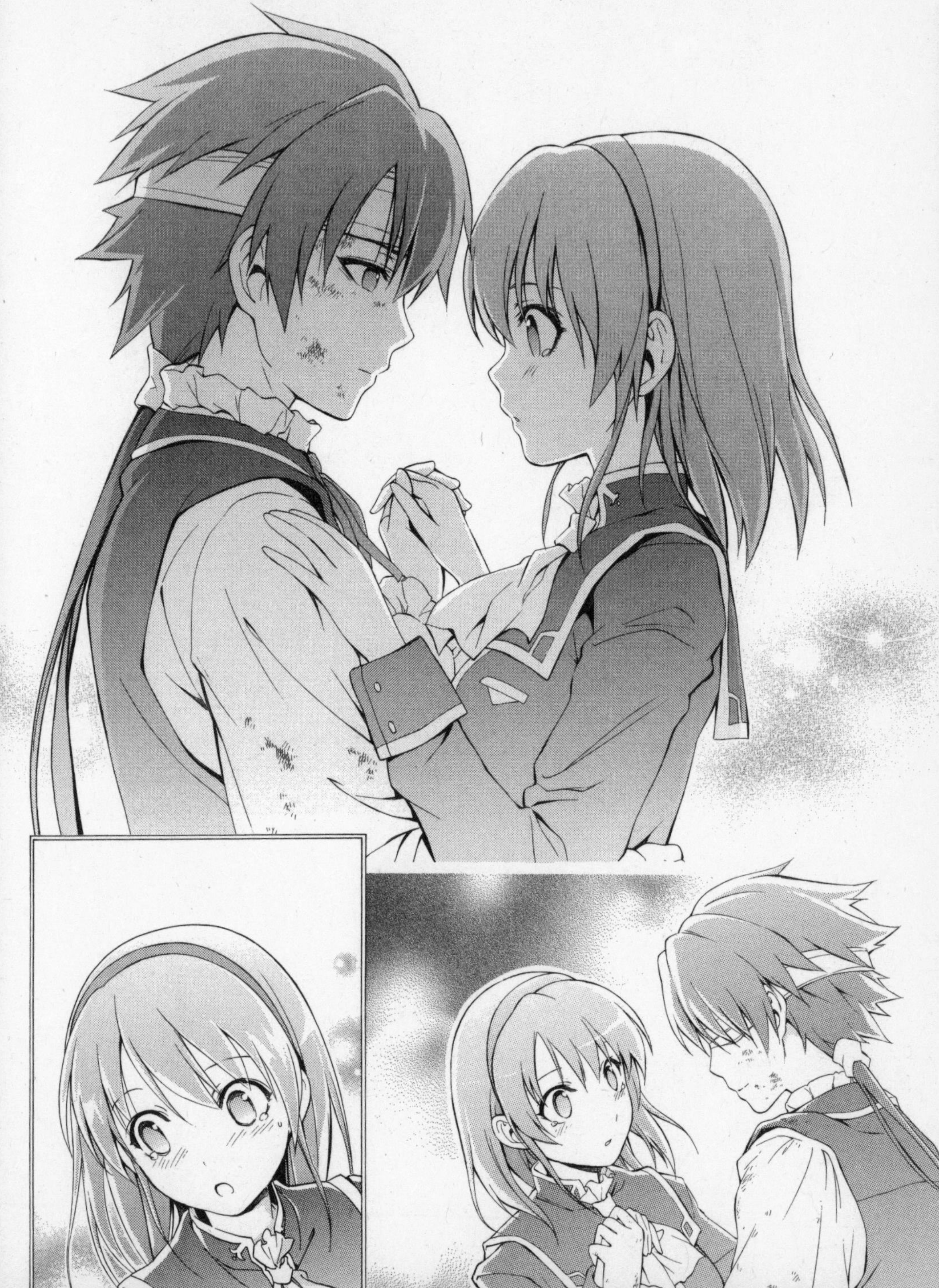

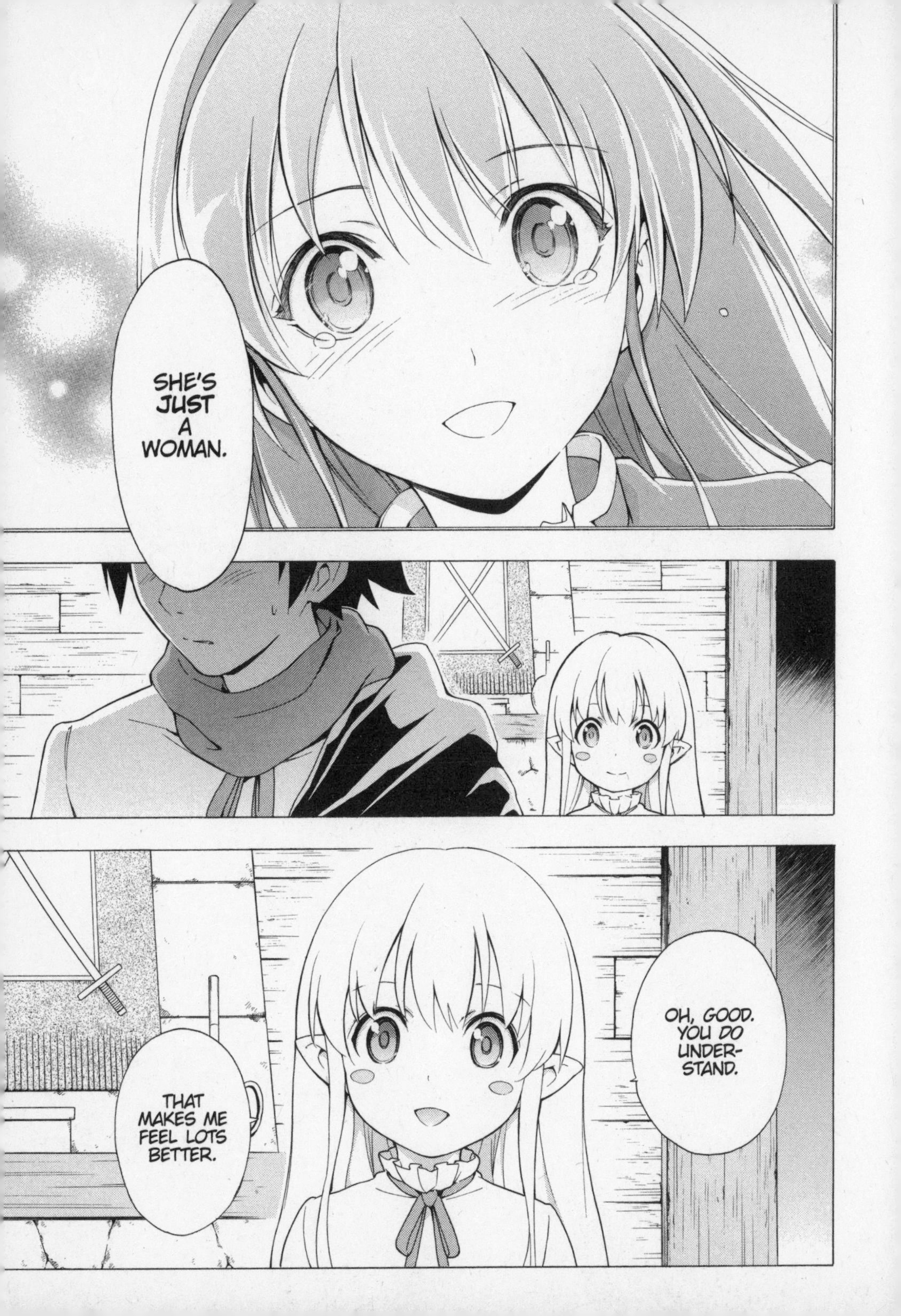
SHE'S JUST A WOMAN.
OH, GOOD. YOU DO UNDER-STAND.
THAT MAKES ME FEEL LOTS BETTER.

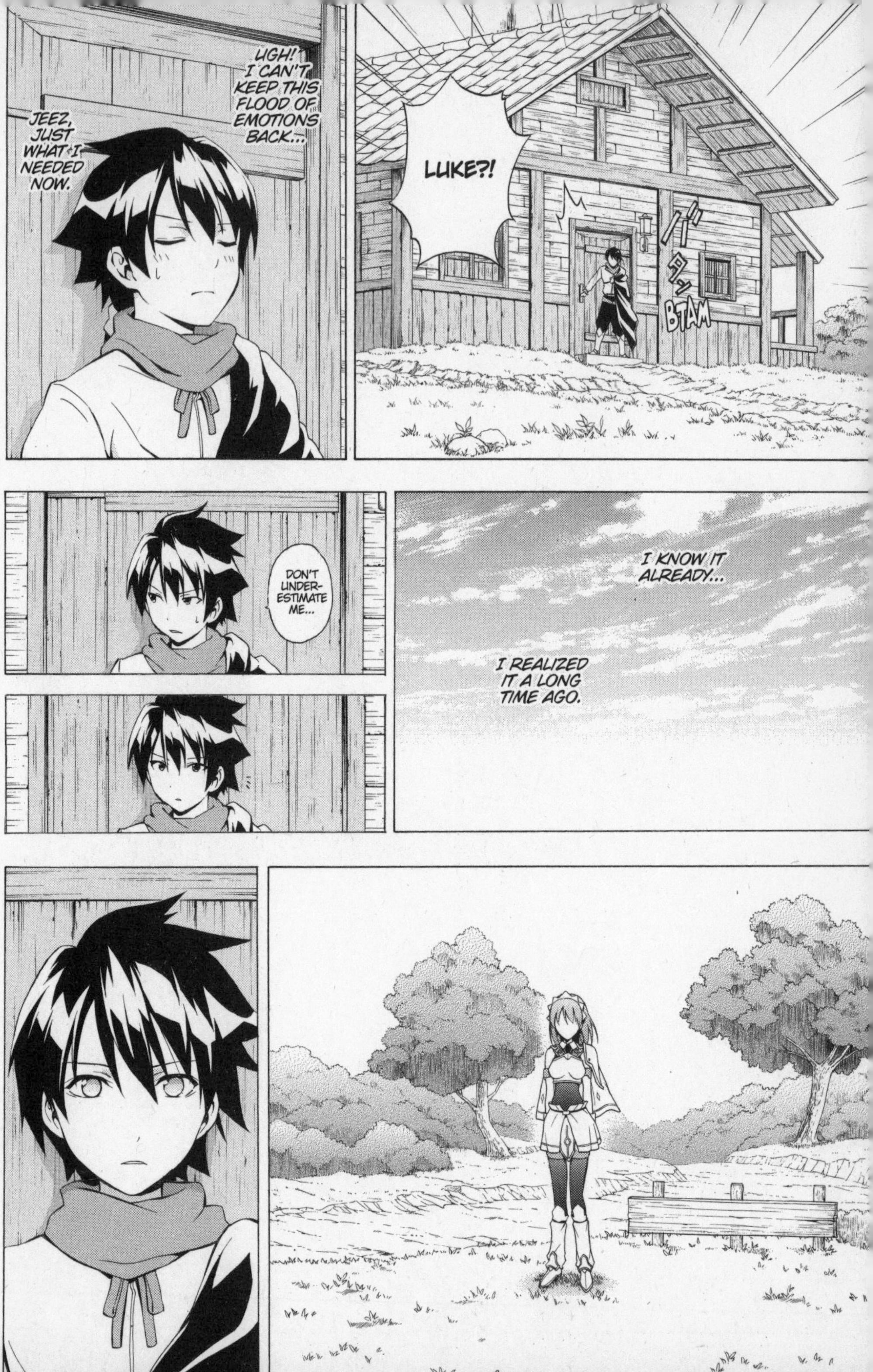
LUKE?!
BTAM
UGH! I CAN'T KEEP THIS FLOOD OF EMOTIONS BACK...
JEEZ, JUST WHAT I NEEDED NOW.
I KNOW IT ALREADY...
I REALIZED IT A LONG TIME AGO.
DON'T UNDER-ESTIMATE ME...

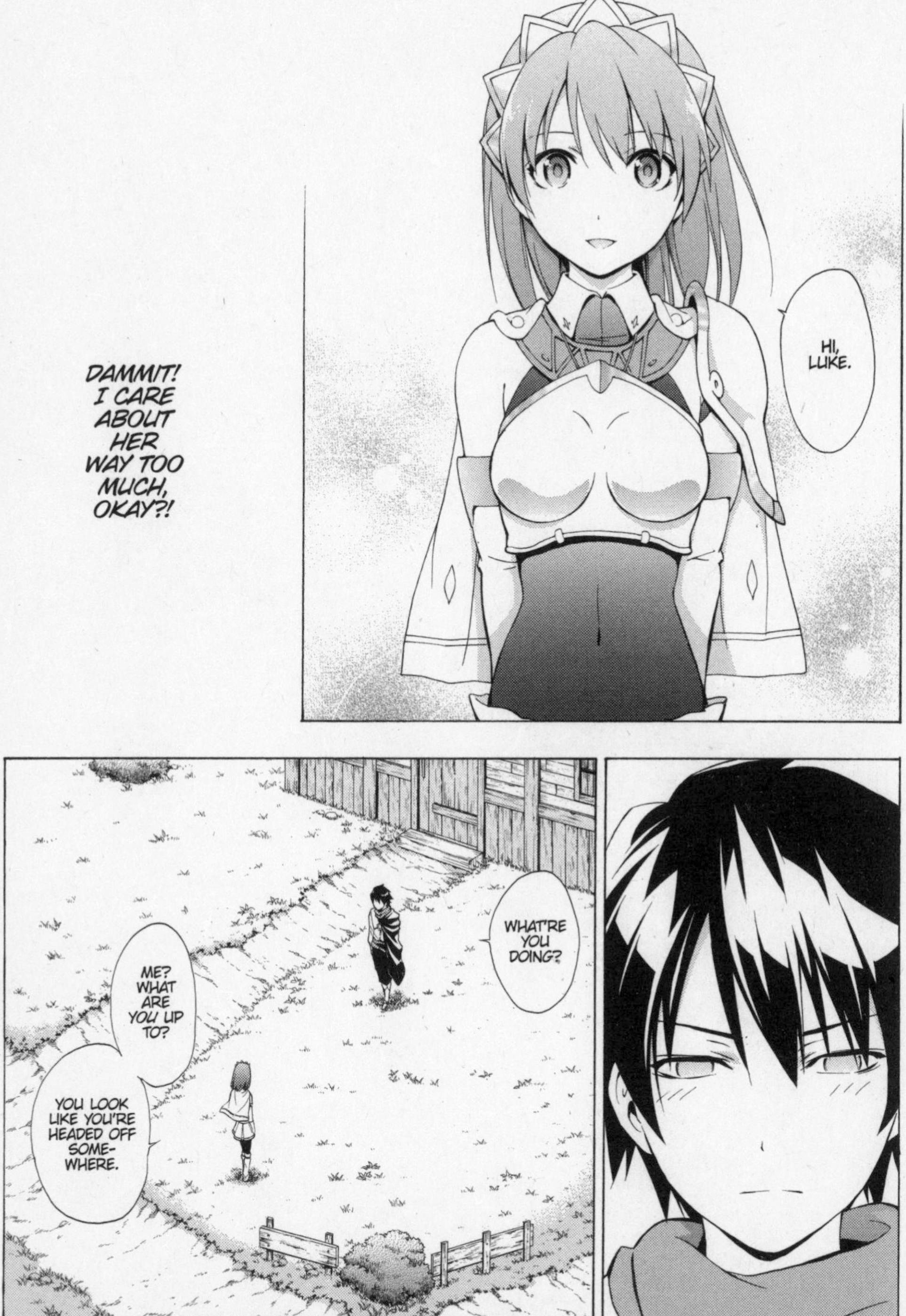
HI, LUKE.
DAMMIT! I CARE ABOUT HER WAY TOO MUCH, OKAY?!
WHAT'RE YOU DOING?
ME? WHAT ARE YOU UP TO?
YOU LOOK LIKE YOU'RE HEADED OFF SOME-WHERE.

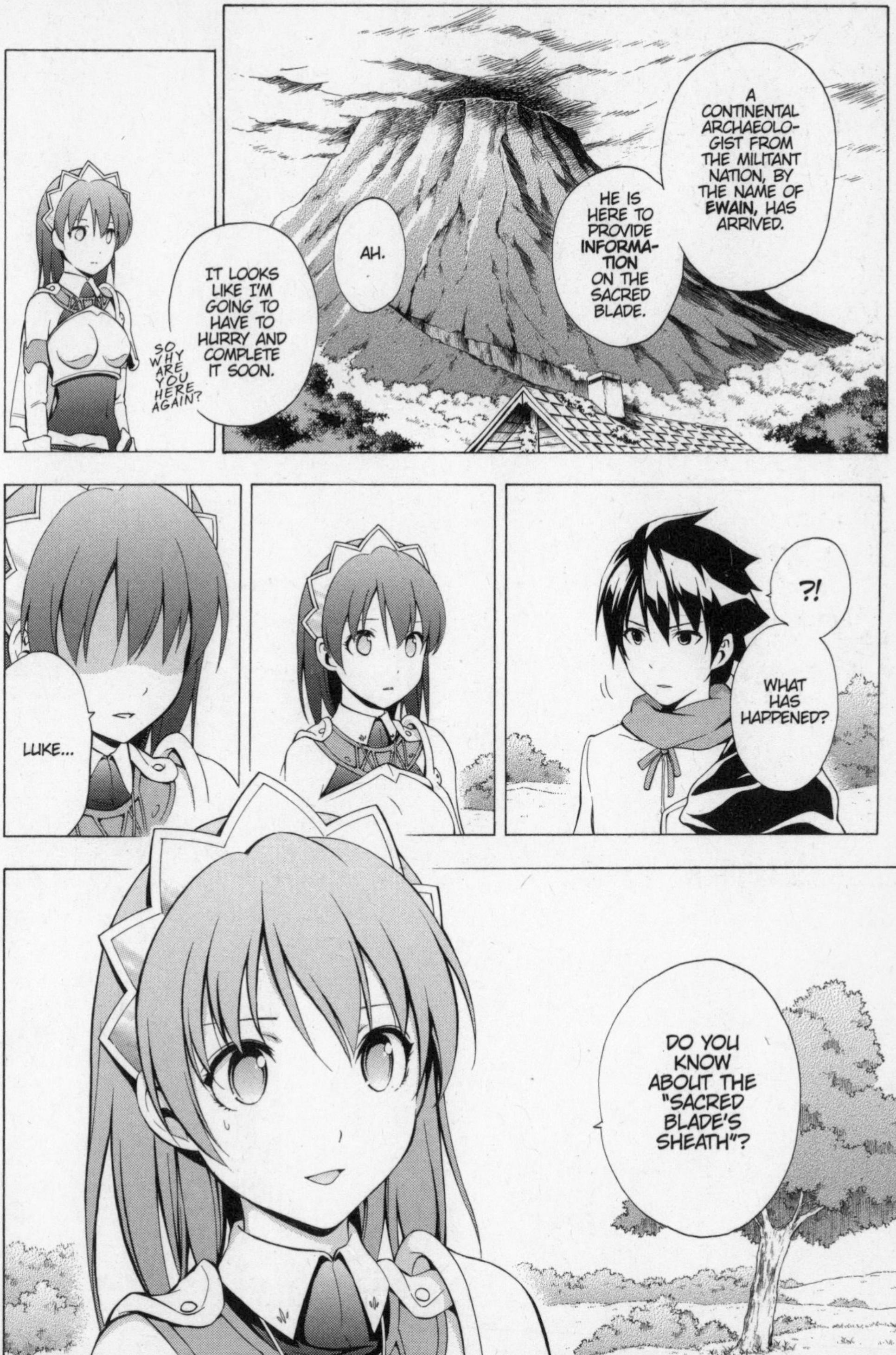
A CONTINENTAL ARCHAEOLOGIST FROM THE MILITANT NATION, BY THE NAME OF EWAIN, HAS ARRIVED.
HE IS HERE TO PROVIDE INFORMATION ON THE SACRED BLADE.
AH.
IT LOOKS LIKE I'M GOING TO HAVE TO HURRY AND COMPLETE IT SOON.
SO WHY ARE YOU HERE AGAIN?
?!
WHAT HAS HAPPENED?
LUKE...
DO YOU KNOW ABOUT THE "SACRED BLADE'S SHEATH"?

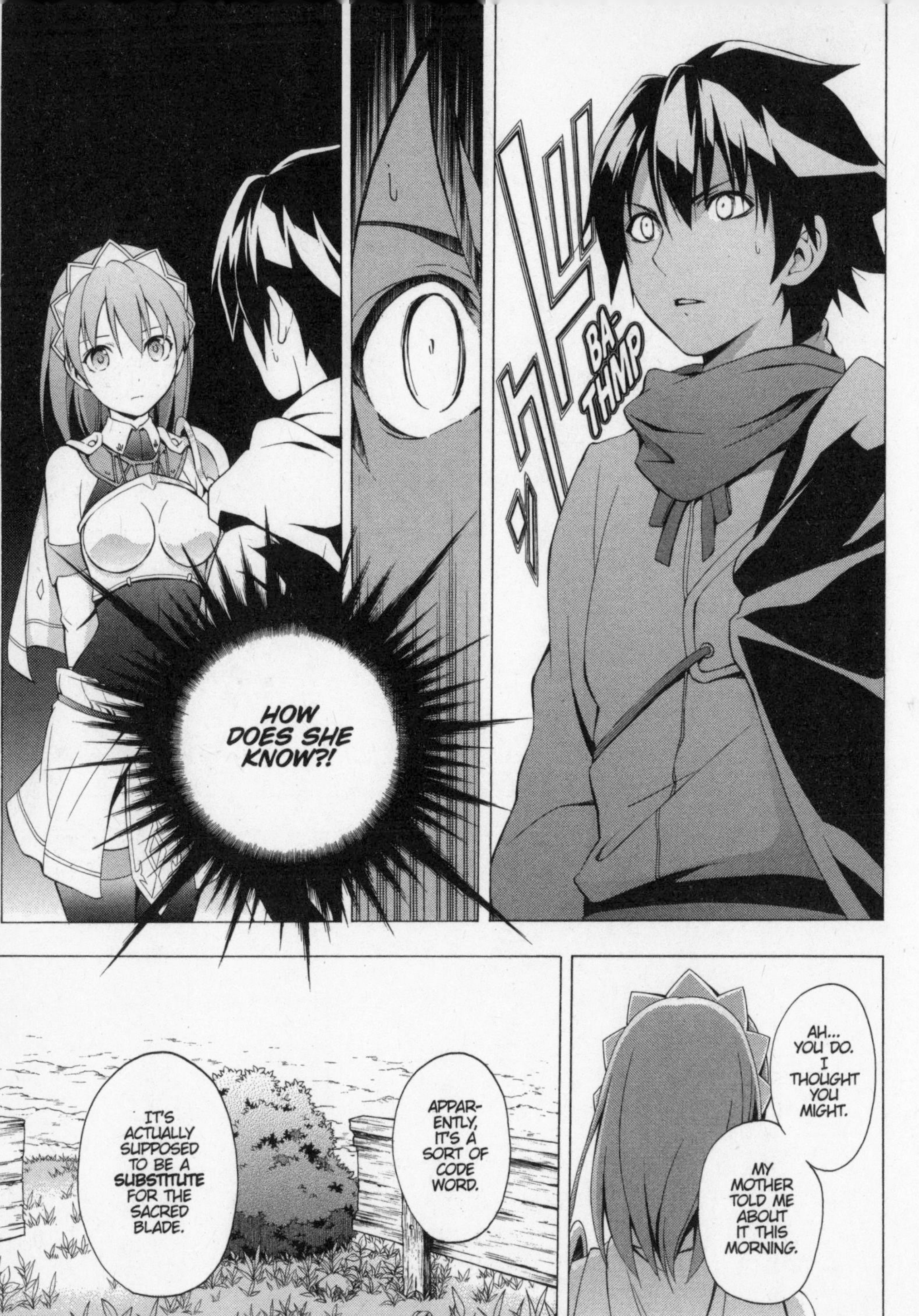
BA-THMP
HOW DOES SHE KNOW?!
AH... YOU DO. I THOUGHT YOU MIGHT.
MY MOTHER TOLD ME ABOUT IT THIS MORNING.
APPAR-ENTLY, IT'S A SORT OF CODE WORD.
IT'S ACTUALLY SUPPOSED TO BE A **SUBSTITUTE** FOR THE SACRED BLADE.

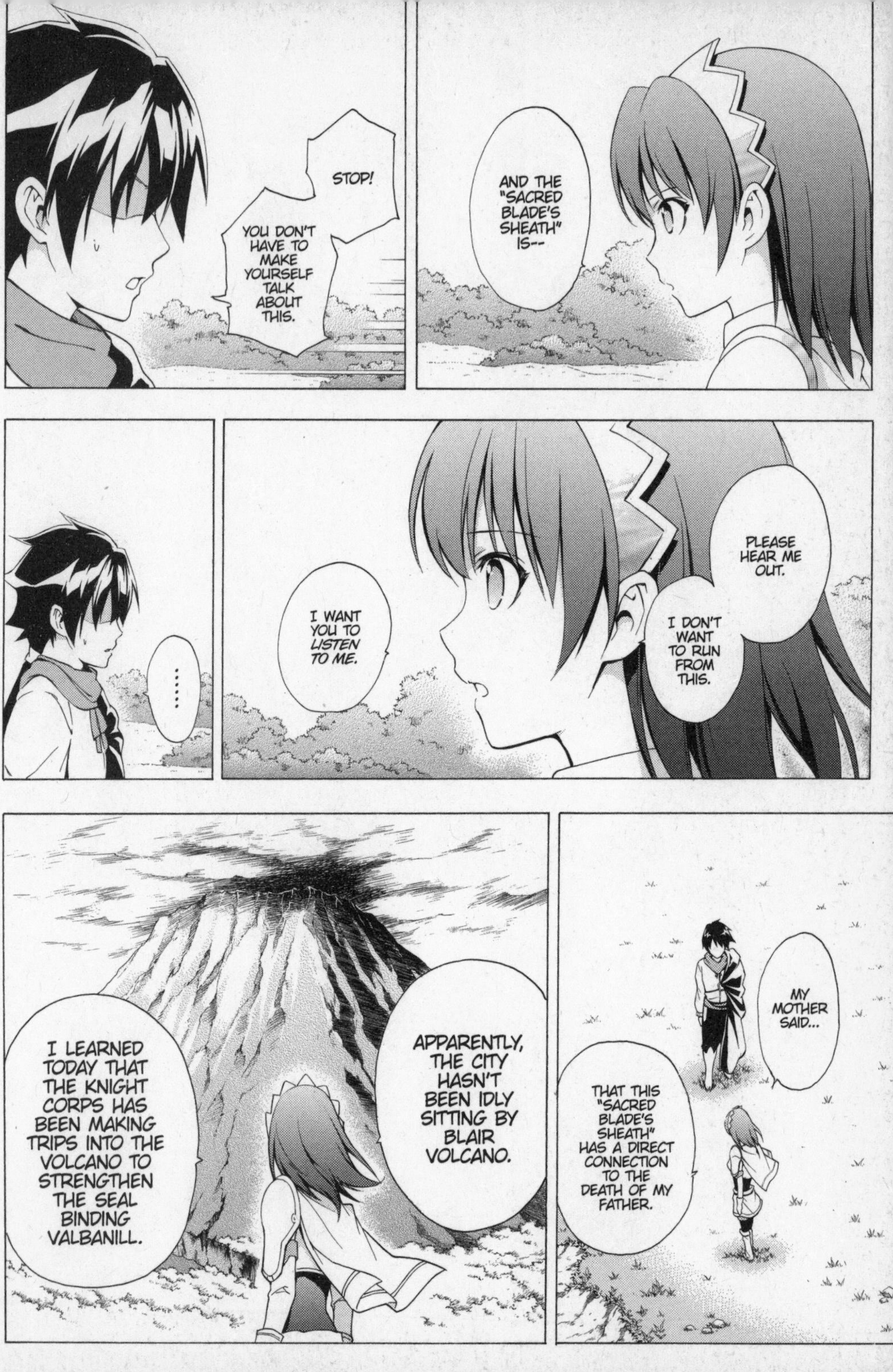
AND THE "SACRED BLADE'S SHEATH" IS--
STOP!
YOU DON'T HAVE TO MAKE YOURSELF TALK ABOUT THIS.
PLEASE HEAR ME OUT.
I DON'T WANT TO RUN FROM THIS.
I WANT YOU TO *LISTEN* TO ME.
......
MY MOTHER SAID...
THAT THIS "SACRED BLADE'S SHEATH" HAS A DIRECT CONNECTION TO THE DEATH OF MY FATHER.
APPARENTLY, THE CITY HASN'T BEEN IDLY SITTING BY BLAIR VOLCANO.
I LEARNED TODAY THAT THE KNIGHT CORPS HAS BEEN MAKING TRIPS INTO THE VOLCANO TO STRENGTHEN THE SEAL BINDING VALBANILL.

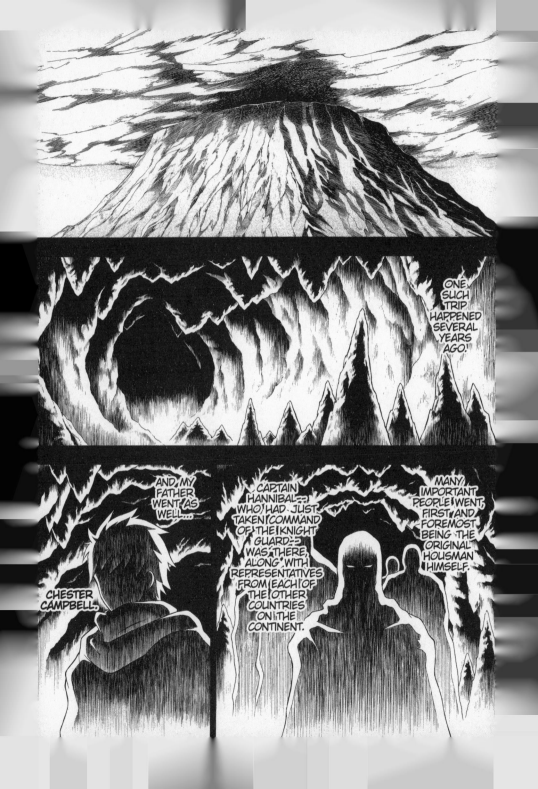

ONE SUCH TRIP HAPPENED SEVERAL YEARS AGO.
MANY IMPORTANT PEOPLE WENT, FIRST AND FOREMOST BEING THE ORIGINAL HOUSMAN HIMSELF.
CAPTAIN HANNIBAL-- WHO HAD JUST TAKEN COMMAND OF THE KNIGHT GUARD-- WAS THERE, ALONG WITH REPRESENTATIVES FROM EACH OF THE OTHER COUNTRIES ON THE CONTINENT.
AND MY FATHER WENT AS WELL...
CHESTER CAMPBELL.

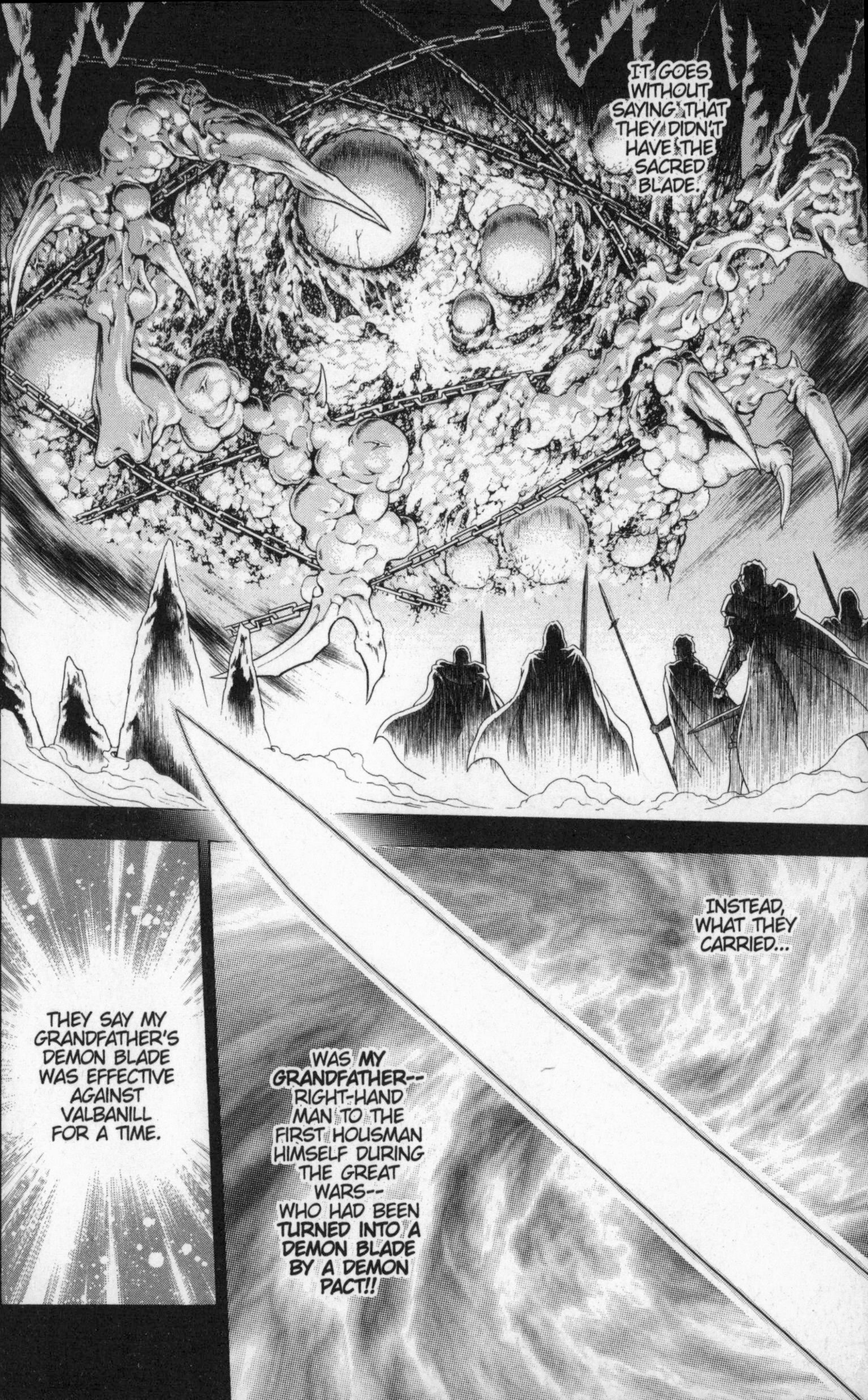
IT GOES WITHOUT SAYING THAT THEY DIDN'T HAVE THE SACRED BLADE.
INSTEAD, WHAT THEY CARRIED...
WAS MY GRANDFATHER-- RIGHT-HAND MAN TO THE FIRST HOUSMAN HIMSELF DURING THE GREAT WARS-- WHO HAD BEEN TURNED INTO A DEMON BLADE BY A DEMON PACT!!
THEY SAY MY GRANDFATHER'S DEMON BLADE WAS EFFECTIVE AGAINST VALBANILL FOR A TIME.

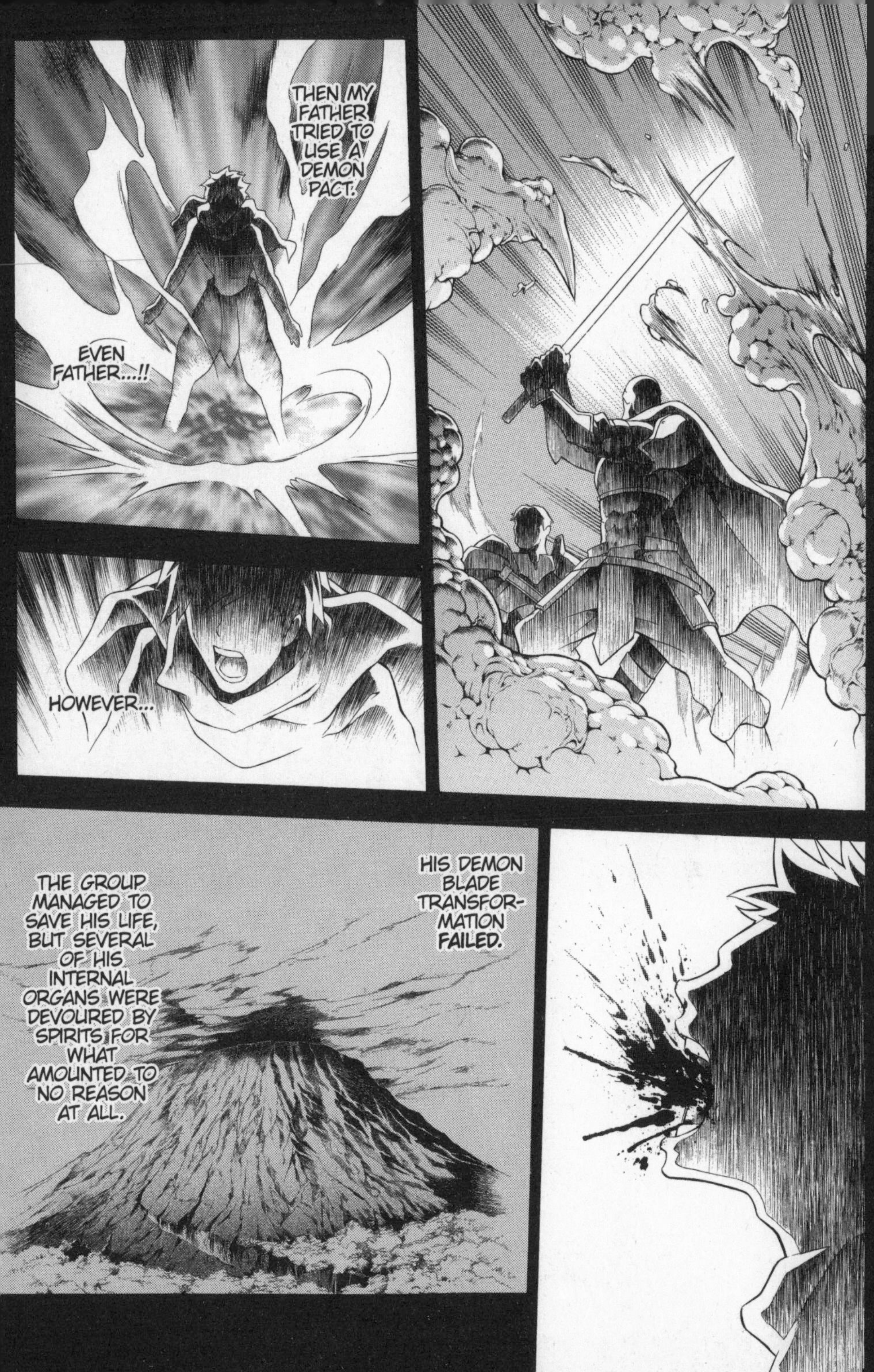
THEN MY FATHER TRIED TO USE A DEMON PACT.
EVEN FATHER...!!
HOWEVER...
HIS DEMON BLADE TRANSFORMATION FAILED.
THE GROUP MANAGED TO SAVE HIS LIFE, BUT SEVERAL OF HIS INTERNAL ORGANS WERE DEVOURED BY SPIRITS FOR WHAT AMOUNTED TO NO REASON AT ALL.

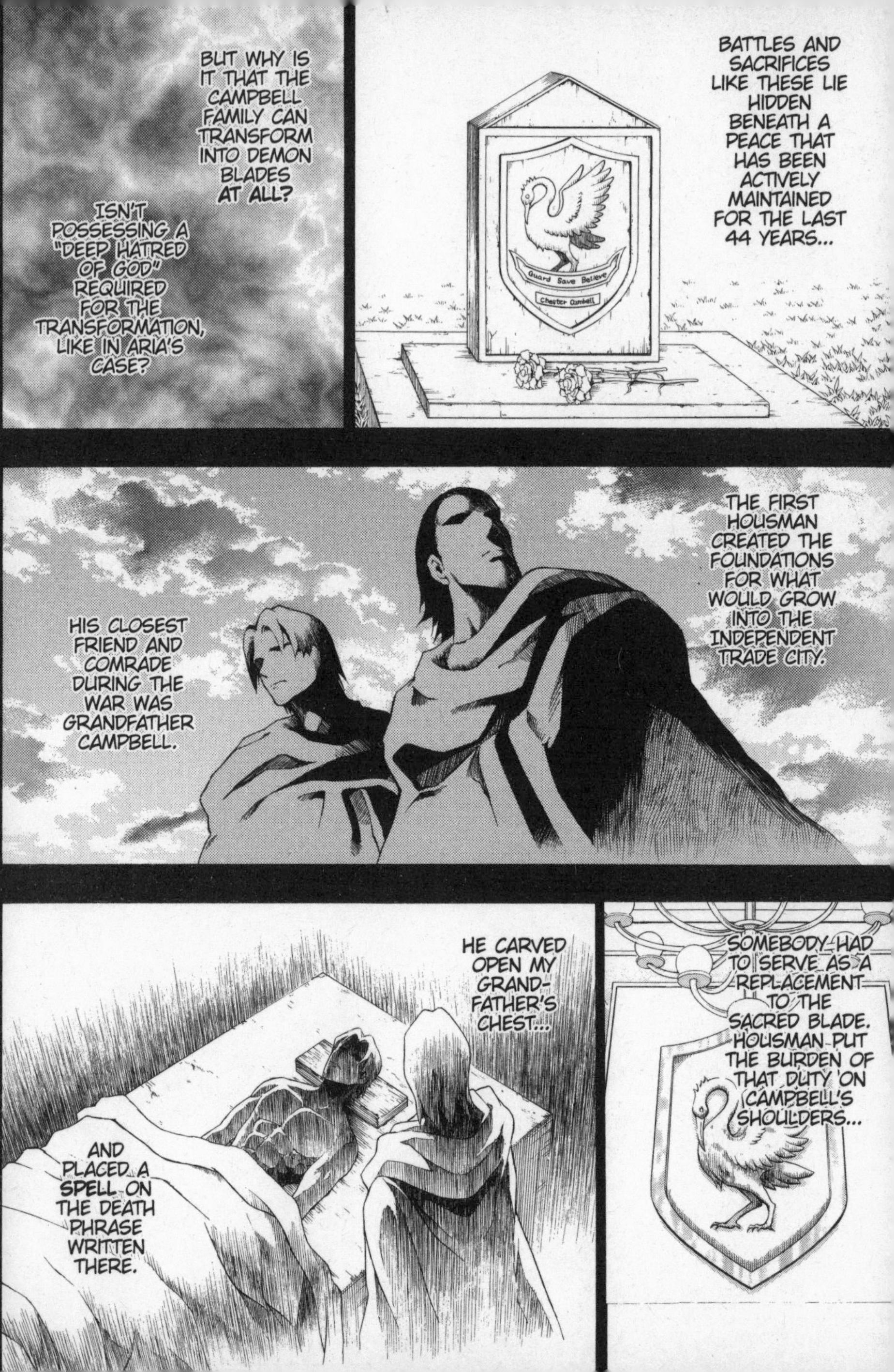
BATTLES AND SACRIFICES LIKE THESE LIE HIDDEN BENEATH A PEACE THAT HAS BEEN ACTIVELY MAINTAINED FOR THE LAST 44 YEARS...
Guard Save Believe
Chester Cambell
BUT WHY IS IT THAT THE CAMPBELL FAMILY CAN TRANSFORM INTO DEMON BLADES AT ALL?
ISN'T POSSESSING A "DEEP HATRED OF GOD" REQUIRED FOR THE TRANSFORMATION, LIKE IN ARIA'S CASE?
THE FIRST HOUSMAN CREATED THE FOUNDATIONS FOR WHAT WOULD GROW INTO THE INDEPENDENT TRADE CITY.
HIS CLOSEST FRIEND AND COMRADE DURING THE WAR WAS GRANDFATHER CAMPBELL.
SOMEBODY HAD TO SERVE AS A REPLACEMENT TO THE SACRED BLADE. HOUSMAN PUT THE BURDEN OF THAT DUTY ON CAMPBELL'S SHOULDERS...
HE CARVED OPEN MY GRAND-FATHER'S CHEST...
AND PLACED A **SPELL** ON THE DEATH PHRASE WRITTEN THERE.

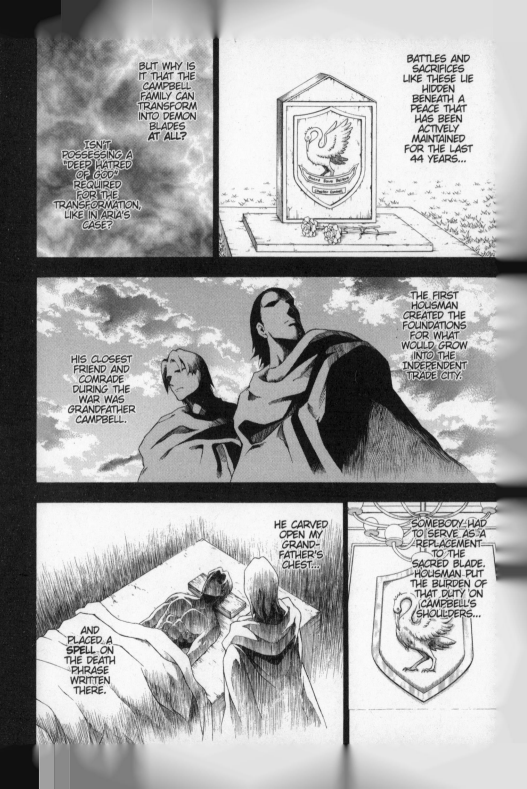

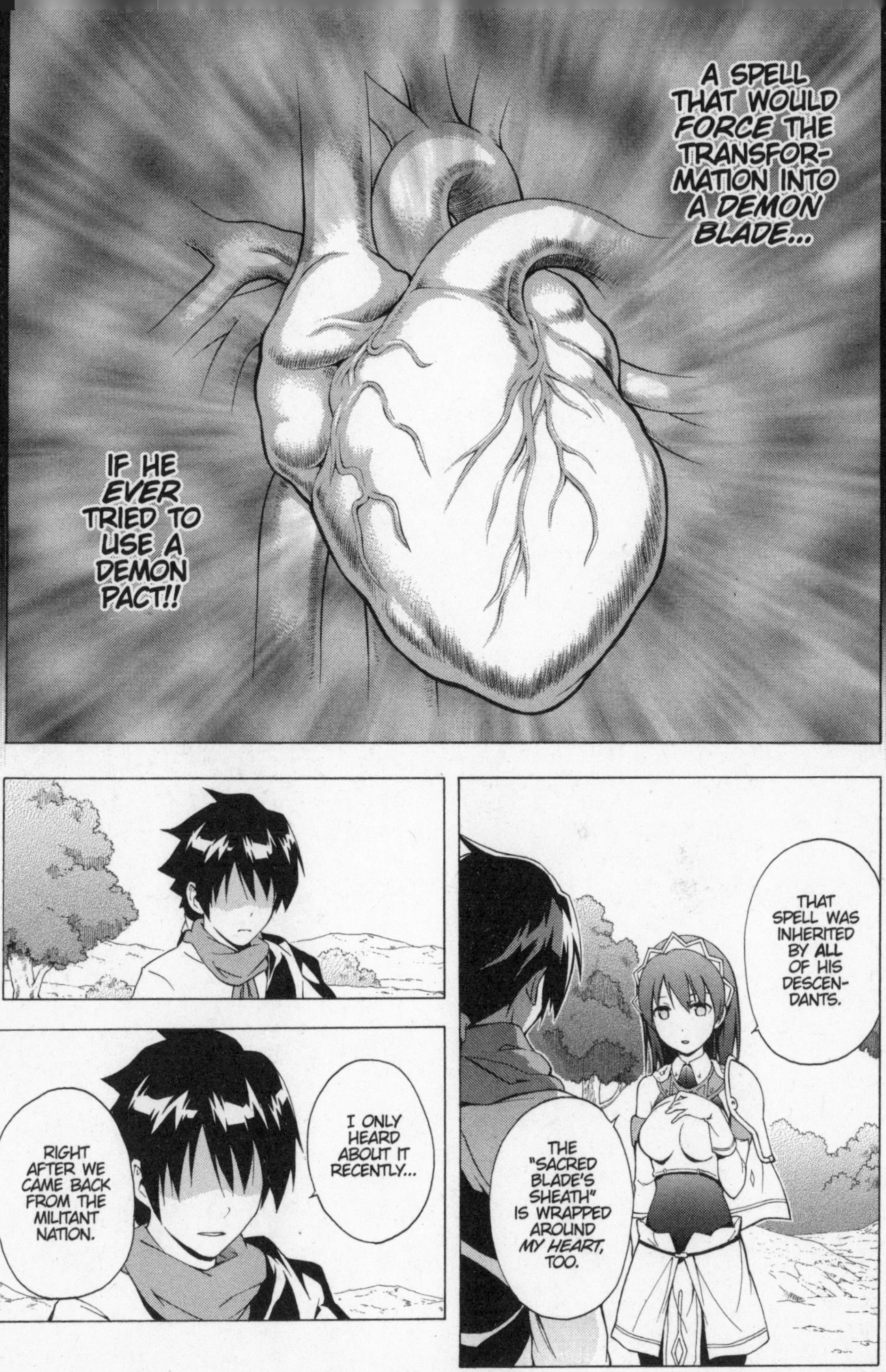
A SPELL THAT WOULD *FORCE* THE TRANSFORMATION INTO A *DEMON BLADE*...
IF HE *EVER* TRIED TO USE A DEMON PACT!!
THAT SPELL WAS INHERITED BY ALL OF HIS DESCENDANTS.
THE "SACRED BLADE'S SHEATH" IS WRAPPED AROUND *MY HEART*, TOO.
I ONLY HEARD ABOUT IT RECENTLY...
RIGHT AFTER WE CAME BACK FROM THE MILITANT NATION.

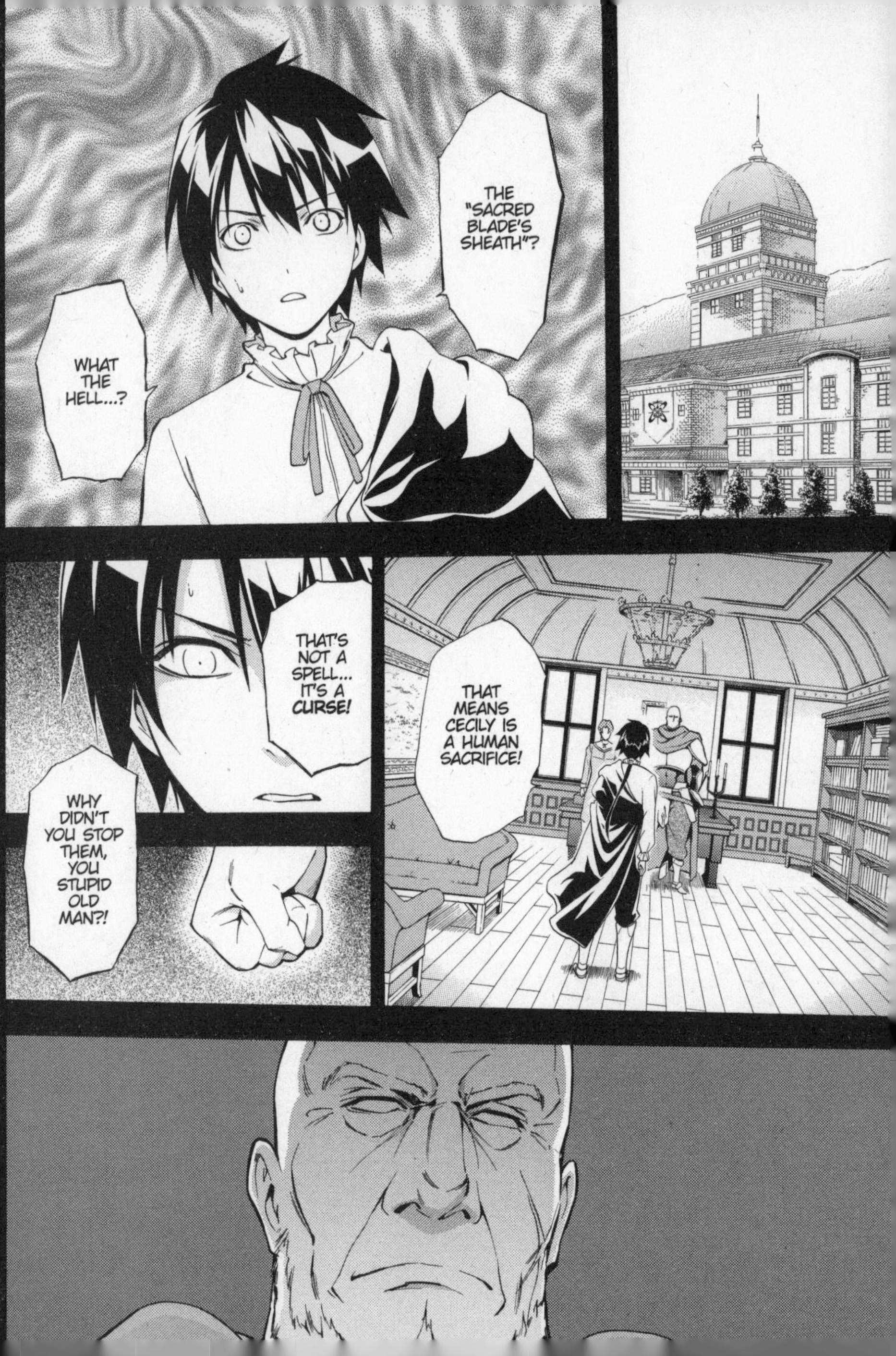
THE "SACRED BLADE'S SHEATH"?
WHAT THE HELL...?
THAT MEANS CECILY IS A HUMAN SACRIFICE!
THAT'S NOT A SPELL... IT'S A **CURSE!**
WHY DIDN'T YOU STOP THEM, YOU STUPID OLD MAN?!

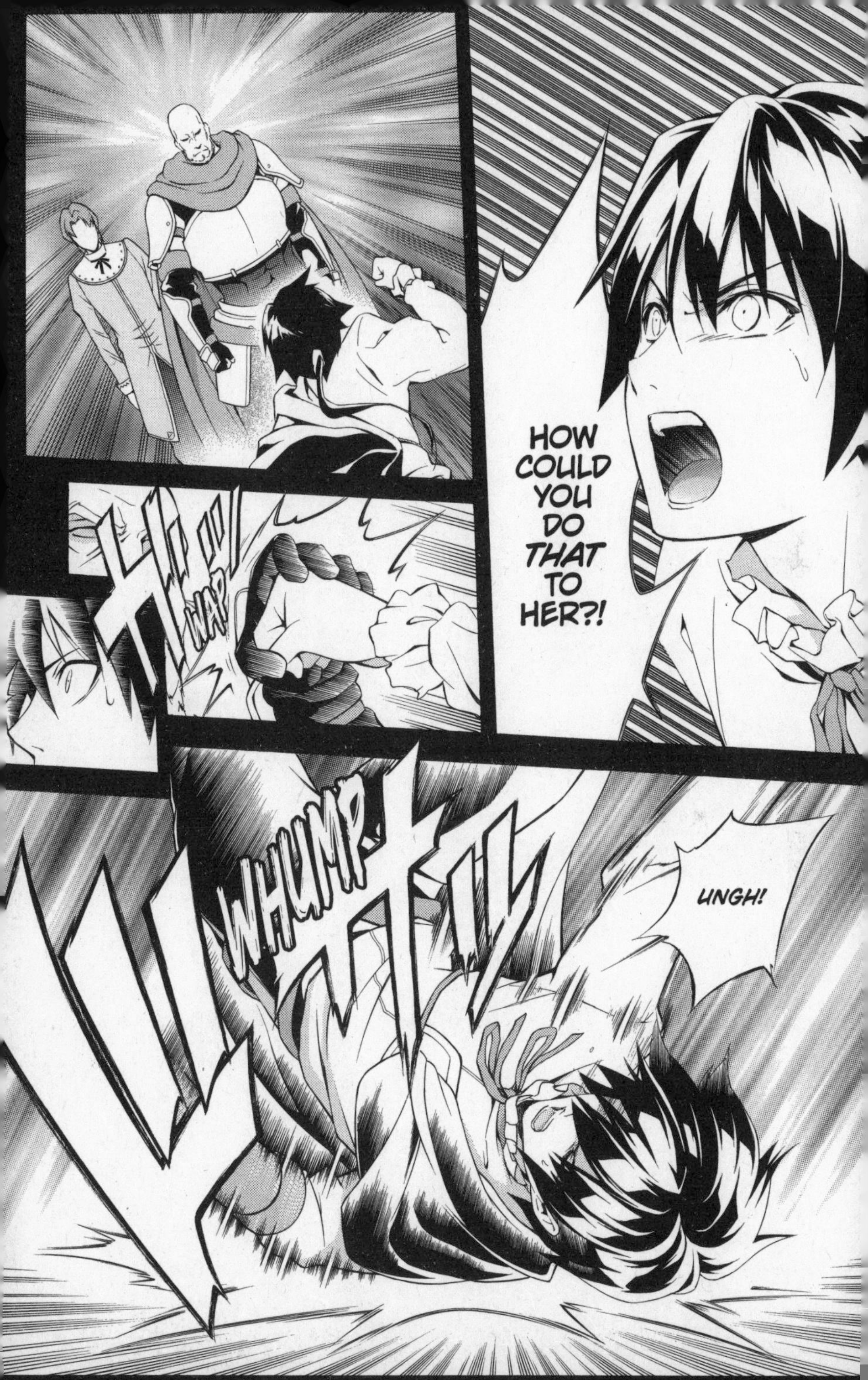
HOW COULD YOU DO *THAT* TO HER?!
WAP
UNGH!
WHUMP

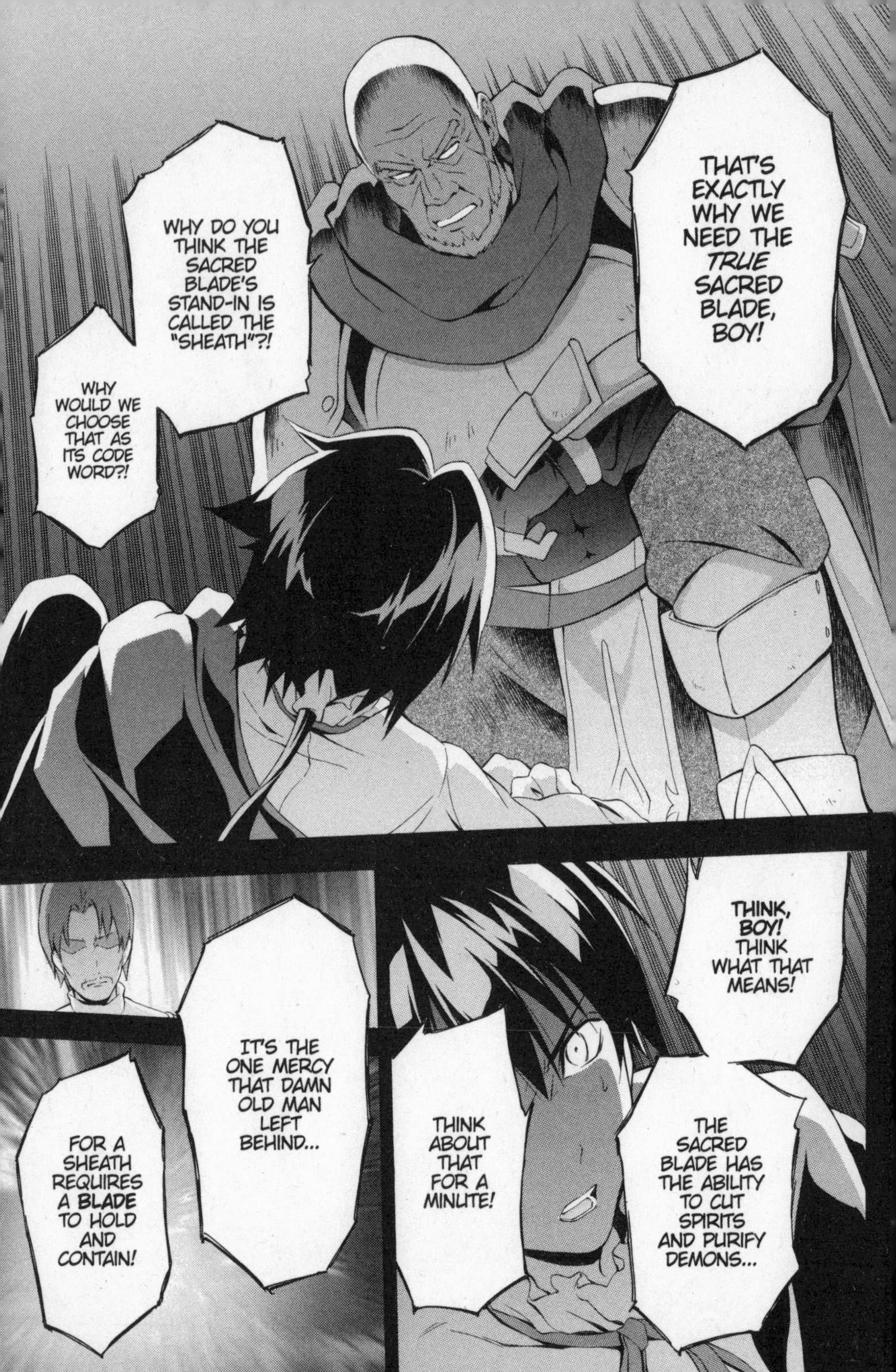
THAT'S EXACTLY WHY WE NEED THE *TRUE* SACRED BLADE, BOY!
WHY DO YOU THINK THE SACRED BLADE'S STAND-IN IS CALLED THE "SHEATH"?!
WHY WOULD WE CHOOSE THAT AS ITS CODE WORD?!
THINK, BOY! THINK WHAT THAT MEANS!
THE SACRED BLADE HAS THE ABILITY TO CUT SPIRITS AND PURIFY DEMONS...
THINK ABOUT THAT FOR A MINUTE!
IT'S THE ONE MERCY THAT DAMN OLD MAN LEFT BEHIND...
FOR A SHEATH REQUIRES A **BLADE** TO HOLD AND CONTAIN!

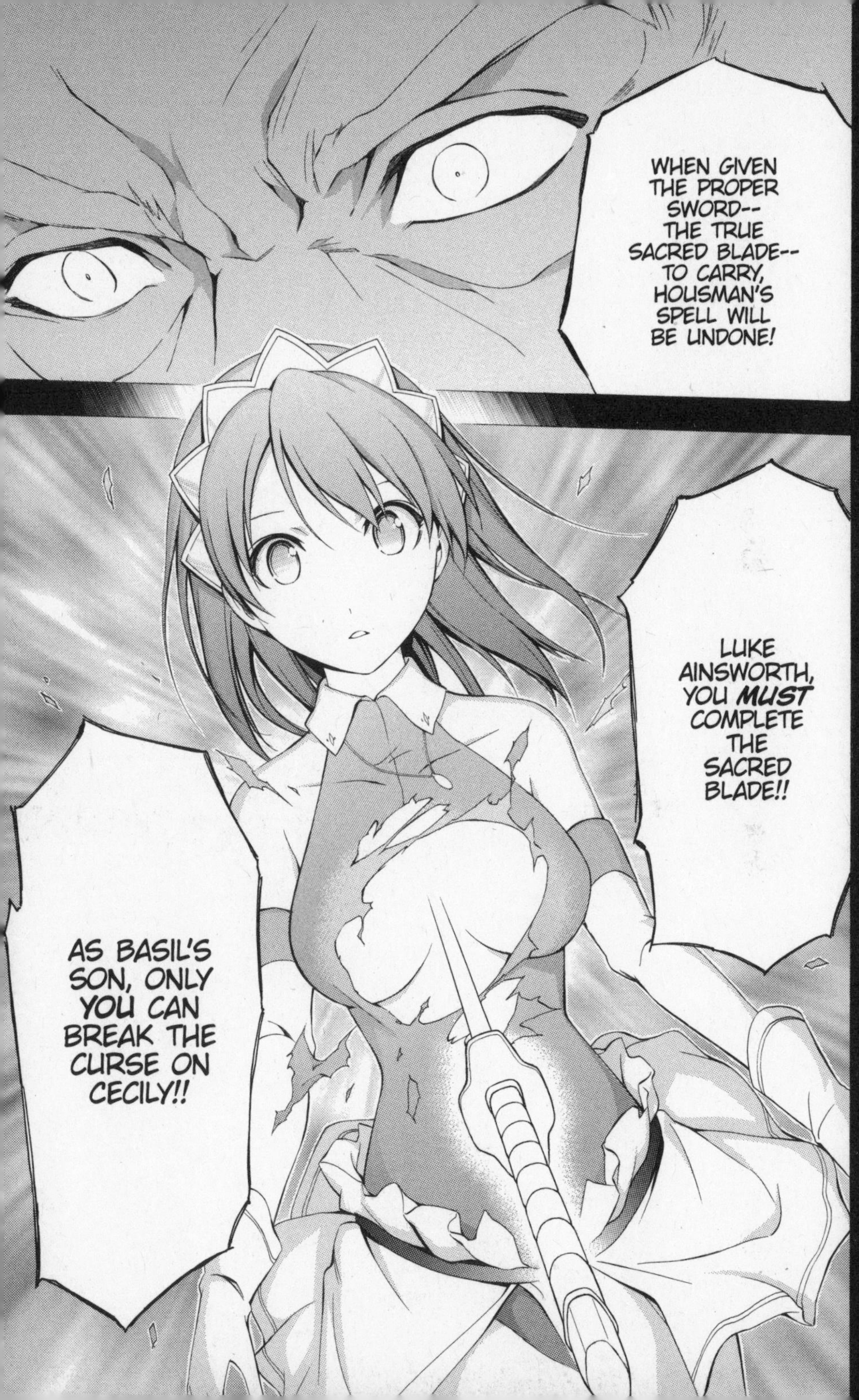
WHEN GIVEN THE PROPER SWORD-- THE TRUE SACRED BLADE-- TO CARRY, HOUSMAN'S SPELL WILL BE UNDONE!
LUKE AINSWORTH, YOU ***MUST*** COMPLETE THE SACRED BLADE!!
AS BASIL'S SON, ONLY **YOU** CAN BREAK THE CURSE ON CECILY!!

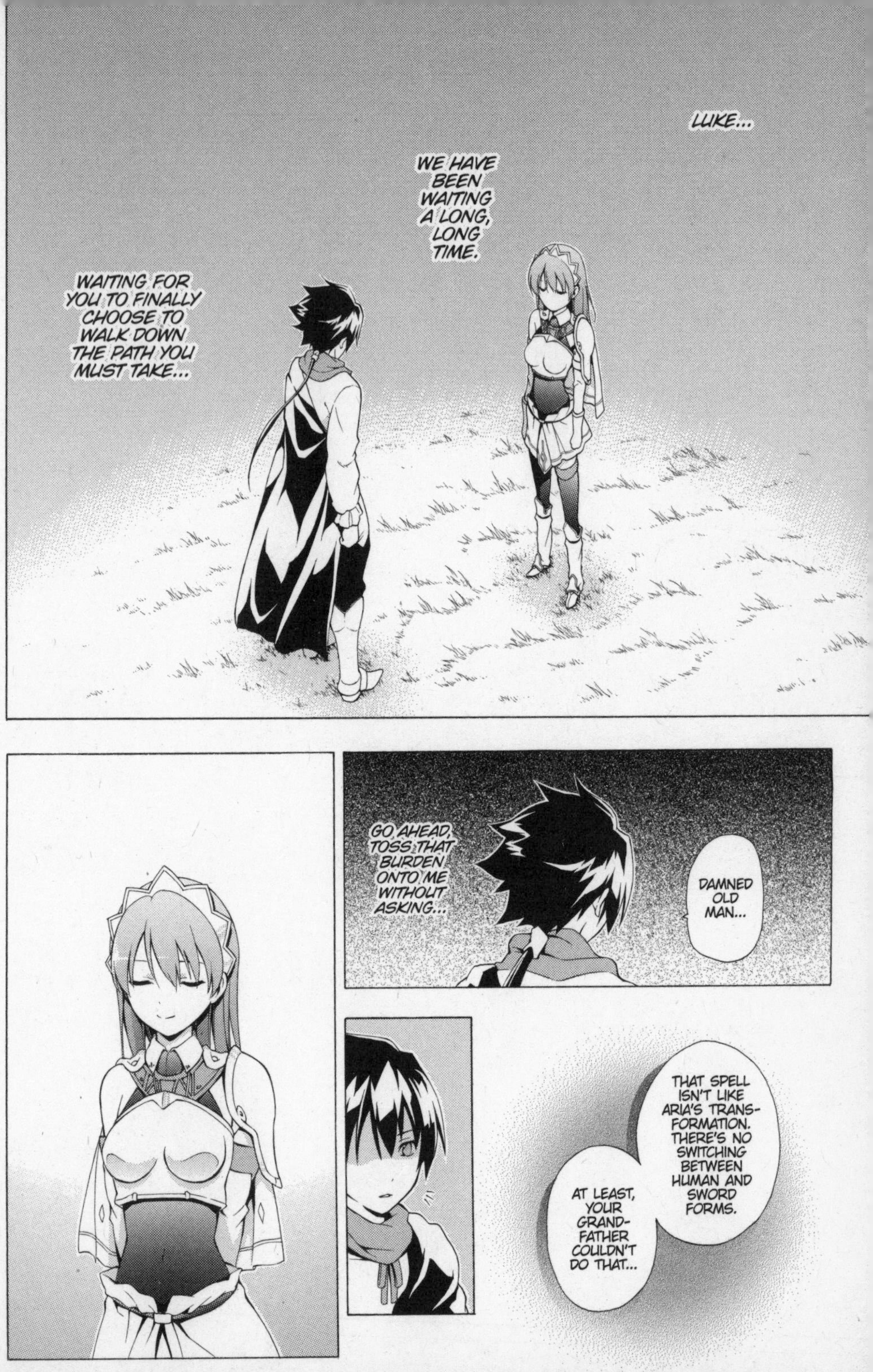
LUKE...
WE HAVE BEEN WAITING A LONG, LONG TIME.
WAITING FOR YOU TO FINALLY CHOOSE TO WALK DOWN THE PATH YOU MUST TAKE...
DAMNED OLD MAN...
GO AHEAD, TOSS THAT BURDEN ONTO ME WITHOUT ASKING...
THAT SPELL ISN'T LIKE ARIA'S TRANS-FORMATION. THERE'S NO SWITCHING BETWEEN HUMAN AND SWORD FORMS.
AT LEAST, YOUR GRAND-FATHER COULDN'T DO THAT...

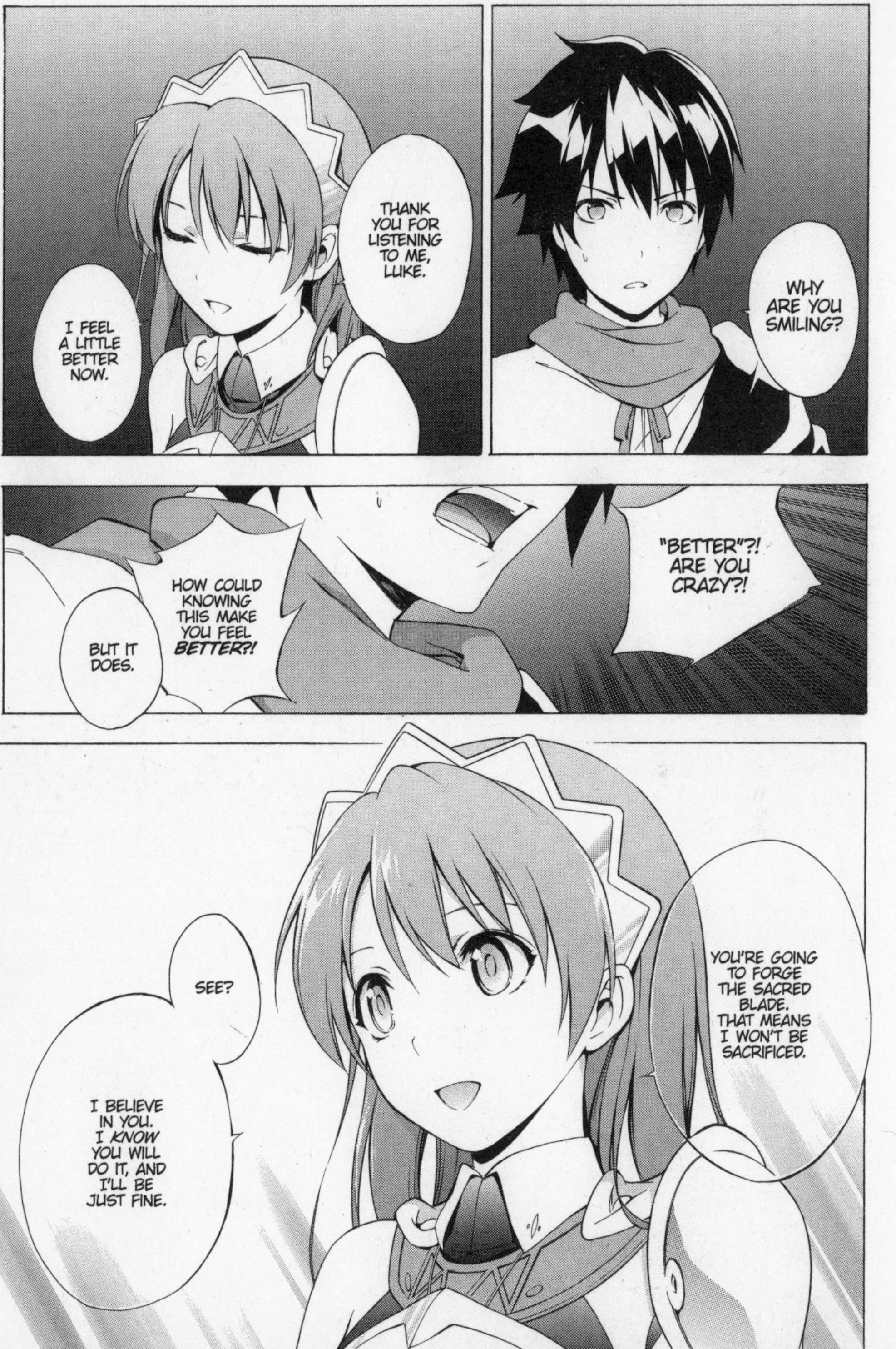
WHY ARE YOU SMILING?
THANK YOU FOR LISTENING TO ME, LUKE.
I FEEL A LITTLE BETTER NOW.
"BETTER"?! ARE YOU CRAZY?!
HOW COULD KNOWING THIS MAKE YOU FEEL *BETTER?!*
BUT IT DOES.
YOU'RE GOING TO FORGE THE SACRED BLADE. THAT MEANS I WON'T BE SACRIFICED.
SEE?
I BELIEVE IN YOU. I *KNOW* YOU WILL DO IT, AND I'LL BE JUST FINE.

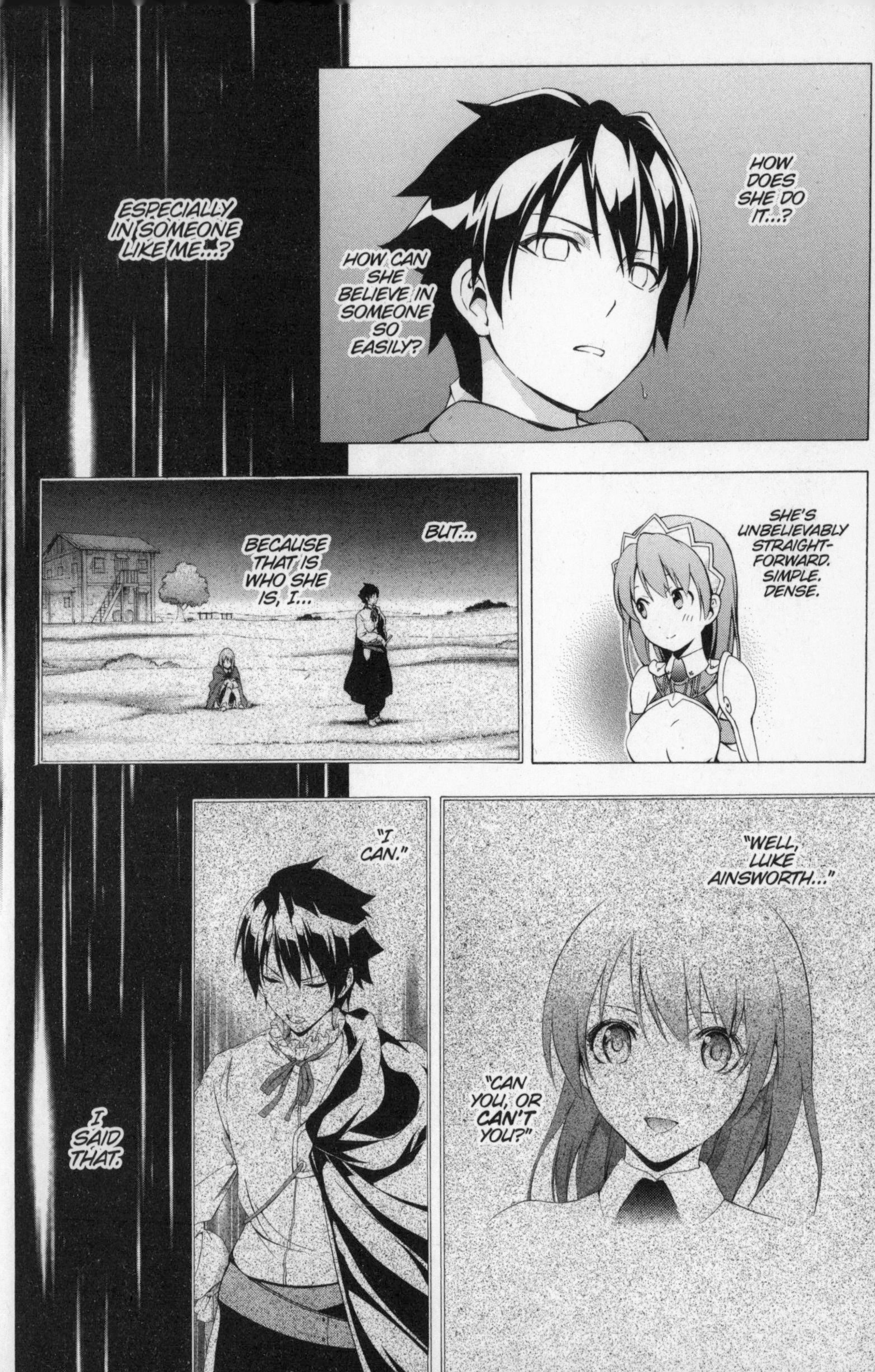
HOW DOES SHE DO IT...?
HOW CAN SHE BELIEVE IN SOMEONE SO EASILY?
ESPECIALLY IN SOMEONE LIKE ME...?
SHE'S UNBELIEVABLY STRAIGHT-FORWARD. SIMPLE. DENSE.
BUT...
BECAUSE THAT IS WHO SHE IS, I...
"WELL, LUKE AINSWORTH..."
"CAN YOU, OR CAN'T YOU?"
"I CAN."
I SAID THAT.

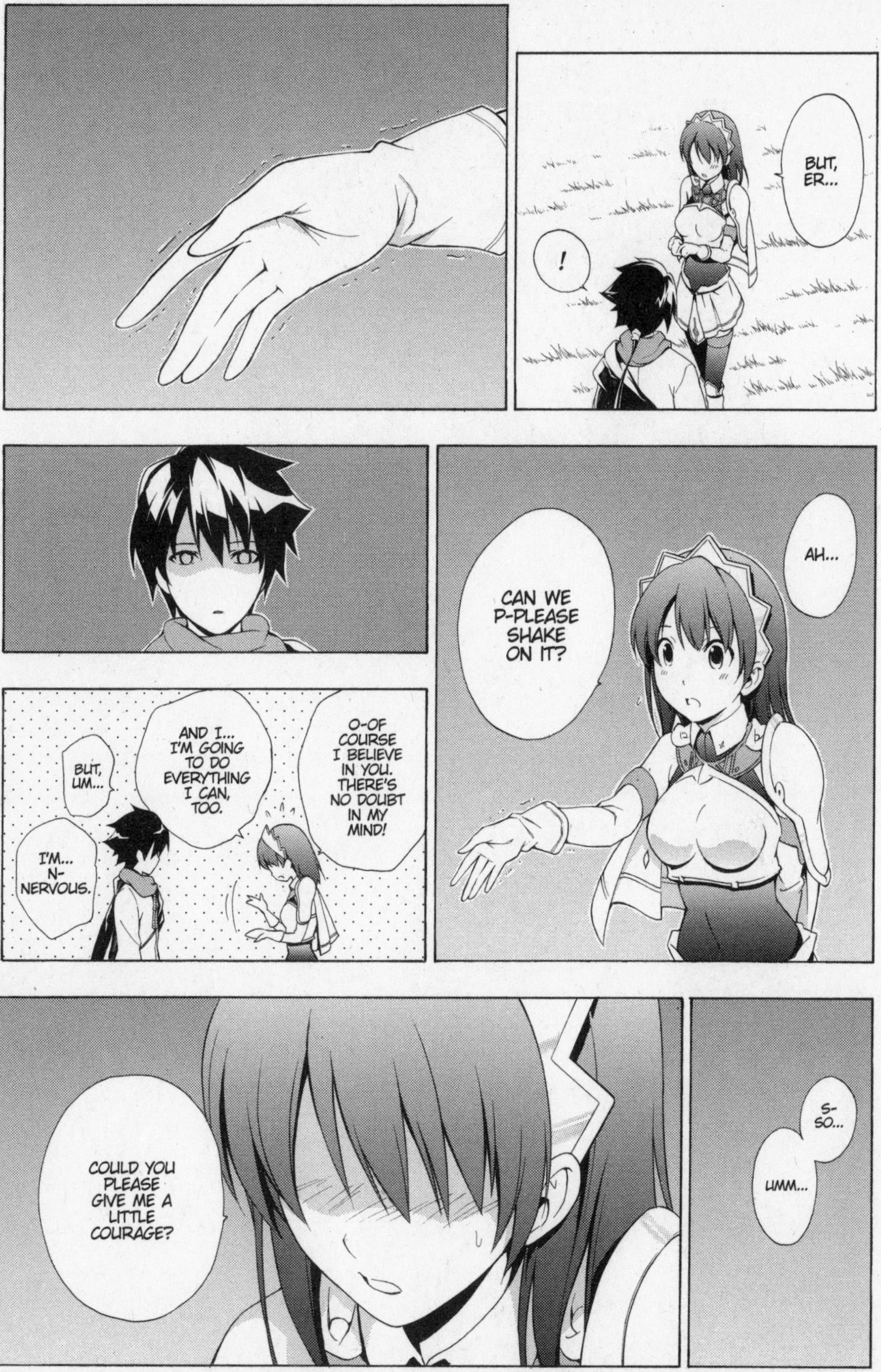
BUT, ER...
!
AH...
CAN WE P-PLEASE SHAKE ON IT?
O-OF COURSE I BELIEVE IN YOU. THERE'S NO DOUBT IN MY MIND!
AND I... I'M GOING TO DO EVERYTHING I CAN, TOO.
BUT, UM...
I'M... N-NERVOUS.
S-SO...
UMM...
COULD YOU PLEASE GIVE ME A LITTLE COURAGE?

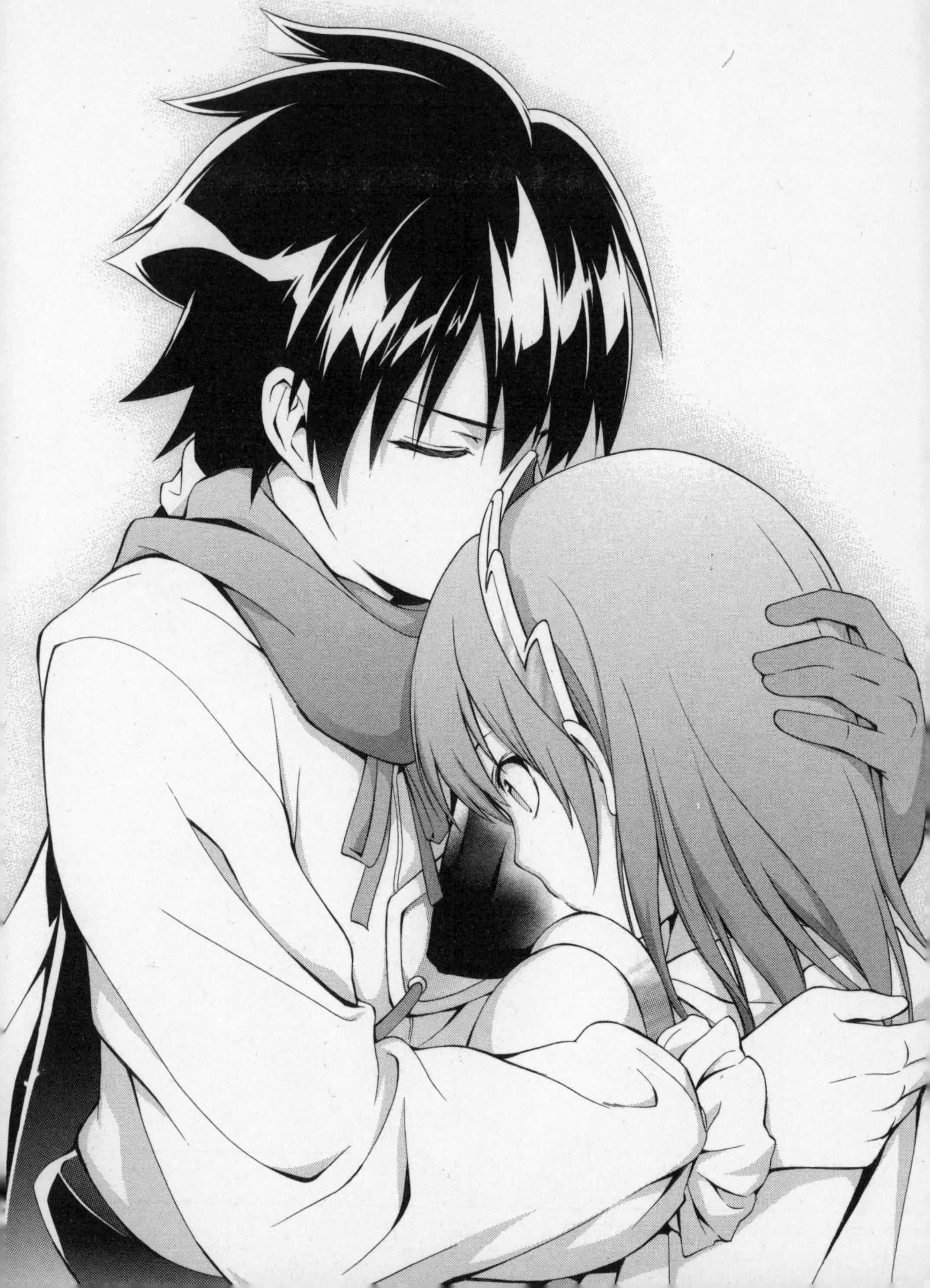

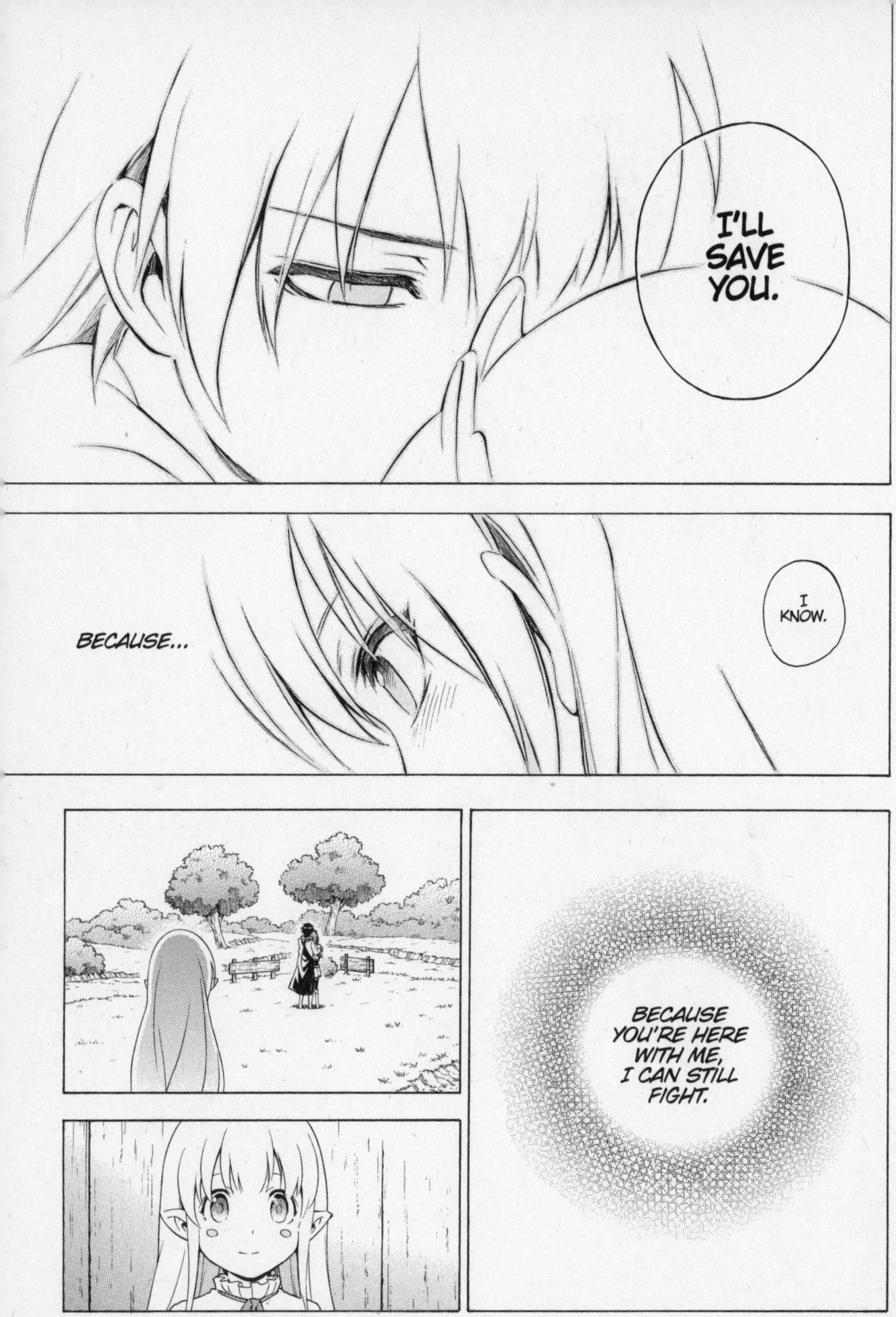
I'LL SAVE YOU.
I KNOW.
BECAUSE...
BECAUSE YOU'RE HERE WITH ME, I CAN STILL FIGHT.

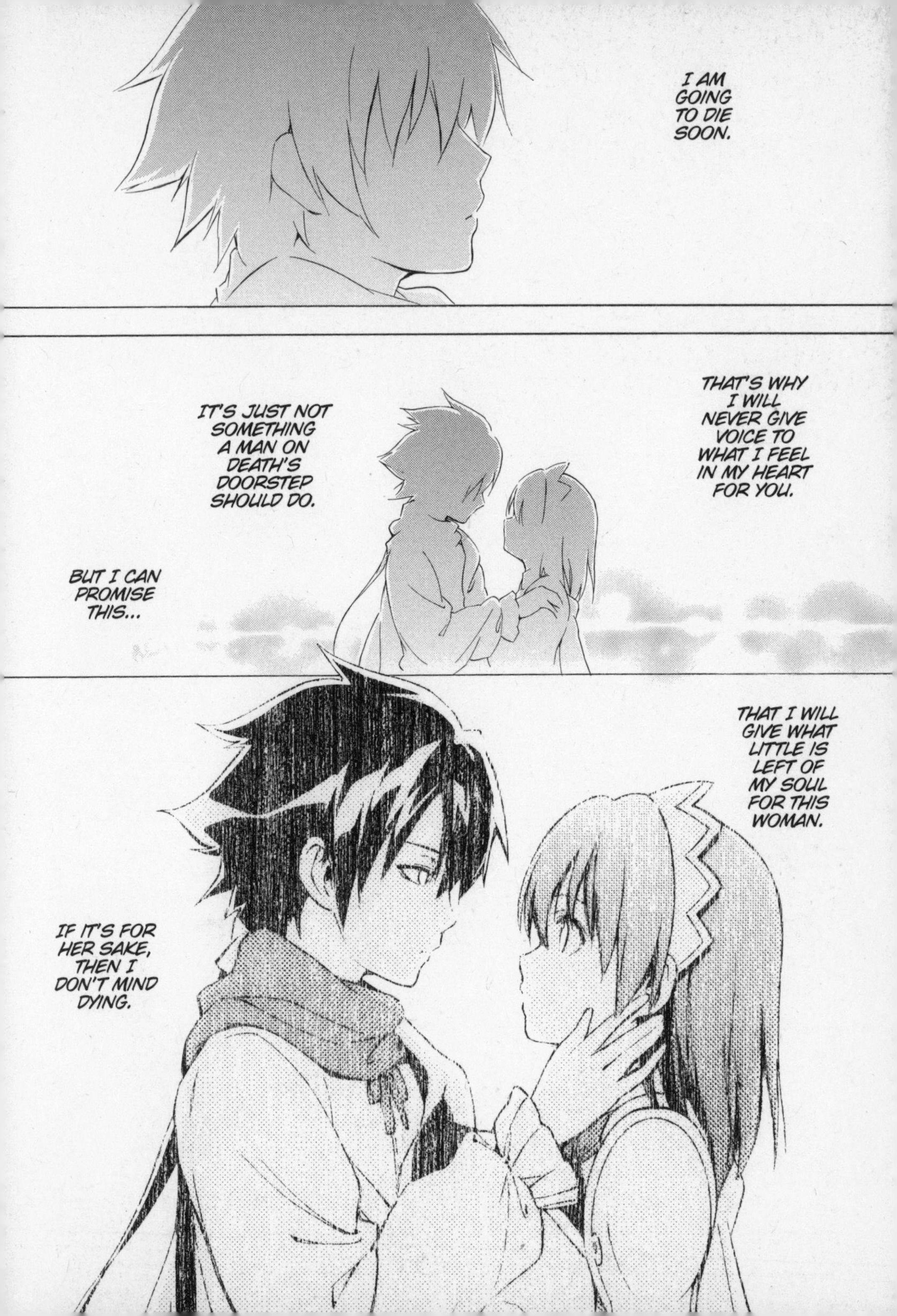
I AM GOING TO DIE SOON.
THAT'S WHY I WILL NEVER GIVE VOICE TO WHAT I FEEL IN MY HEART FOR YOU.
IT'S JUST NOT SOMETHING A MAN ON DEATH'S DOORSTEP SHOULD DO.
BUT I CAN PROMISE THIS...
THAT I WILL GIVE WHAT LITTLE IS LEFT OF MY SOUL FOR THIS WOMAN.
IF IT'S FOR HER SAKE, THEN I DON'T MIND DYING.

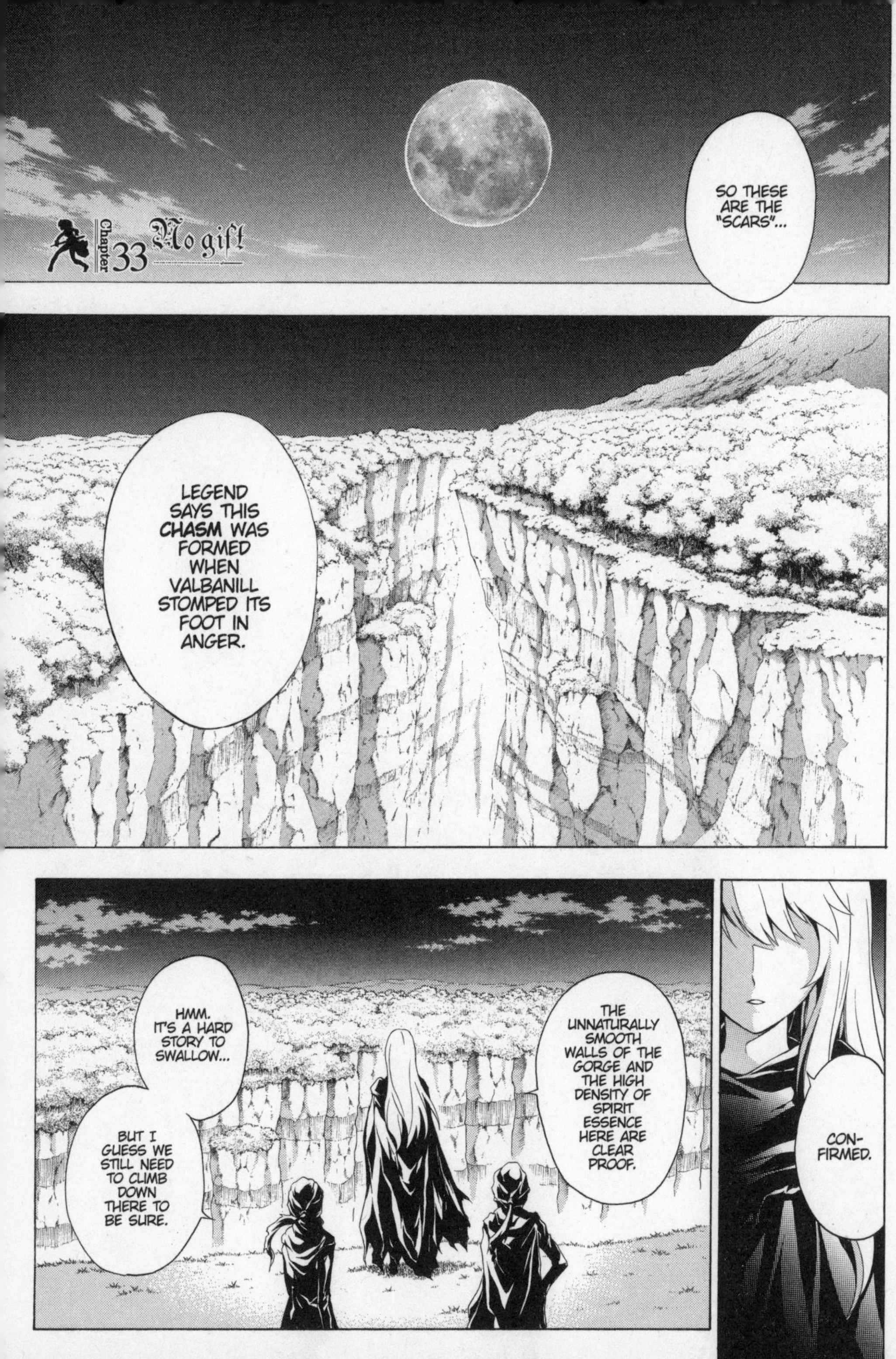
Chapter 33 No gift
SO THESE ARE THE "SCARS"...
LEGEND SAYS THIS CHASM WAS FORMED WHEN VALBANILL STOMPED ITS FOOT IN ANGER.
CON-FIRMED.
THE UNNATURALLY SMOOTH WALLS OF THE GORGE AND THE HIGH DENSITY OF SPIRIT ESSENCE HERE ARE CLEAR PROOF.
HMM. IT'S A HARD STORY TO SWALLOW...
BUT I GUESS WE STILL NEED TO CLIMB DOWN THERE TO BE SURE.

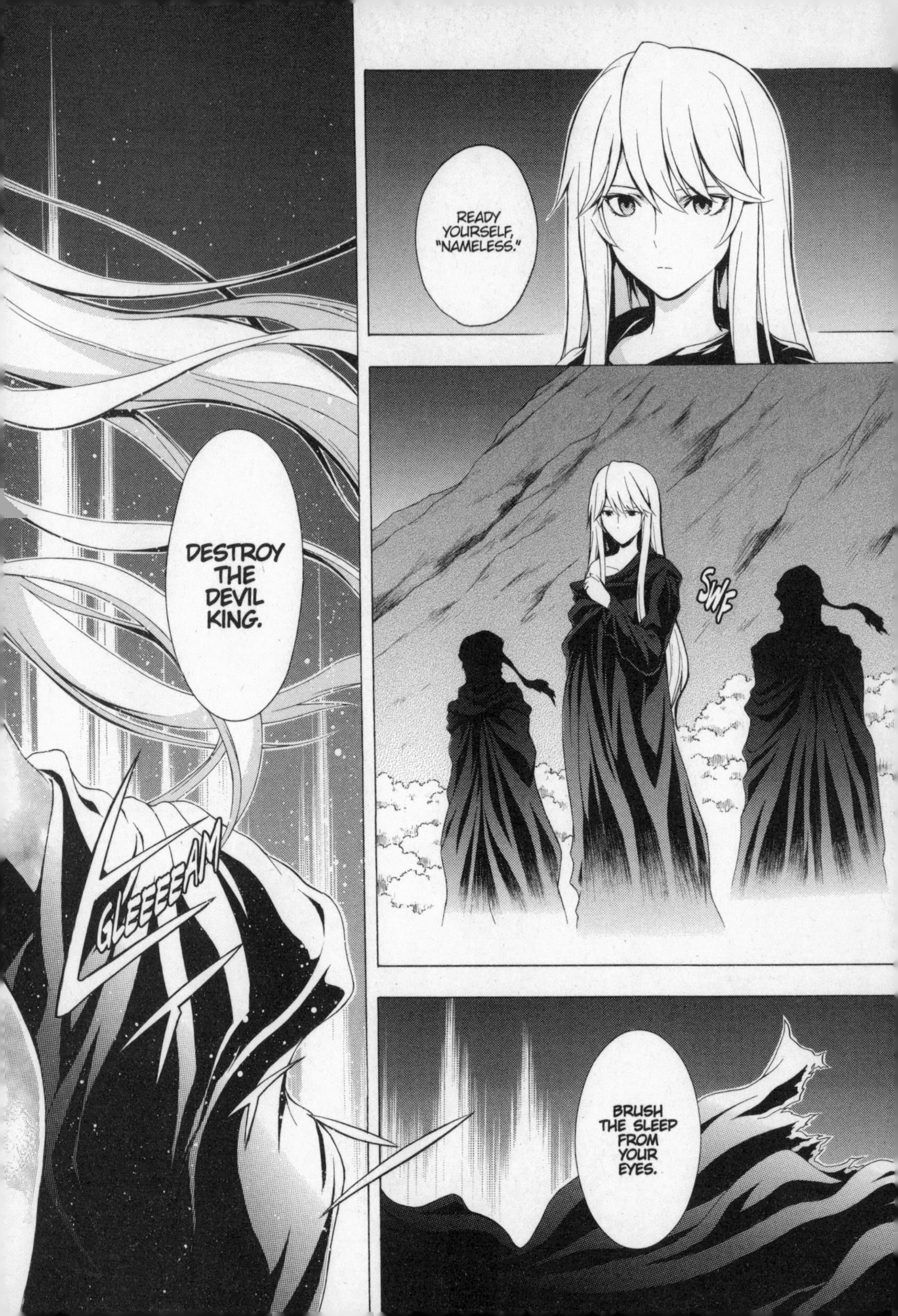
READY YOURSELF, "NAMELESS."
SWF
BRUSH THE SLEEP FROM YOUR EYES.
DESTROY THE DEVIL KING.
GLEEEEAM

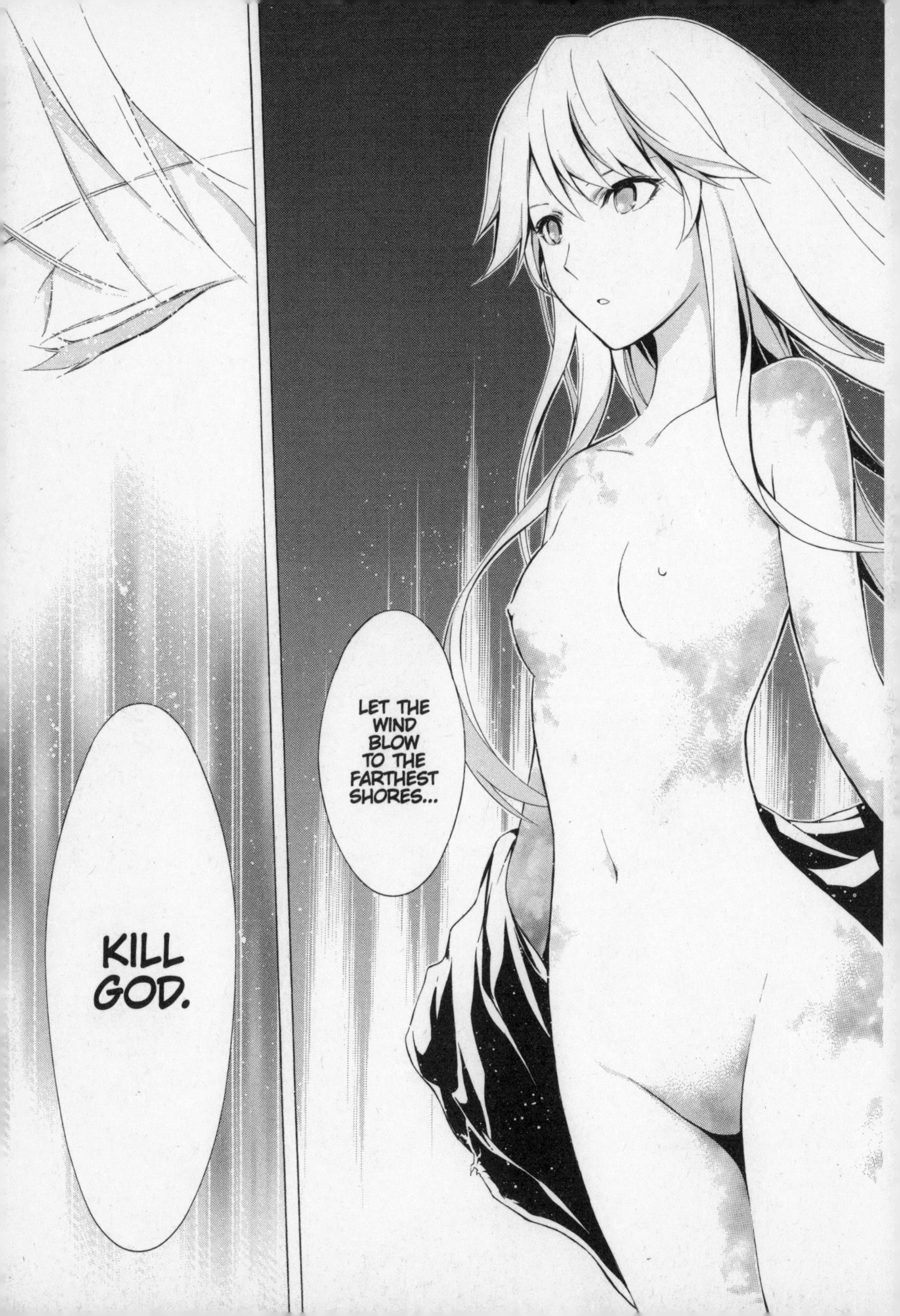
LET THE WIND BLOW TO THE FARTHEST SHORES...
KILL GOD.

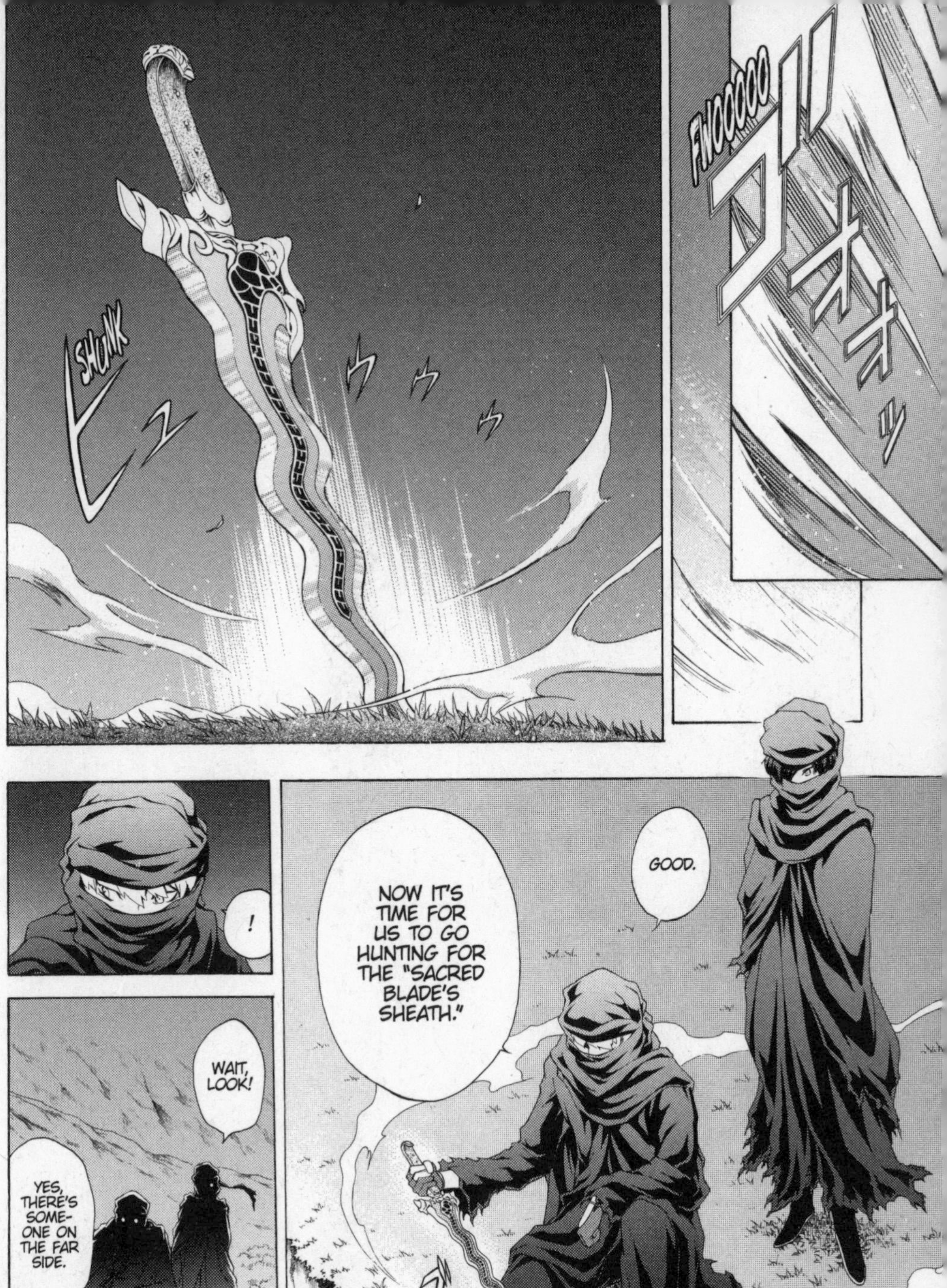
FWOOOOO
SHUNK
GOOD.
NOW IT'S TIME FOR US TO GO HUNTING FOR THE "SACRED BLADE'S SHEATH."
!
WAIT, LOOK!
YES, THERE'S SOME-ONE ON THE FAR SIDE.

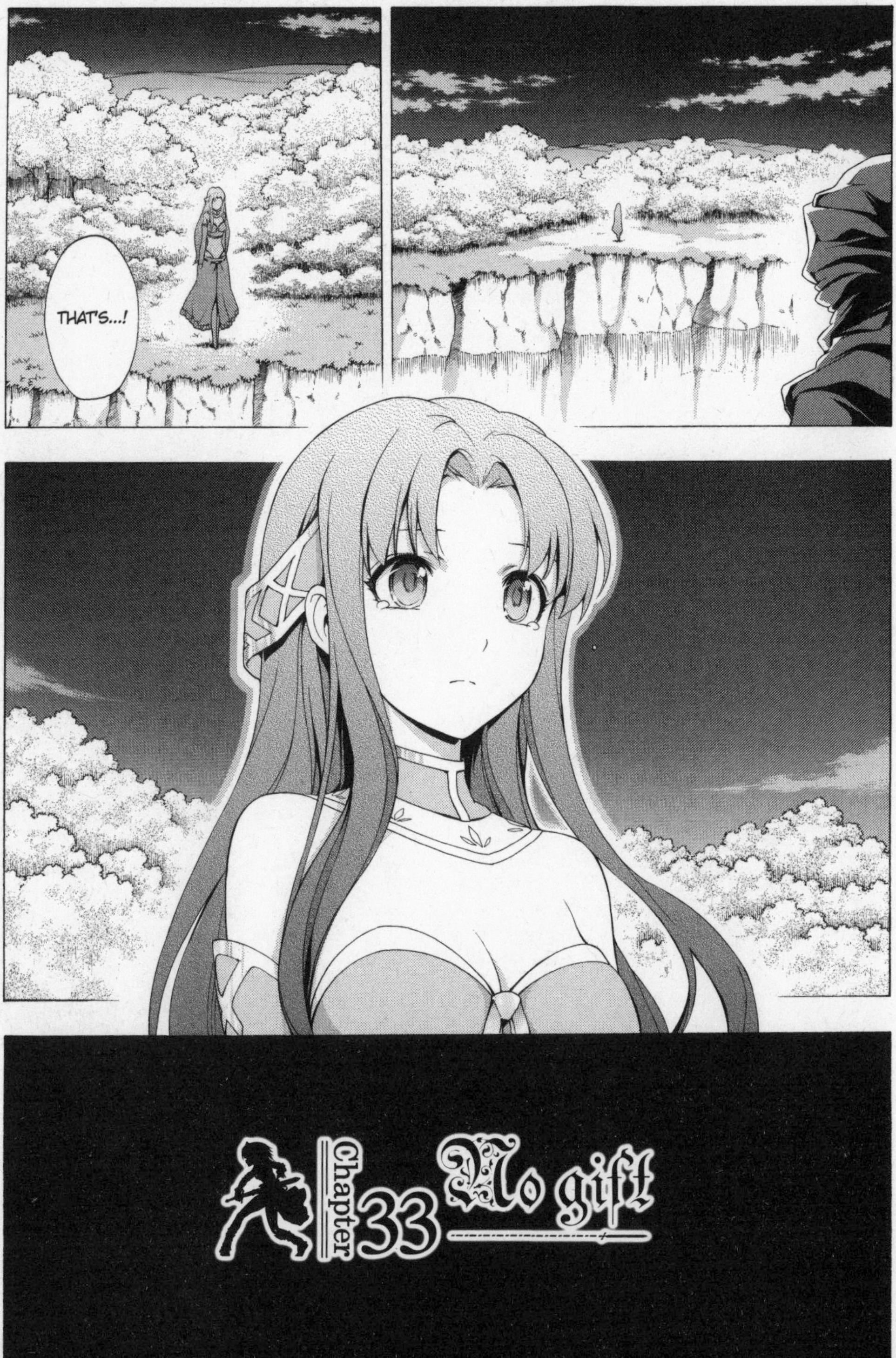
THAT'S...!
Chapter 33
No gift

SEVERAL HOURS EARLIER...

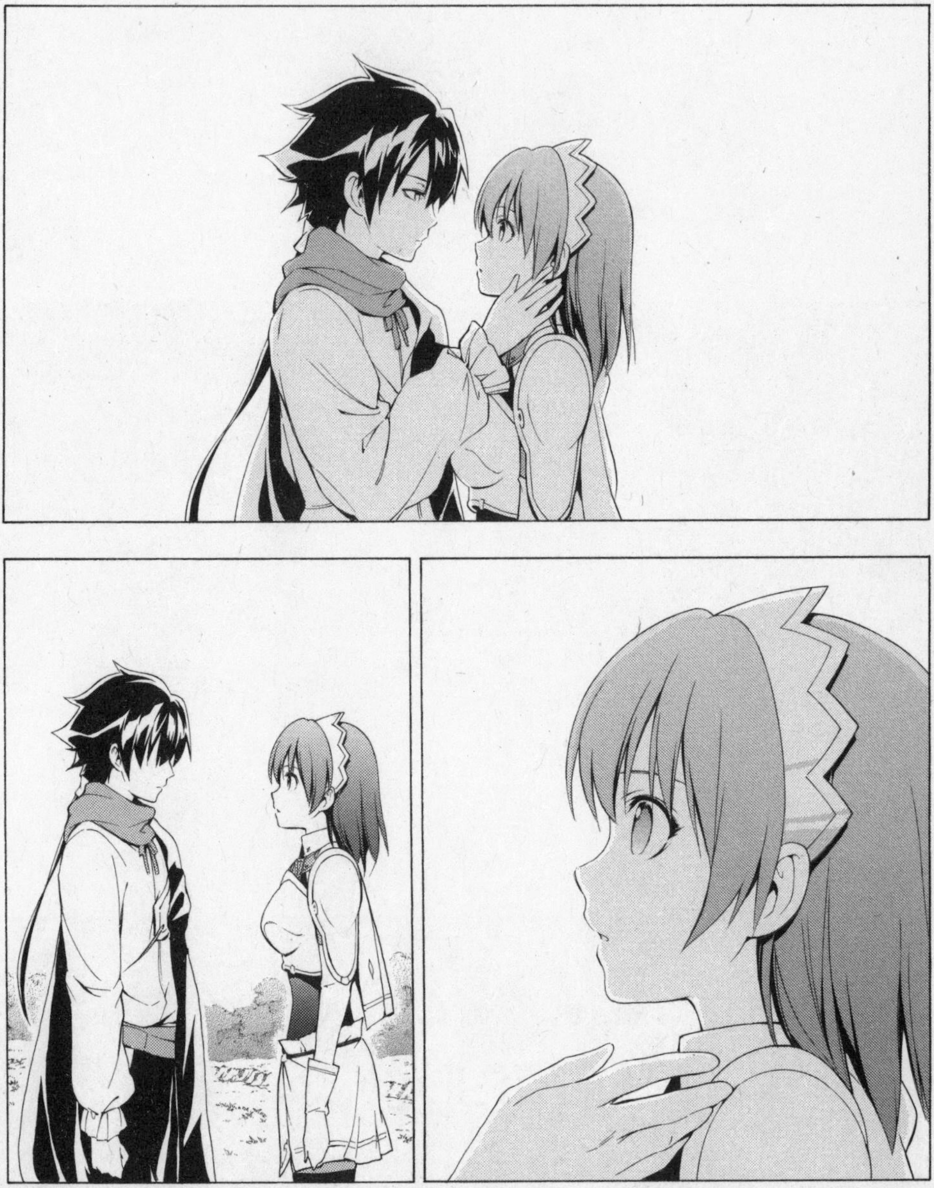

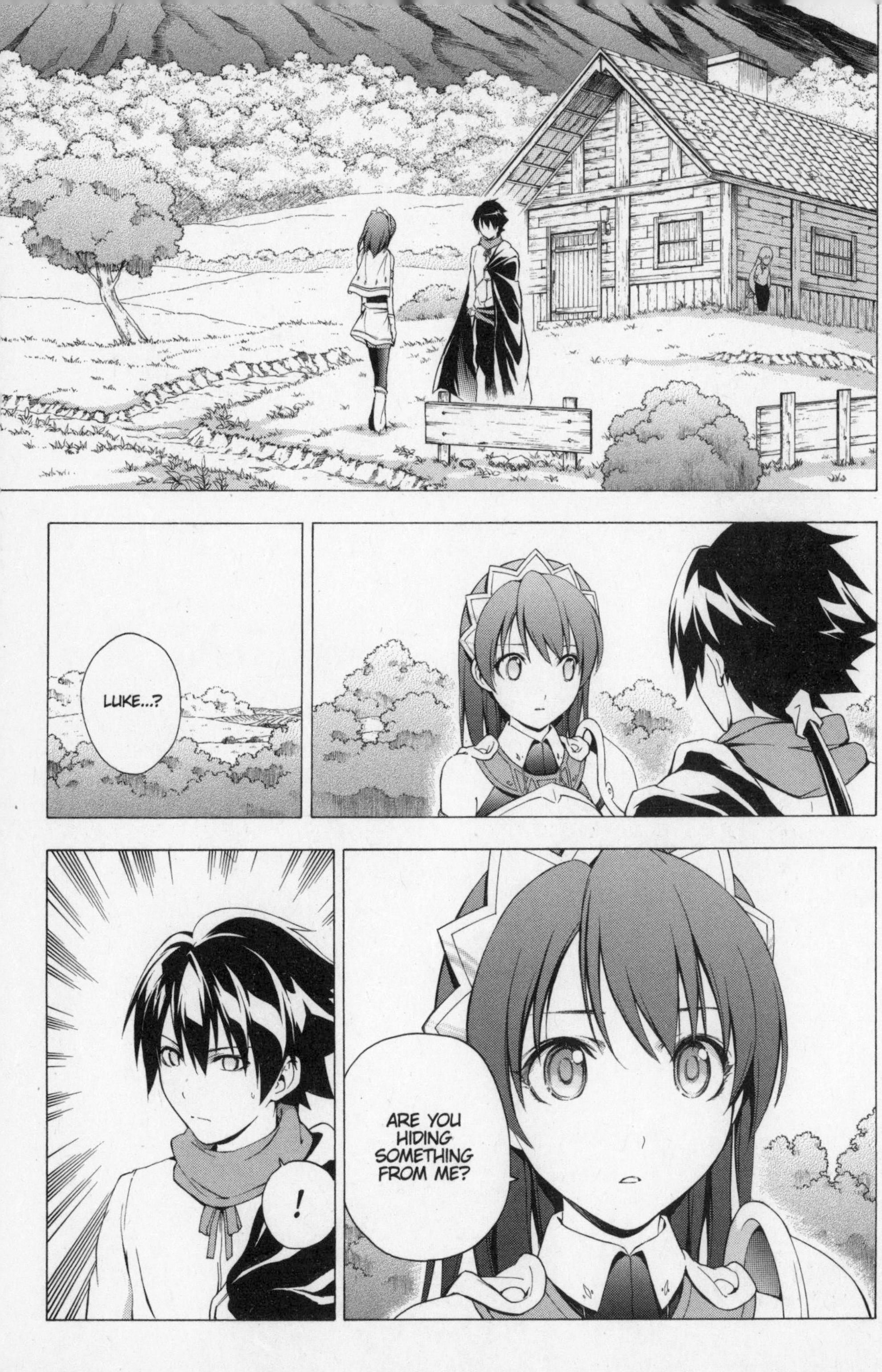
LUKE...?
ARE YOU HIDING SOMETHING FROM ME?
!

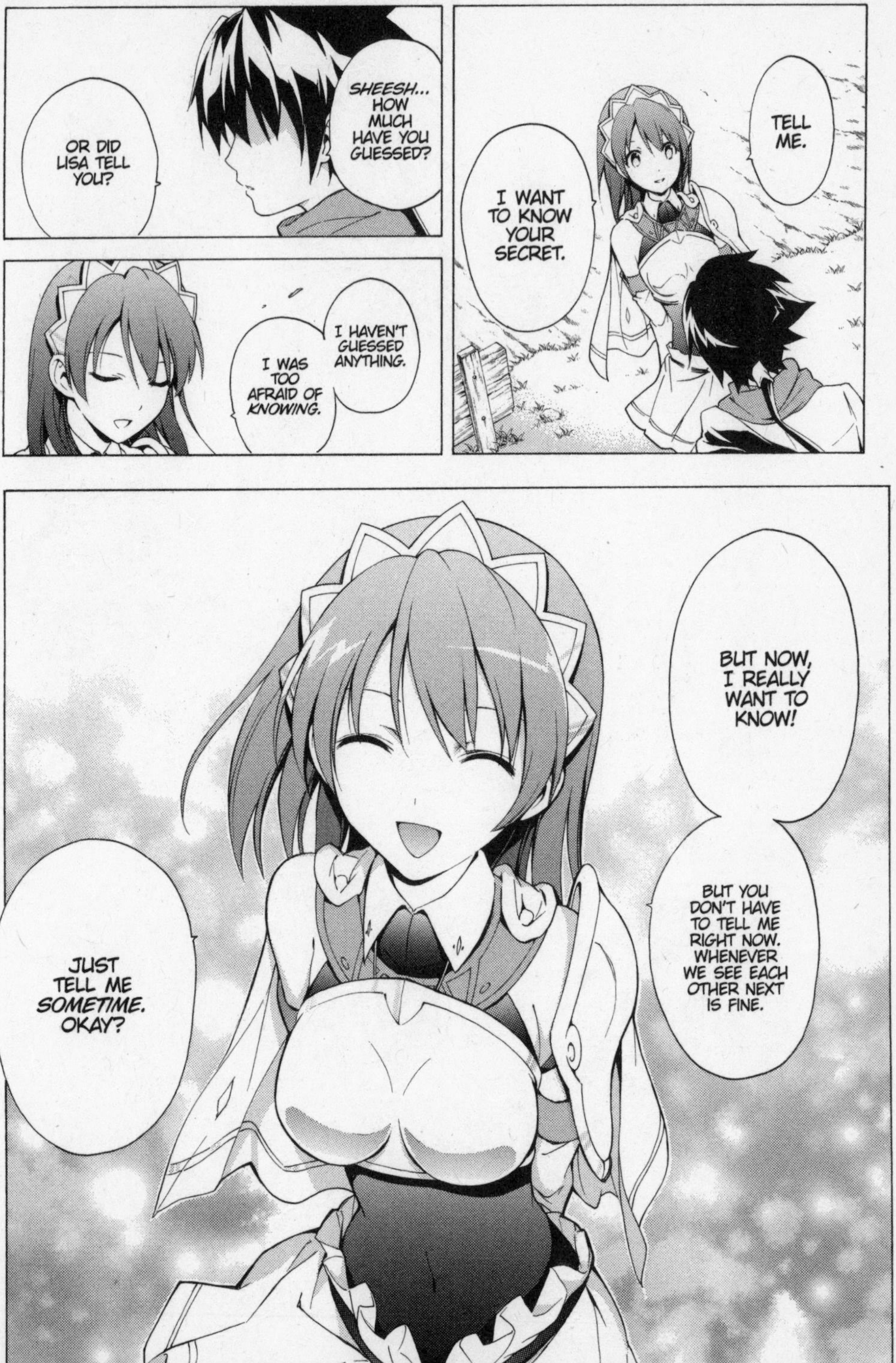
TELL ME.
I WANT TO KNOW YOUR SECRET.
SHEESH... HOW MUCH HAVE YOU GUESSED?
OR DID LISA TELL YOU?
I HAVEN'T GUESSED ANYTHING.
I WAS TOO AFRAID OF *KNOWING.*
BUT NOW, I REALLY WANT TO KNOW!
BUT YOU DON'T HAVE TO TELL ME RIGHT NOW. WHENEVER WE SEE EACH OTHER NEXT IS FINE.
JUST TELL ME *SOMETIME.* OKAY?

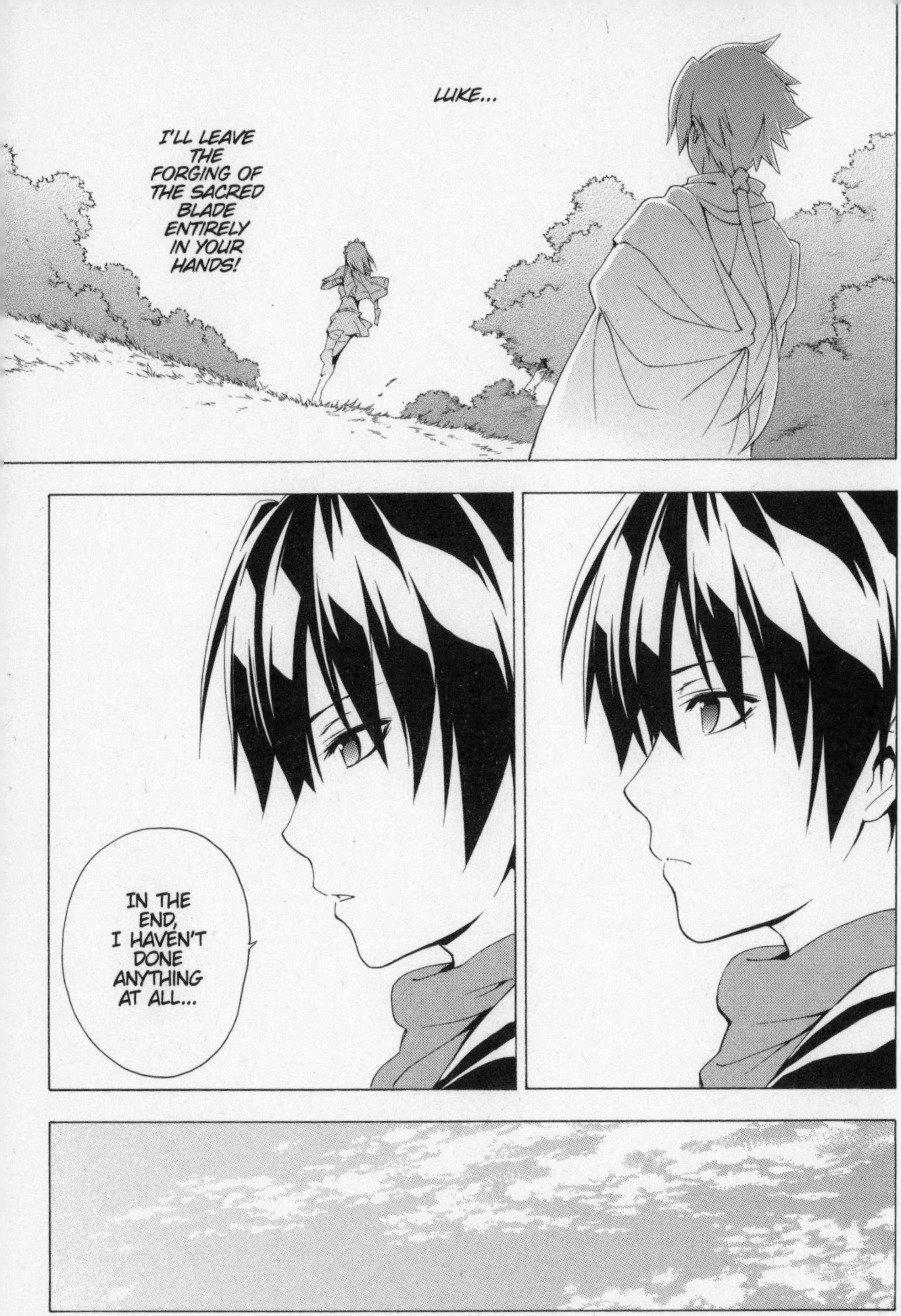
LUKE...
I'LL LEAVE THE FORGING OF THE SACRED BLADE ENTIRELY IN YOUR HANDS!
IN THE END, I HAVEN'T DONE ANYTHING AT ALL...

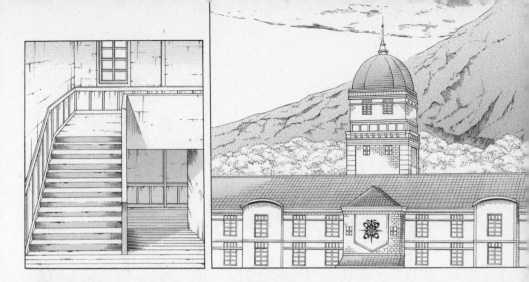

—PUBLIC OFFICES, BASEMENT STORAGE ROOM—

ARE YOU THE ARCHAE-OLOGIST WHO CAME FROM THE MILITANT NATION?

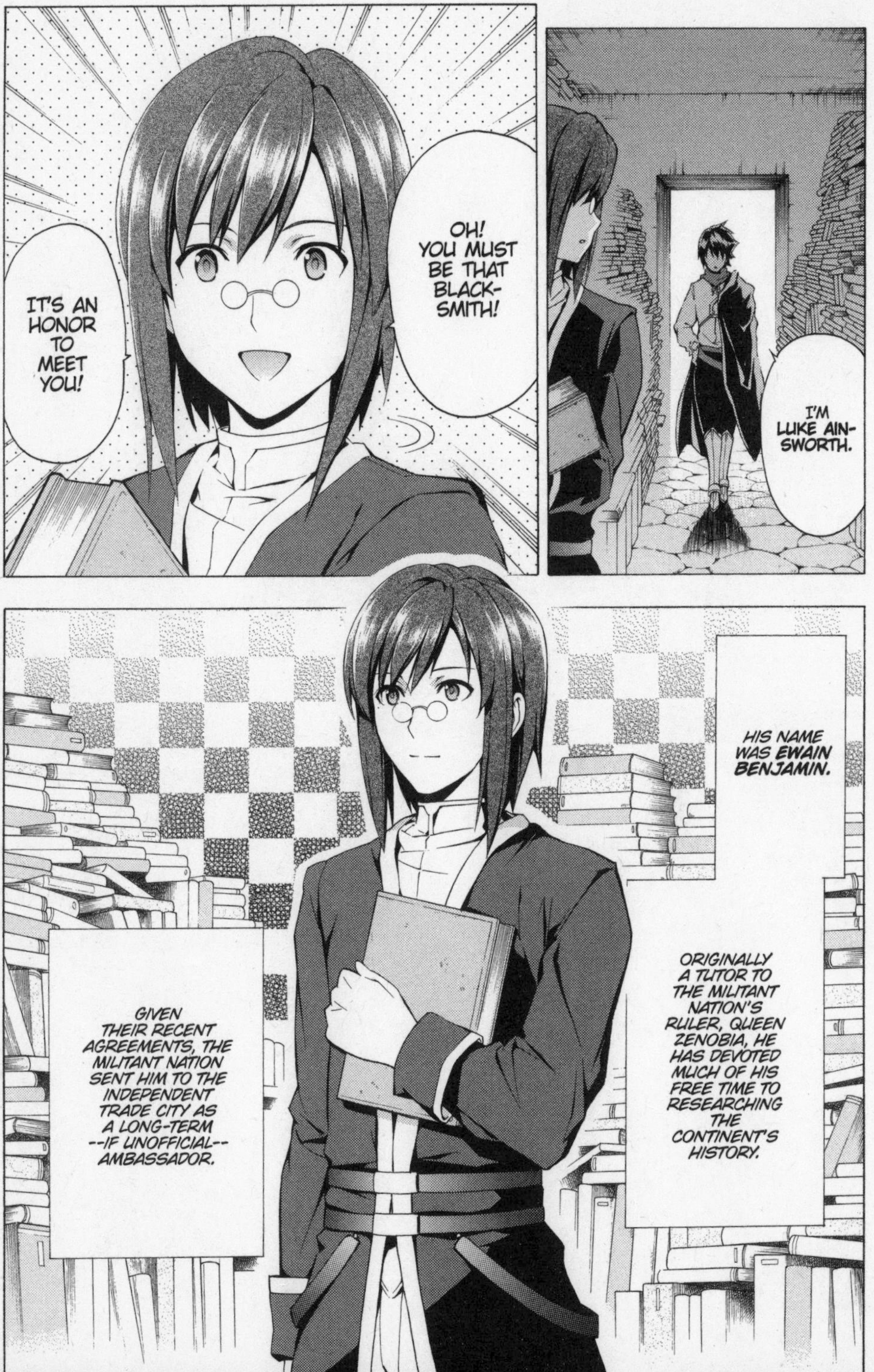
I'M LUKE AIN-SWORTH.
OH! YOU MUST BE THAT BLACK-SMITH!
IT'S AN HONOR TO MEET YOU!
HIS NAME WAS EWAIN BENJAMIN.
ORIGINALLY A TUTOR TO THE MILITANT NATION'S RULER, QUEEN ZENOBIA, HE HAS DEVOTED MUCH OF HIS FREE TIME TO RESEARCHING THE CONTINENT'S HISTORY.
GIVEN THEIR RECENT AGREEMENTS, THE MILITANT NATION SENT HIM TO THE INDEPENDENT TRADE CITY AS A LONG-TERM --IF UNOFFICIAL-- AMBASSADOR.

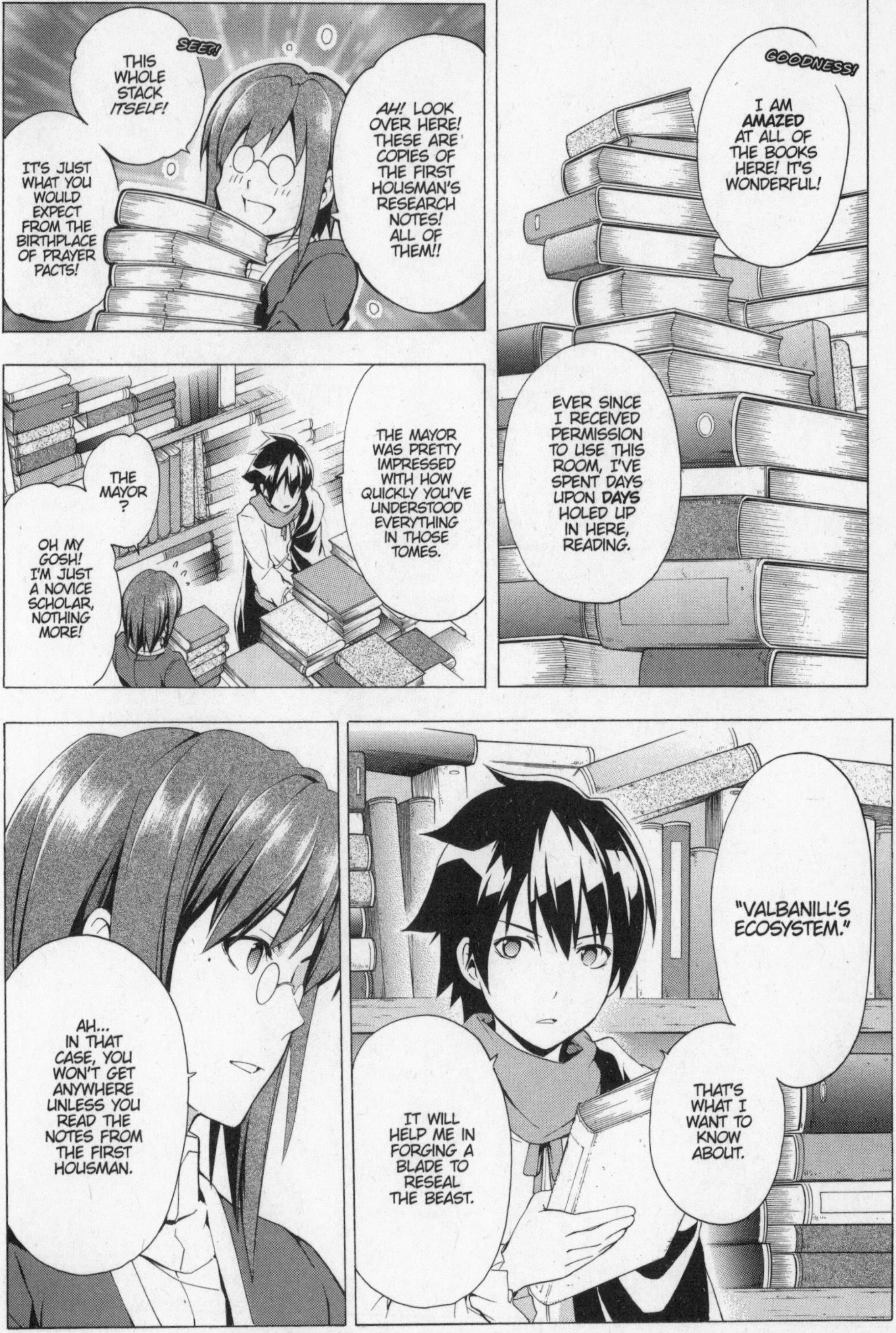
GOODNESS!
I AM AMAZED AT ALL OF THE BOOKS HERE! IT'S WONDERFUL!
EVER SINCE I RECEIVED PERMISSION TO USE THIS ROOM, I'VE SPENT DAYS UPON DAYS HOLED UP IN HERE, READING.
AH! LOOK OVER HERE! THESE ARE COPIES OF THE FIRST HOUSMAN'S RESEARCH NOTES! ALL OF THEM!!
SEE?!
THIS WHOLE STACK ITSELF!
IT'S JUST WHAT YOU WOULD EXPECT FROM THE BIRTHPLACE OF PRAYER PACTS!
THE MAYOR WAS PRETTY IMPRESSED WITH HOW QUICKLY YOU'VE UNDERSTOOD EVERYTHING IN THOSE TOMES.
THE MAYOR?
OH MY GOSH! I'M JUST A NOVICE SCHOLAR, NOTHING MORE!
"VALBANILL'S ECOSYSTEM."
THAT'S WHAT I WANT TO KNOW ABOUT.
IT WILL HELP ME IN FORGING A BLADE TO RESEAL THE BEAST.
AH... IN THAT CASE, YOU WON'T GET ANYWHERE UNLESS YOU READ THE NOTES FROM THE FIRST HOUSMAN.

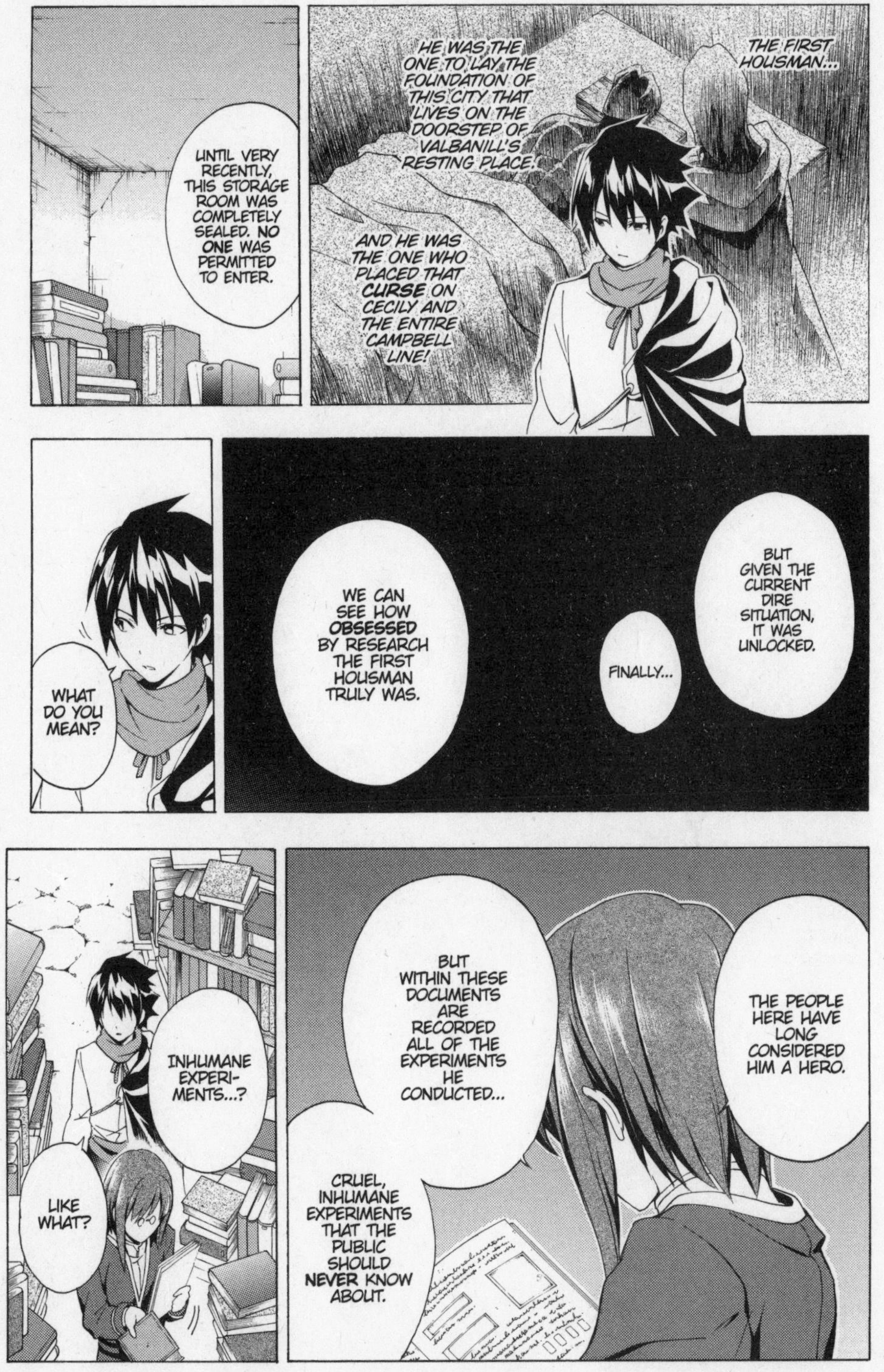
THE FIRST HOUSMAN...
HE WAS THE ONE TO LAY THE FOUNDATION OF THIS CITY THAT LIVES ON THE DOORSTEP OF VALBANILL'S RESTING PLACE.
AND HE WAS THE ONE WHO PLACED THAT CURSE ON CECILY AND THE ENTIRE CAMPBELL LINE!
UNTIL VERY RECENTLY, THIS STORAGE ROOM WAS COMPLETELY SEALED. NO ONE WAS PERMITTED TO ENTER.
BUT GIVEN THE CURRENT DIRE SITUATION, IT WAS UNLOCKED.
FINALLY...
WE CAN SEE HOW OBSESSED BY RESEARCH THE FIRST HOUSMAN TRULY WAS.
WHAT DO YOU MEAN?
THE PEOPLE HERE HAVE LONG CONSIDERED HIM A HERO.
BUT WITHIN THESE DOCUMENTS ARE RECORDED ALL OF THE EXPERIMENTS HE CONDUCTED...
CRUEL, INHUMANE EXPERIMENTS THAT THE PUBLIC SHOULD NEVER KNOW ABOUT.
INHUMANE EXPERI-MENTS...?
LIKE WHAT?

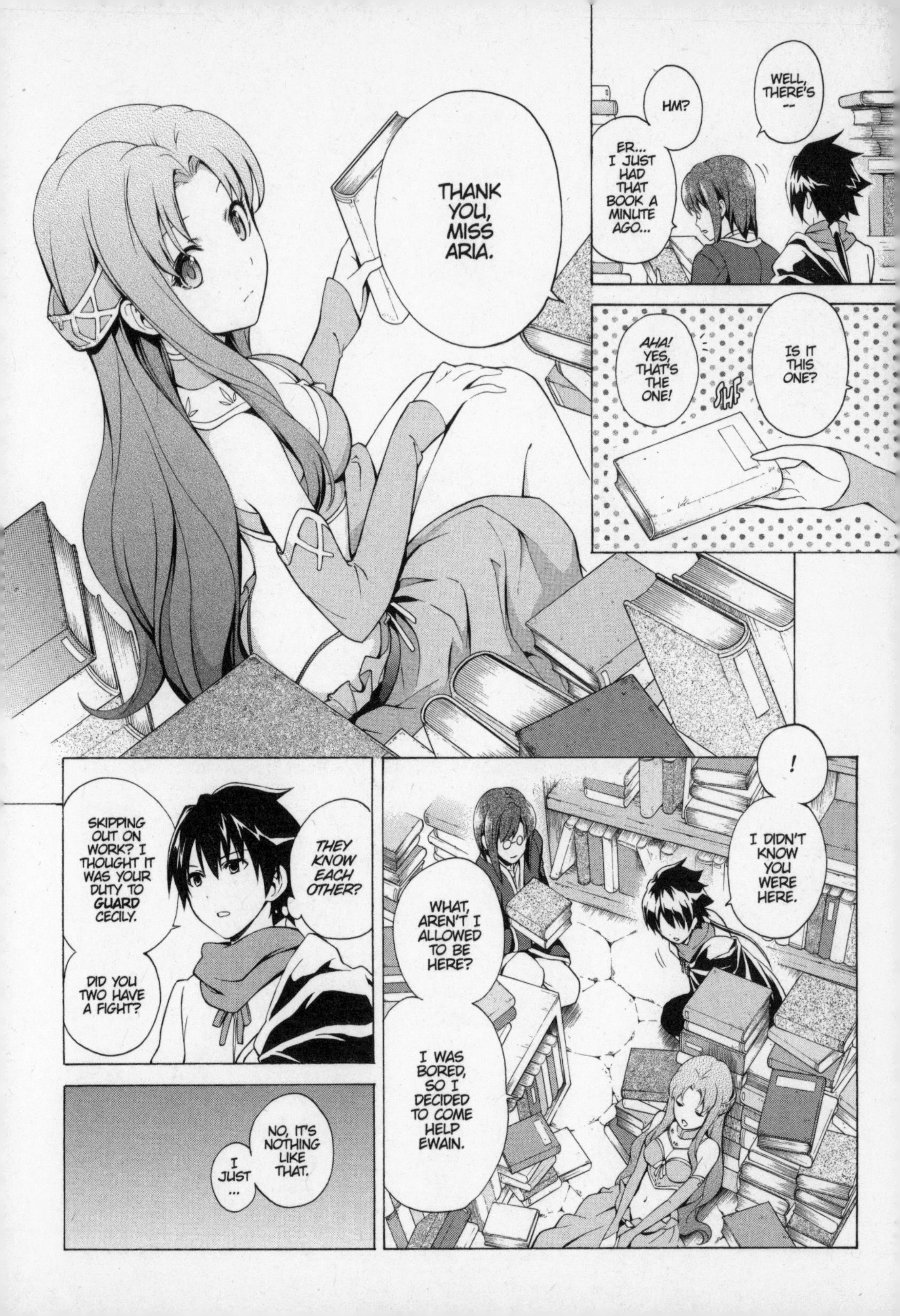
WELL, THERE'S --
HM?
ER... I JUST HAD THAT BOOK A MINUTE AGO...
IS IT THIS ONE?
AHA! YES, THAT'S THE ONE!
SHF
THANK YOU, MISS ARIA.
!
I DIDN'T KNOW YOU WERE HERE.
WHAT, AREN'T I ALLOWED TO BE HERE?
I WAS BORED, SO I DECIDED TO COME HELP EWAIN.
THEY KNOW EACH OTHER?
SKIPPING OUT ON WORK? I THOUGHT IT WAS YOUR DUTY TO GUARD CECILY.
DID YOU TWO HAVE A FIGHT?
NO, IT'S NOTHING LIKE THAT.
I JUST ...

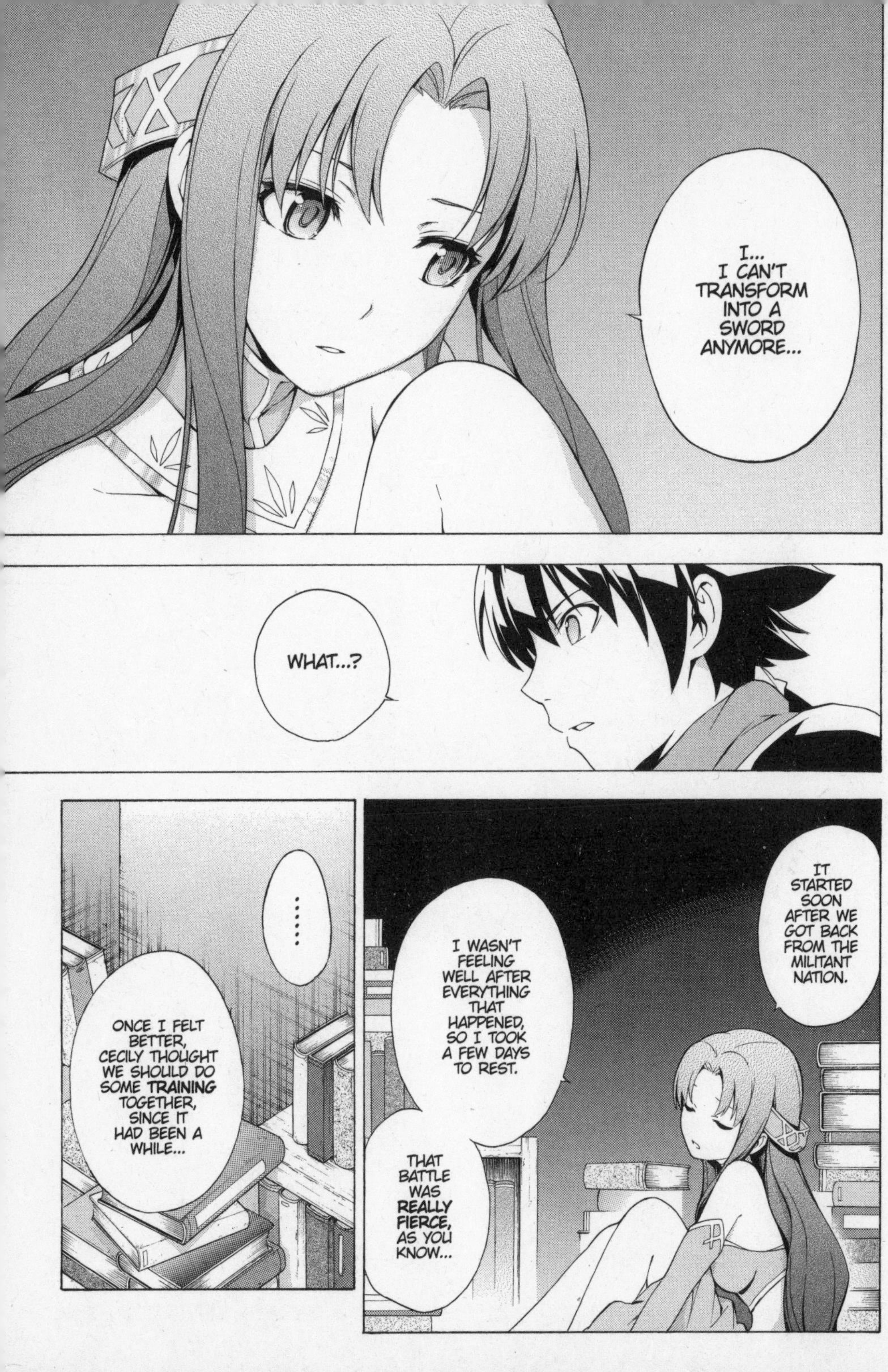
I... I CAN'T TRANSFORM INTO A SWORD ANYMORE...
WHAT...?
IT STARTED SOON AFTER WE GOT BACK FROM THE MILITANT NATION.
I WASN'T FEELING WELL AFTER EVERYTHING THAT HAPPENED, SO I TOOK A FEW DAYS TO REST.
THAT BATTLE WAS REALLY FIERCE, AS YOU KNOW...
......
ONCE I FELT BETTER, CECILY THOUGHT WE SHOULD DO SOME TRAINING TOGETHER, SINCE IT HAD BEEN A WHILE...

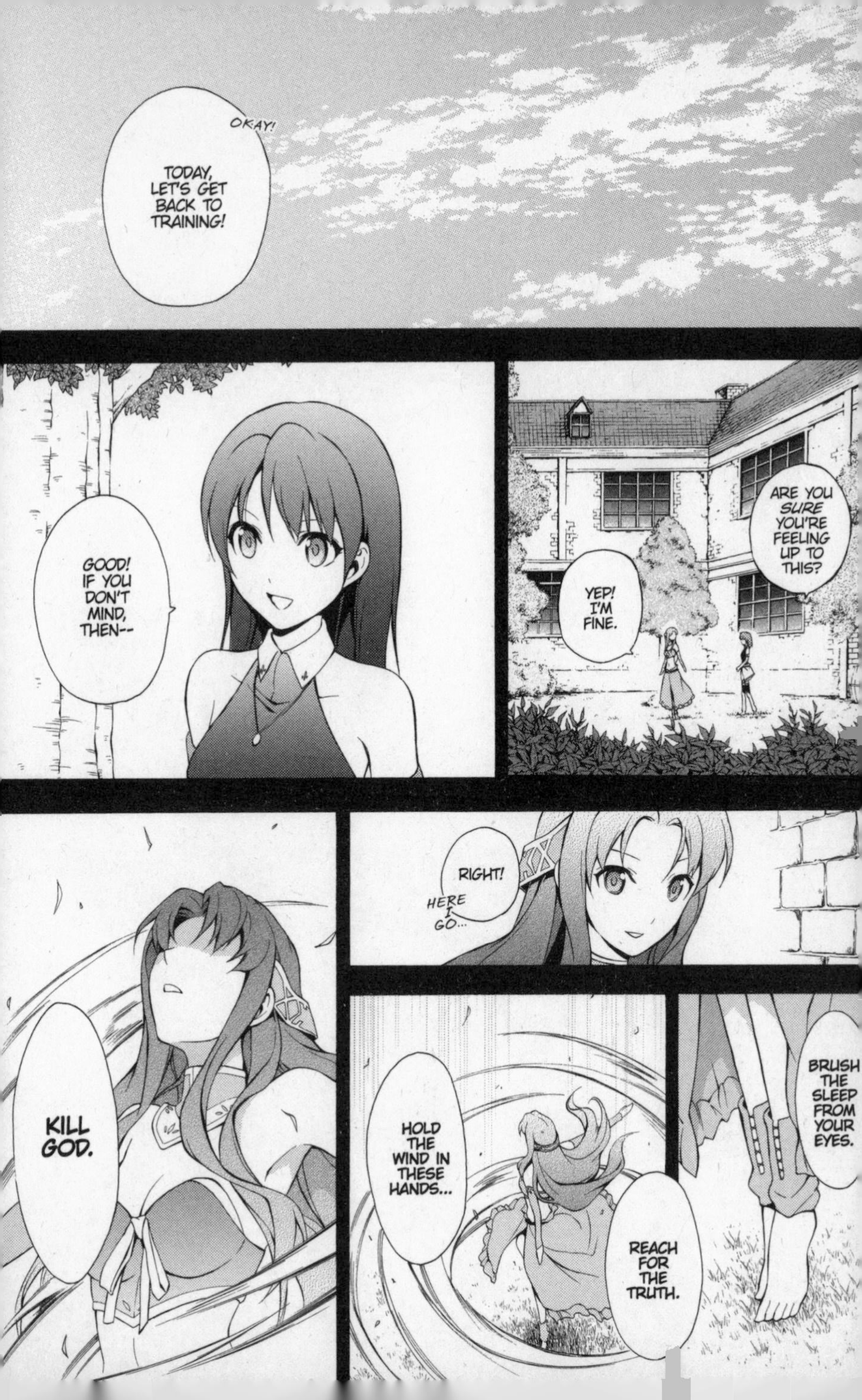
TODAY, LET'S GET BACK TO TRAINING!
OKAY!
ARE YOU SURE YOU'RE FEELING UP TO THIS?
YEP! I'M FINE.
GOOD! IF YOU DON'T MIND, THEN--
RIGHT!
HERE I GO...
BRUSH THE SLEEP FROM YOUR EYES.
HOLD THE WIND IN THESE HANDS...
REACH FOR THE TRUTH.
KILL GOD.

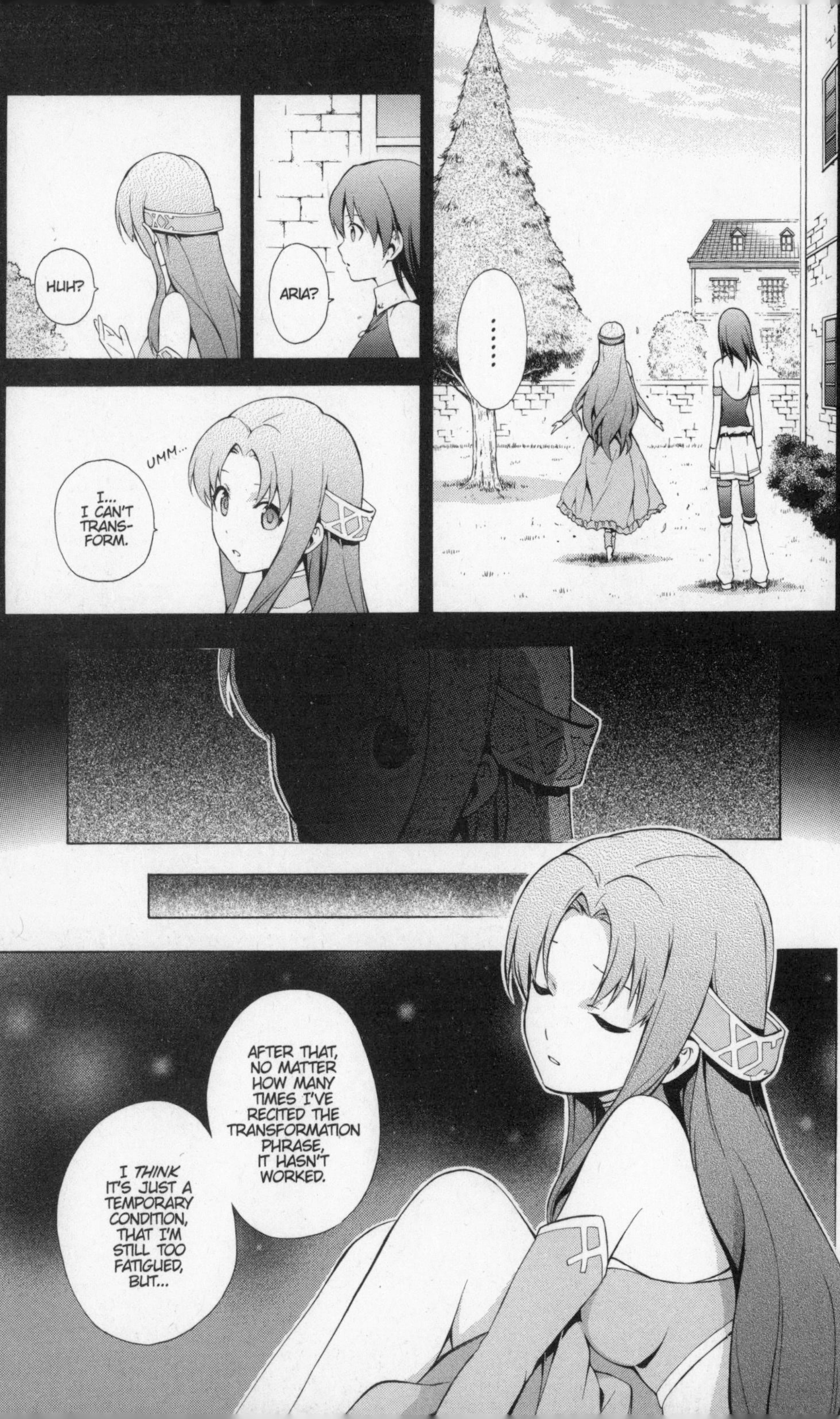
......
ARIA?
HUH?
UMM...
I... I CAN'T TRANS-FORM.
AFTER THAT, NO MATTER HOW MANY TIMES I'VE RECITED THE TRANSFORMATION PHRASE, IT HASN'T WORKED.
I *THINK* IT'S JUST A TEMPORARY CONDITION, THAT I'M STILL TOO FATIGUED, BUT...

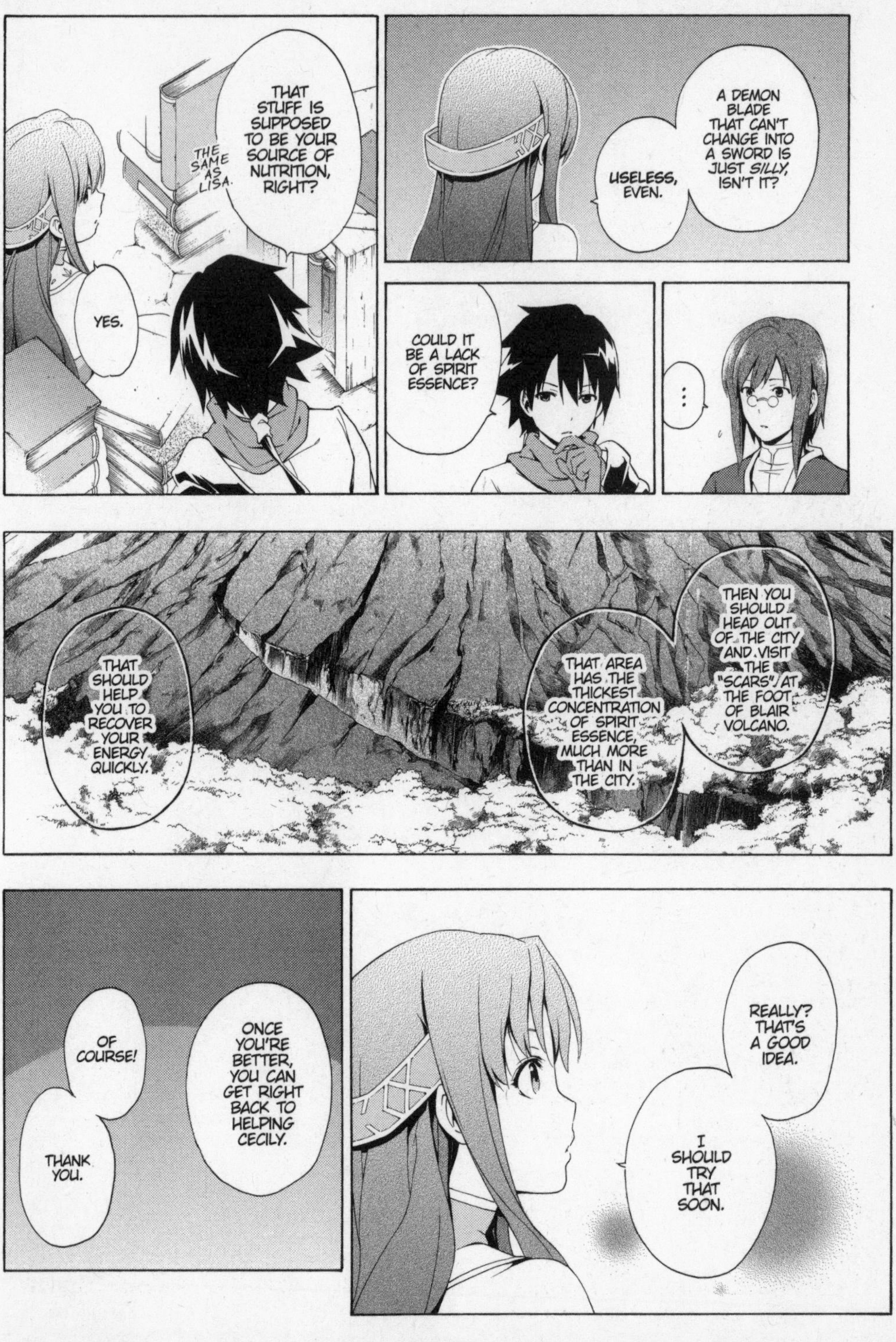
A DEMON BLADE THAT CAN'T CHANGE INTO A SWORD IS JUST *SILLY*, ISN'T IT?
USELESS, EVEN.
...
COULD IT BE A LACK OF SPIRIT ESSENCE?
THAT STUFF IS SUPPOSED TO BE YOUR SOURCE OF NUTRITION, RIGHT?
THE SAME AS LISA.
YES.
THEN YOU SHOULD HEAD OUT OF THE CITY AND VISIT THE "SCARS" AT THE FOOT OF BLAIR VOLCANO.
THAT AREA HAS THE THICKEST CONCENTRATION OF SPIRIT ESSENCE, MUCH MORE THAN IN THE CITY.
THAT SHOULD HELP YOU TO RECOVER YOUR ENERGY QUICKLY.
REALLY? THAT'S A GOOD IDEA.
I SHOULD TRY THAT SOON.
ONCE YOU'RE BETTER, YOU CAN GET RIGHT BACK TO HELPING CECILY.
OF COURSE!
THANK YOU.

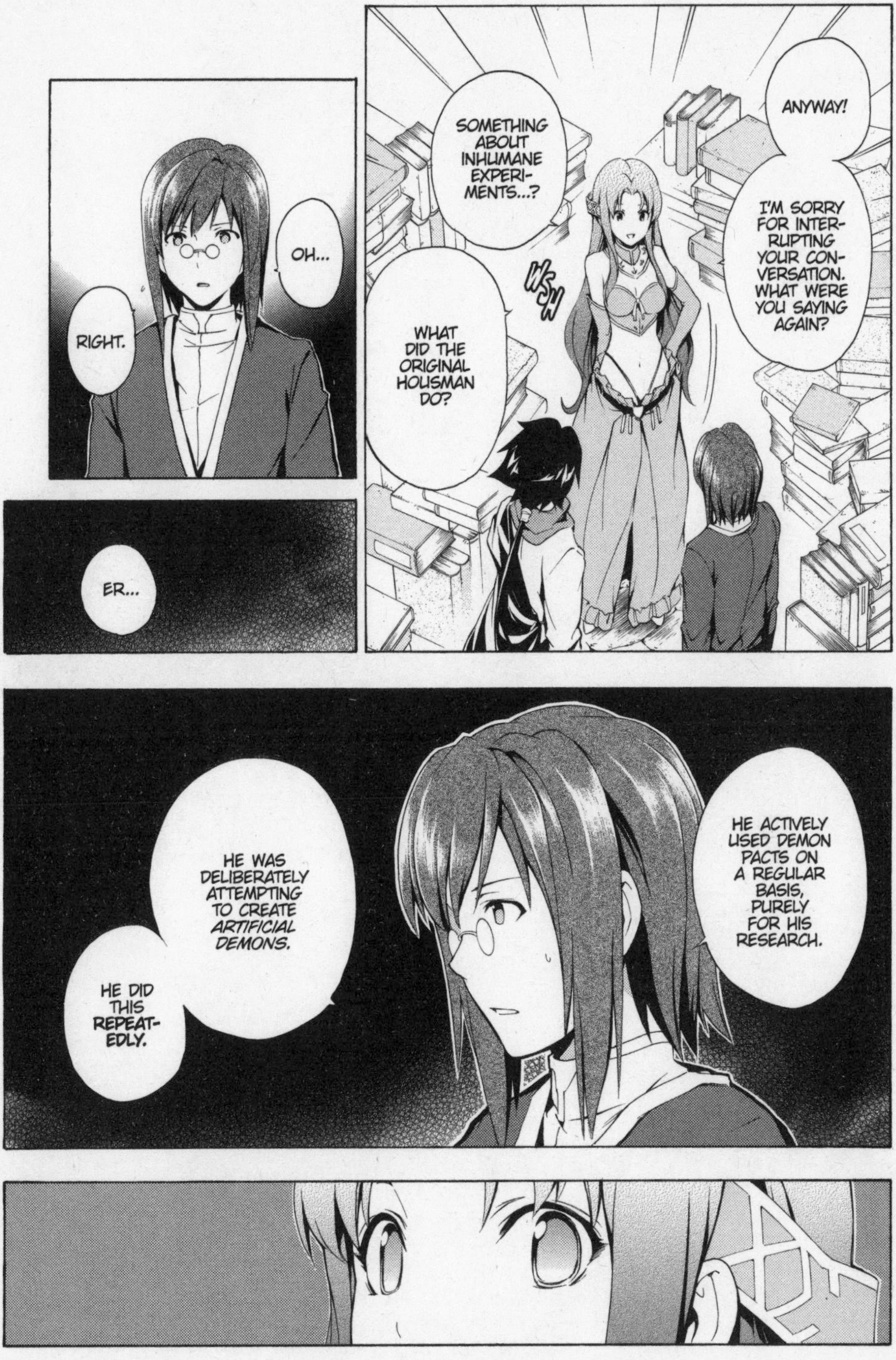
ANYWAY!
I'M SORRY FOR INTER-RUPTING YOUR CON-VERSATION. WHAT WERE YOU SAYING AGAIN?
SOMETHING ABOUT INHUMANE EXPERI-MENTS...?
WSH
WHAT DID THE ORIGINAL HOUSMAN DO?
OH...
RIGHT.
ER...
HE ACTIVELY USED DEMON PACTS ON A REGULAR BASIS, PURELY FOR HIS RESEARCH.
HE WAS DELIBERATELY ATTEMPTING TO CREATE *ARTIFICIAL DEMONS.*
HE DID THIS REPEAT-EDLY.

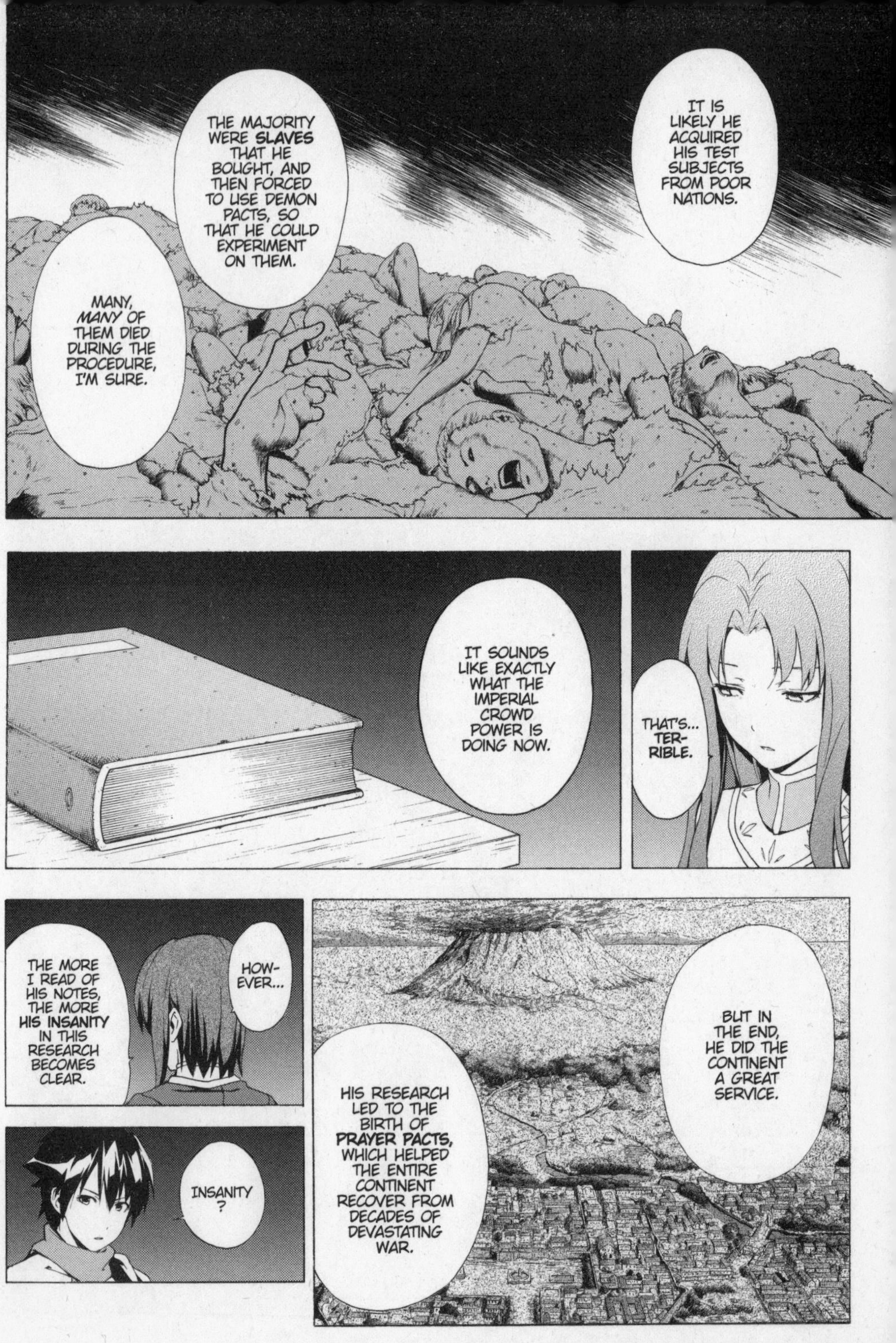
IT IS LIKELY HE ACQUIRED HIS TEST SUBJECTS FROM POOR NATIONS.
THE MAJORITY WERE **SLAVES** THAT HE BOUGHT, AND THEN FORCED TO USE DEMON PACTS, SO THAT HE COULD EXPERIMENT ON THEM.
MANY, *MANY* OF THEM DIED DURING THE PROCEDURE, I'M SURE.
THAT'S... **TER-RIBLE.**
IT SOUNDS LIKE EXACTLY WHAT THE IMPERIAL CROWD POWER IS DOING NOW.
BUT IN THE END, HE DID THE CONTINENT A GREAT SERVICE.
HIS RESEARCH LED TO THE BIRTH OF **PRAYER PACTS,** WHICH HELPED THE ENTIRE CONTINENT RECOVER FROM DECADES OF DEVASTATING WAR.
HOW-EVER...
THE MORE I READ OF HIS NOTES, THE MORE **HIS INSANITY** IN THIS RESEARCH BECOMES CLEAR.
INSANITY ?

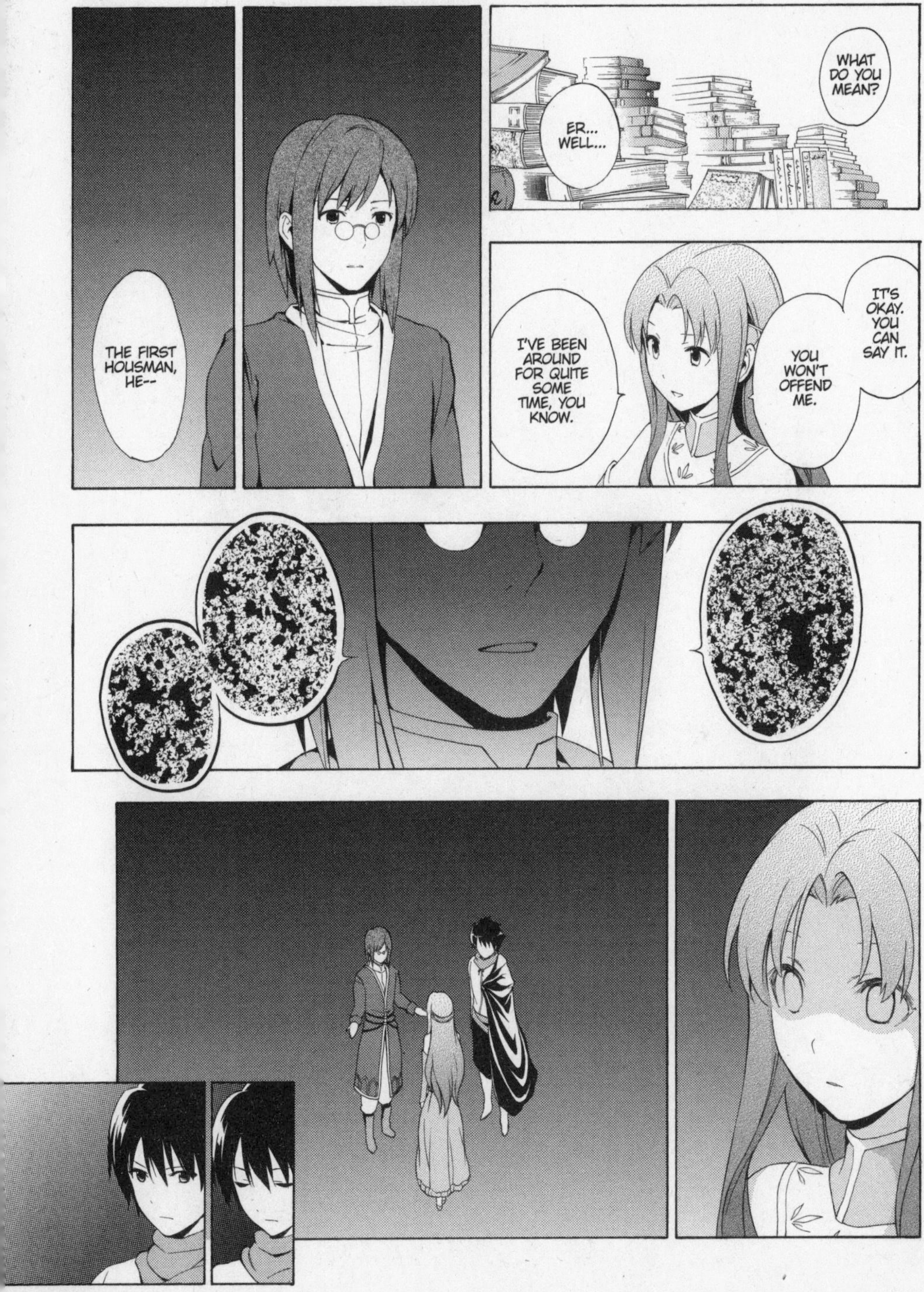
WHAT DO YOU MEAN?
ER... WELL...
IT'S OKAY. YOU CAN SAY IT.
YOU WON'T OFFEND ME.
I'VE BEEN AROUND FOR QUITE SOME TIME, YOU KNOW.
THE FIRST HOUSMAN, HE--

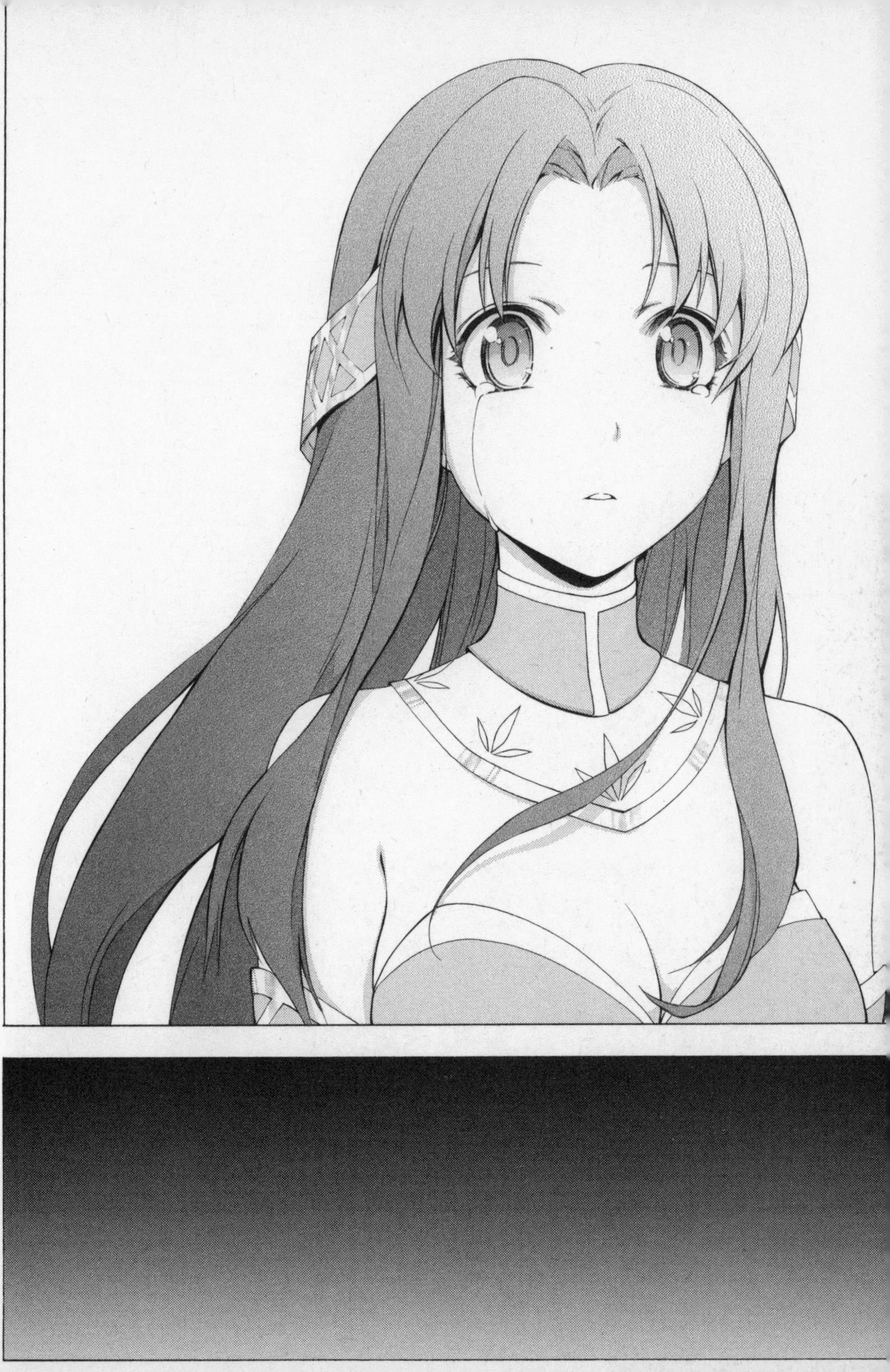

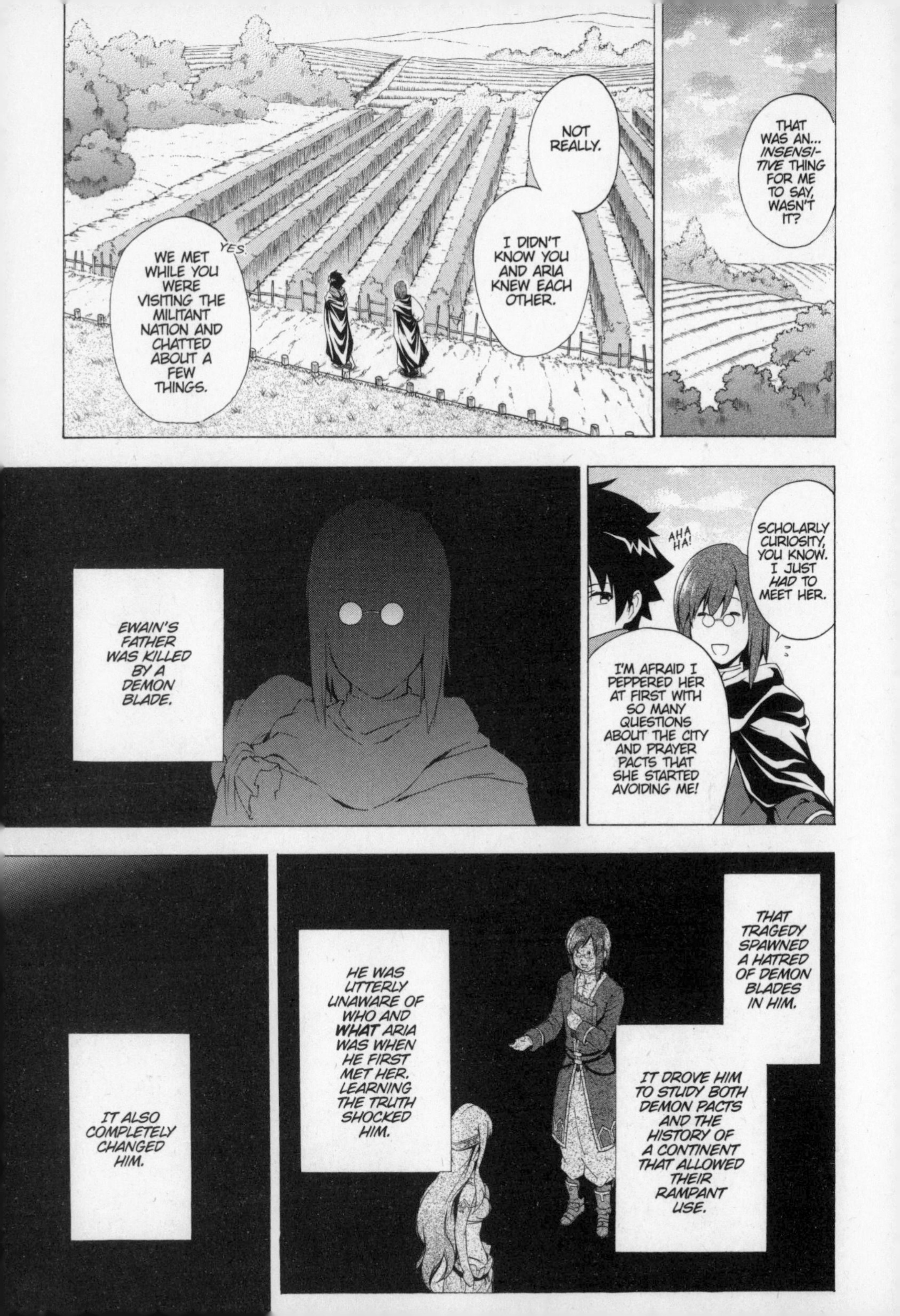
THAT WAS AN... INSENSITIVE THING FOR ME TO SAY, WASN'T IT?
NOT REALLY.
I DIDN'T KNOW YOU AND ARIA KNEW EACH OTHER.
YES.
WE MET WHILE YOU WERE VISITING THE MILITANT NATION AND CHATTED ABOUT A FEW THINGS.
AHA HA!
SCHOLARLY CURIOSITY, YOU KNOW. I JUST HAD TO MEET HER.
I'M AFRAID I PEPPERED HER AT FIRST WITH SO MANY QUESTIONS ABOUT THE CITY AND PRAYER PACTS THAT SHE STARTED AVOIDING ME!
EWAIN'S FATHER WAS KILLED BY A DEMON BLADE.
THAT TRAGEDY SPAWNED A HATRED OF DEMON BLADES IN HIM.
IT DROVE HIM TO STUDY BOTH DEMON PACTS AND THE HISTORY OF A CONTINENT THAT ALLOWED THEIR RAMPANT USE.
HE WAS UTTERLY UNAWARE OF WHO AND WHAT ARIA WAS WHEN HE FIRST MET HER. LEARNING THE TRUTH SHOCKED HIM.
IT ALSO COMPLETELY CHANGED HIM.

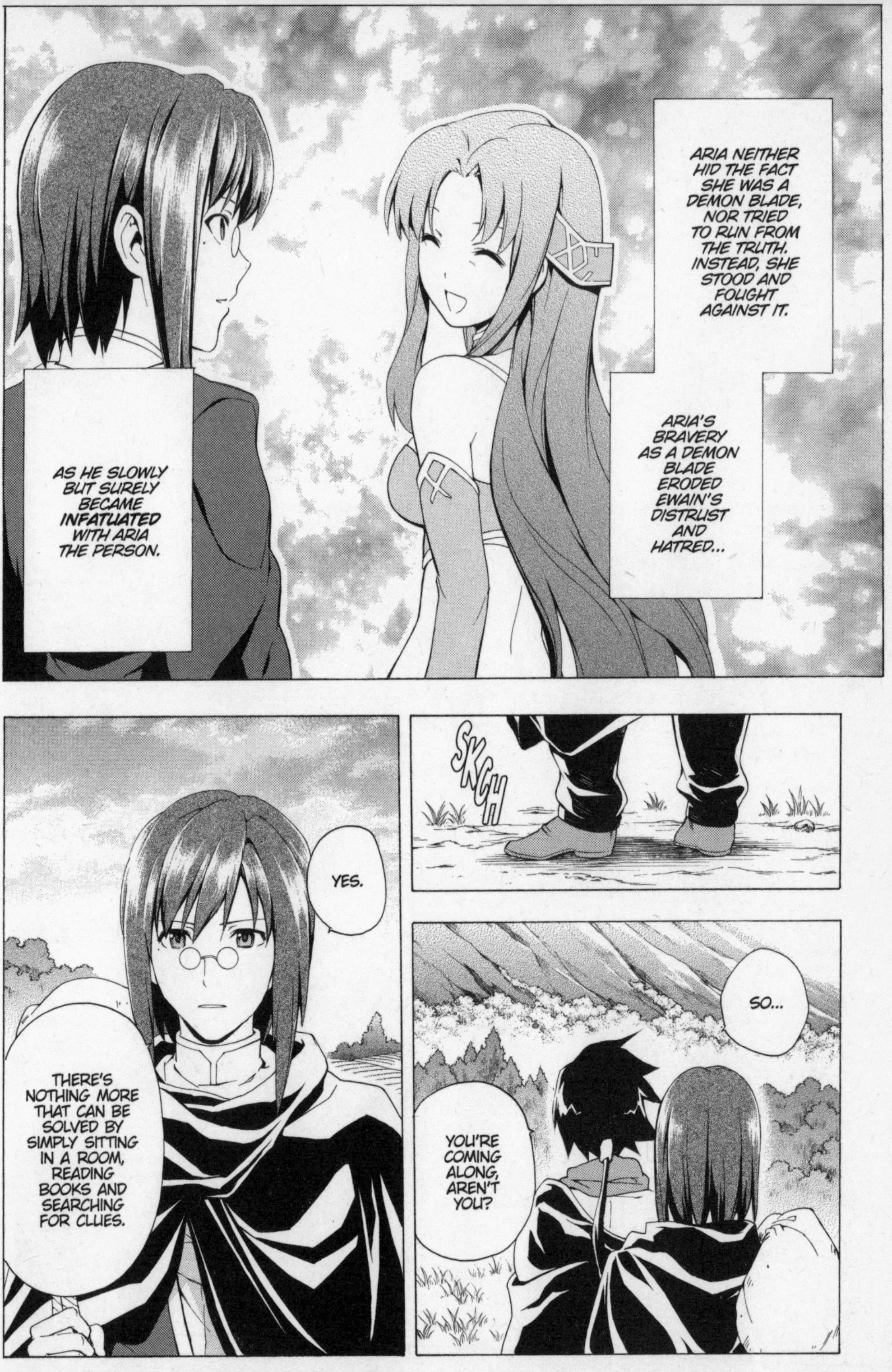
ARIA NEITHER HID THE FACT SHE WAS A DEMON BLADE, NOR TRIED TO RUN FROM THE TRUTH. INSTEAD, SHE STOOD AND FOUGHT AGAINST IT.
ARIA'S BRAVERY AS A DEMON BLADE ERODED EWAIN'S DISTRUST AND HATRED...
AS HE SLOWLY BUT SURELY BECAME **INFATUATED** WITH ARIA THE PERSON.
SKCH
SO...
YOU'RE COMING ALONG, AREN'T YOU?
YES.
THERE'S NOTHING MORE THAT CAN BE SOLVED BY SIMPLY SITTING IN A ROOM, READING BOOKS AND SEARCHING FOR CLUES.

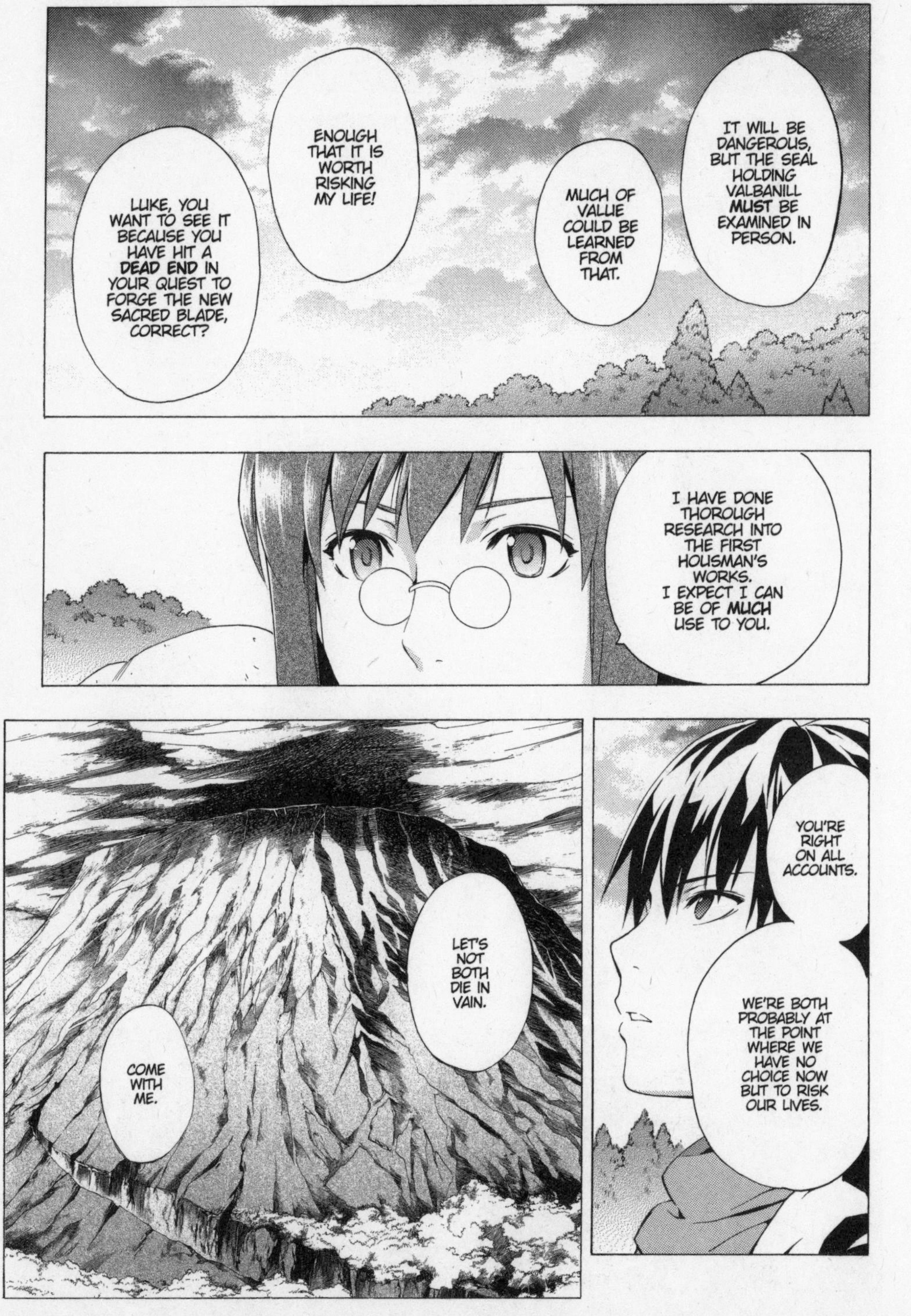
IT WILL BE DANGEROUS, BUT THE SEAL HOLDING VALBANILL **MUST** BE EXAMINED IN PERSON.
MUCH OF VALUE COULD BE LEARNED FROM THAT.
ENOUGH THAT IT IS WORTH RISKING MY LIFE!
LUKE, YOU WANT TO SEE IT BECAUSE YOU HAVE HIT A **DEAD END** IN YOUR QUEST TO FORGE THE NEW SACRED BLADE, CORRECT?
I HAVE DONE THOROUGH RESEARCH INTO THE FIRST HOUSMAN'S WORKS. I EXPECT I CAN BE OF **MUCH** USE TO YOU.
YOU'RE RIGHT ON ALL ACCOUNTS.
WE'RE BOTH PROBABLY AT THE POINT WHERE WE HAVE NO CHOICE NOW BUT TO RISK OUR LIVES.
LET'S NOT BOTH DIE IN VAIN.
COME WITH ME.

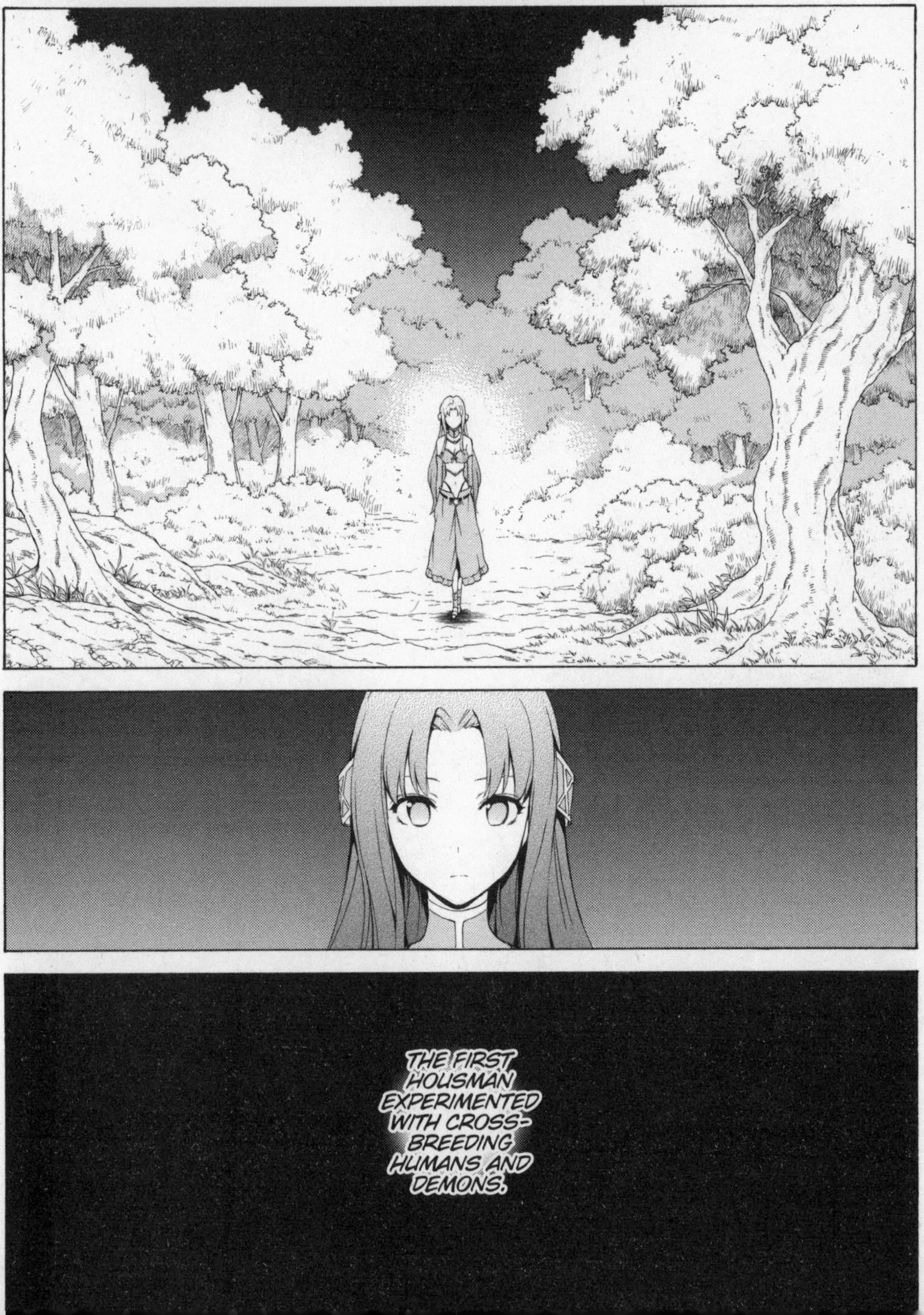
THE FIRST HOUSMAN EXPERIMENTED WITH CROSS-BREEDING HUMANS AND DEMONS.

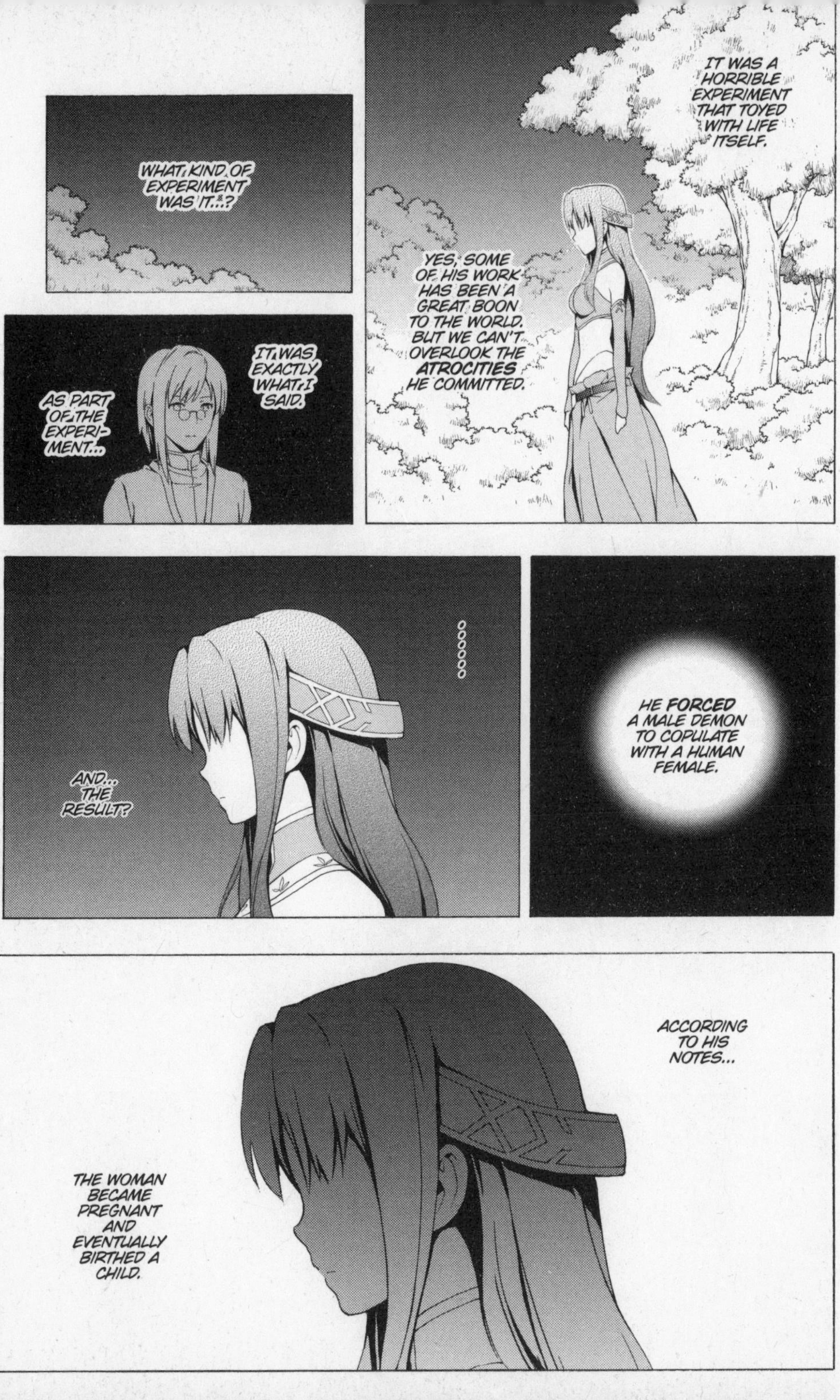
IT WAS A HORRIBLE EXPERIMENT THAT TOYED WITH LIFE ITSELF.
YES, SOME OF HIS WORK HAS BEEN A GREAT BOON TO THE WORLD. BUT WE CAN'T OVERLOOK THE ATROCITIES HE COMMITTED.
WHAT KIND OF EXPERIMENT WAS IT...?
IT WAS EXACTLY WHAT I SAID.
AS PART OF THE EXPERI-MENT...
HE FORCED A MALE DEMON TO COPULATE WITH A HUMAN FEMALE.
......
AND... THE RESULT?
ACCORDING TO HIS NOTES...
THE WOMAN BECAME PREGNANT AND EVENTUALLY BIRTHED A CHILD.

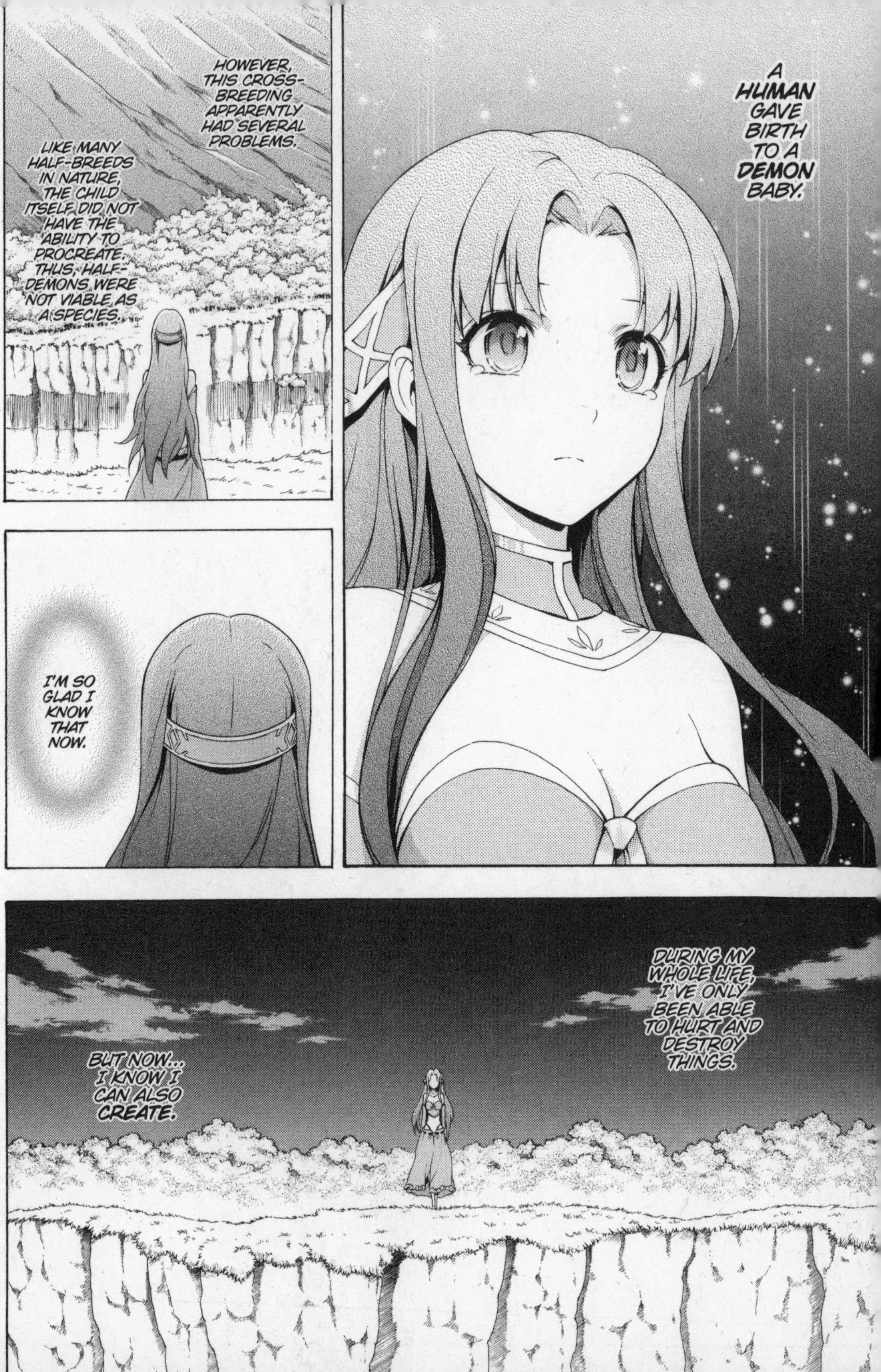
A HUMAN GAVE BIRTH TO A DEMON BABY.
HOWEVER, THIS CROSS-BREEDING APPARENTLY HAD SEVERAL PROBLEMS.
LIKE MANY HALF-BREEDS IN NATURE, THE CHILD ITSELF DID NOT HAVE THE ABILITY TO PROCREATE. THUS, HALF-DEMONS WERE NOT VIABLE AS A SPECIES.
I'M SO GLAD I KNOW THAT NOW.
DURING MY WHOLE LIFE, I'VE ONLY BEEN ABLE TO HURT AND DESTROY THINGS.
BUT NOW... I KNOW I CAN ALSO CREATE.

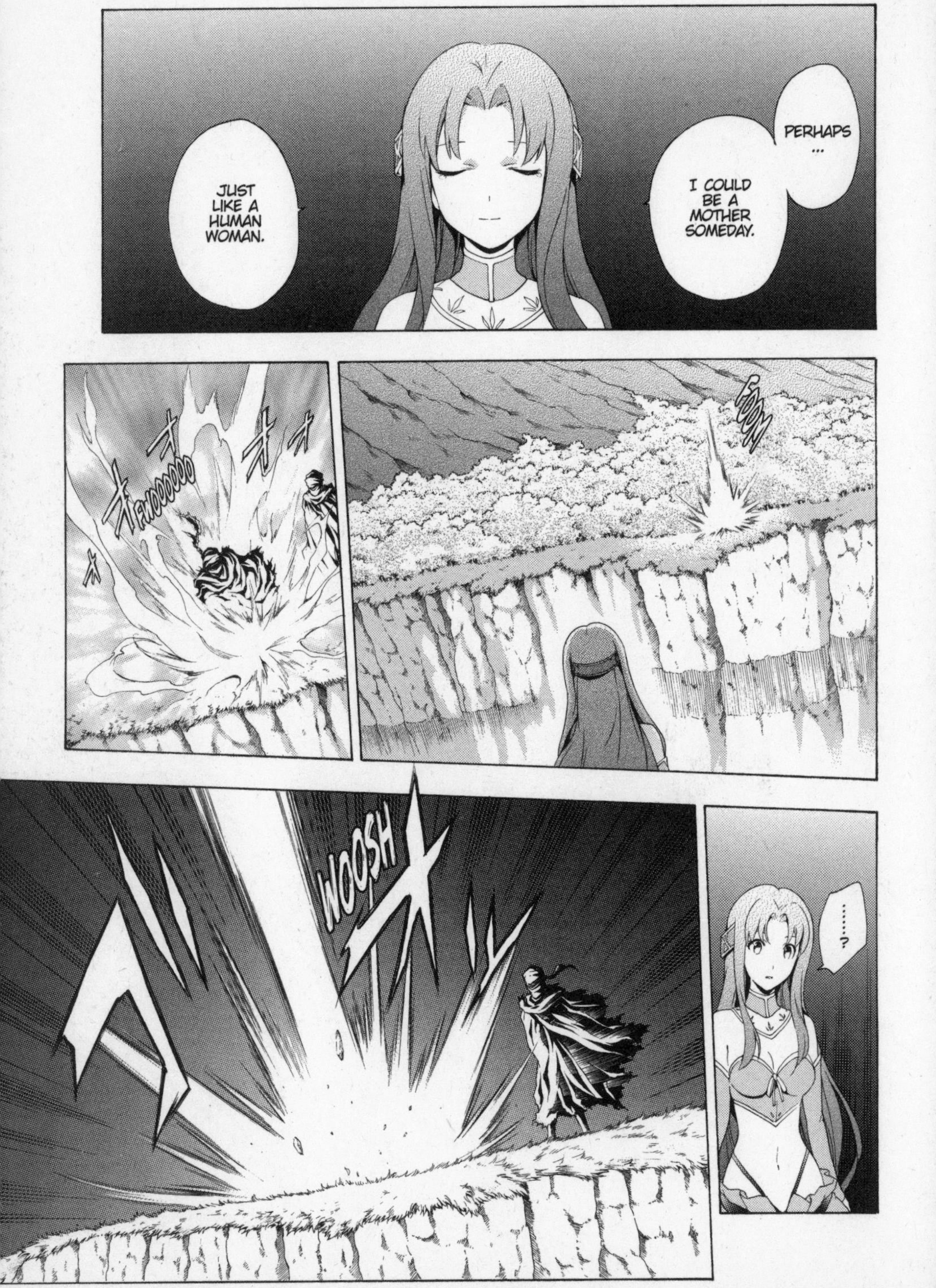
PERHAPS ...
I COULD BE A MOTHER SOMEDAY.
JUST LIKE A HUMAN WOMAN.
FOOM
FWOOOOOO
......?
WOOSH

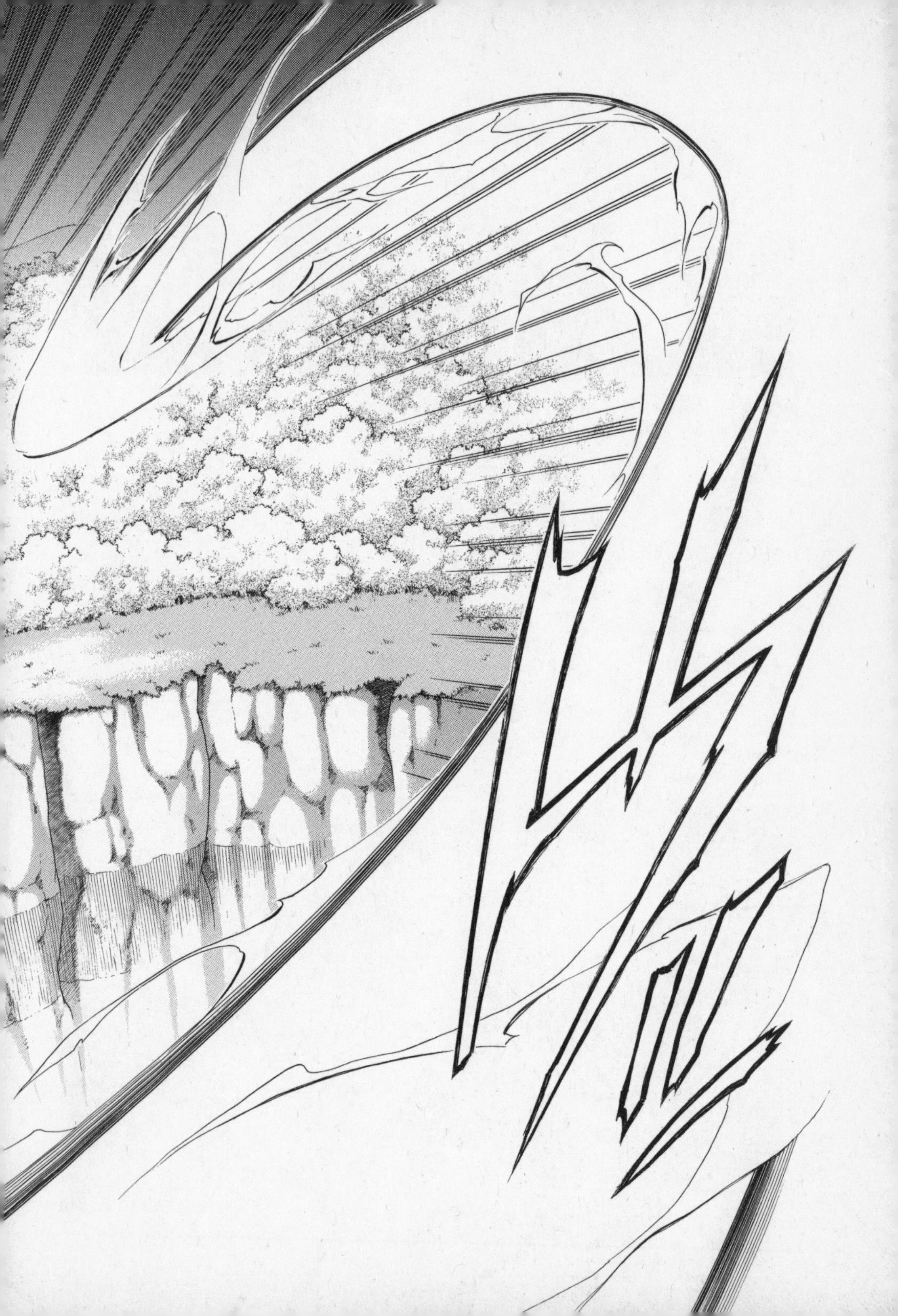

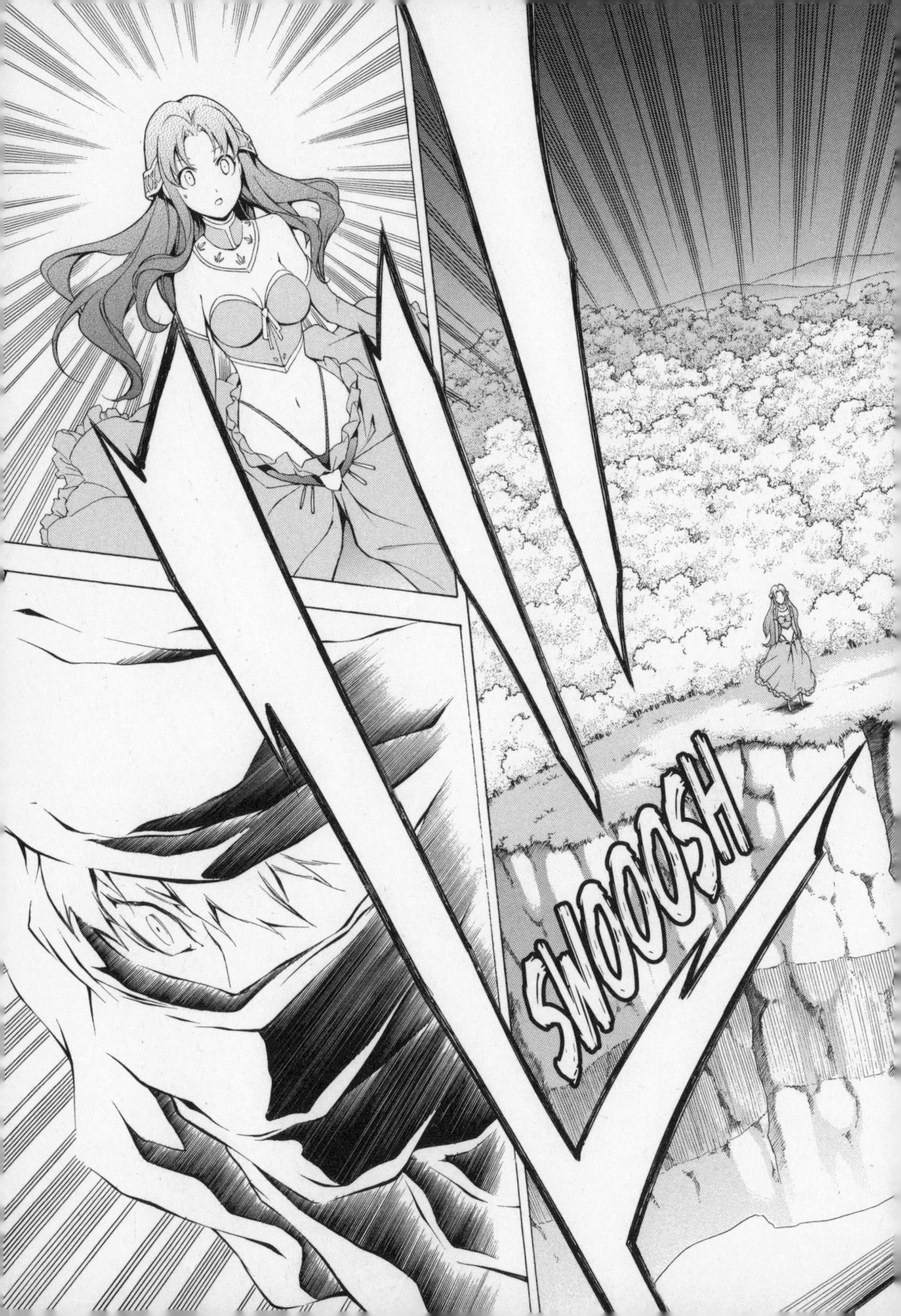
SWOOOSH

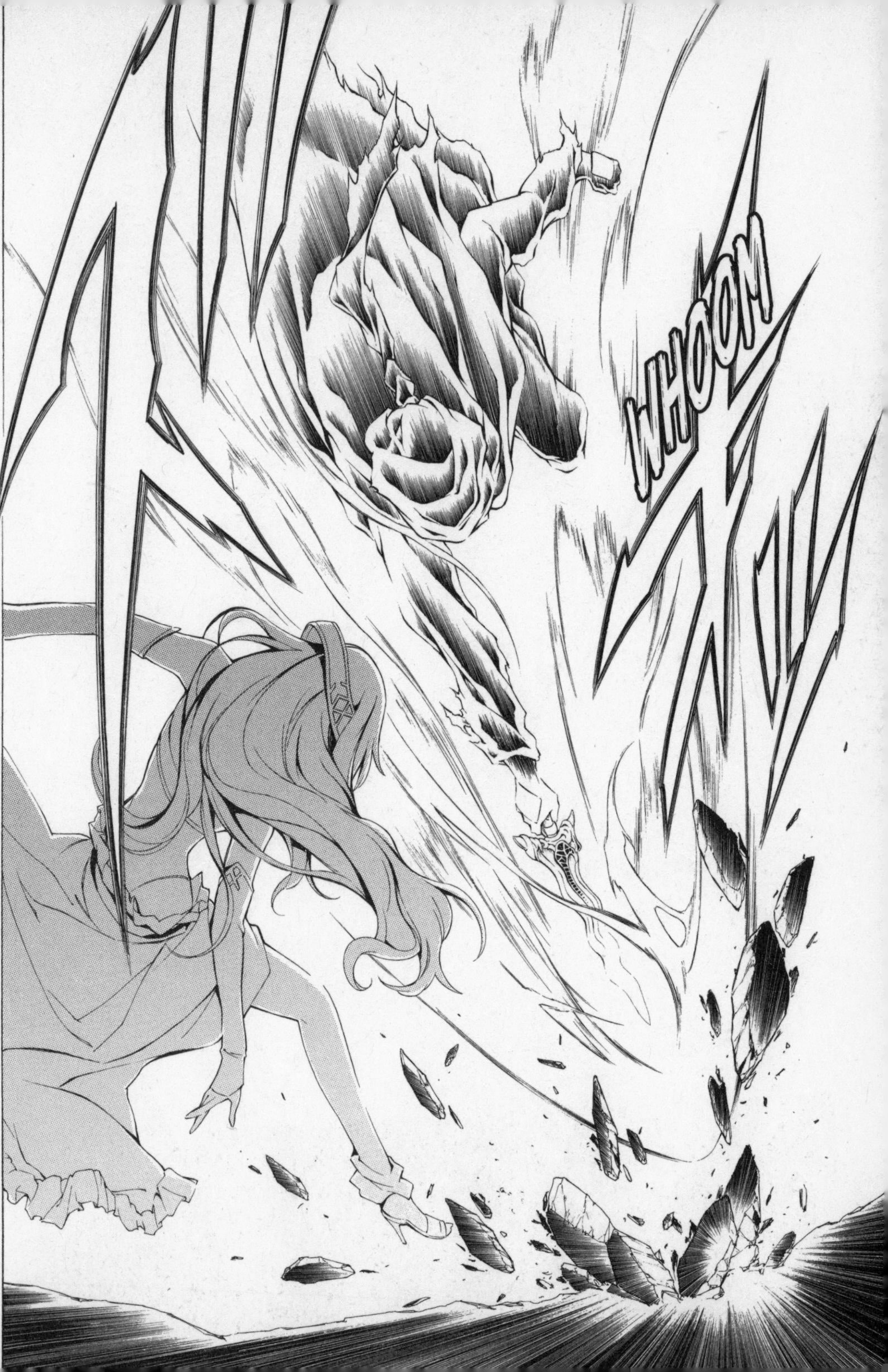
WHOOM

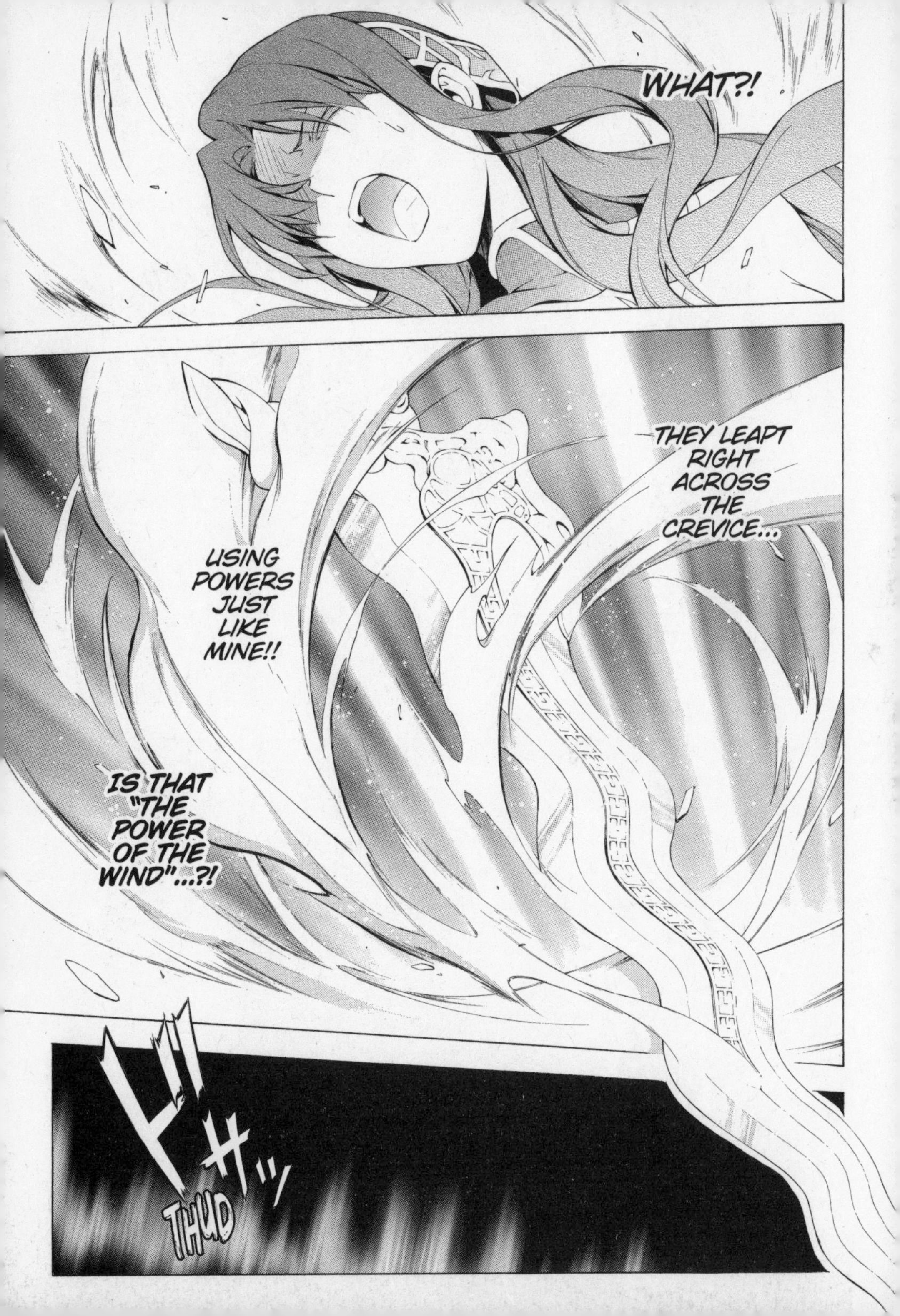
WHAT?!
THEY LEAPT RIGHT ACROSS THE CREVICE...
USING POWERS JUST LIKE MINE!!
IS THAT "THE POWER OF THE WIND"...?!
THUD

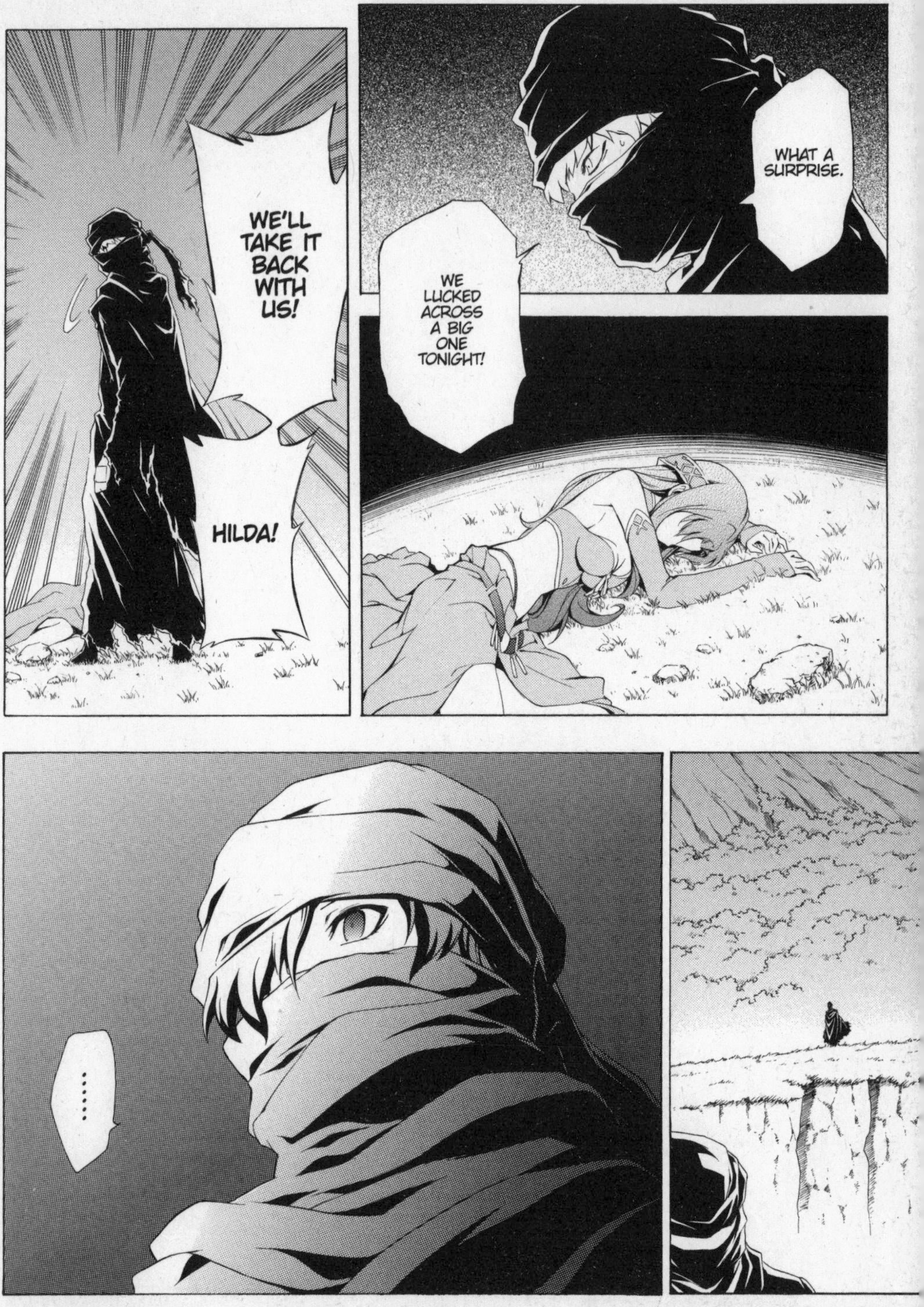
WHAT A SURPRISE.
WE LUCKED ACROSS A BIG ONE TONIGHT!
WE'LL TAKE IT BACK WITH US!
HILDA!
......

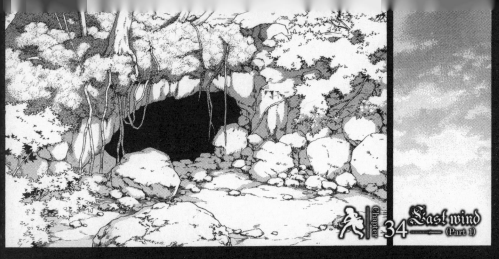

I'M NOT GOING TO RUN AND HIDE ANYMORE.

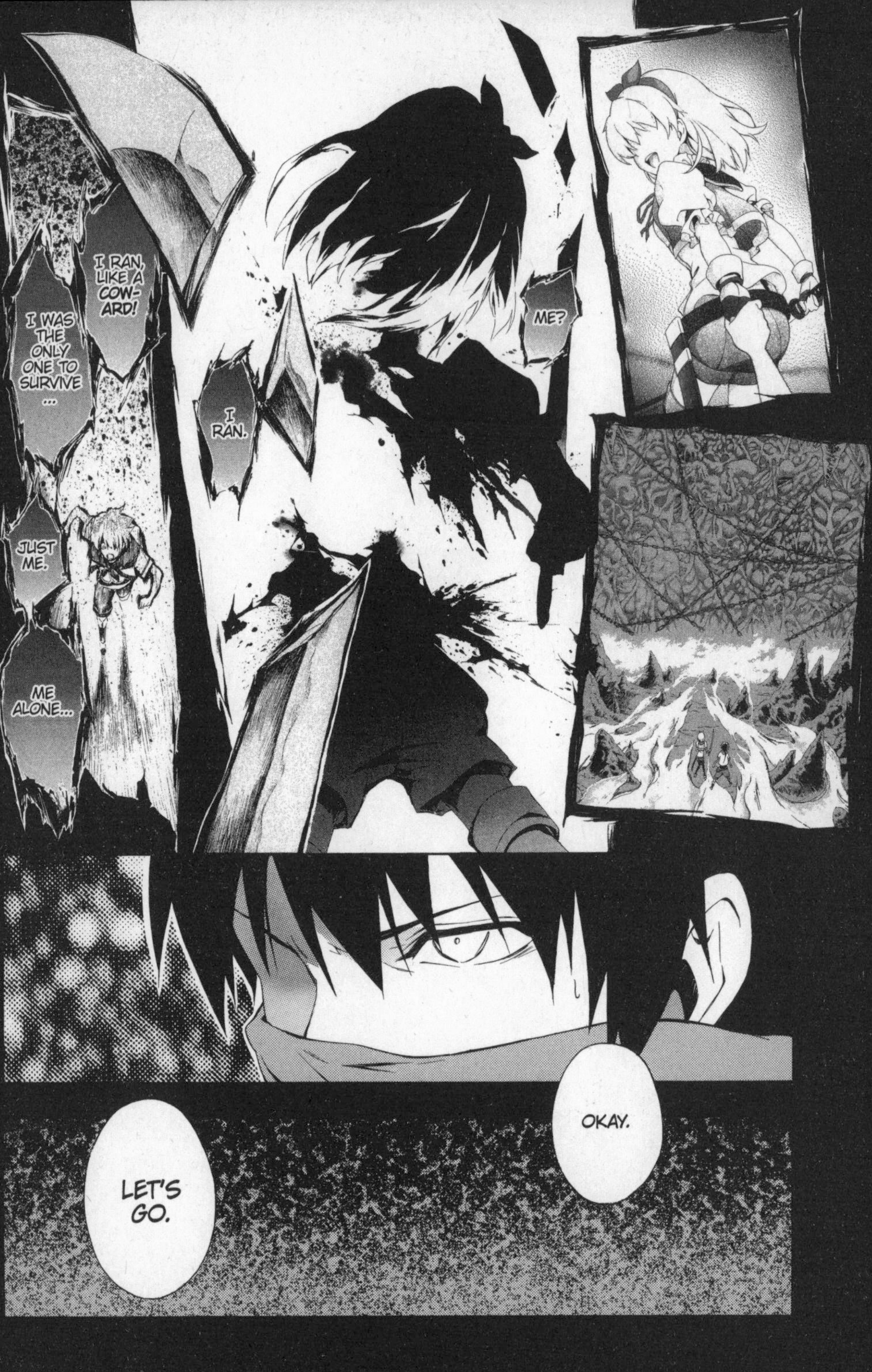
ME?
I RAN.
I RAN, LIKE A COW-ARD!
I WAS THE ONLY ONE TO SURVIVE ...
JUST ME.
ME ALONE...
OKAY.
LET'S GO.

Chapter 34 Last wind (Part 1)

The Sacred Blacksmith
聖剣の刀鍛冶

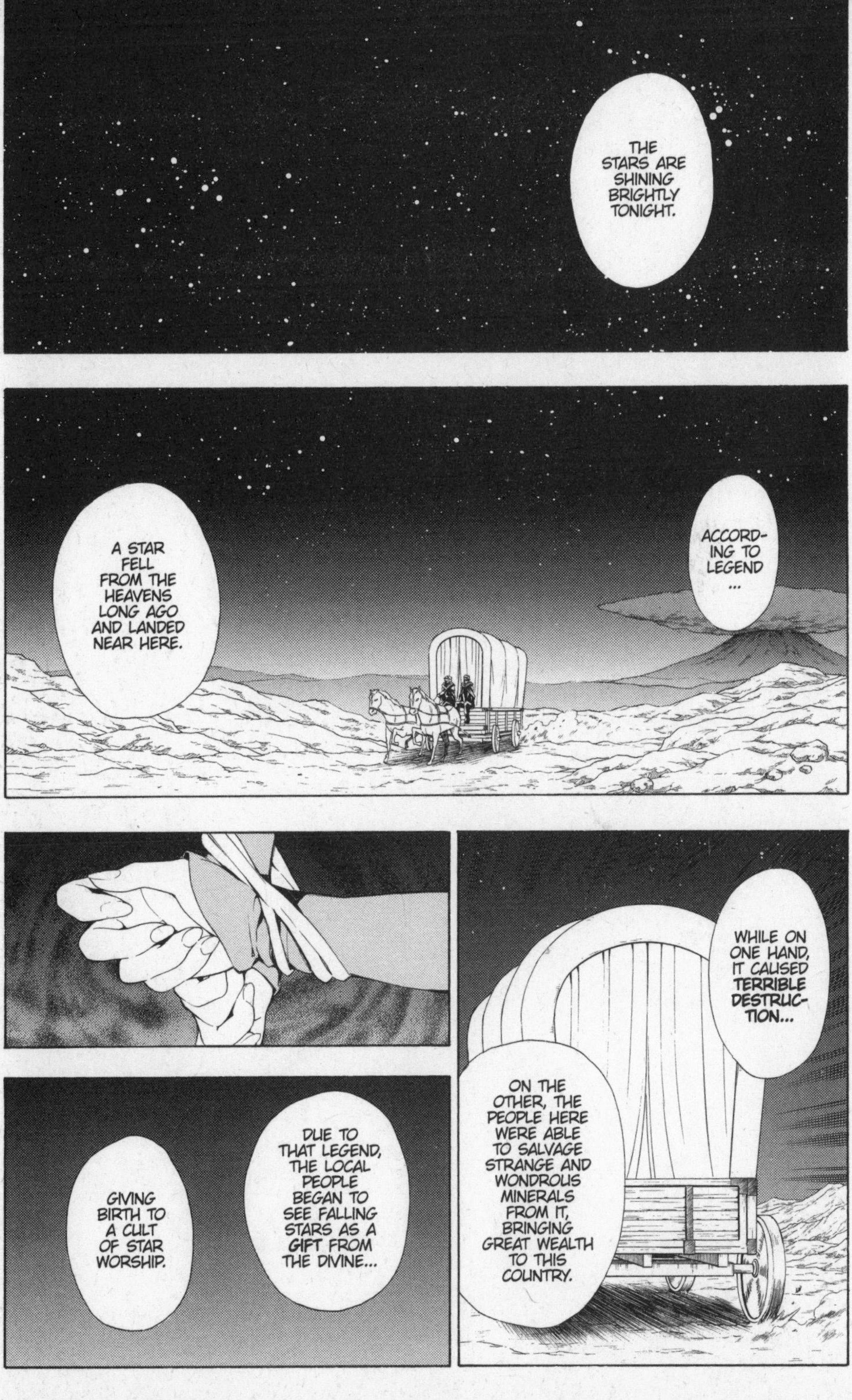
THE STARS ARE SHINING BRIGHTLY TONIGHT.
ACCORDING TO LEGEND...
A STAR FELL FROM THE HEAVENS LONG AGO AND LANDED NEAR HERE.
WHILE ON ONE HAND, IT CAUSED TERRIBLE DESTRUCTION...
ON THE OTHER, THE PEOPLE HERE WERE ABLE TO SALVAGE STRANGE AND WONDROUS MINERALS FROM IT, BRINGING GREAT WEALTH TO THIS COUNTRY.
DUE TO THAT LEGEND, THE LOCAL PEOPLE BEGAN TO SEE FALLING STARS AS A GIFT FROM THE DIVINE...
GIVING BIRTH TO A CULT OF STAR WORSHIP.

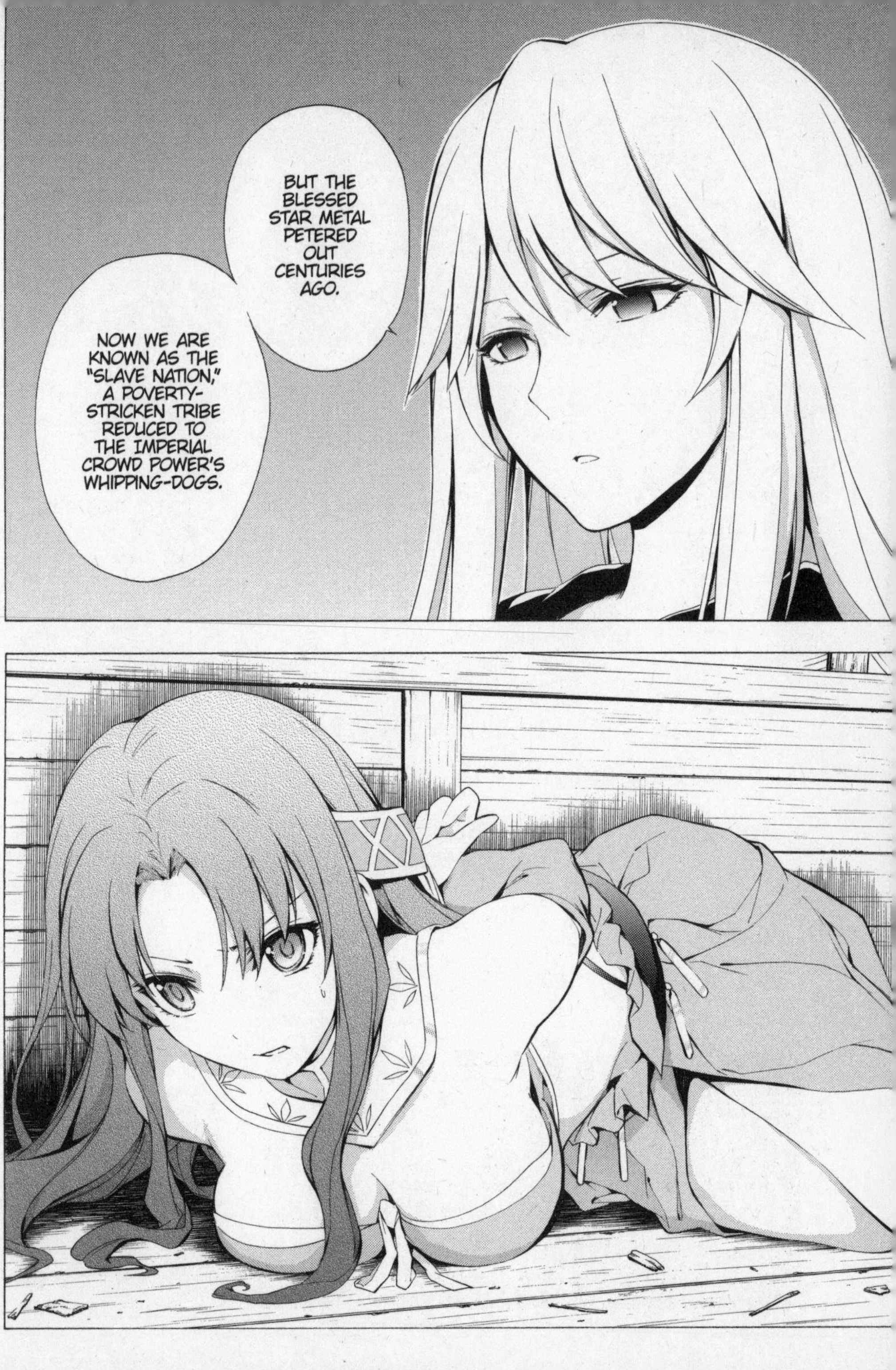
BUT THE BLESSED STAR METAL PETERED OUT CENTURIES AGO.
NOW WE ARE KNOWN AS THE "SLAVE NATION," A POVERTY-STRICKEN TRIBE REDUCED TO THE IMPERIAL CROWD POWER'S WHIPPING-DOGS.

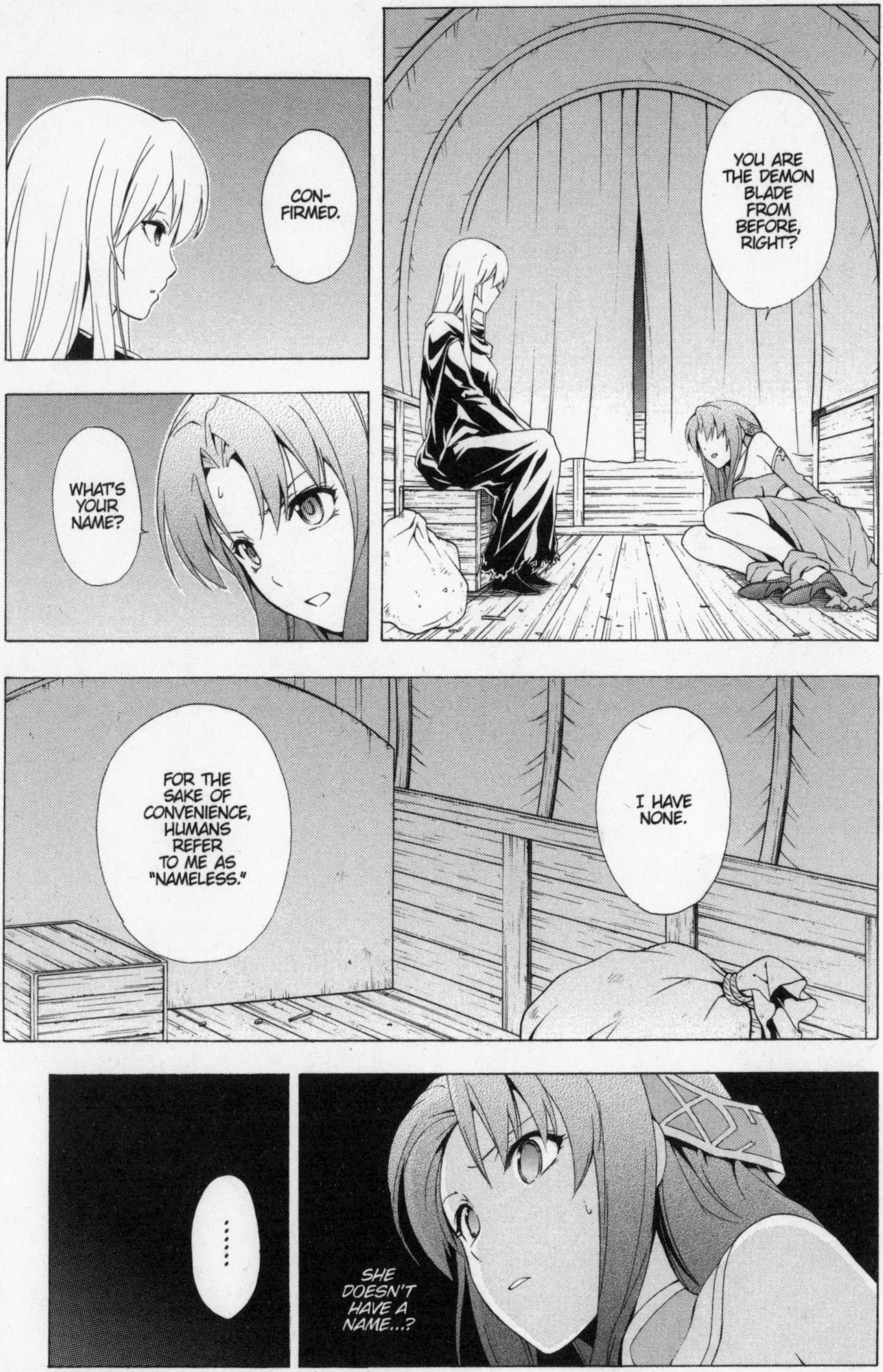
YOU ARE THE DEMON BLADE FROM BEFORE, RIGHT?
CON-FIRMED.
WHAT'S YOUR NAME?
I HAVE NONE.
FOR THE SAKE OF CONVENIENCE, HUMANS REFER TO ME AS "NAMELESS."
SHE DOESN'T HAVE A NAME...?
......

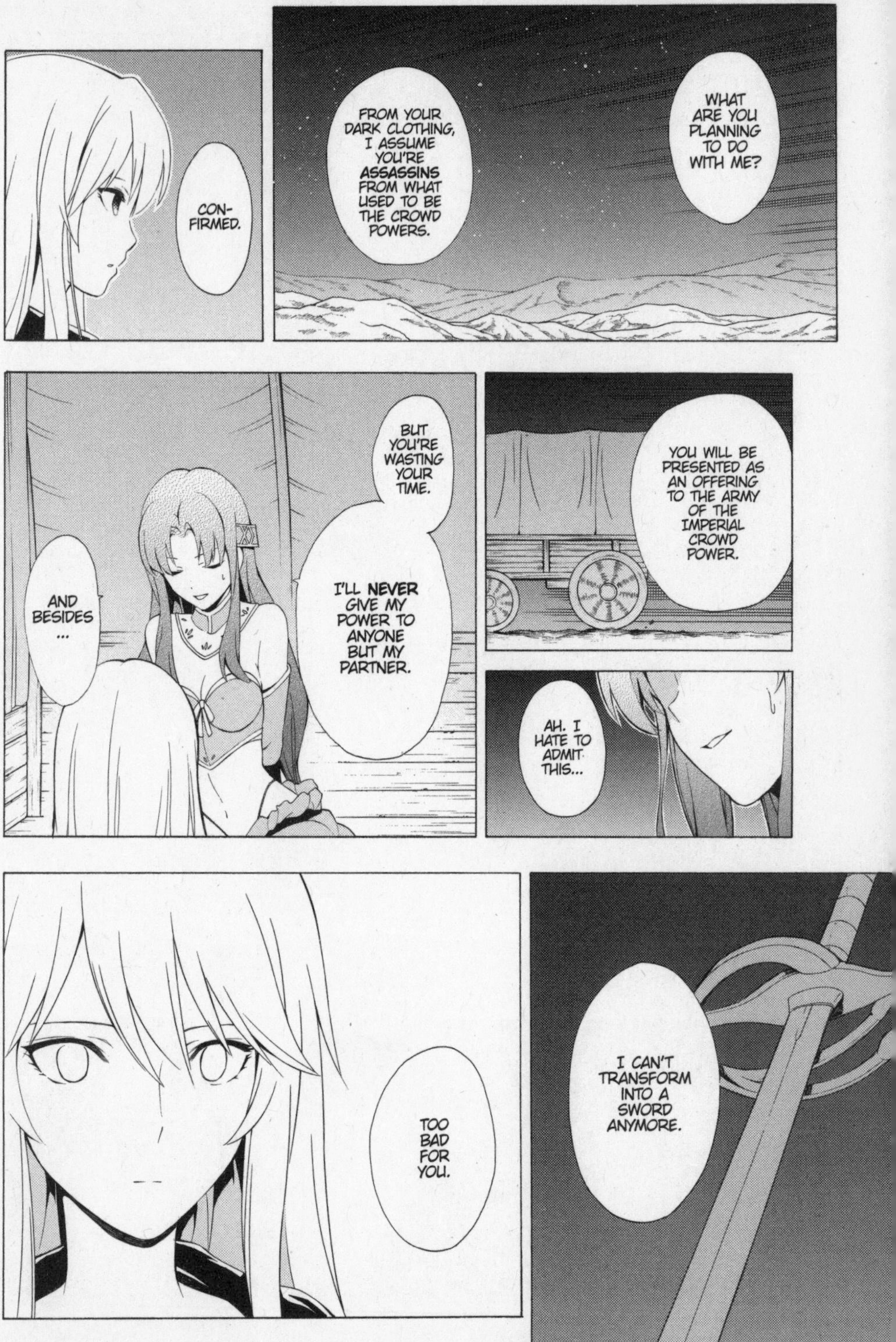
WHAT ARE YOU PLANNING TO DO WITH ME?
FROM YOUR DARK CLOTHING, I ASSUME YOU'RE **ASSASSINS** FROM WHAT USED TO BE THE CROWD POWERS.
CON-FIRMED.
YOU WILL BE PRESENTED AS AN OFFERING TO THE ARMY OF THE IMPERIAL CROWD POWER.
AH. I HATE TO ADMIT THIS...
BUT YOU'RE WASTING YOUR TIME.
I'LL **NEVER** GIVE MY POWER TO ANYONE BUT MY PARTNER.
AND BESIDES ...
I CAN'T TRANSFORM INTO A SWORD ANYMORE.
TOO BAD FOR YOU.

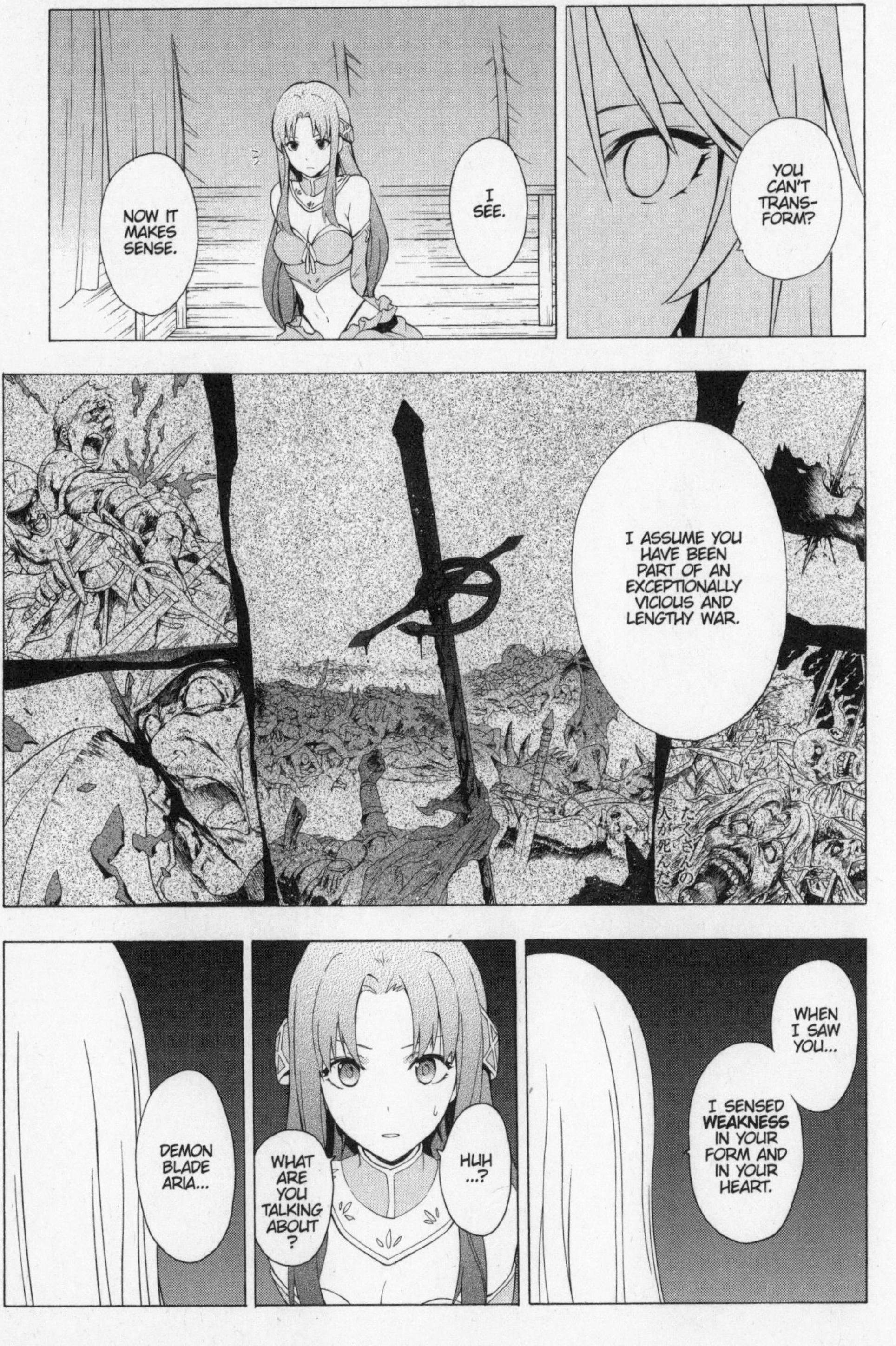
YOU CAN'T TRANSFORM?
I SEE.
NOW IT MAKES SENSE.
I ASSUME YOU HAVE BEEN PART OF AN EXCEPTIONALLY VICIOUS AND LENGTHY WAR.
たくさんの人が死んだ
WHEN I SAW YOU...
I SENSED **WEAKNESS** IN YOUR FORM AND IN YOUR HEART.
HUH...?
WHAT ARE YOU TALKING ABOUT?
DEMON BLADE ARIA...

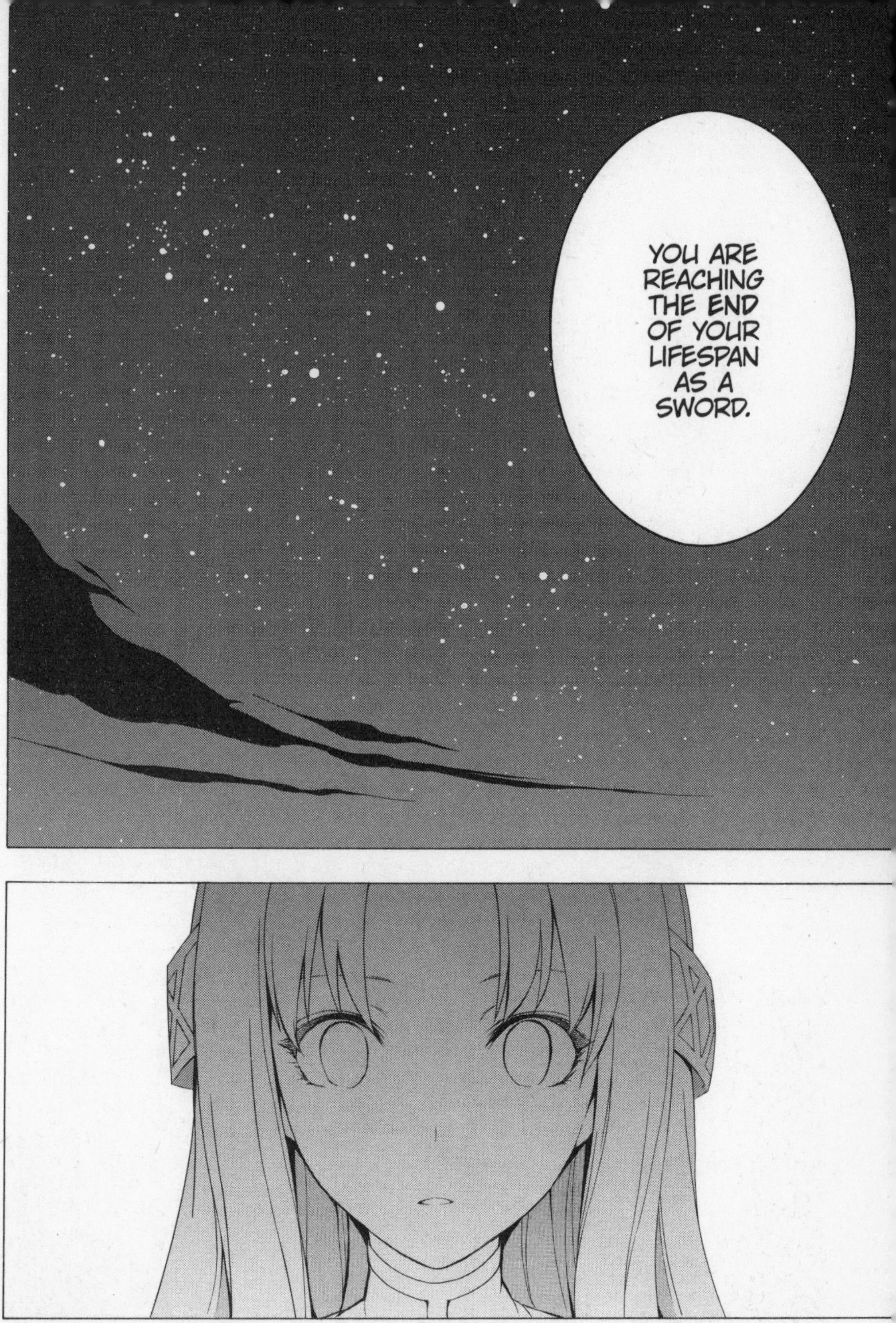
YOU ARE REACHING THE END OF YOUR LIFESPAN AS A SWORD.

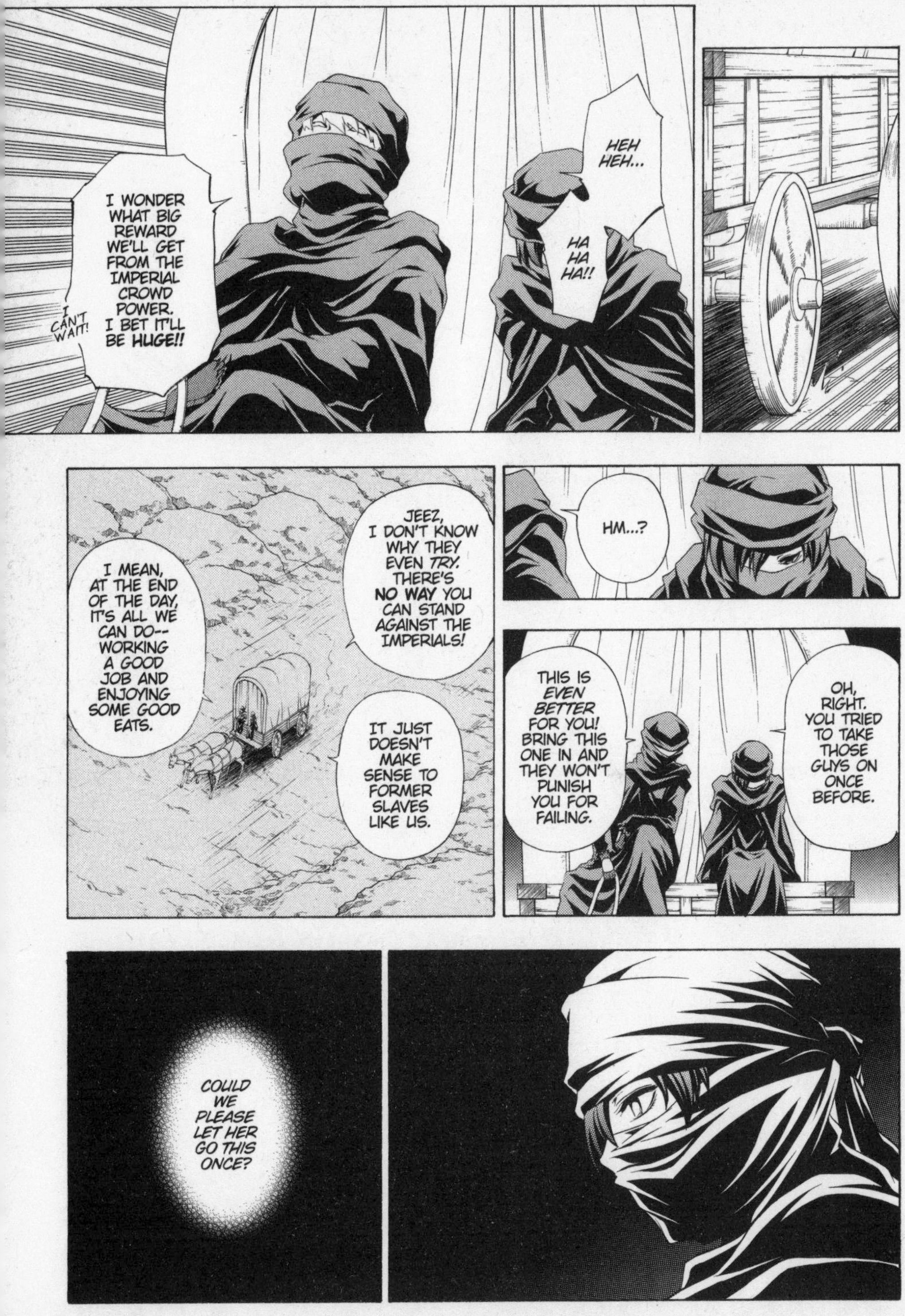
HEH HEH...
HA HA HA!!
I WONDER WHAT BIG REWARD WE'LL GET FROM THE IMPERIAL CROWD POWER. I BET IT'LL BE **HUGE!!**
I CAN'T WAIT!
HM...?
OH, RIGHT. YOU TRIED TO TAKE THOSE GUYS ON ONCE BEFORE.
THIS IS *EVEN BETTER* FOR YOU! BRING THIS ONE IN AND THEY WON'T PUNISH YOU FOR FAILING.
JEEZ, I DON'T KNOW WHY THEY EVEN *TRY*. THERE'S **NO WAY** YOU CAN STAND AGAINST THE IMPERIALS!
IT JUST DOESN'T MAKE SENSE TO FORMER SLAVES LIKE US.
I MEAN, AT THE END OF THE DAY, IT'S ALL WE CAN DO-- WORKING A GOOD JOB AND ENJOYING SOME GOOD EATS.
COULD WE PLEASE LET HER GO THIS ONCE?

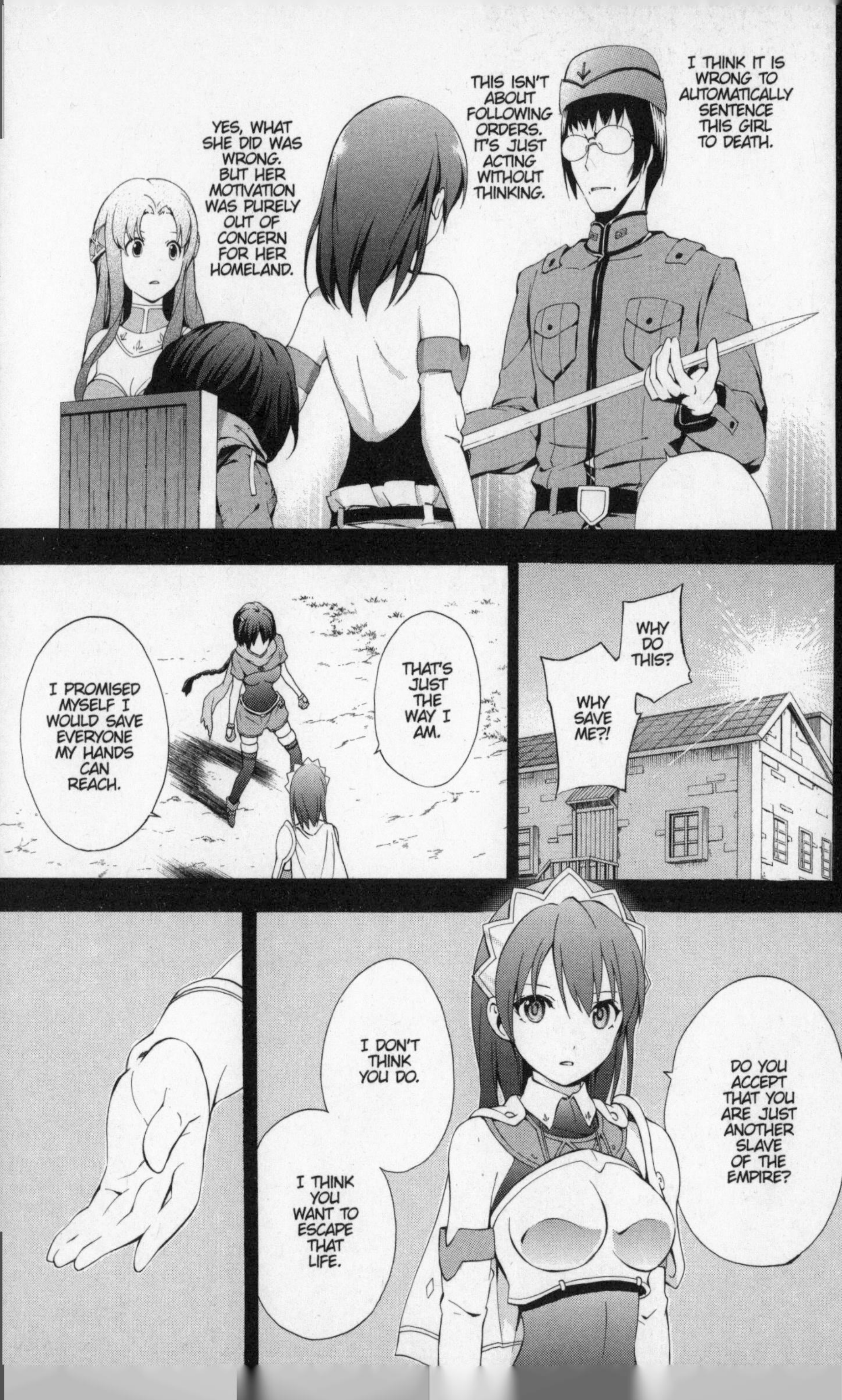
I THINK IT IS WRONG TO AUTOMATICALLY SENTENCE THIS GIRL TO DEATH.
THIS ISN'T ABOUT FOLLOWING ORDERS. IT'S JUST ACTING WITHOUT THINKING.
YES, WHAT SHE DID WAS WRONG. BUT HER MOTIVATION WAS PURELY OUT OF CONCERN FOR HER HOMELAND.
WHY DO THIS?
WHY SAVE ME?!
THAT'S JUST THE WAY I AM.
I PROMISED MYSELF I WOULD SAVE EVERYONE MY HANDS CAN REACH.
DO YOU ACCEPT THAT YOU ARE JUST ANOTHER SLAVE OF THE EMPIRE?
I DON'T THINK YOU DO.
I THINK YOU WANT TO ESCAPE THAT LIFE.

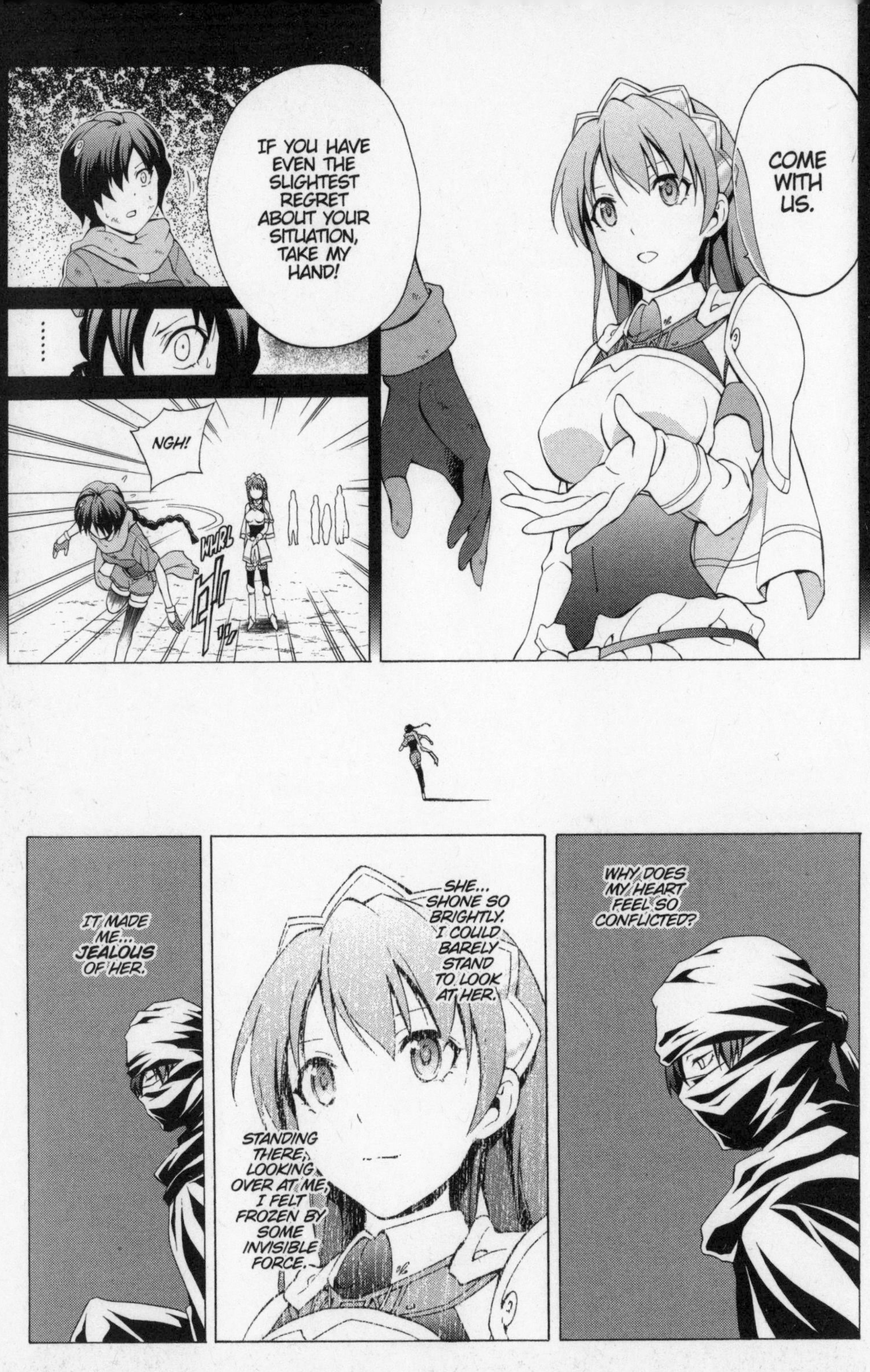
COME WITH US.
IF YOU HAVE EVEN THE SLIGHTEST REGRET ABOUT YOUR SITUATION, TAKE MY HAND!
......
NGH!
WHRL
WHY DOES MY HEART FEEL SO CONFLICTED?
SHE... SHONE SO BRIGHTLY. I COULD BARELY STAND TO LOOK AT HER.
STANDING THERE, LOOKING OVER AT ME, I FELT FROZEN BY SOME INVISIBLE FORCE.
IT MADE ME... JEALOUS OF HER.

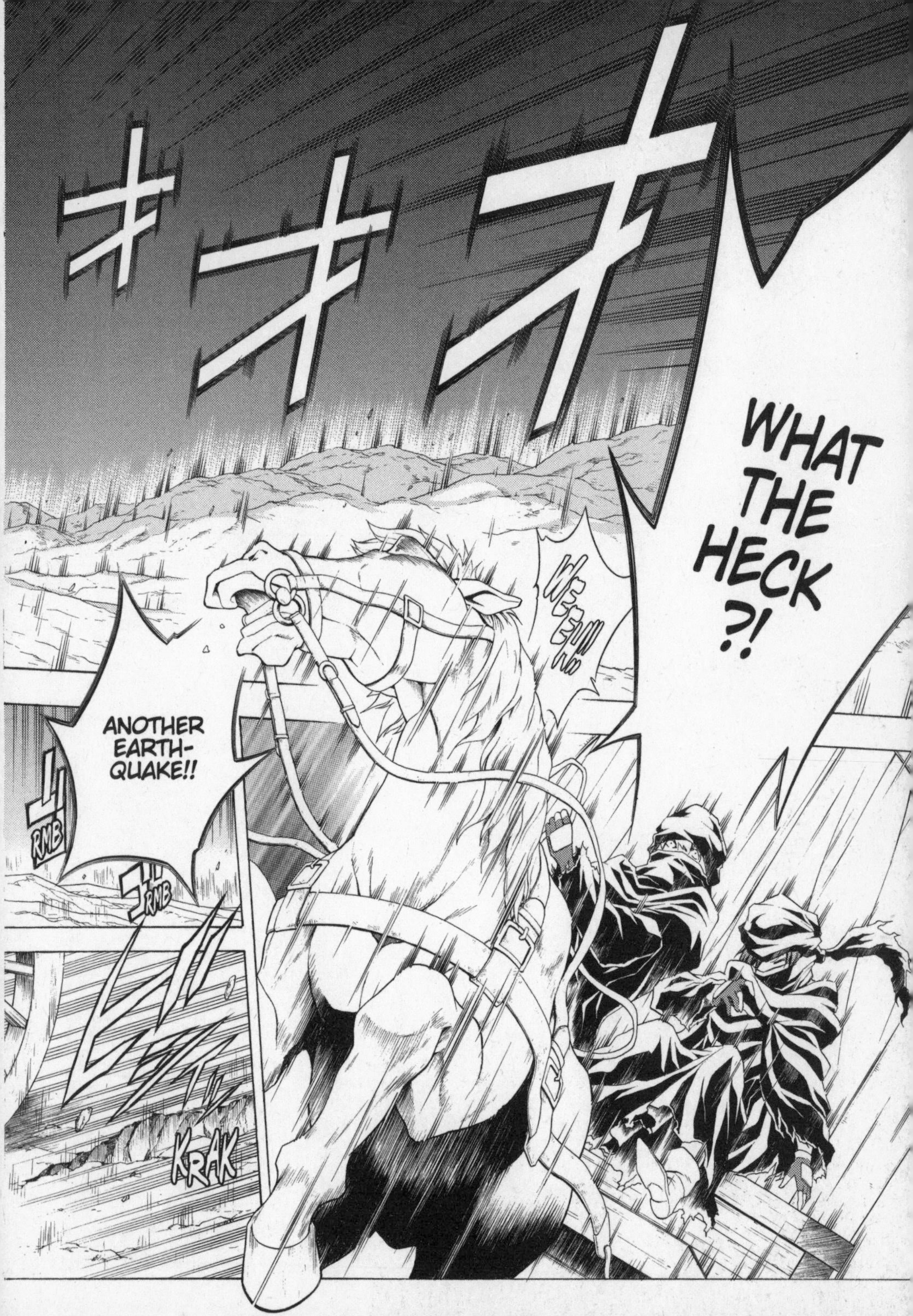
WHAT THE HECK ?!
ANOTHER EARTH-QUAKE!!
RMB
RMB
KRAK

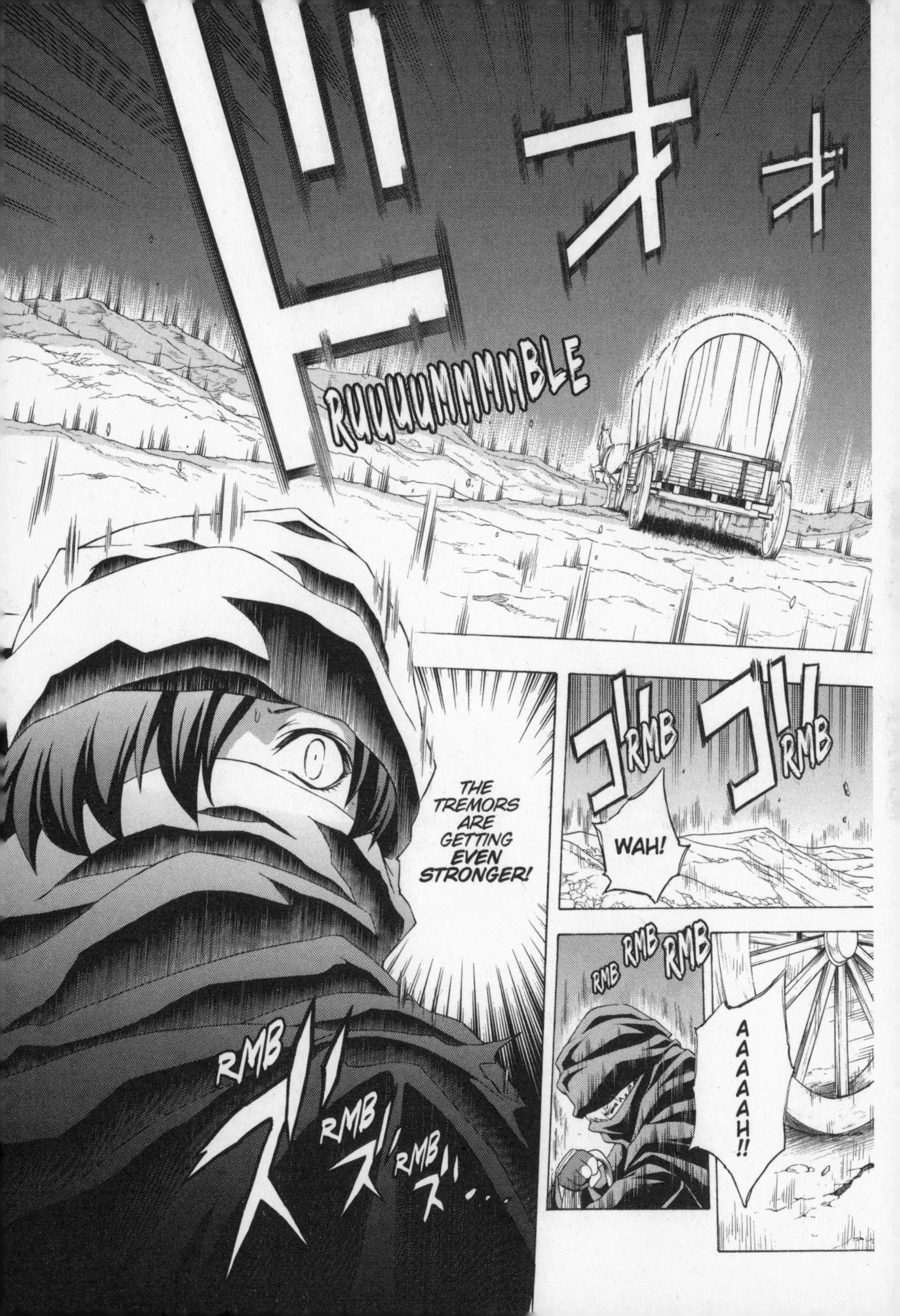

ドォォ
RUUUUMMMMMBLE
ゴ RMB ゴ RMB
WAH!
RMB RMB RMB
AAAAAAH!!
THE TREMORS ARE GETTING EVEN STRONGER!
RMB ズ RMB ズ RMB ズ...

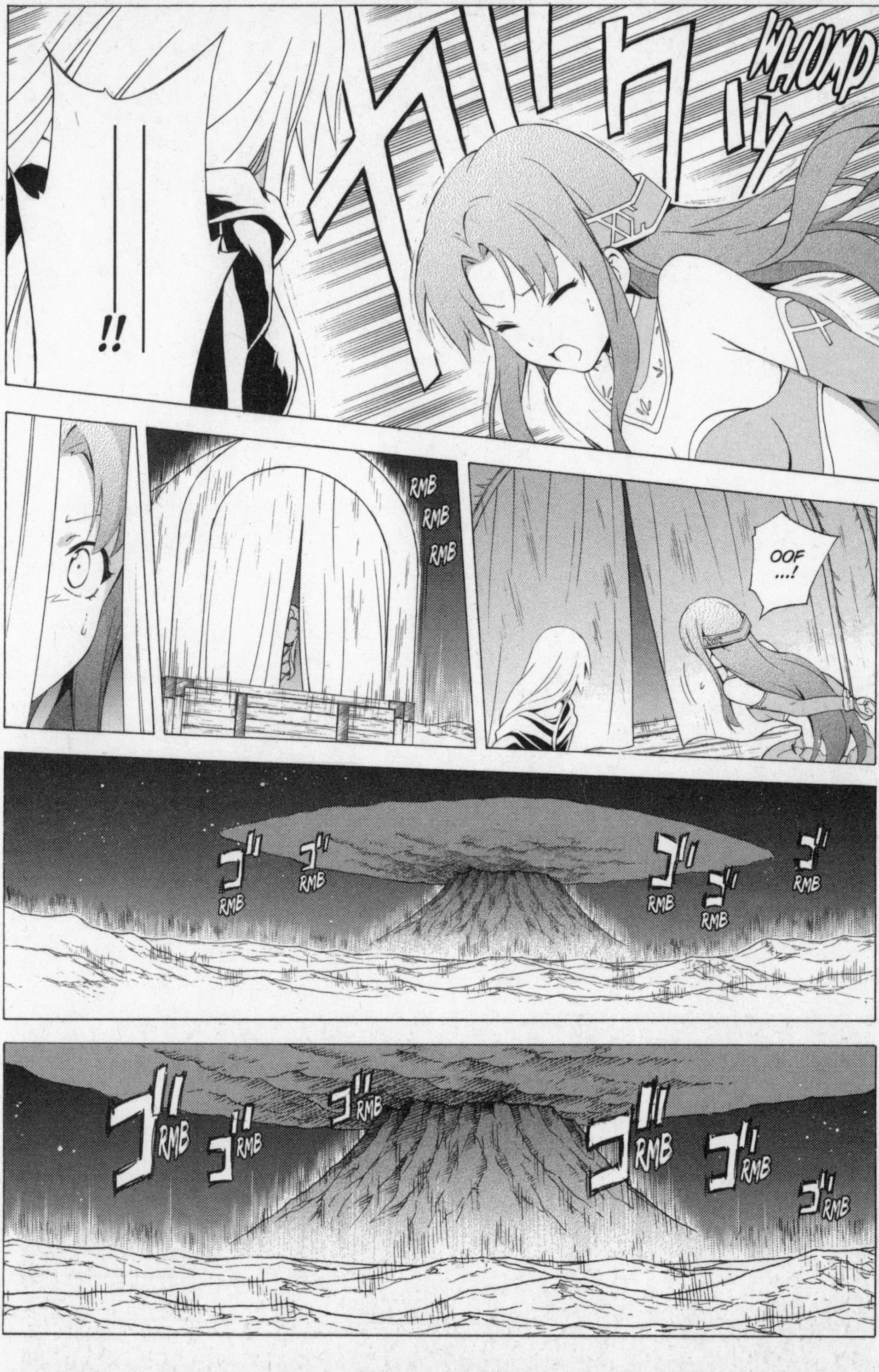
WHUMP
!!
OOF ...!
RMB
RMB
RMB
RMB
RMB
RMB
RMB
RMB
RMB
RMB
RMB
RMB
RMB
RMB
RMB

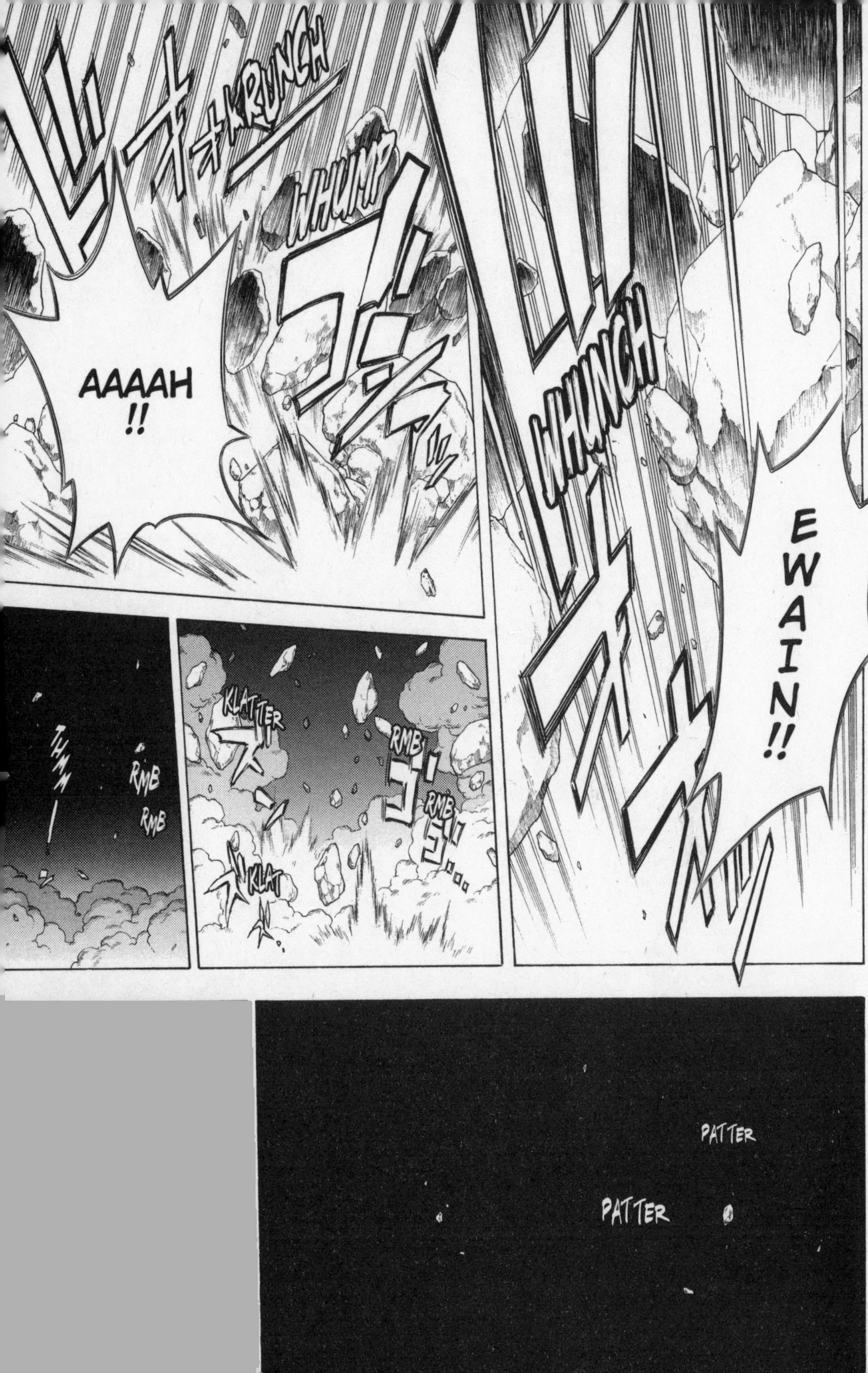
WHUNCH
EWAIN!!
KRUNCH
WHUMP
AAAAH!!
KLATTER
RMB
RMB
KLAT
THMM
RMB
RMB
PATTER
PATTER

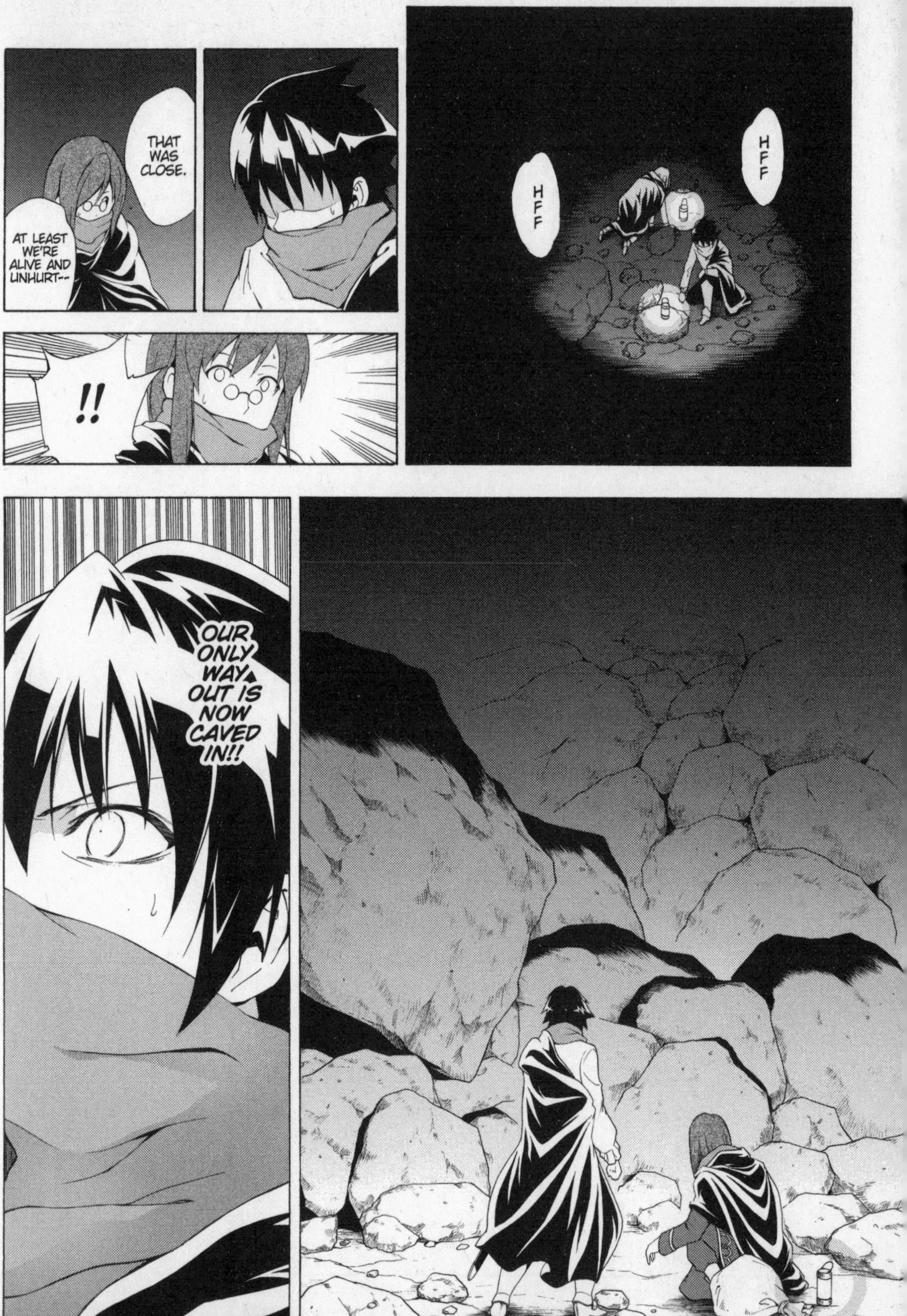
HFF
HFF
THAT WAS CLOSE.
AT LEAST WE'RE ALIVE AND UNHURT--
!!
OUR ONLY WAY OUT IS NOW CAVED IN!!

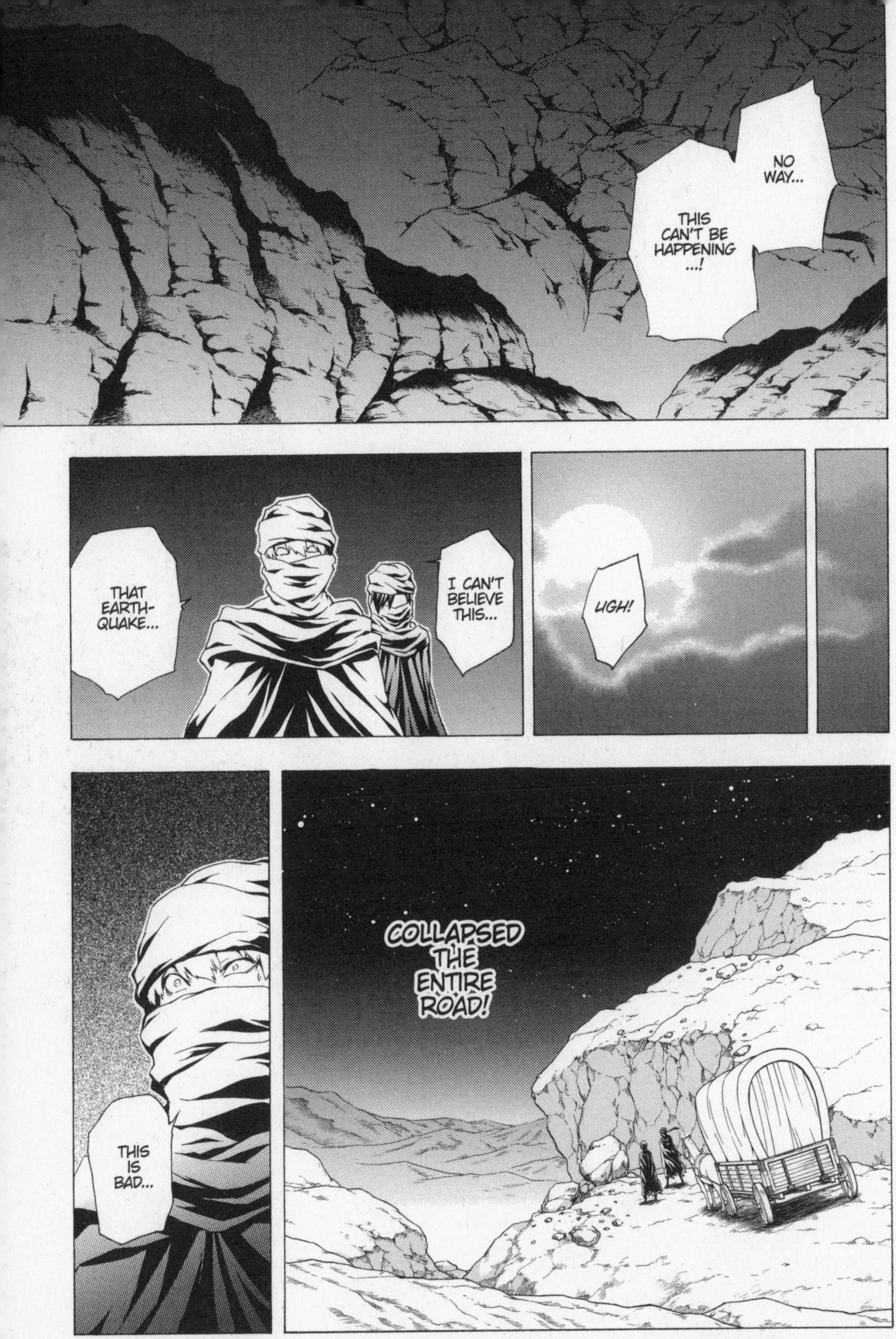
NO WAY...
THIS CAN'T BE HAPPENING ...!
UGH!
I CAN'T BELIEVE THIS...
THAT EARTH-QUAKE...
COLLAPSED THE ENTIRE ROAD!
THIS IS BAD...

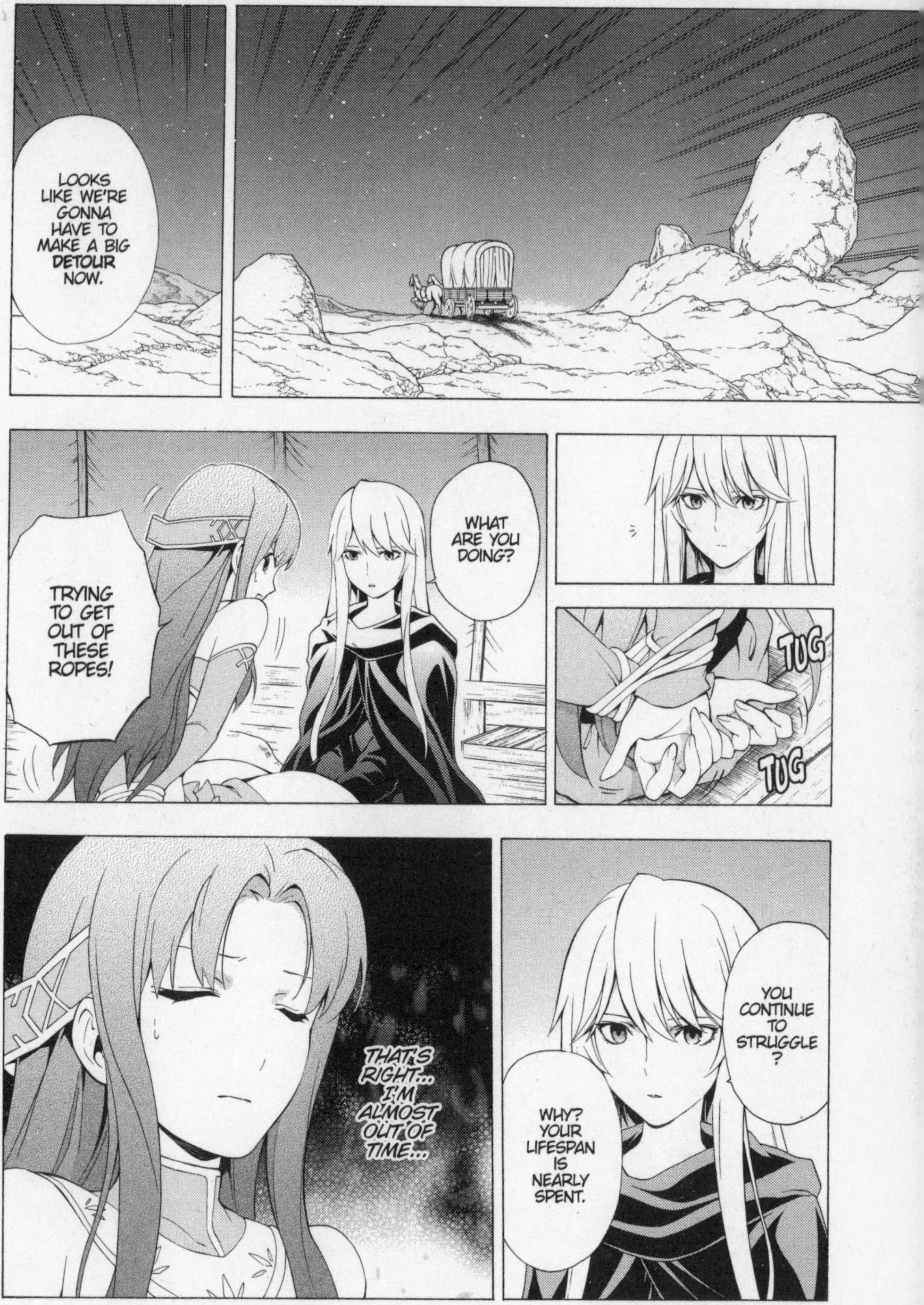
LOOKS LIKE WE'RE GONNA HAVE TO MAKE A BIG DETOUR NOW.
TUG
TUG
WHAT ARE YOU DOING?
TRYING TO GET OUT OF THESE ROPES!
YOU CONTINUE TO STRUGGLE?
WHY? YOUR LIFESPAN IS NEARLY SPENT.
THAT'S RIGHT... I'M ALMOST OUT OF TIME...

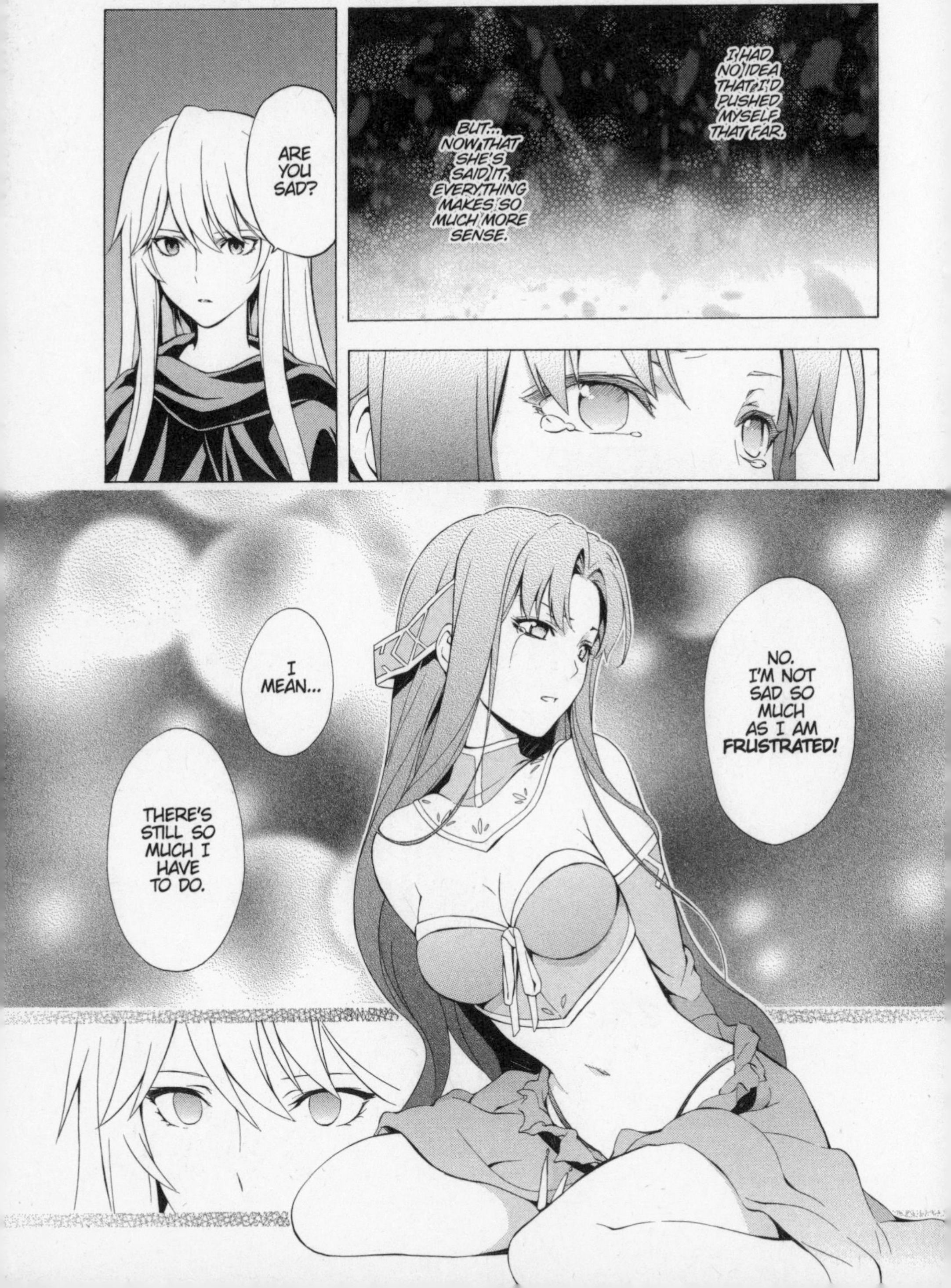
I HAD NO IDEA THAT I'D PUSHED MYSELF THAT FAR.
BUT... NOW THAT SHE'S SAID IT, EVERYTHING MAKES SO MUCH MORE SENSE.
ARE YOU SAD?
NO. I'M NOT SAD SO MUCH AS I AM FRUSTRATED!
I MEAN...
THERE'S STILL SO MUCH I HAVE TO DO.

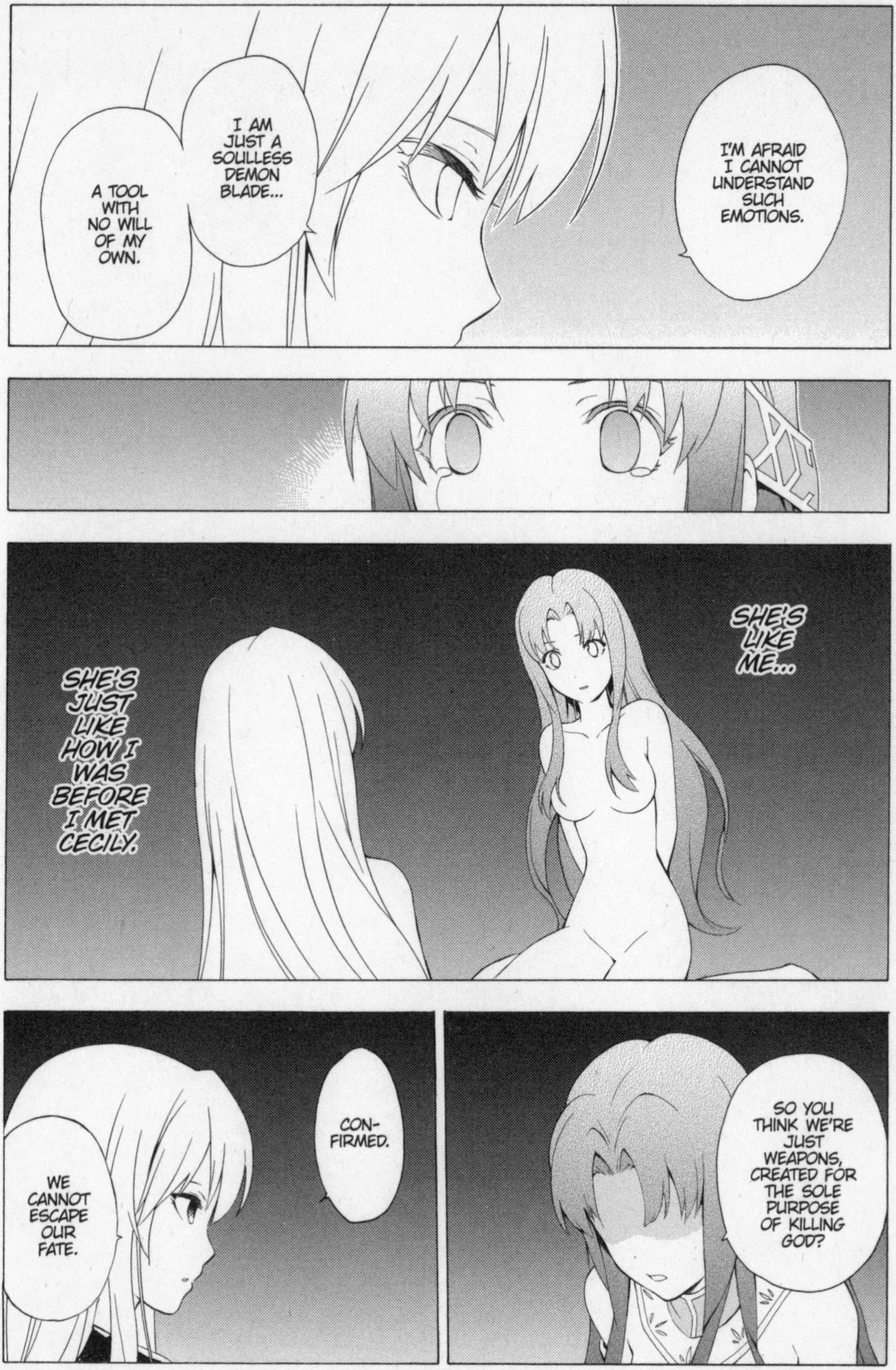
I'M AFRAID I CANNOT UNDERSTAND SUCH EMOTIONS.
I AM JUST A SOULLESS DEMON BLADE...
A TOOL WITH NO WILL OF MY OWN.
SHE'S LIKE ME...
SHE'S JUST LIKE HOW I WAS BEFORE I MET CECILY.
SO YOU THINK WE'RE JUST WEAPONS, CREATED FOR THE SOLE PURPOSE OF KILLING GOD?
CON-FIRMED.
WE CANNOT ESCAPE OUR FATE.

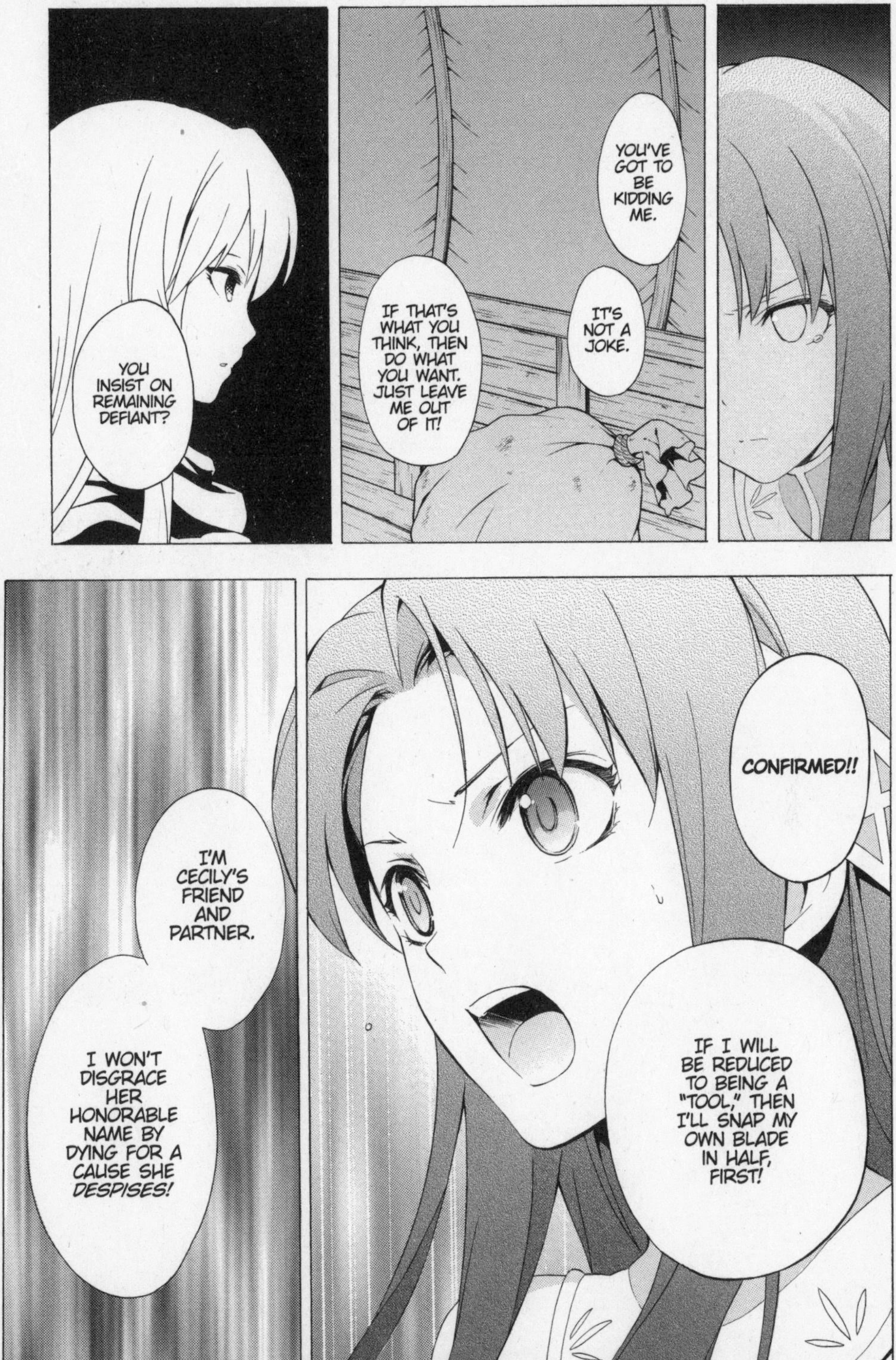
YOU'VE GOT TO BE KIDDING ME.
IT'S NOT A JOKE.
IF THAT'S WHAT YOU THINK, THEN DO WHAT YOU WANT. JUST LEAVE ME OUT OF IT!
YOU INSIST ON REMAINING DEFIANT?
CONFIRMED!!
IF I WILL BE REDUCED TO BEING A "TOOL," THEN I'LL SNAP MY OWN BLADE IN HALF, FIRST!
I'M CECILY'S FRIEND AND PARTNER.
I WON'T DISGRACE HER HONORABLE NAME BY DYING FOR A CAUSE SHE *DESPISES*!

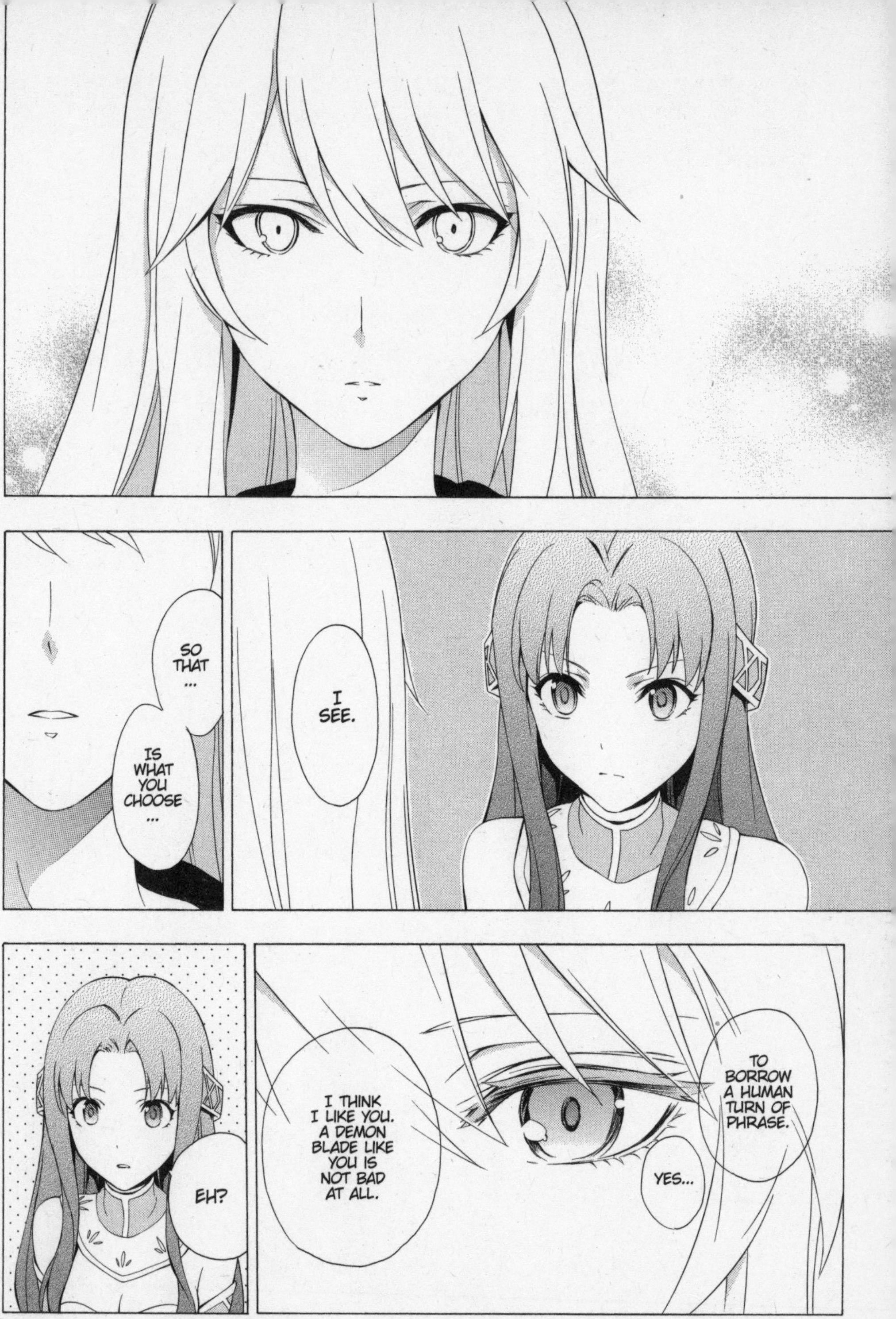
I SEE.
SO THAT ...
IS WHAT YOU CHOOSE ...
YES...
TO BORROW A HUMAN TURN OF PHRASE.
I THINK I LIKE YOU. A DEMON BLADE LIKE YOU IS NOT BAD AT ALL.
EH?

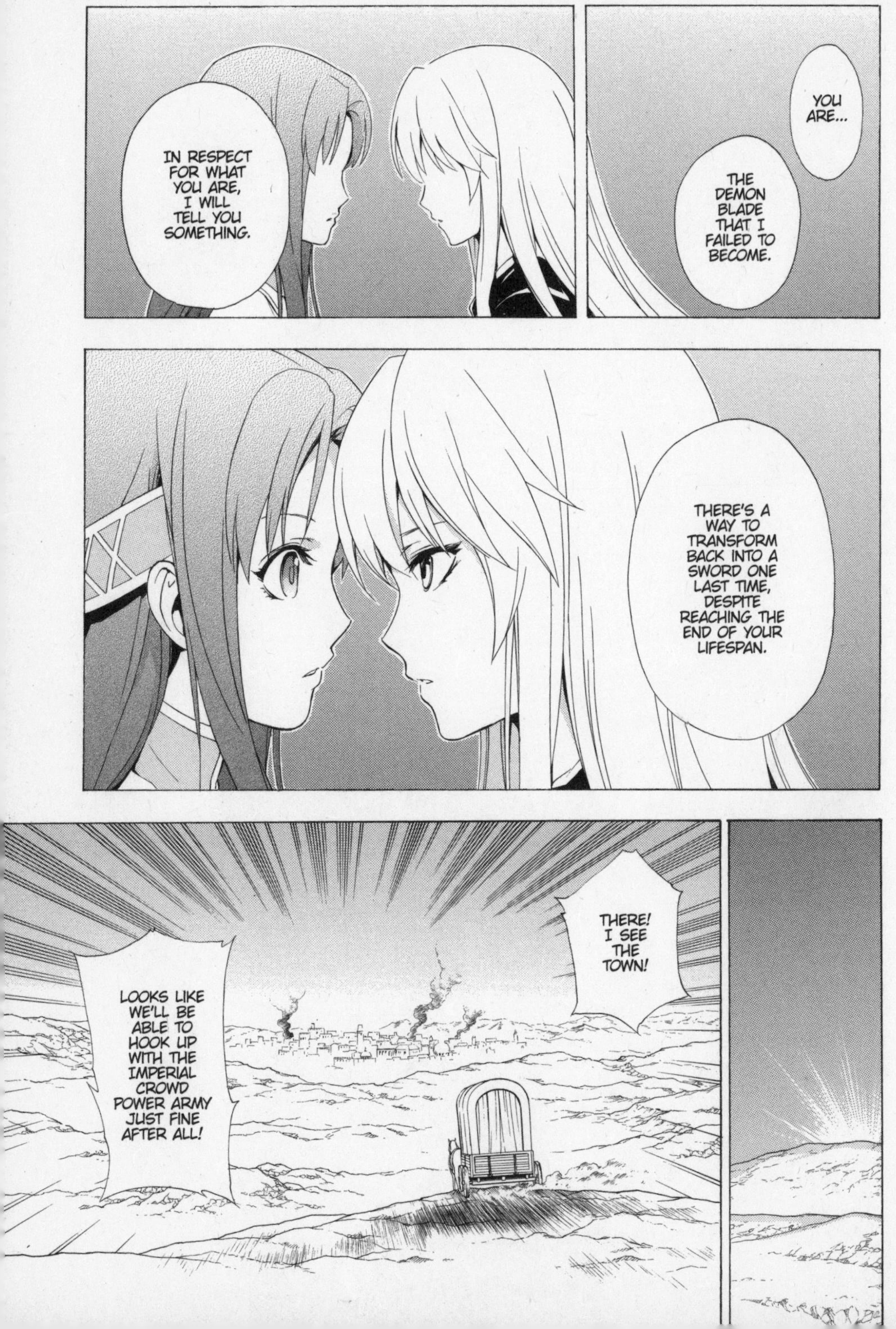
YOU ARE...
THE DEMON BLADE THAT I FAILED TO BECOME.
IN RESPECT FOR WHAT YOU ARE, I WILL TELL YOU SOMETHING.
THERE'S A WAY TO TRANSFORM BACK INTO A SWORD ONE LAST TIME, DESPITE REACHING THE END OF YOUR LIFESPAN.
THERE! I SEE THE TOWN!
LOOKS LIKE WE'LL BE ABLE TO HOOK UP WITH THE IMPERIAL CROWD POWER ARMY JUST FINE AFTER ALL!

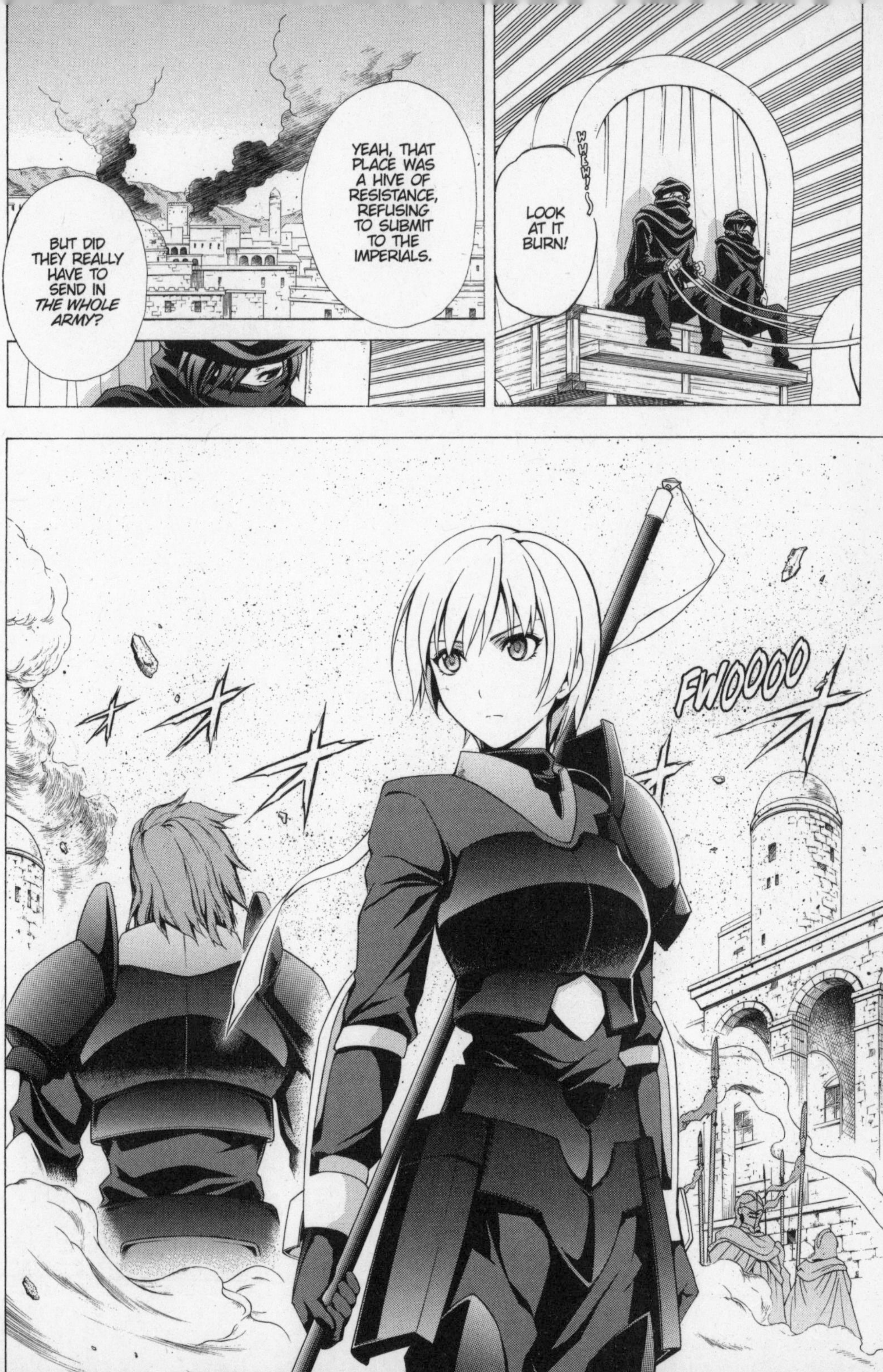
WHEW!~
LOOK AT IT BURN!
YEAH, THAT PLACE WAS A HIVE OF RESISTANCE, REFUSING TO SUBMIT TO THE IMPERIALS.
BUT DID THEY REALLY HAVE TO SEND IN *THE WHOLE ARMY?*
FWOOOO

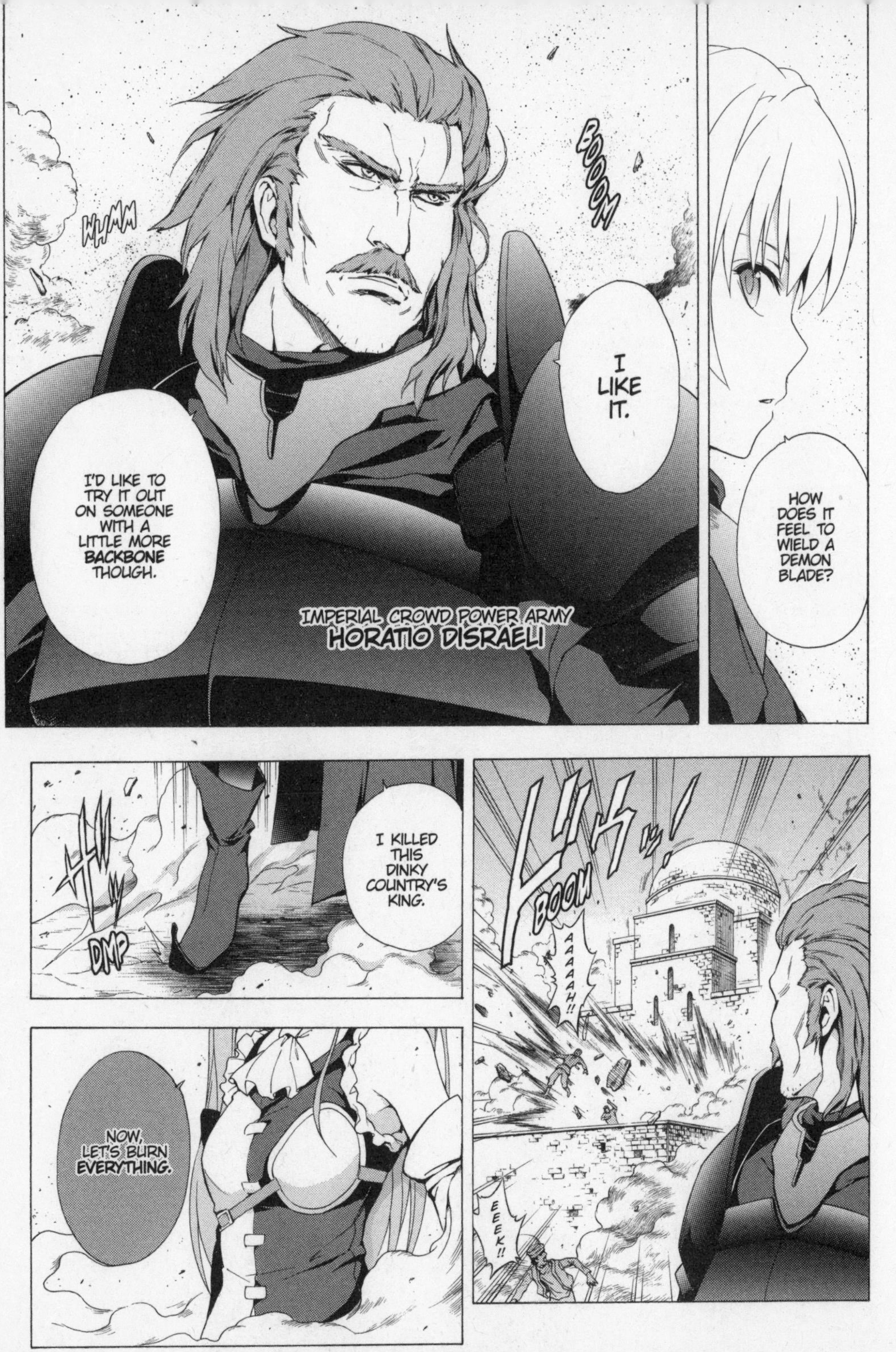
HOW DOES IT FEEL TO WIELD A DEMON BLADE?
BOOOOM
I LIKE IT.
WHMM
I'D LIKE TO TRY IT OUT ON SOMEONE WITH A LITTLE MORE BACKBONE THOUGH.
IMPERIAL CROWD POWER ARMY
HORATIO DISRAELI
BOOM
AAAAAAH!!
EEEEK!!
I KILLED THIS DINKY COUNTRY'S KING.
DMP
NOW, LET'S BURN EVERYTHING.

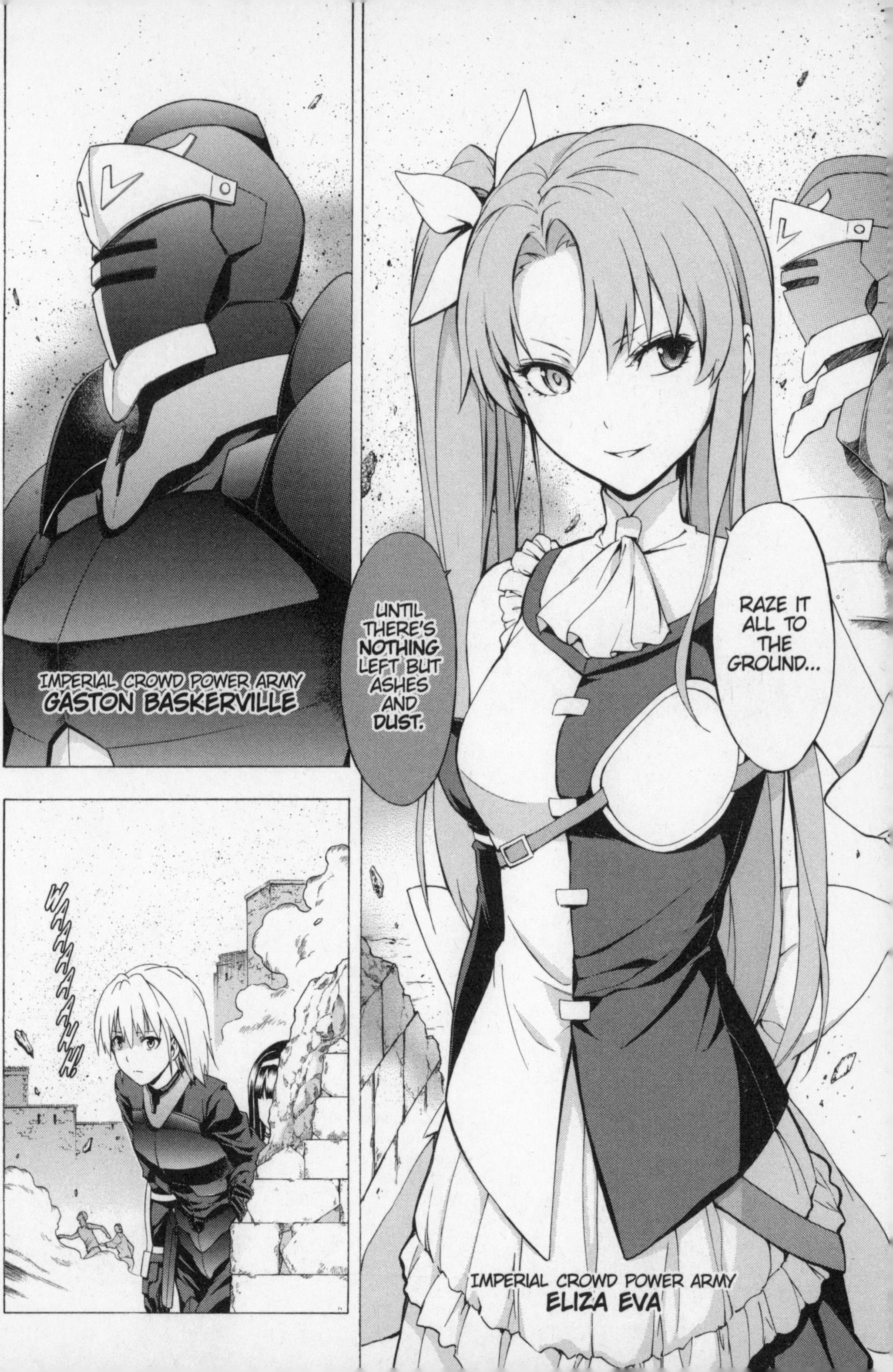
RAZE IT ALL TO THE GROUND...
UNTIL THERE'S NOTHING LEFT BUT ASHES AND DUST.
IMPERIAL CROWD POWER ARMY
ELIZA EVA
IMPERIAL CROWD POWER ARMY
GASTON BASKERVILLE
WAAAAAHH!!

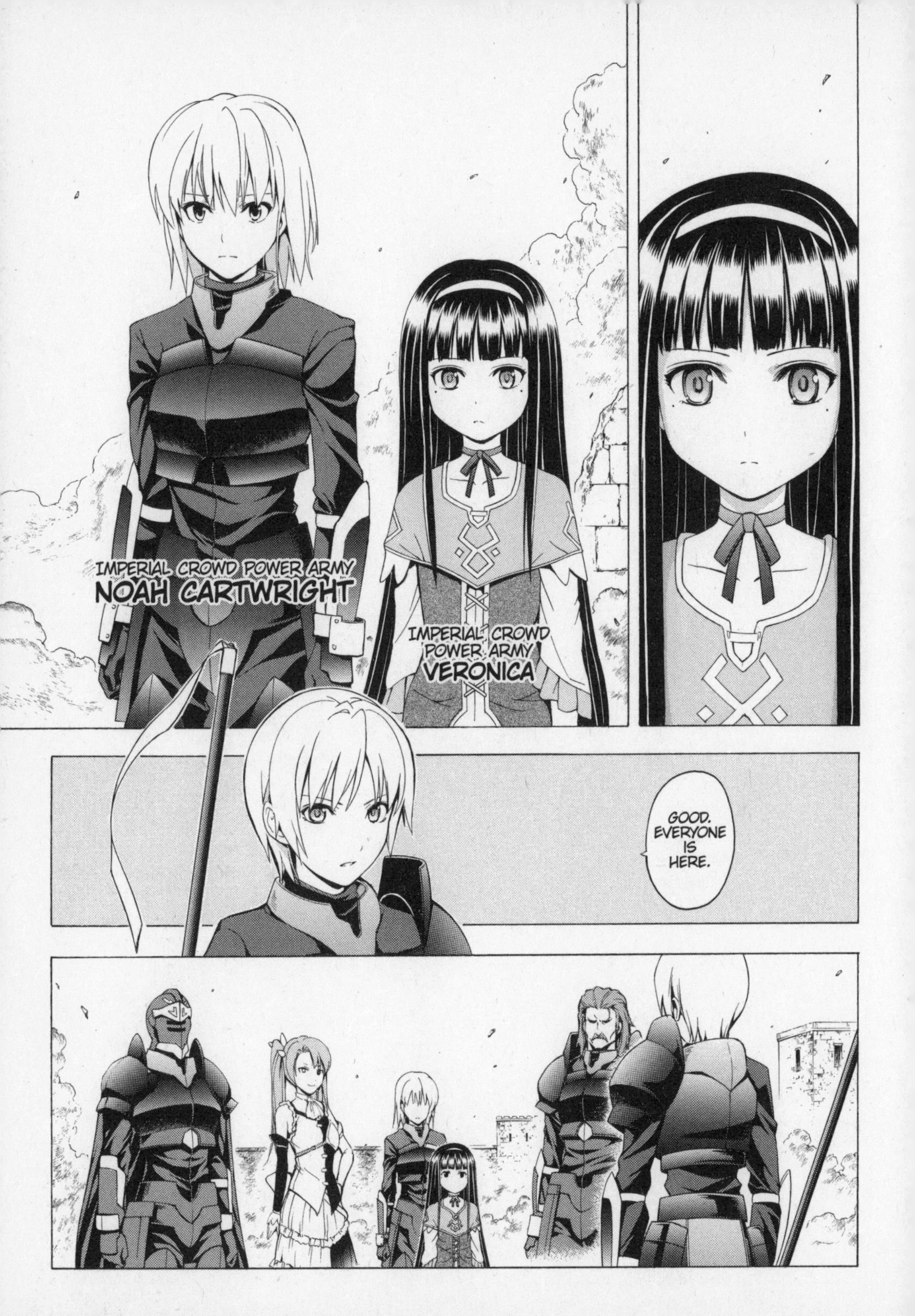
IMPERIAL CROWD POWER ARMY
NOAH CARTWRIGHT
IMPERIAL CROWD POWER ARMY
VERONICA
GOOD. EVERYONE IS HERE.

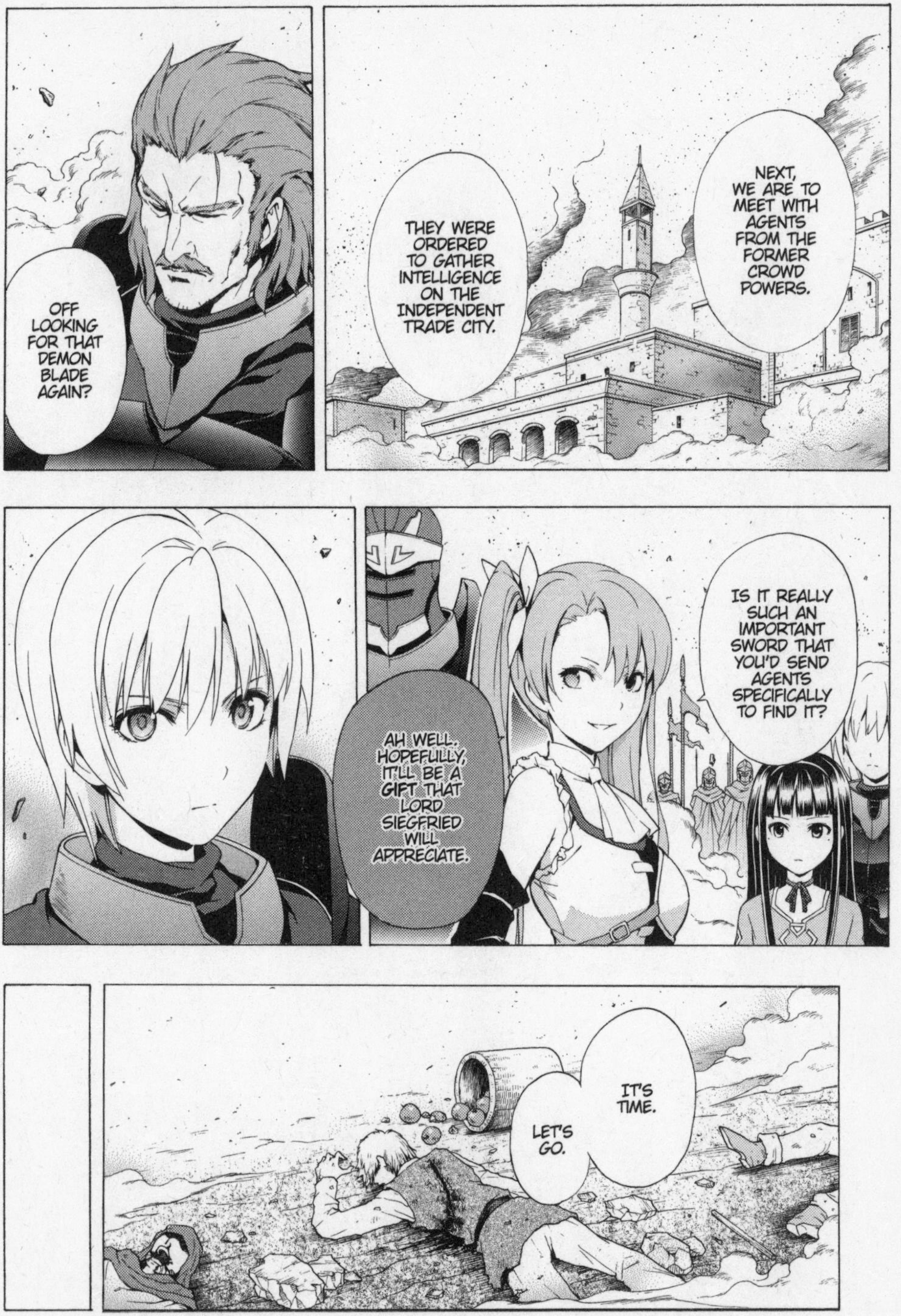
NEXT, WE ARE TO MEET WITH AGENTS FROM THE FORMER CROWD POWERS.
THEY WERE ORDERED TO GATHER INTELLIGENCE ON THE INDEPENDENT TRADE CITY.
OFF LOOKING FOR THAT DEMON BLADE AGAIN?
IS IT REALLY SUCH AN IMPORTANT SWORD THAT YOU'D SEND AGENTS SPECIFICALLY TO FIND IT?
AH WELL. HOPEFULLY, IT'LL BE A GIFT THAT LORD SIEGFRIED WILL APPRECIATE.
IT'S TIME.
LET'S GO.

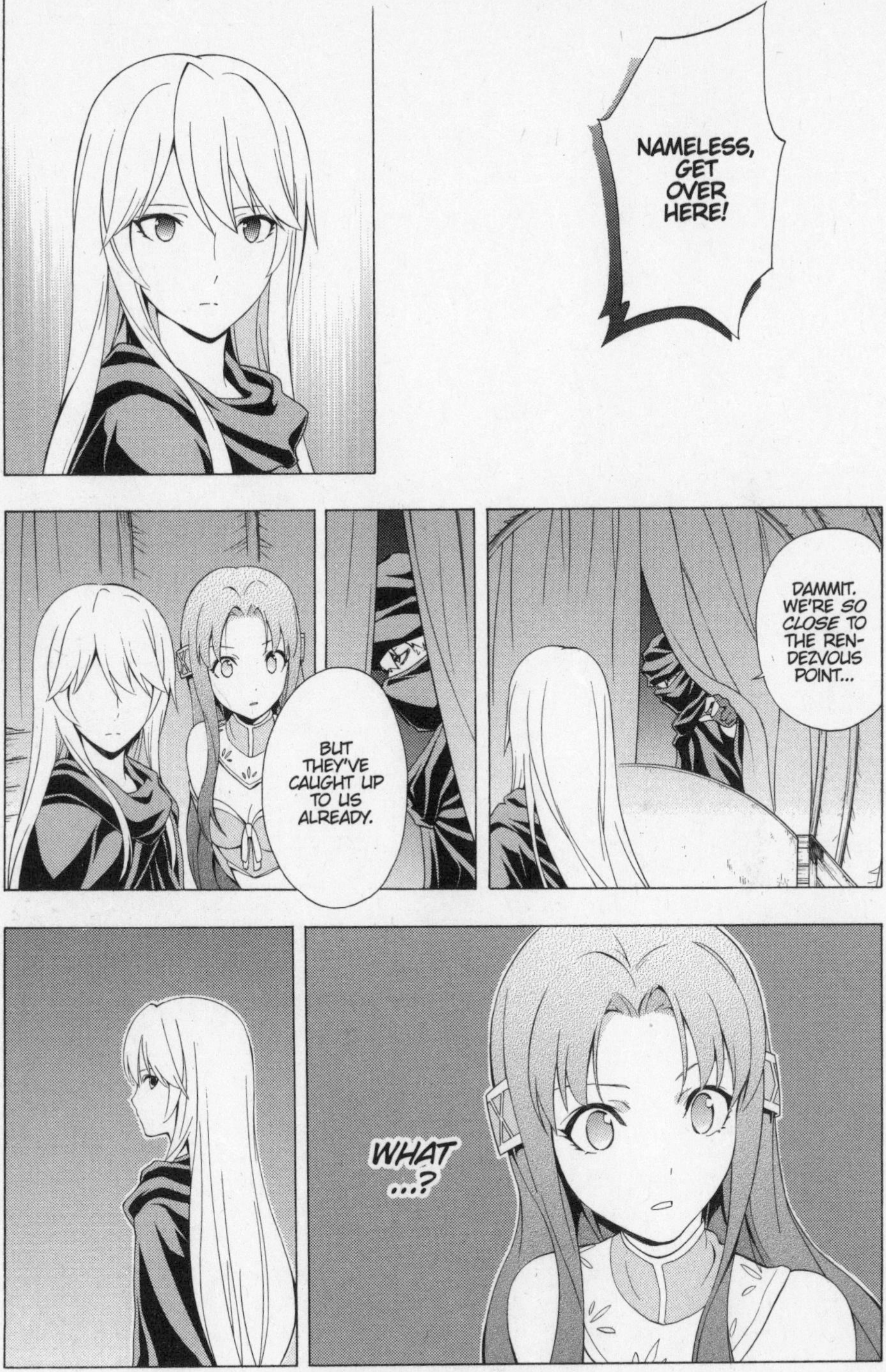
NAMELESS, GET OVER HERE!
DAMMIT. WE'RE SO *CLOSE* TO THE REN-DEZVOUS POINT...
BUT THEY'VE CAUGHT UP TO US ALREADY.
WHAT ...?

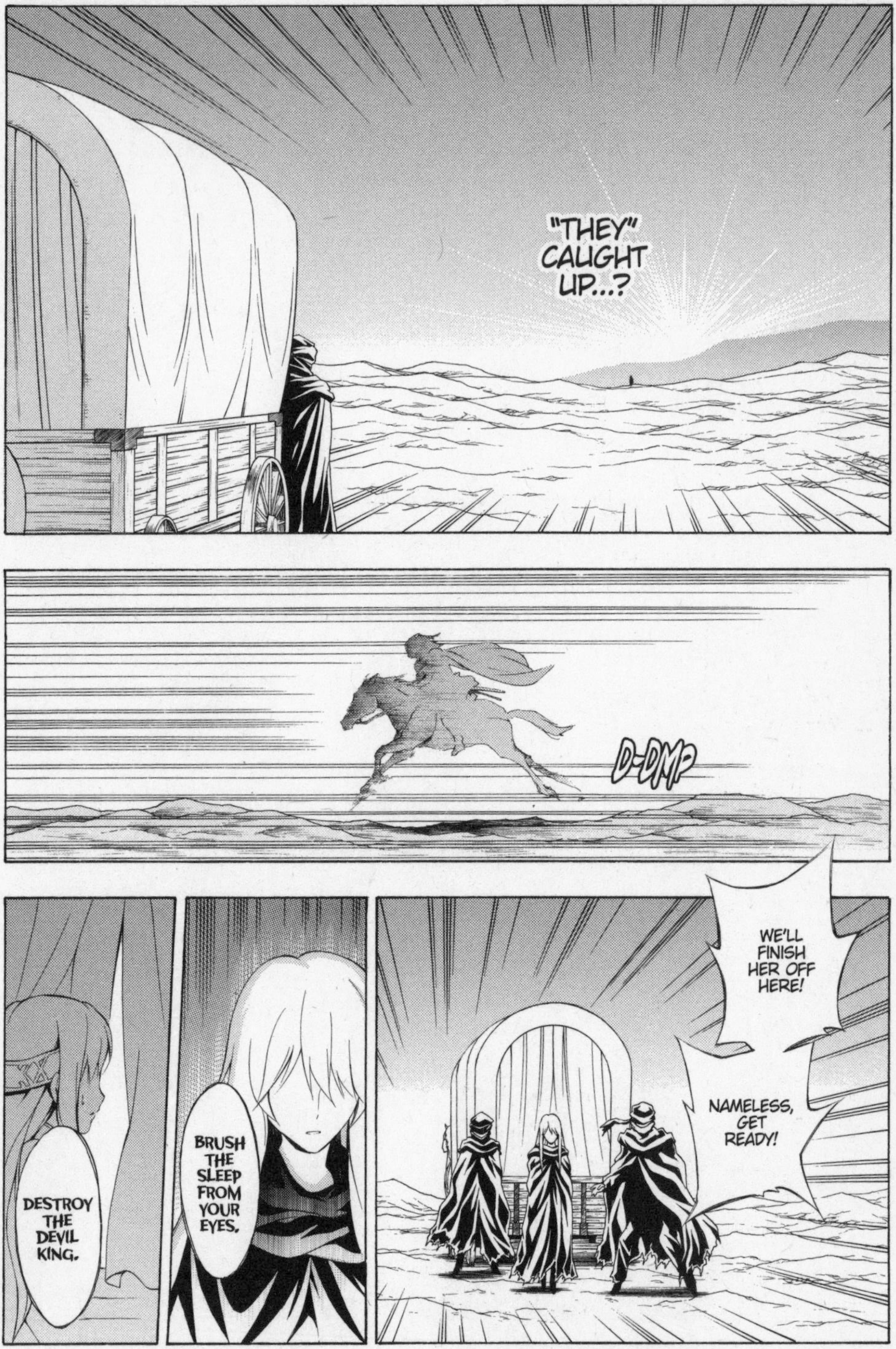
"THEY" CAUGHT UP...?
D-DMP
WE'LL FINISH HER OFF HERE!
NAMELESS, GET READY!
BRUSH THE SLEEP FROM YOUR EYES.
DESTROY THE DEVIL KING.

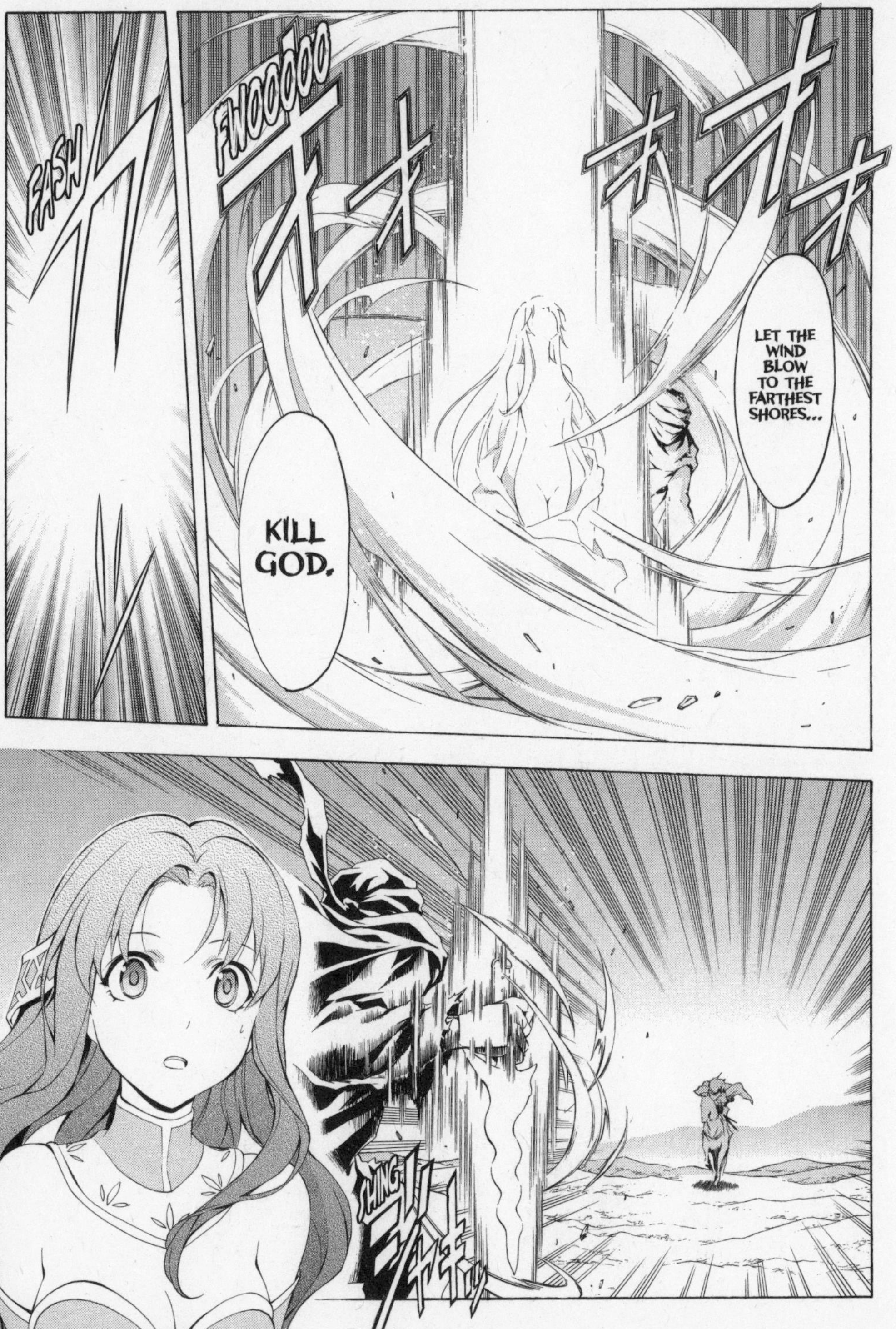
FWOOOOO
LET THE WIND BLOW TO THE FARTHEST SHORES...
KILL GOD.
FASH
SHING

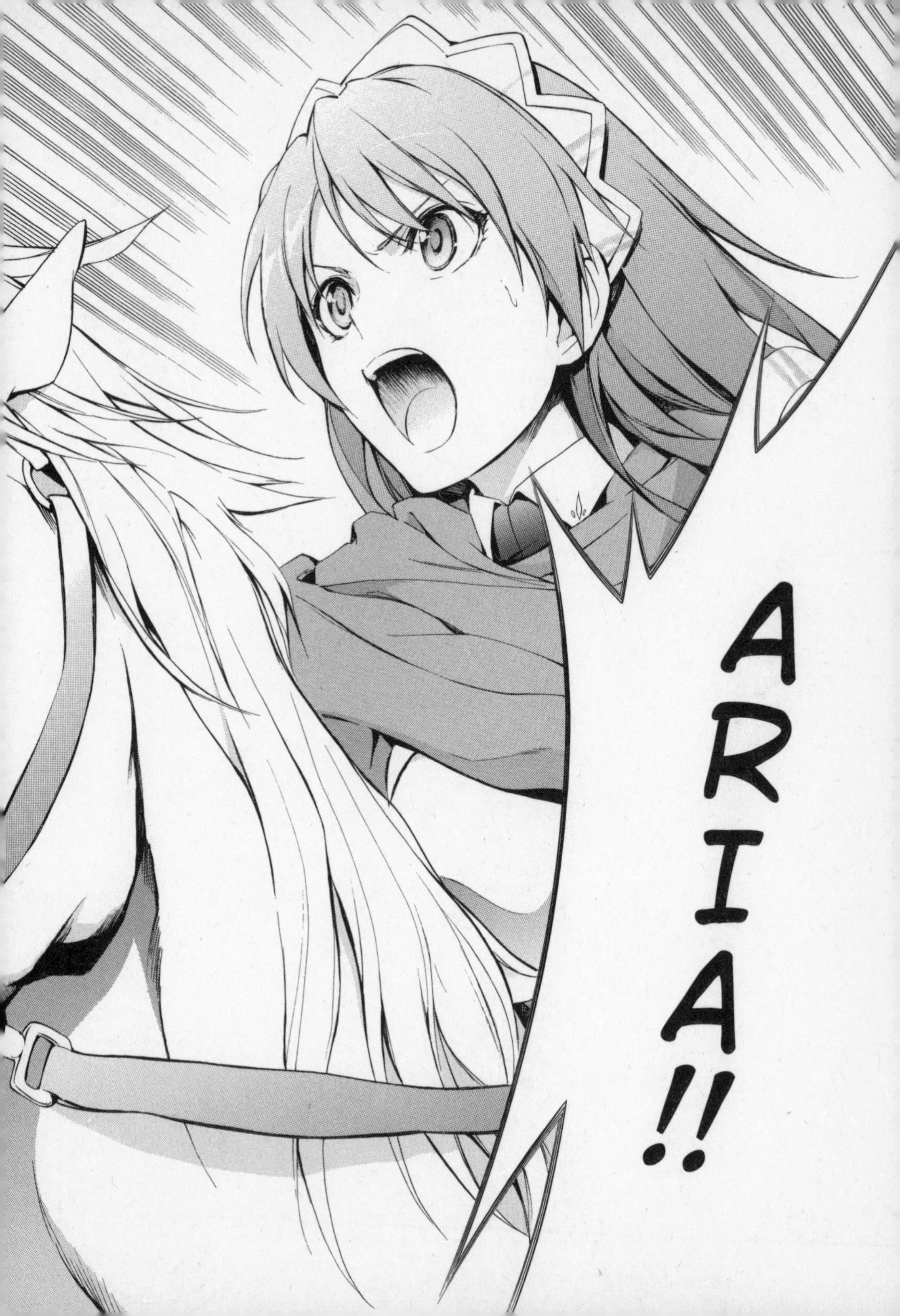
ARIA!!

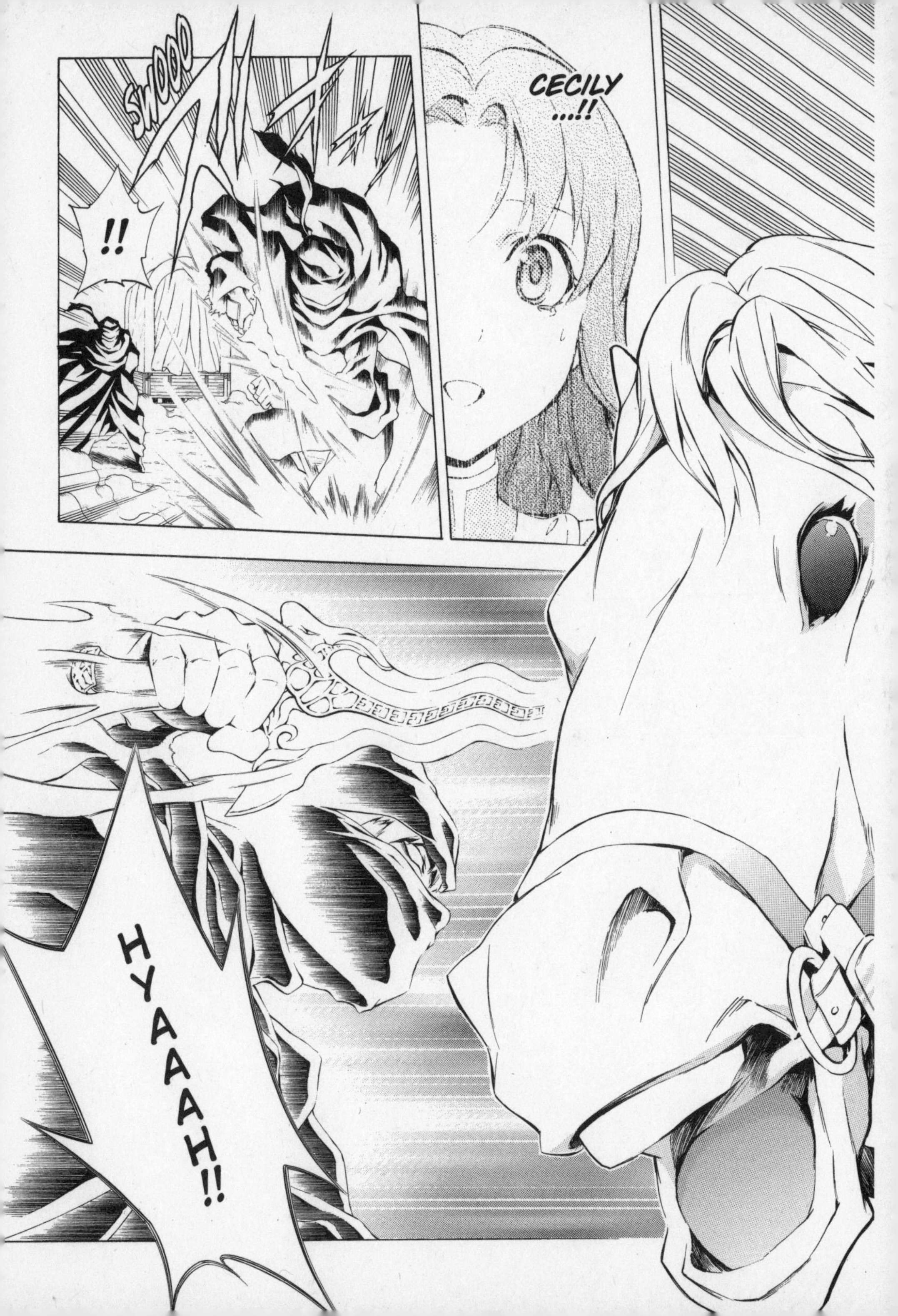
CECILY ...!!
SWOOO
!!
HYAAAH!!

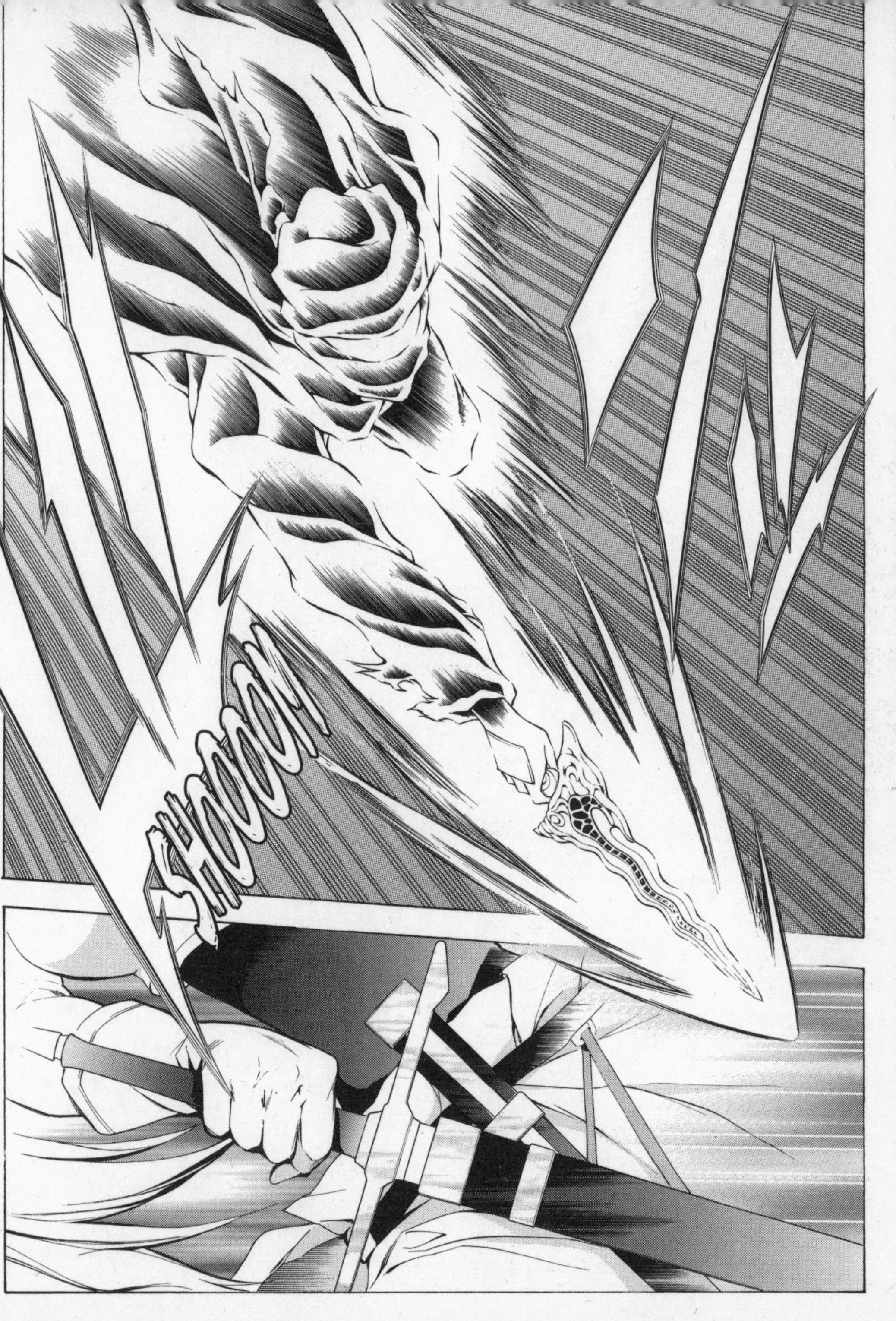
SHOOOOM

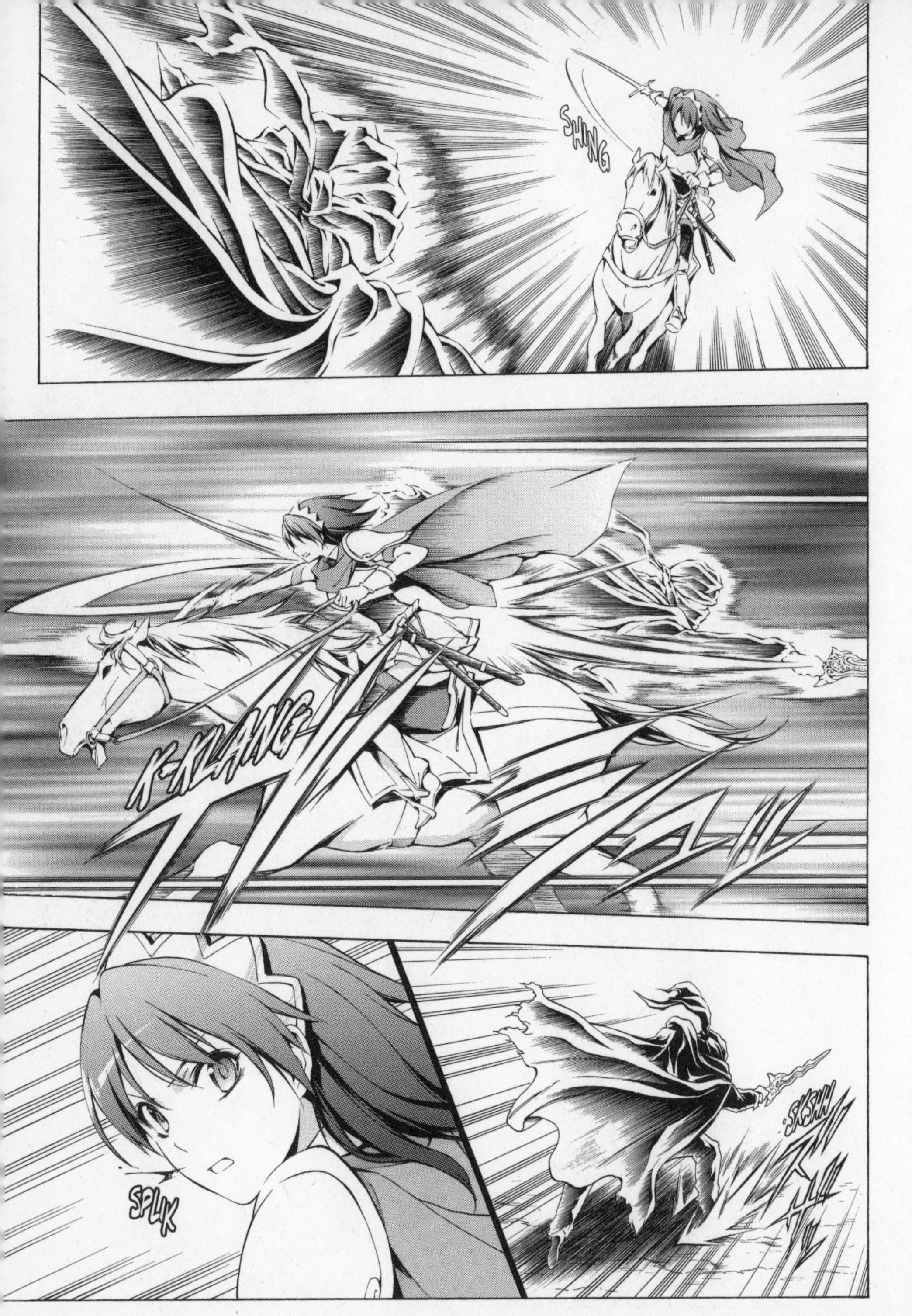
SHING
K-KLANG
SKSHH
SPLIK

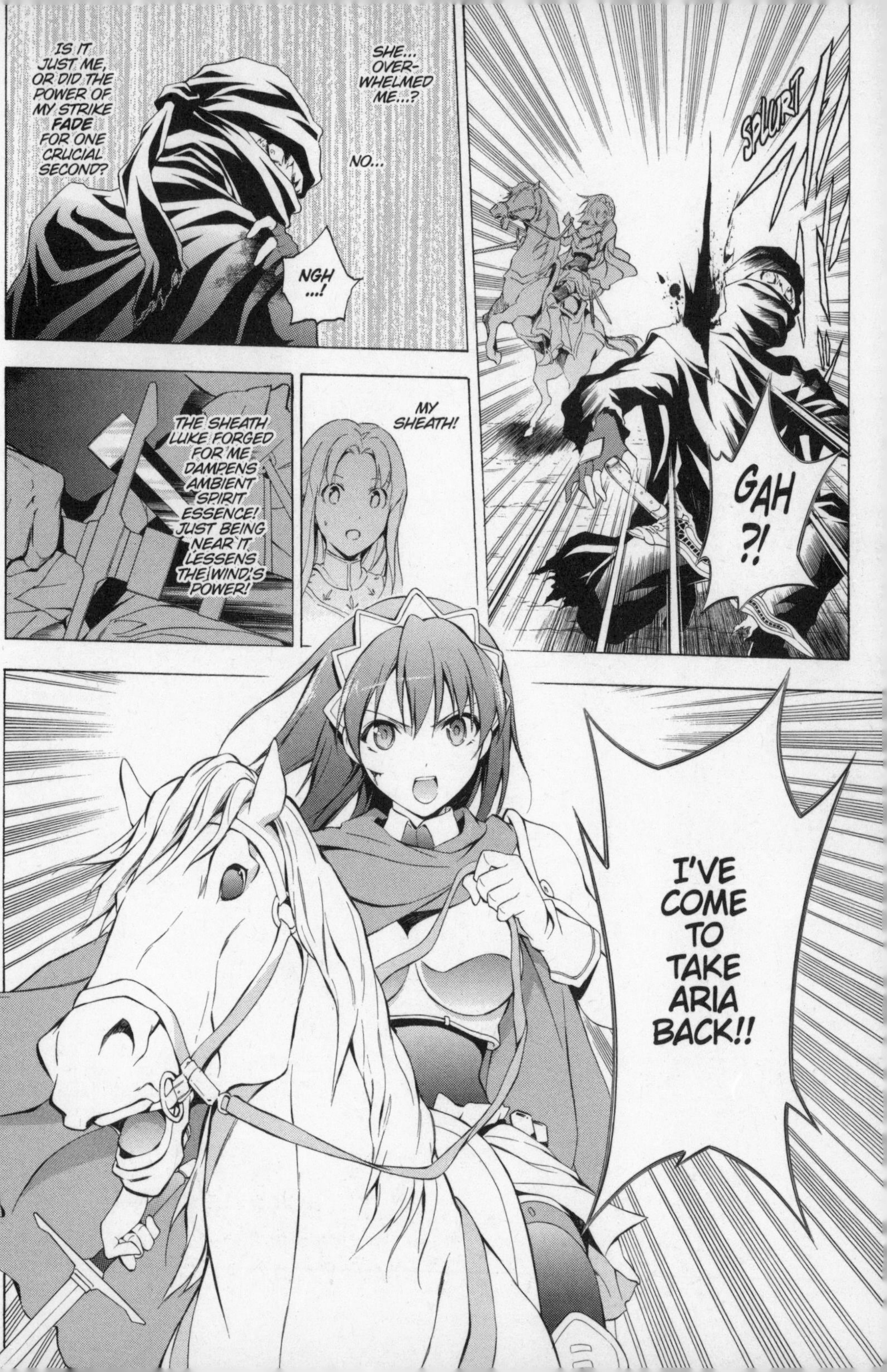
SPLURT
GAH ?!
SHE... OVER-WHELMED ME...?
IS IT JUST ME, OR DID THE POWER OF MY STRIKE FADE FOR ONE CRUCIAL SECOND?
NO...
NGH ...!
MY SHEATH!
THE SHEATH LUKE FORGED FOR ME DAMPENS AMBIENT SPIRIT ESSENCE! JUST BEING NEAR IT LESSENS THE WIND'S POWER!
I'VE COME TO TAKE ARIA BACK!!

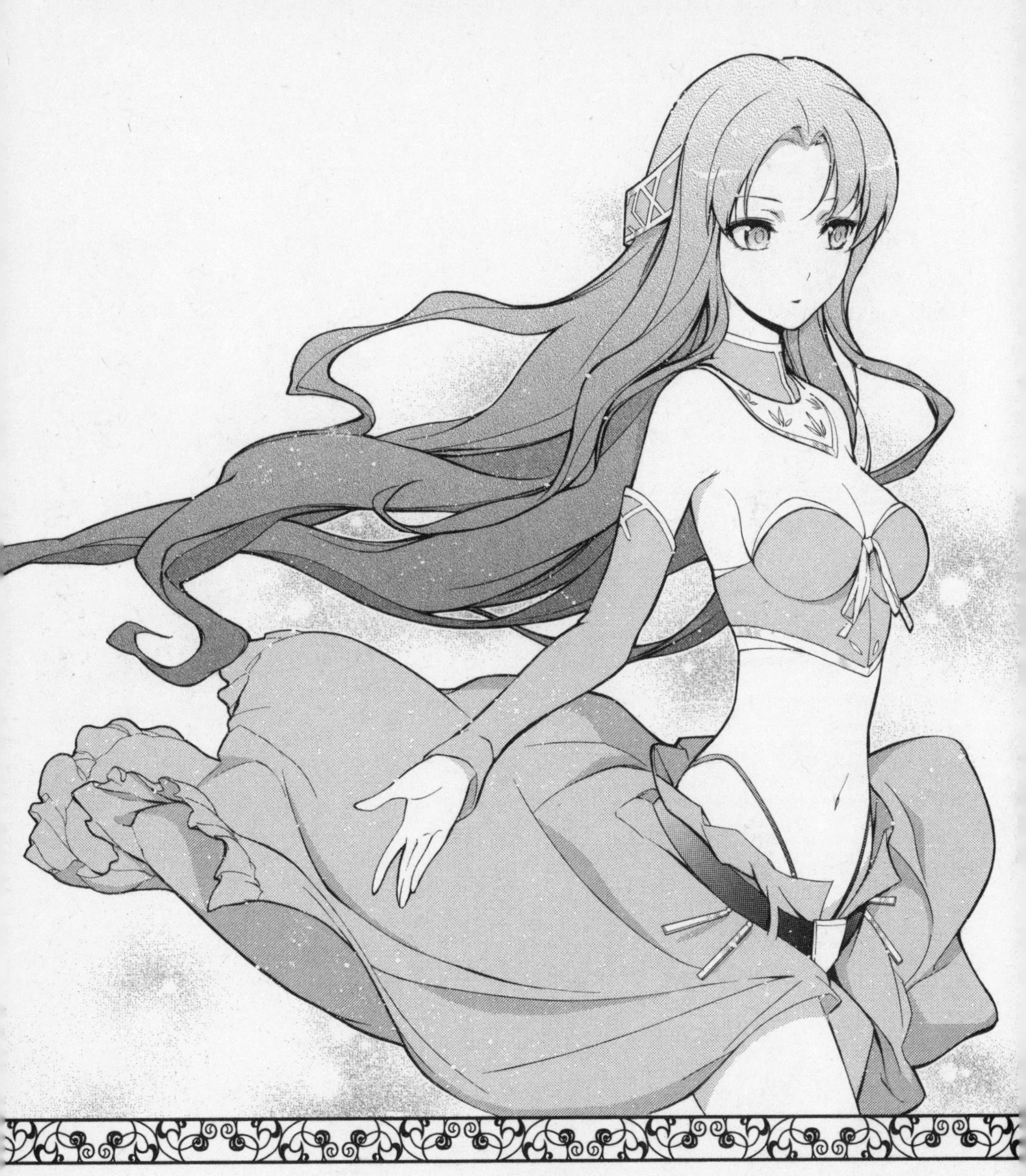

Chapter 35 East wind (Part 2)

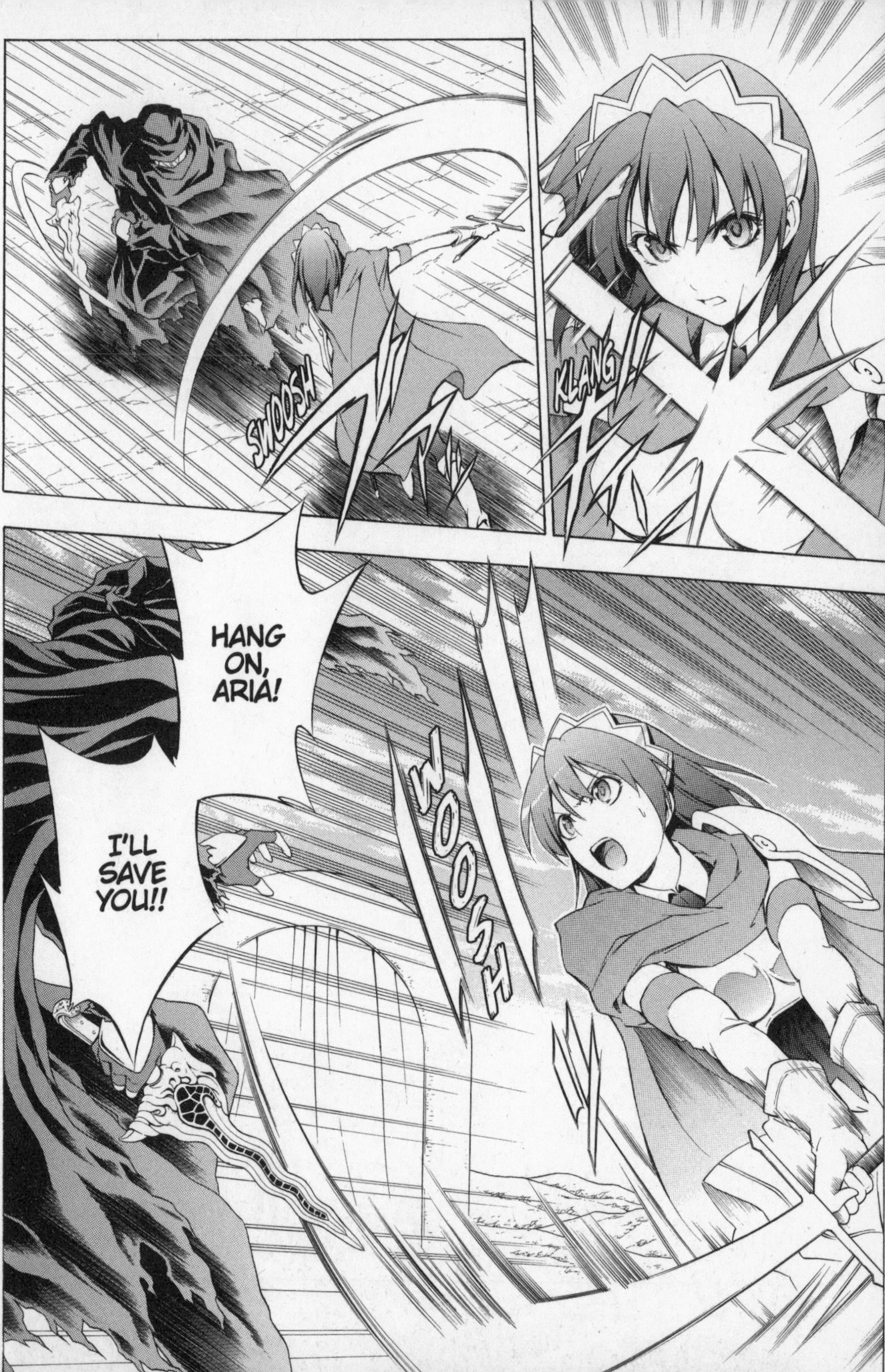
KLANG
SWOOSH
HANG ON, ARIA!
I'LL SAVE YOU!!
WOOSH

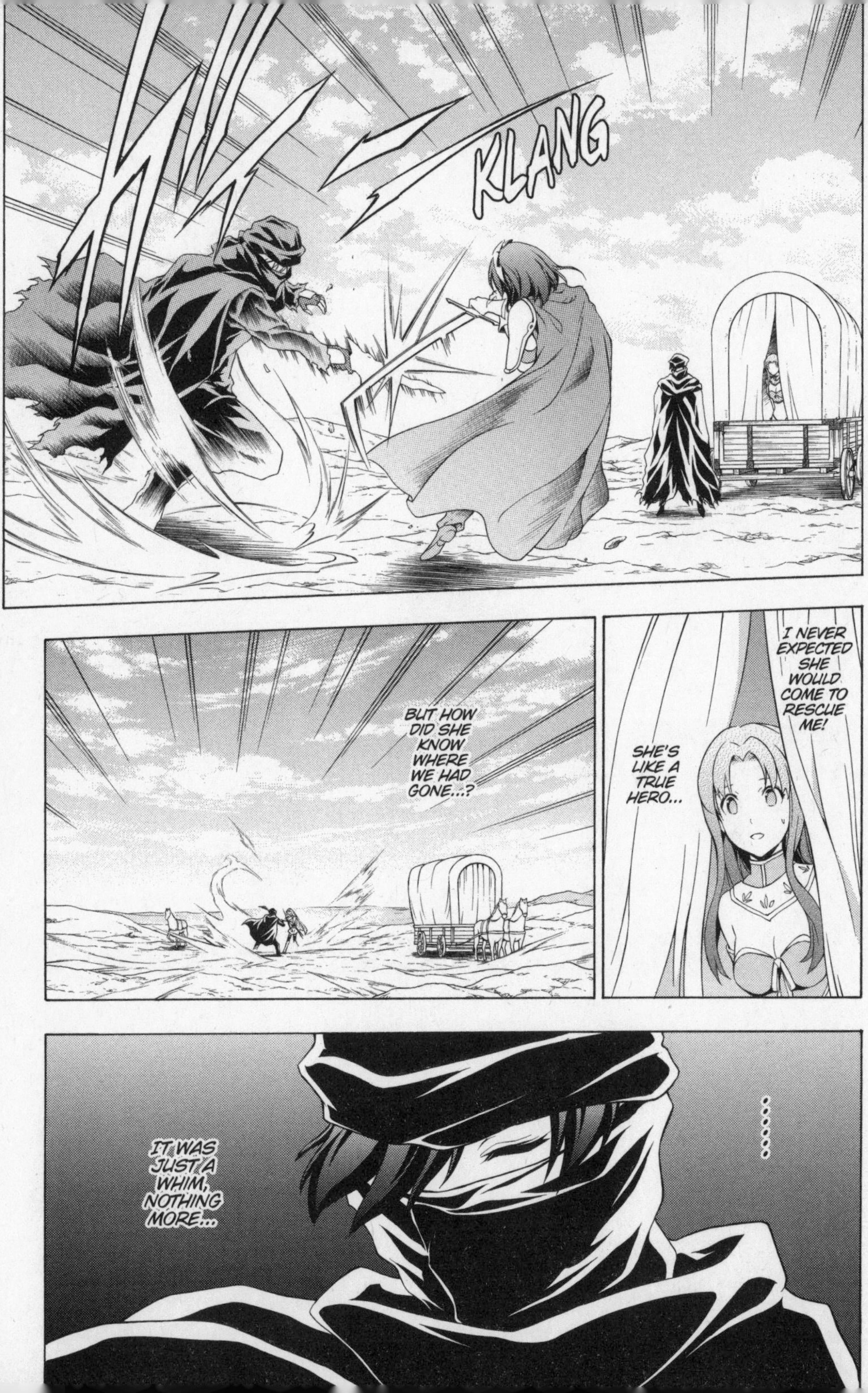
KLANG
I NEVER EXPECTED SHE WOULD COME TO RESCUE ME!
SHE'S LIKE A TRUE HERO...
BUT HOW DID SHE KNOW WHERE WE HAD GONE...?
......
IT WAS JUST A WHIM, NOTHING MORE...

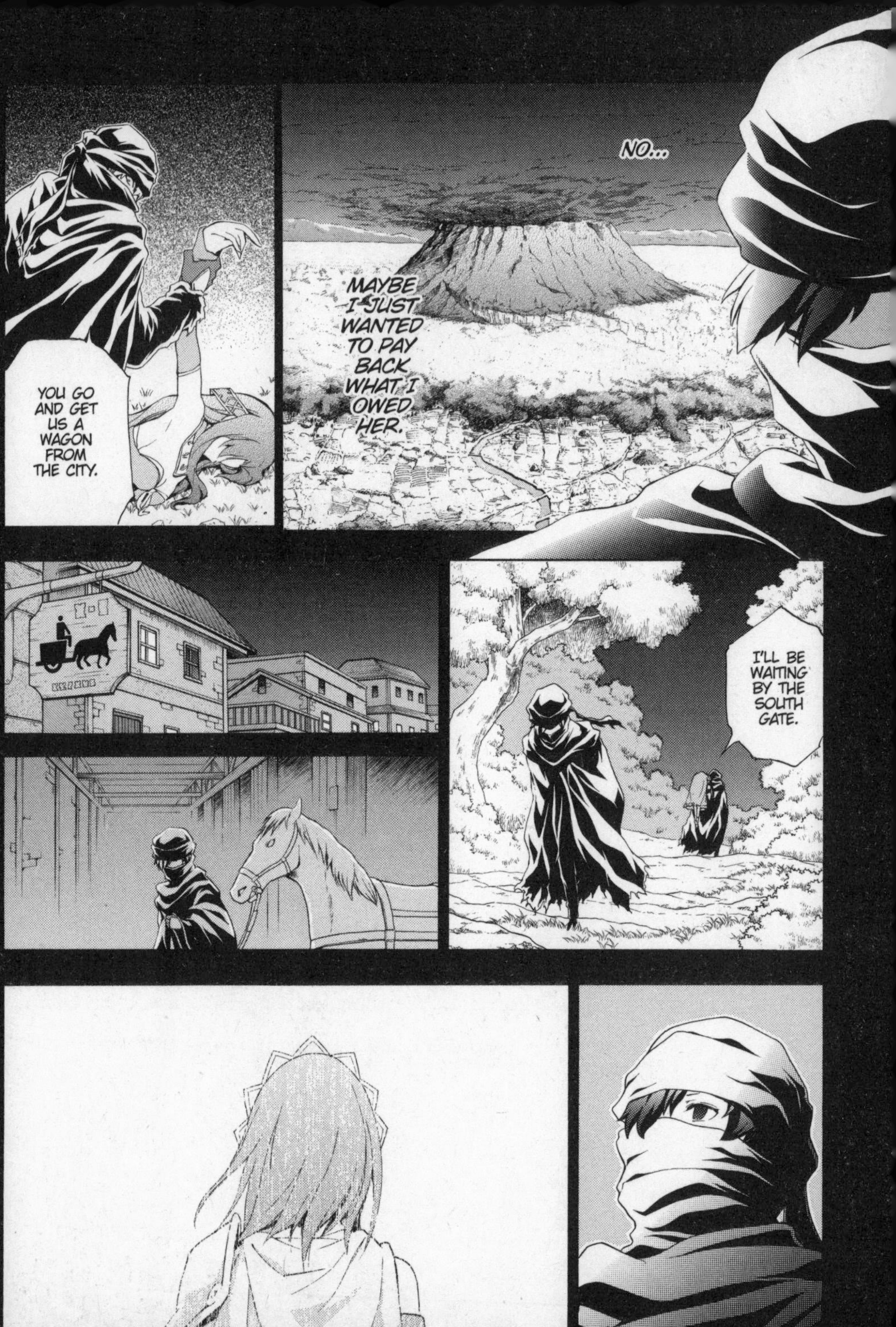
NO...
MAYBE I JUST WANTED TO PAY BACK WHAT I OWED HER.
YOU GO AND GET US A WAGON FROM THE CITY.
I'LL BE WAITING BY THE SOUTH GATE.

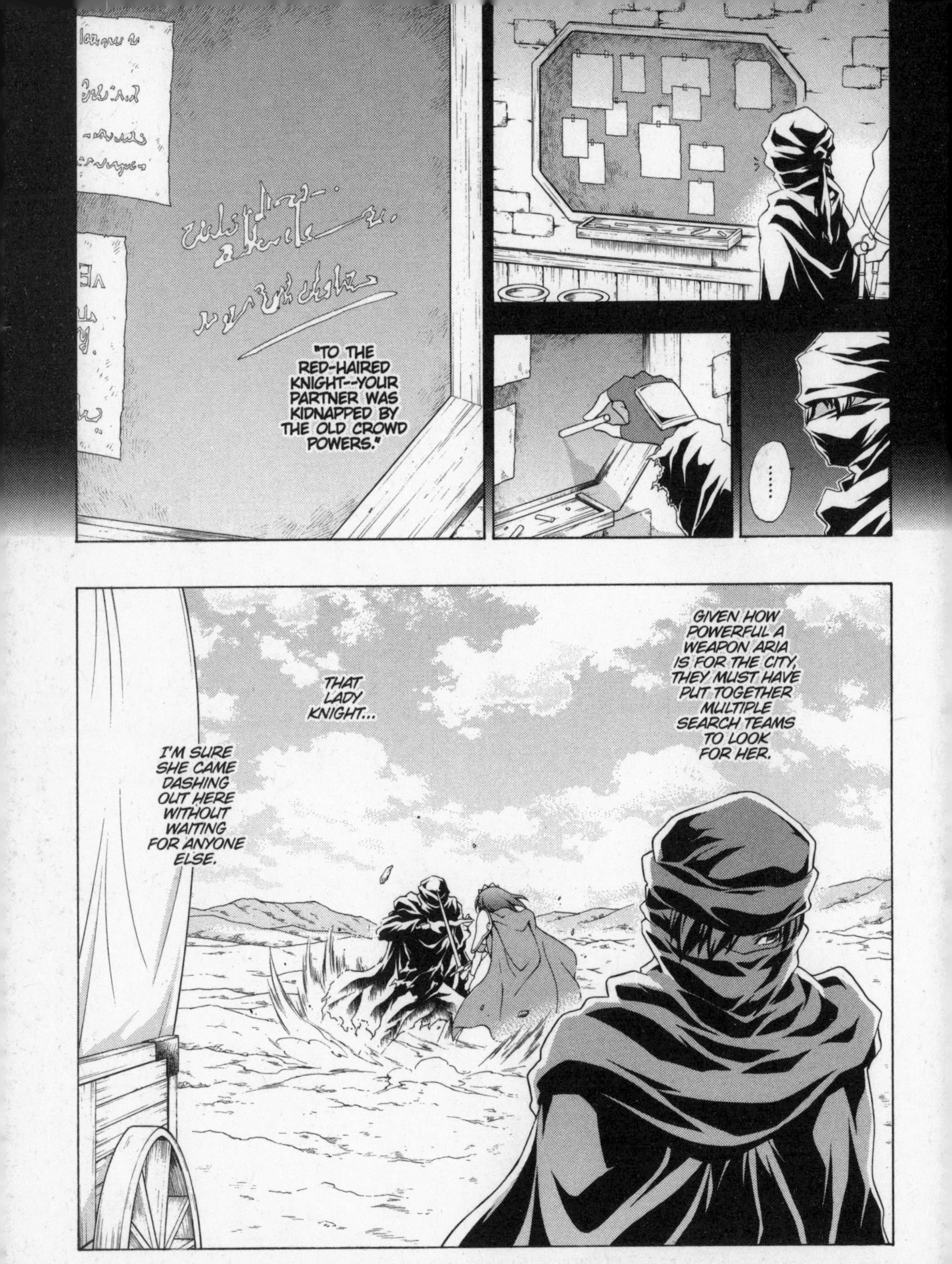
......
"TO THE RED-HAIRED KNIGHT--YOUR PARTNER WAS KIDNAPPED BY THE OLD CROWD POWERS."
GIVEN HOW POWERFUL A WEAPON ARIA IS FOR THE CITY, THEY MUST HAVE PUT TOGETHER MULTIPLE SEARCH TEAMS TO LOOK FOR HER.
THAT LADY KNIGHT...
I'M SURE SHE CAME DASHING OUT HERE WITHOUT WAITING FOR ANYONE ELSE.

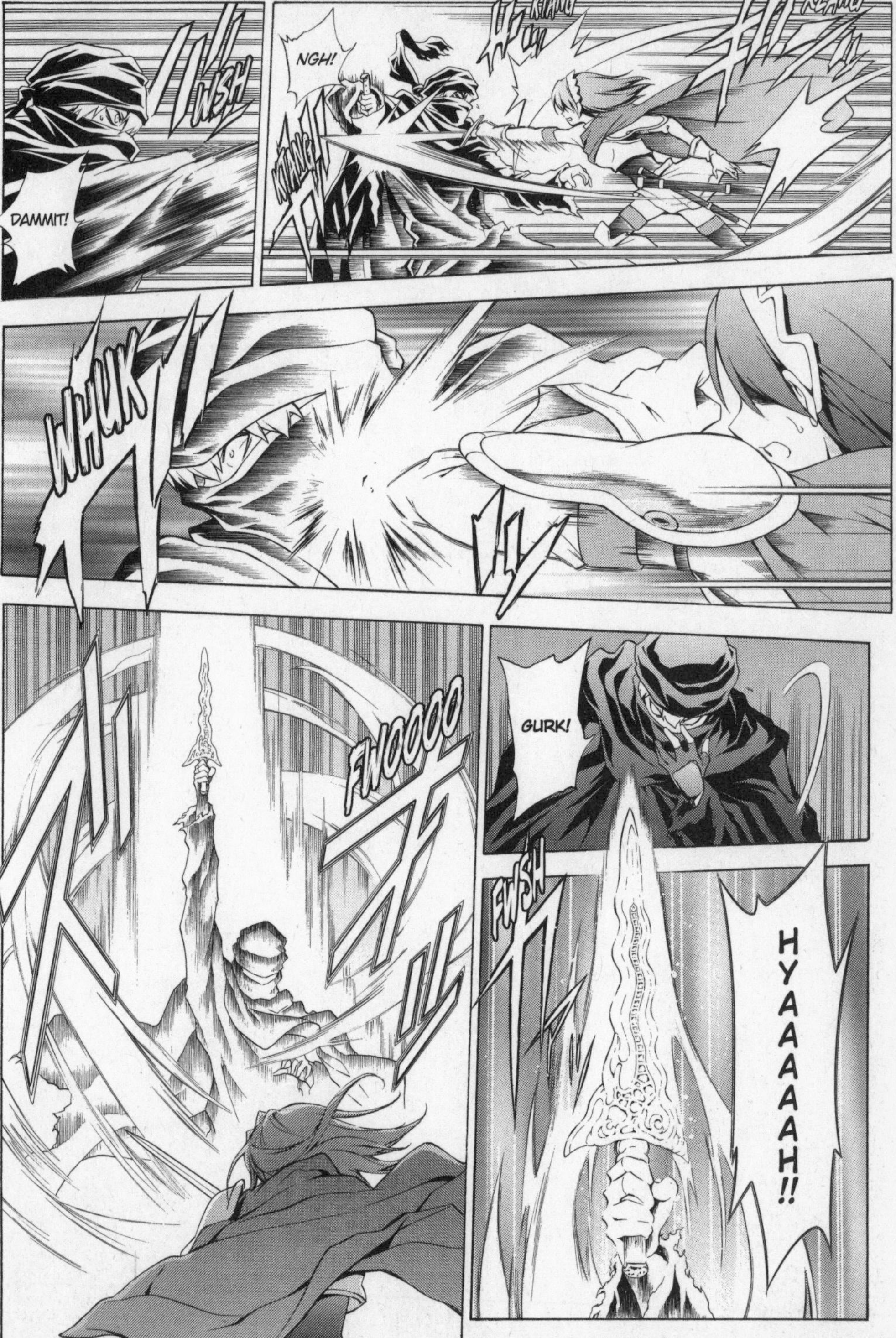
KLANG
KTANG
NGH!
KTANG
WSH
DAMMIT!
WHUK
GURK!
FWSH
HYAAAAAH!!
FWOOOO

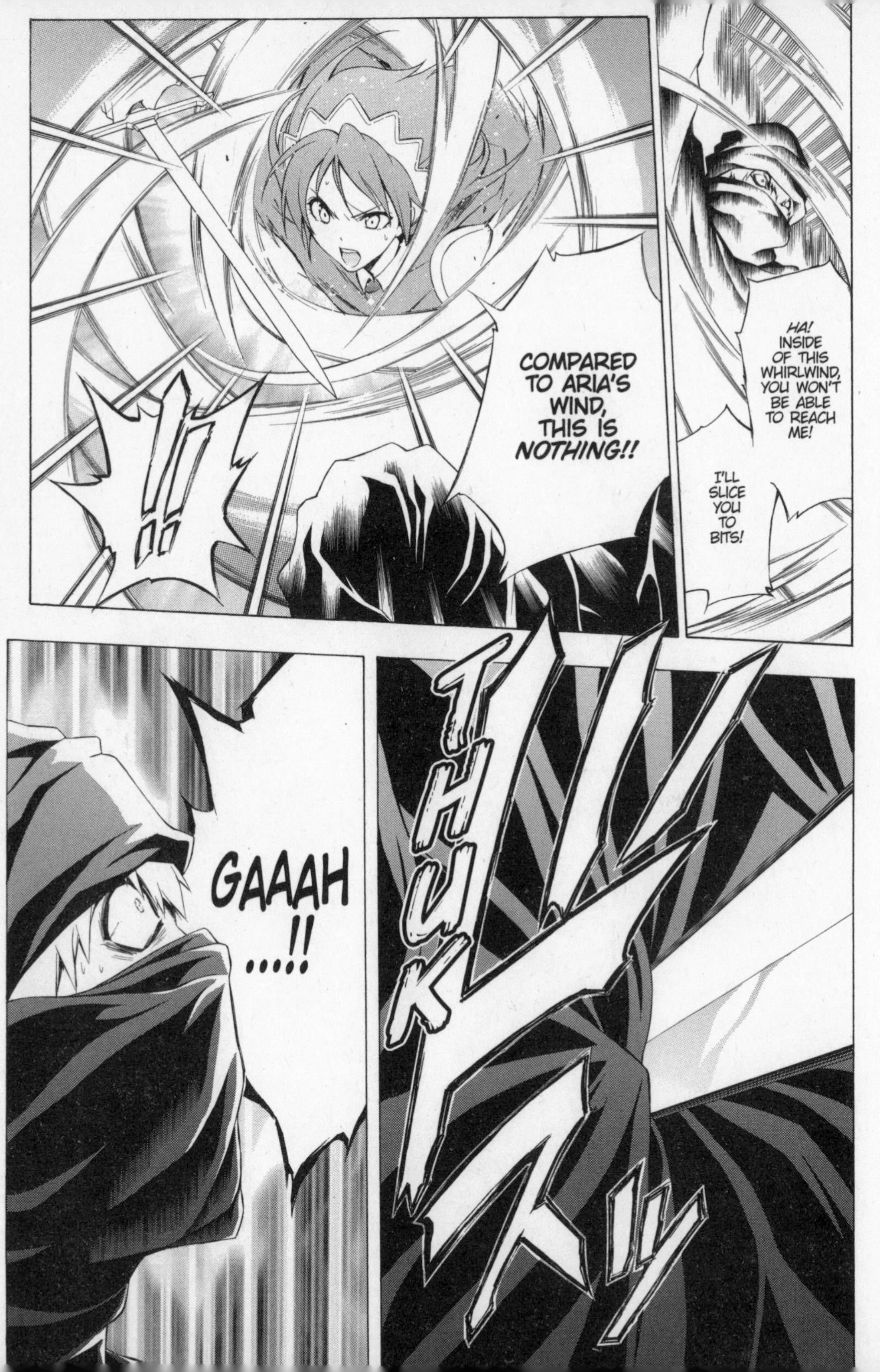
HA! INSIDE OF THIS WHIRLWIND, YOU WON'T BE ABLE TO REACH ME!
I'LL SLICE YOU TO BITS!
COMPARED TO ARIA'S WIND, THIS IS *NOTHING!!*
!!
THUK
GAAAH ...!!

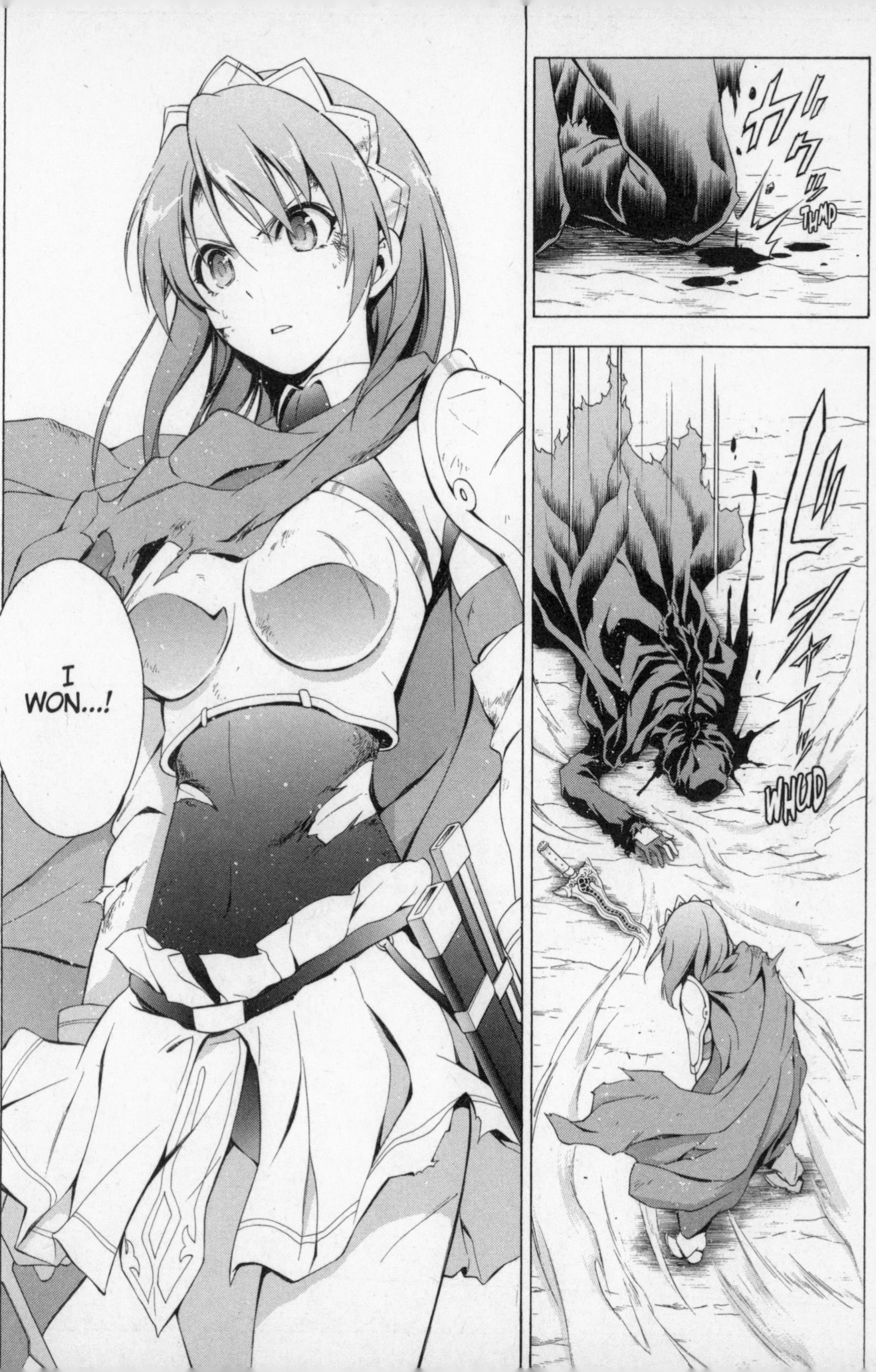
THMP
WHUD
I WON...!

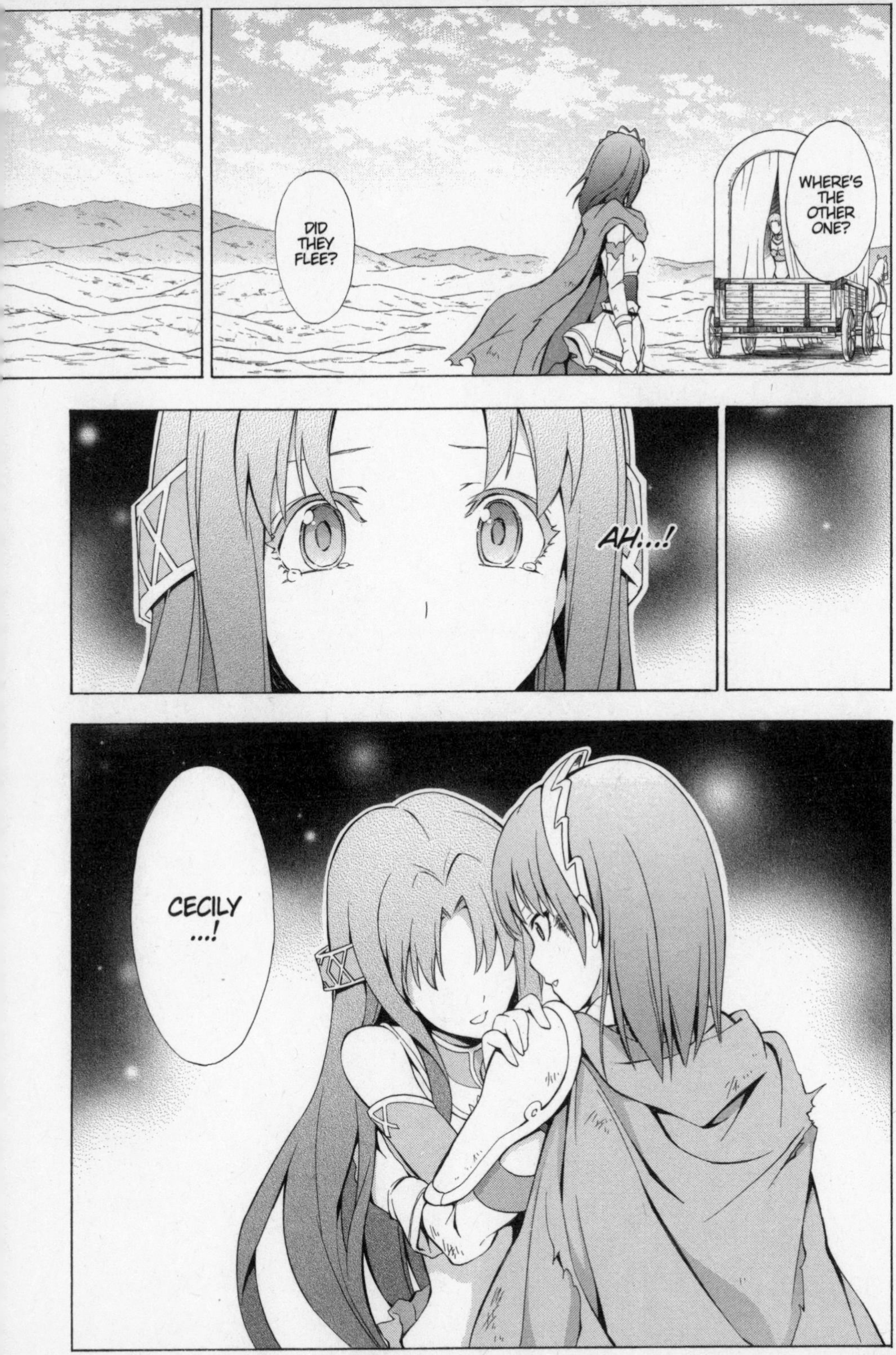
WHERE'S THE OTHER ONE?
DID THEY FLEE?
AH...!
CECILY ...!

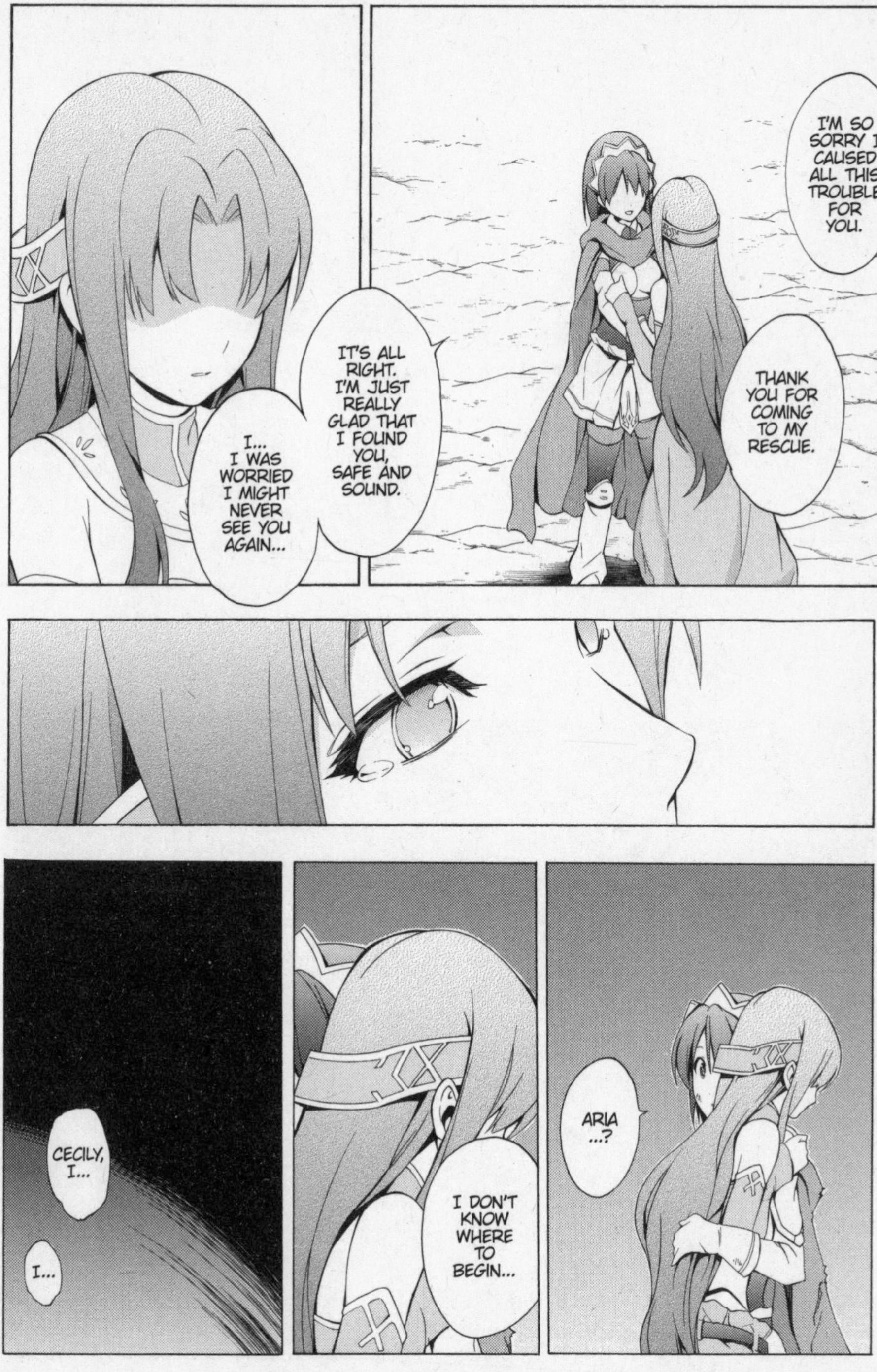
I'M SO SORRY I CAUSED ALL THIS TROUBLE FOR YOU.
THANK YOU FOR COMING TO MY RESCUE.
IT'S ALL RIGHT. I'M JUST REALLY GLAD THAT I FOUND YOU, SAFE AND SOUND.
I... I WAS WORRIED I MIGHT NEVER SEE YOU AGAIN...
ARIA ...?
I DON'T KNOW WHERE TO BEGIN...
CECILY, I...
I...

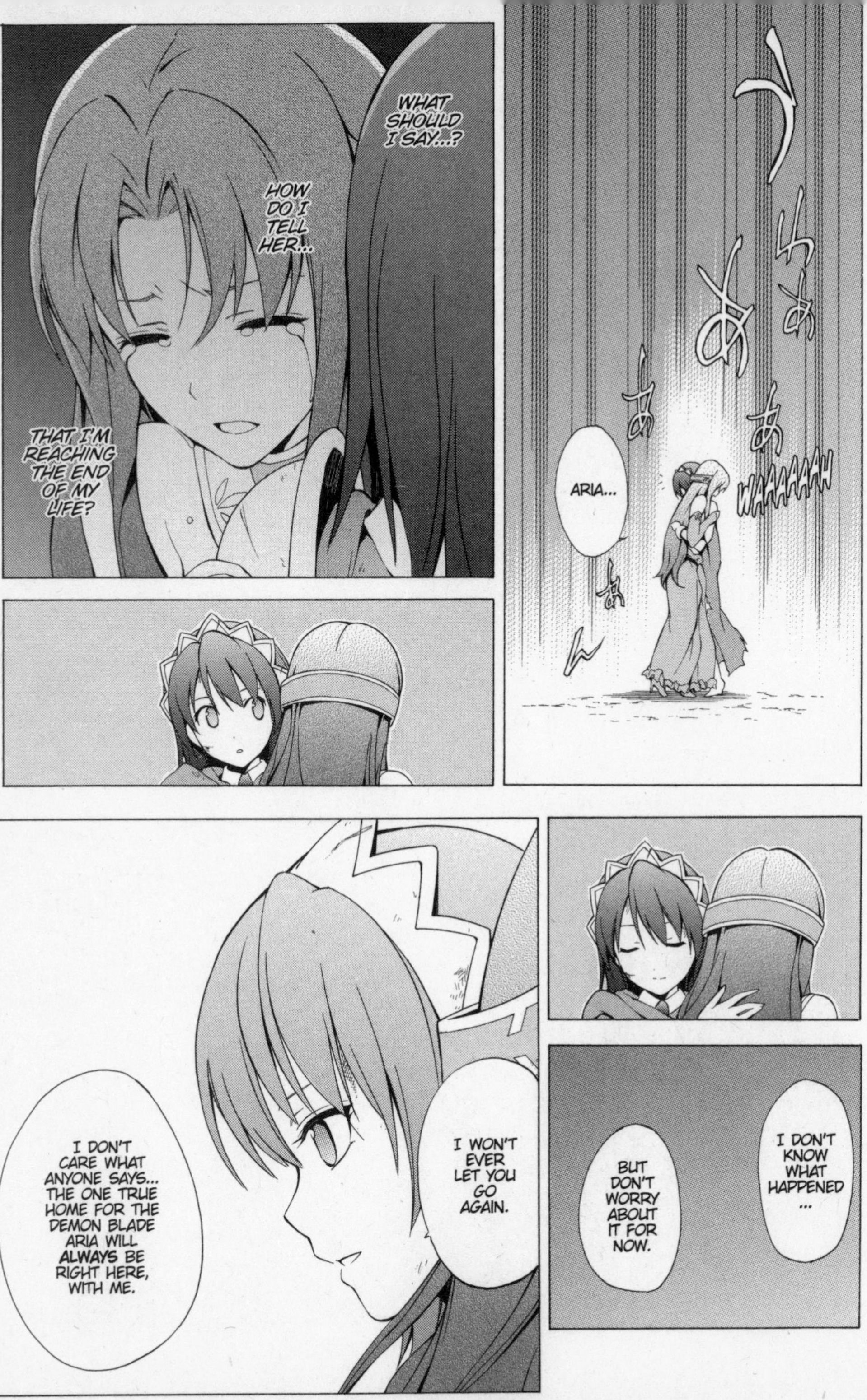
WAAAAAAH
ARIA...
WHAT SHOULD I SAY...?
HOW DO I TELL HER...
THAT I'M REACHING THE END OF MY LIFE?
I DON'T KNOW WHAT HAPPENED ...
BUT DON'T WORRY ABOUT IT FOR NOW.
I WON'T EVER LET YOU GO AGAIN.
I DON'T CARE WHAT ANYONE SAYS... THE ONE TRUE HOME FOR THE DEMON BLADE ARIA WILL **ALWAYS** BE RIGHT HERE, WITH ME.

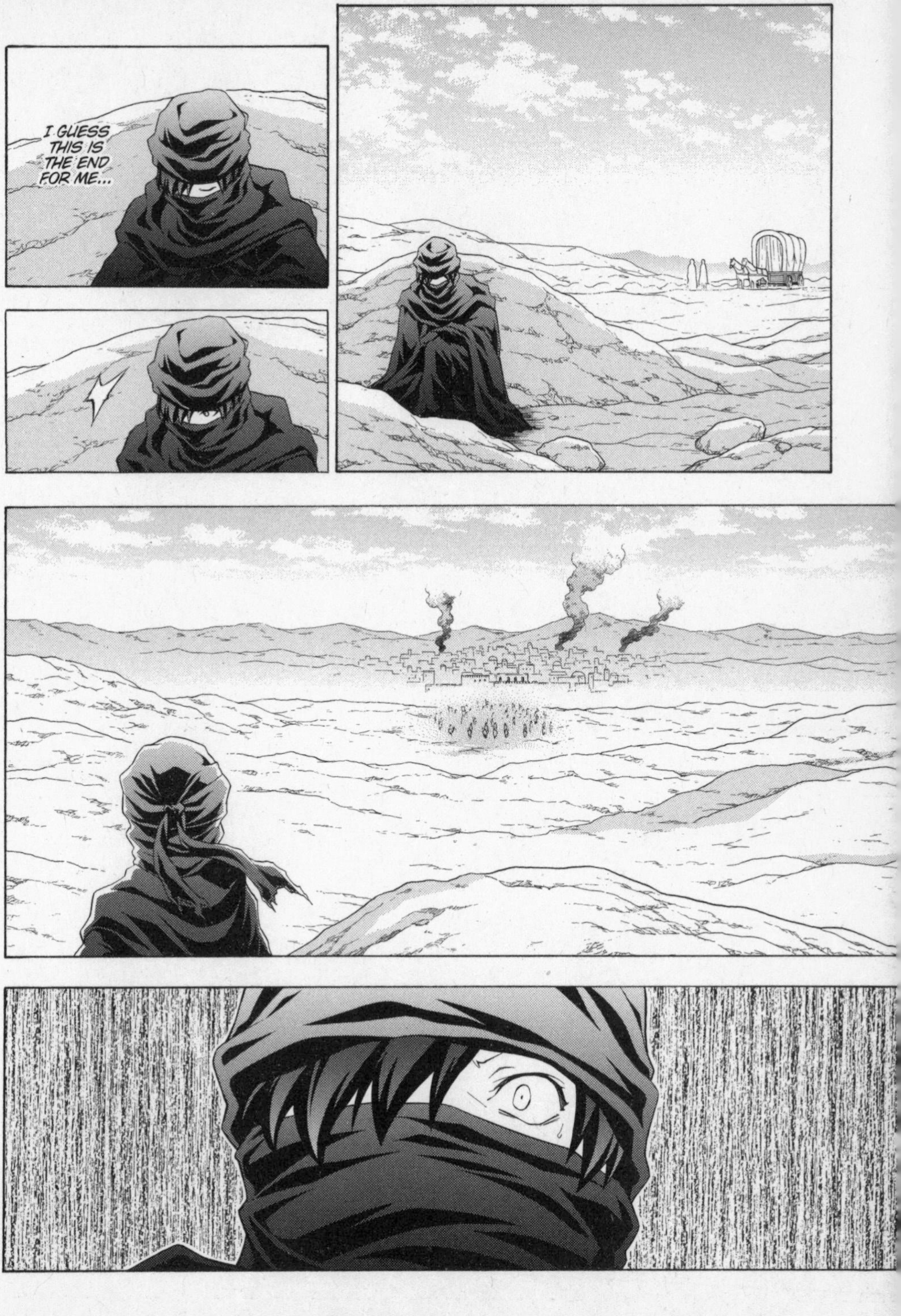
I GUESS THIS IS THE END FOR ME...

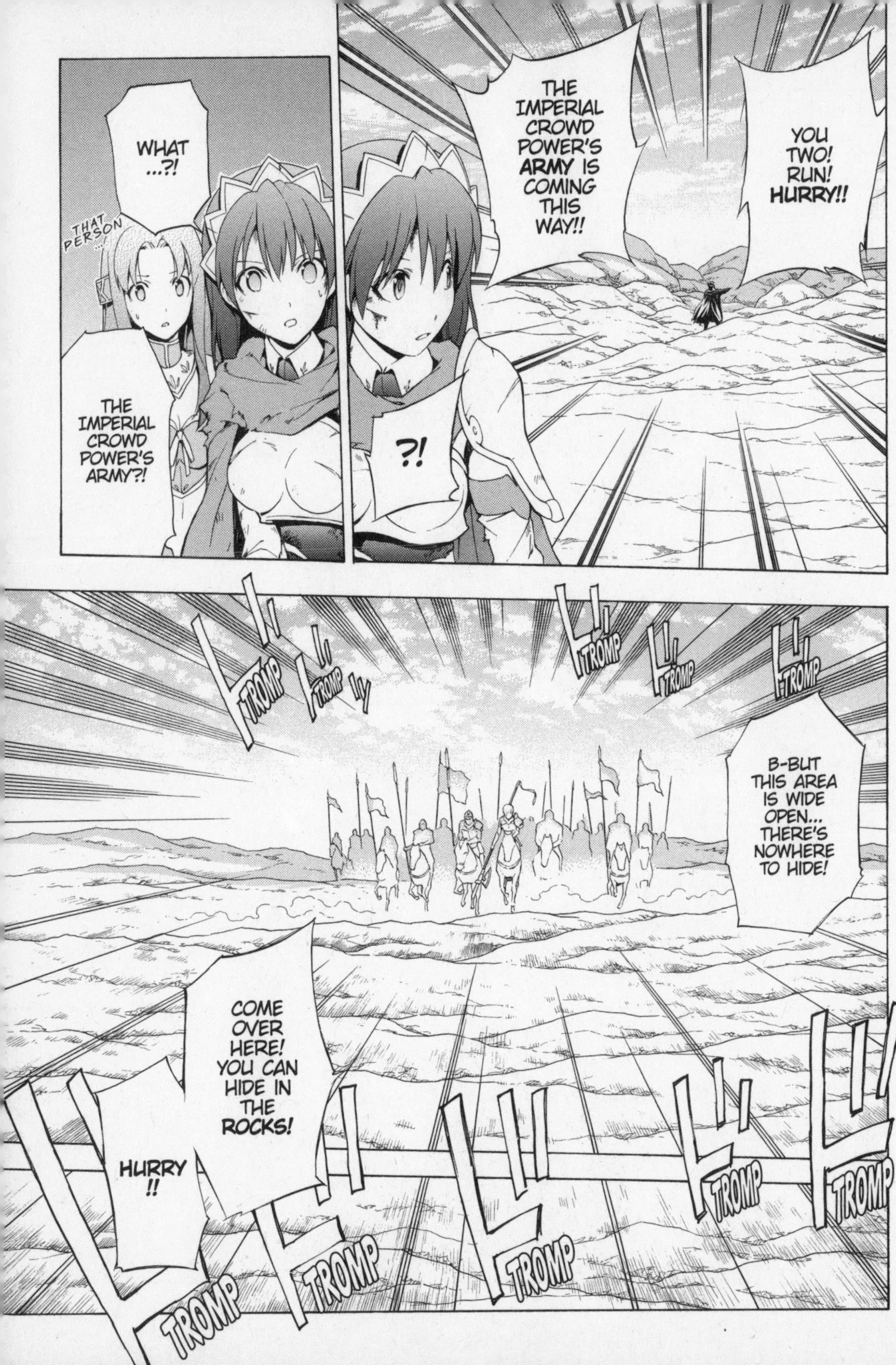
YOU TWO! RUN! HURRY!!
THE IMPERIAL CROWD POWER'S ARMY IS COMING THIS WAY!!
?!
WHAT ...?!
THAT PERSON ...
THE IMPERIAL CROWD POWER'S ARMY?!
TROMP
TROMP
TROMP
TROMP
TROMP
B-BUT THIS AREA IS WIDE OPEN... THERE'S NOWHERE TO HIDE!
COME OVER HERE! YOU CAN HIDE IN THE ROCKS!
HURRY !!
TROMP
TROMP
TROMP
TROMP
TROMP

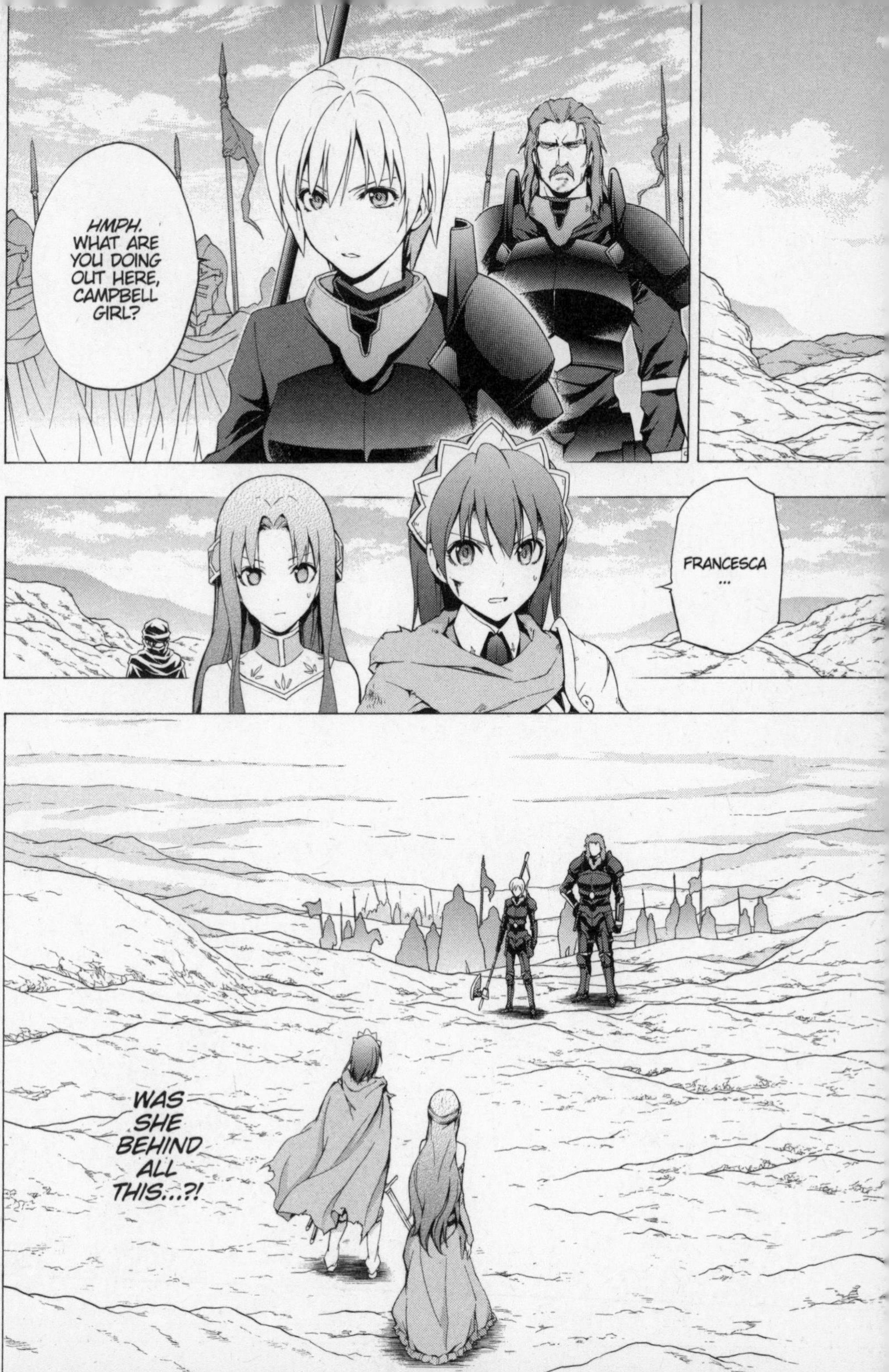
HMPH. WHAT ARE YOU DOING OUT HERE, CAMPBELL GIRL?
FRANCESCA ...
WAS SHE BEHIND ALL THIS...?!

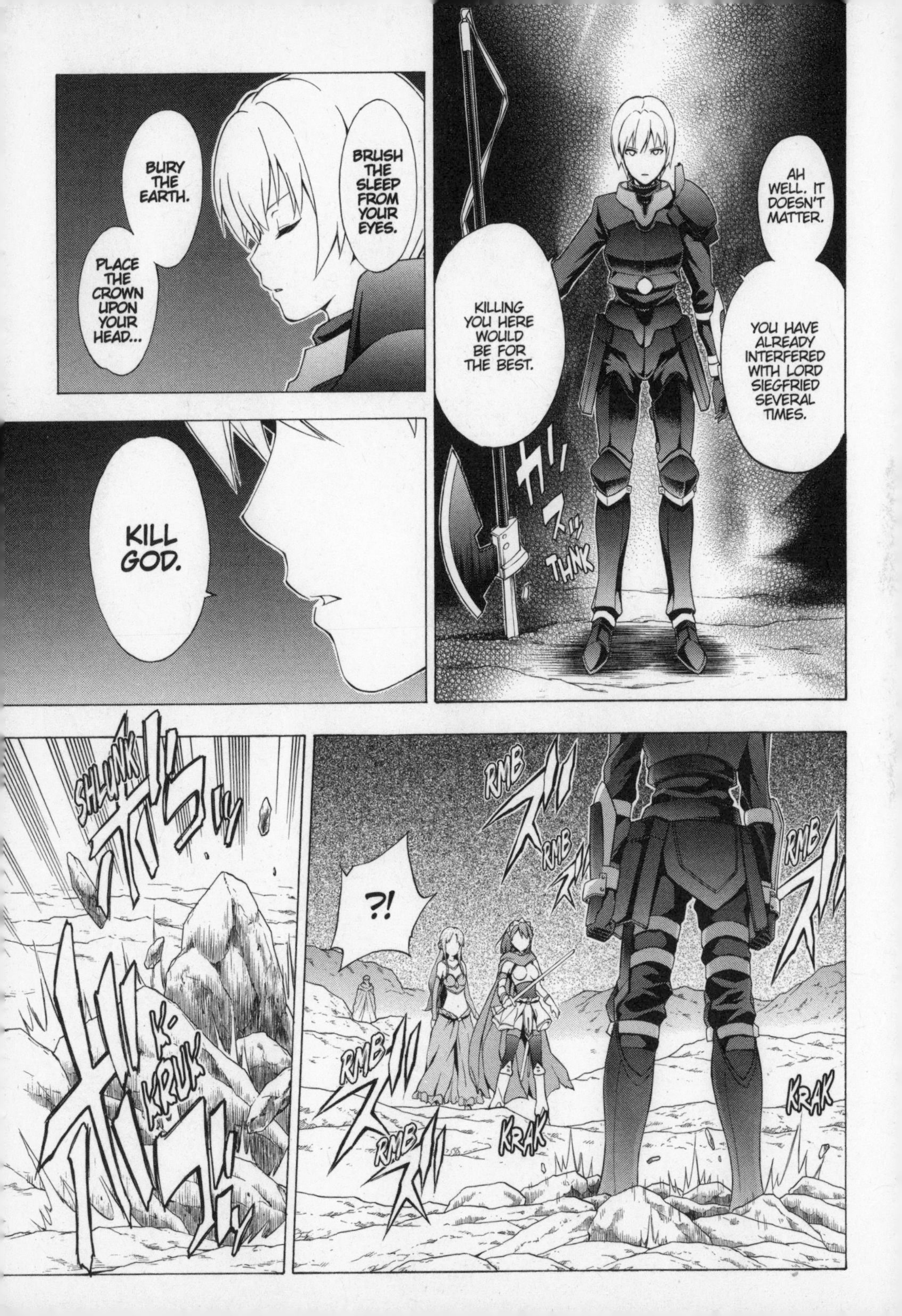
AH WELL. IT DOESN'T MATTER.
YOU HAVE ALREADY INTERFERED WITH LORD SIEGFRIED SEVERAL TIMES.
KILLING YOU HERE WOULD BE FOR THE BEST.
THNK
BRUSH THE SLEEP FROM YOUR EYES.
BURY THE EARTH.
PLACE THE CROWN UPON YOUR HEAD...
KILL GOD.
RMB
RMB
RMB
?!
RMB
RMB
KRAK
KRAK
SHLUNK
KRUK

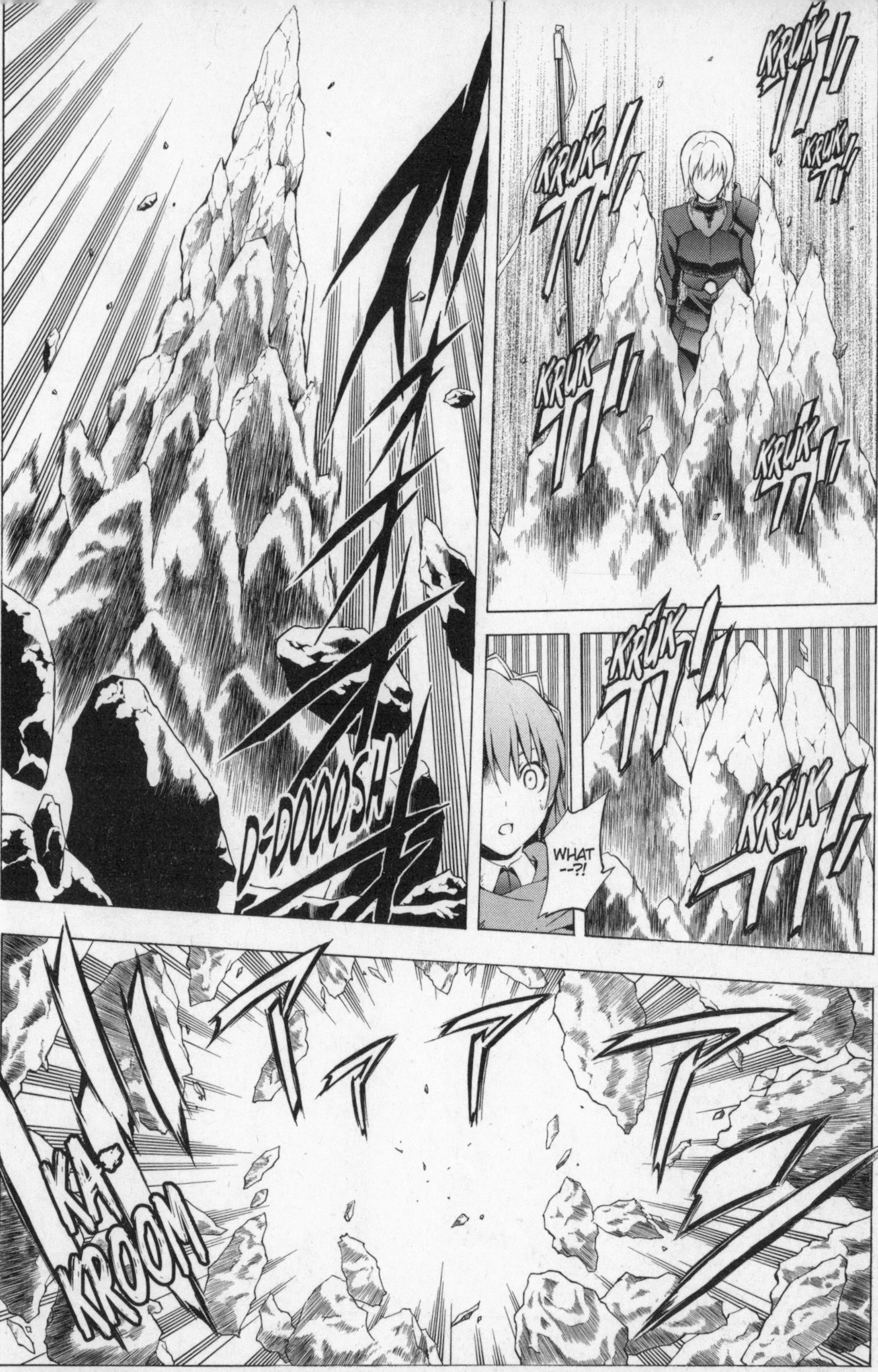
KRUK!!
KRUK!!
KRUK!!
KRUK!!
KRUK!!
KRUK!!
KRUK!!
WHAT --?!
D-DOOOSH
KA-KROOM

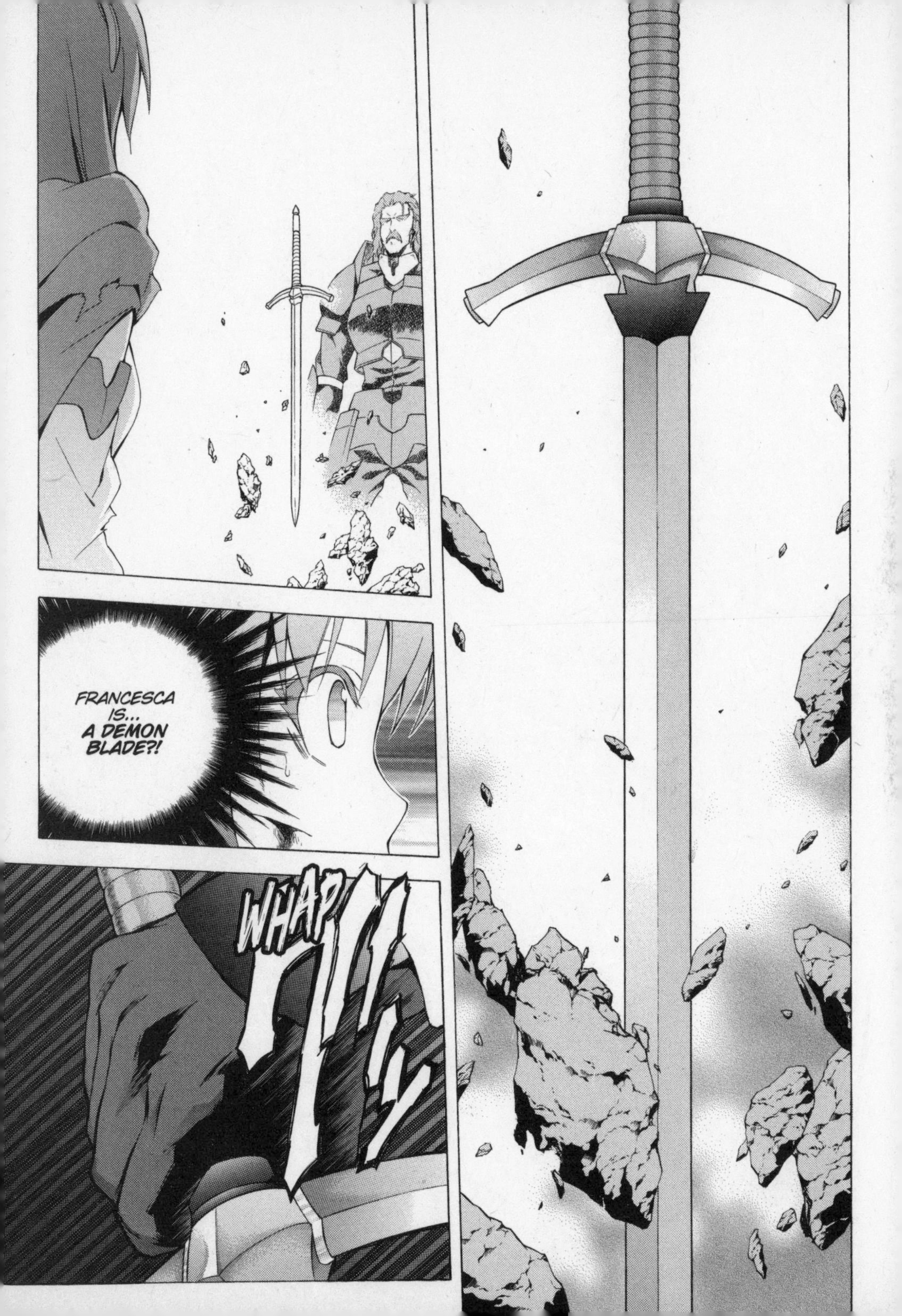
FRANCESCA IS... A DEMON BLADE?!
WHAP

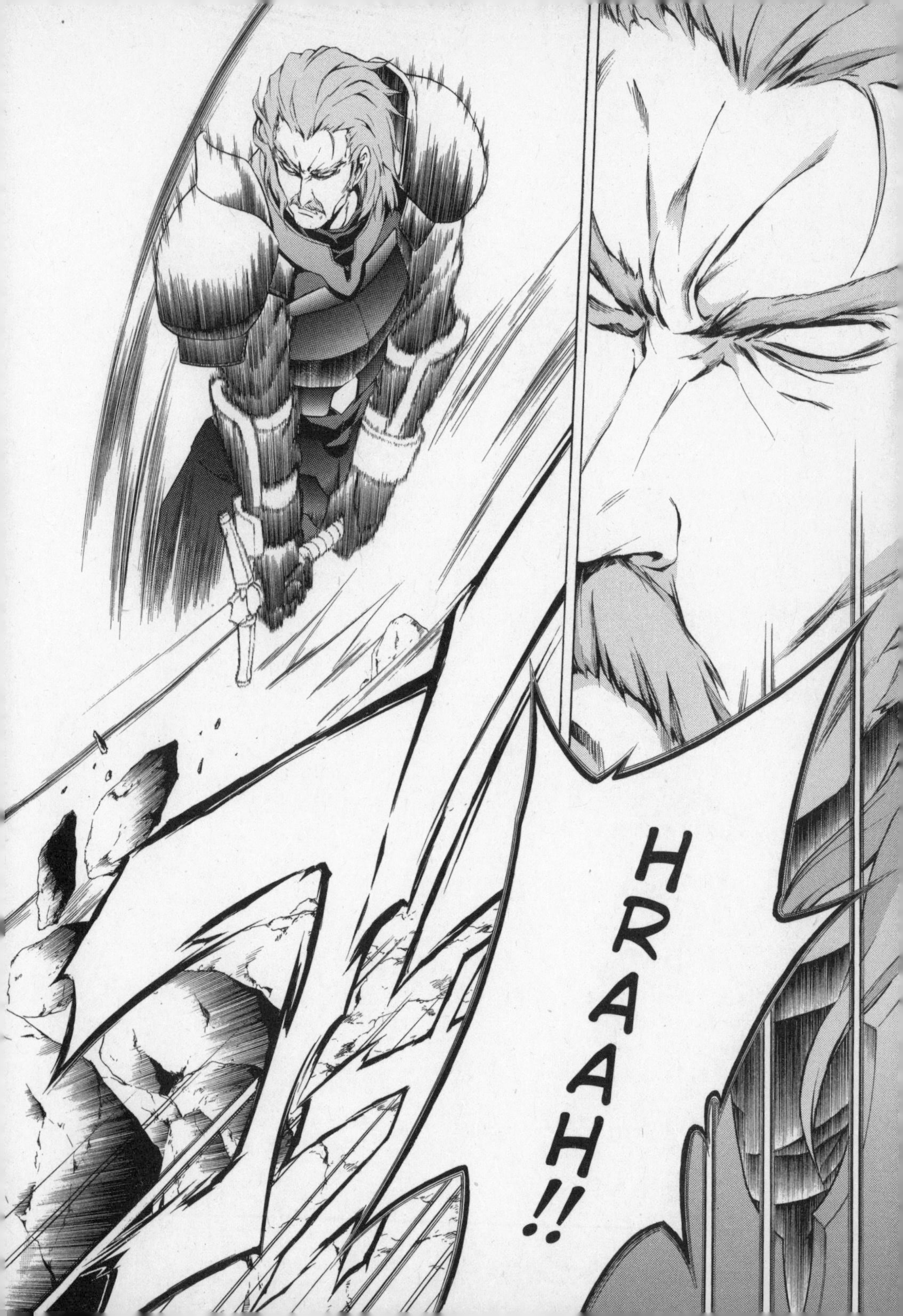
HRAAH!!

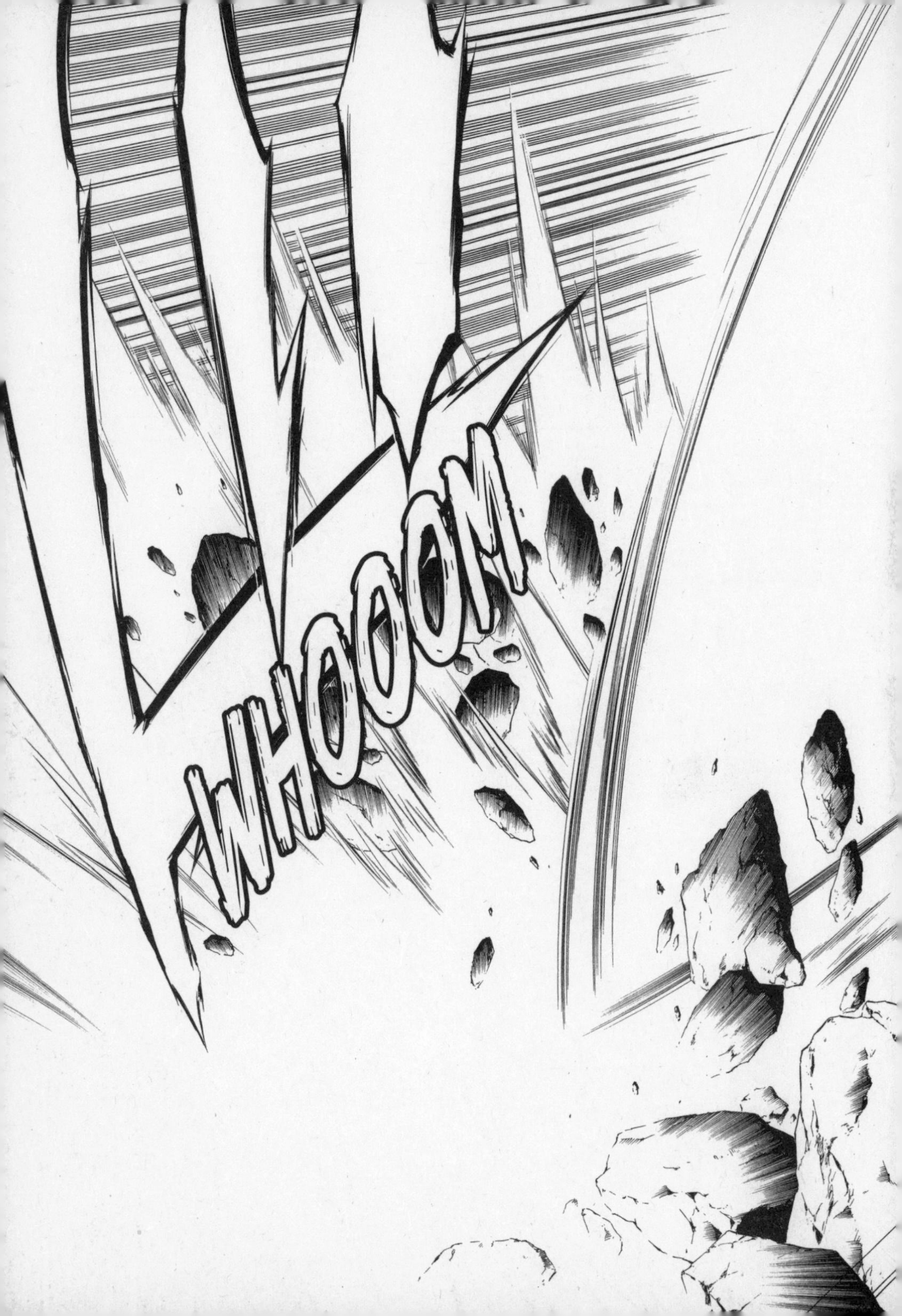
WHOOOM

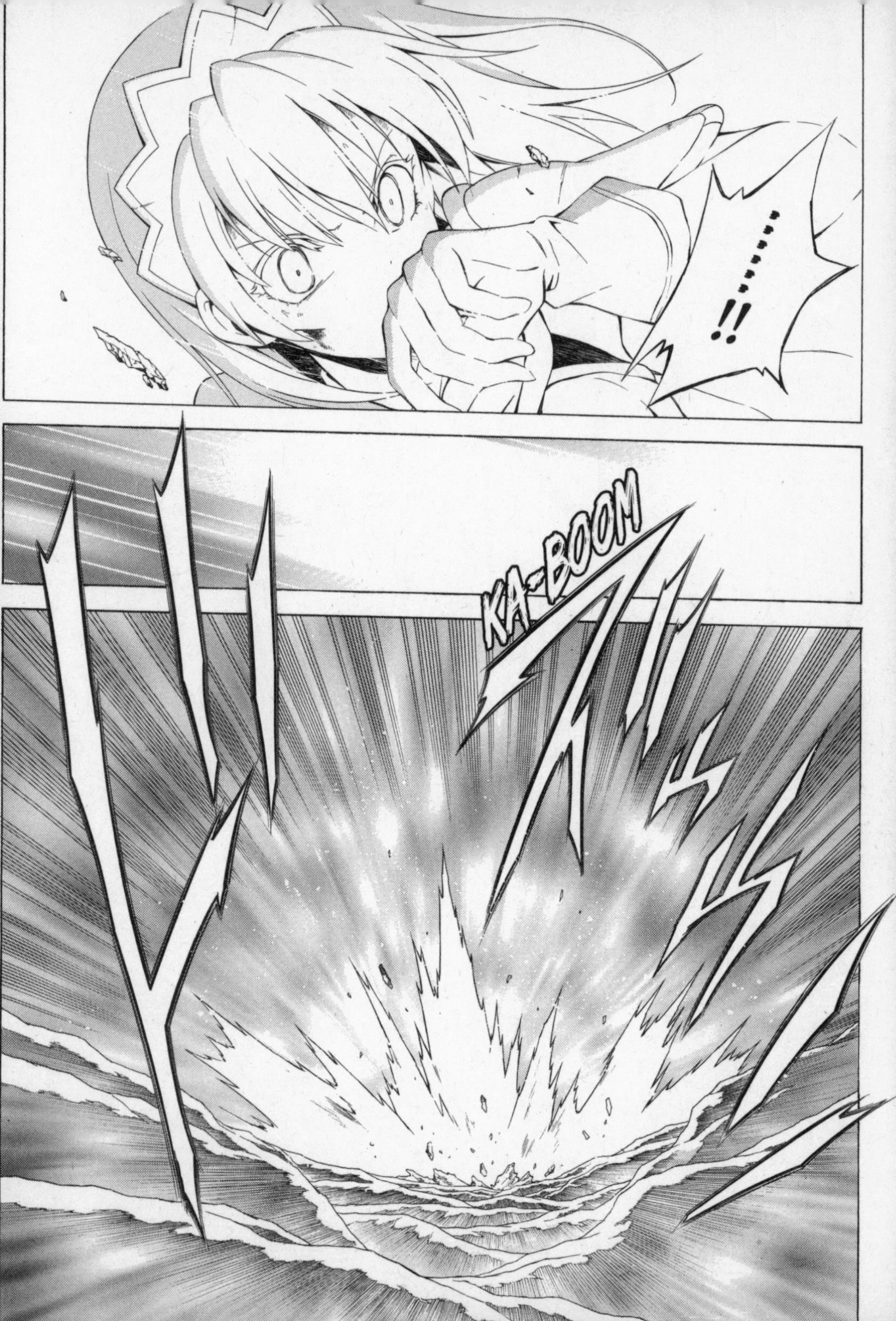
......!!
KA-BOOM

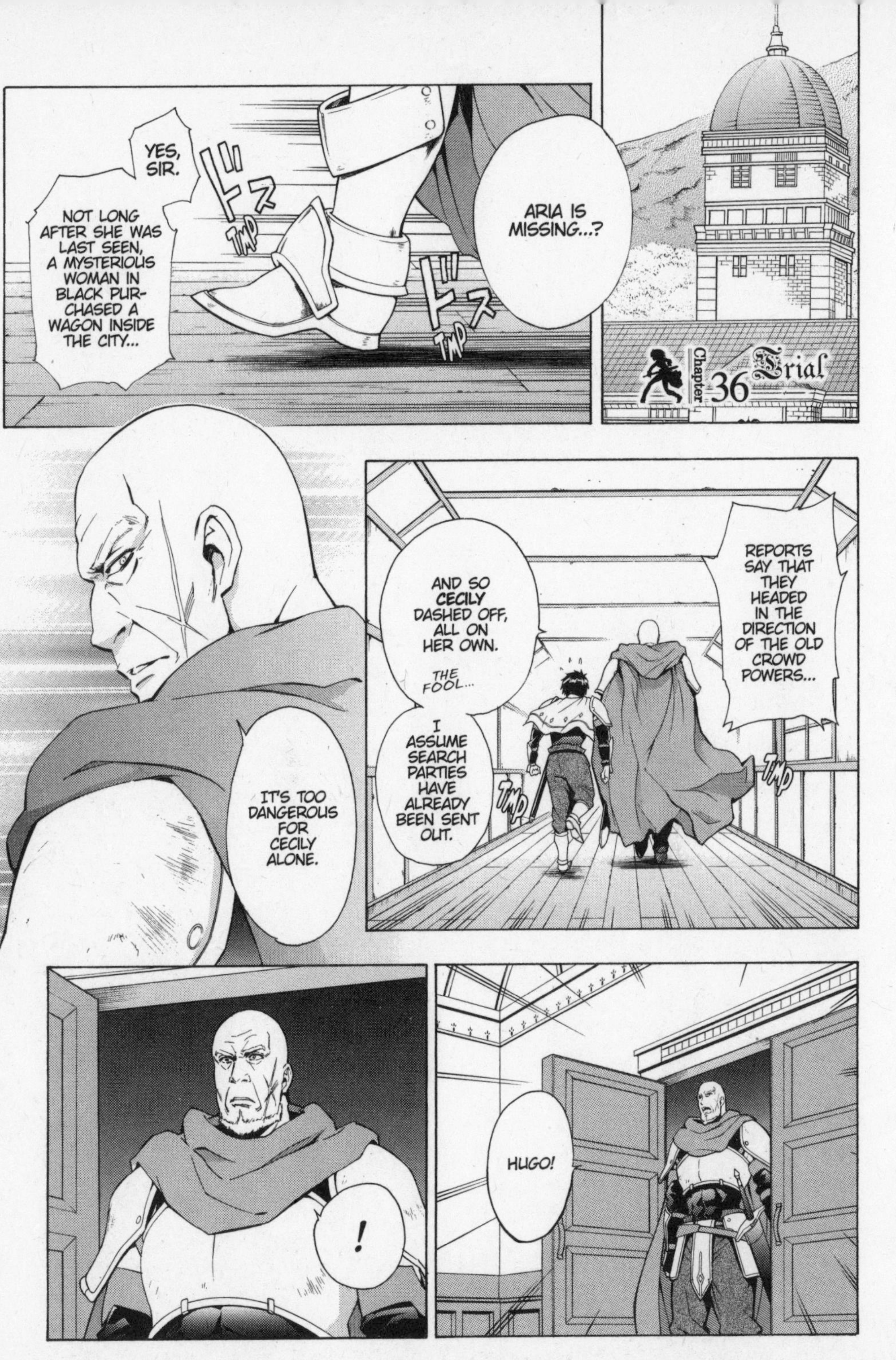
Chapter 36 Trial
ARIA IS MISSING...?
ドス TMP
ドス TMP
YES, SIR.
NOT LONG AFTER SHE WAS LAST SEEN, A MYSTERIOUS WOMAN IN BLACK PURCHASED A WAGON INSIDE THE CITY...
REPORTS SAY THAT THEY HEADED IN THE DIRECTION OF THE OLD CROWD POWERS...
AND SO CECILY DASHED OFF, ALL ON HER OWN.
THE FOOL...
I ASSUME SEARCH PARTIES HAVE ALREADY BEEN SENT OUT.
TMP
TMP
IT'S TOO DANGEROUS FOR CECILY ALONE.
HUGO!
!

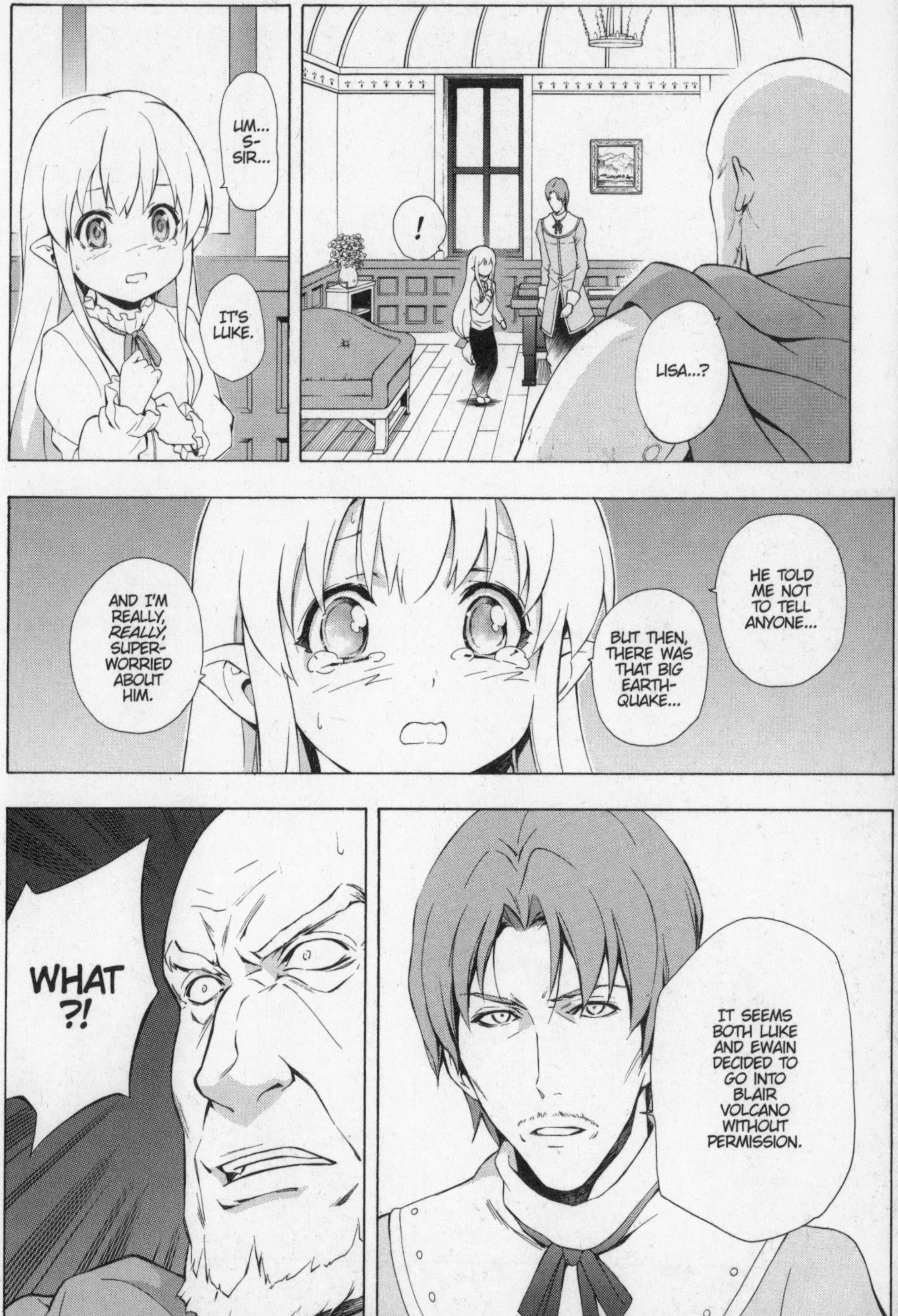
!
LISA...?
UM... S-SIR...
IT'S LUKE.
HE TOLD ME NOT TO TELL ANYONE...
BUT THEN, THERE WAS THAT BIG EARTHQUAKE...
AND I'M REALLY, *REALLY,* SUPER-WORRIED ABOUT HIM.
IT SEEMS BOTH LUKE AND EWAIN DECIDED TO GO INTO BLAIR VOLCANO WITHOUT PERMISSION.
WHAT?!

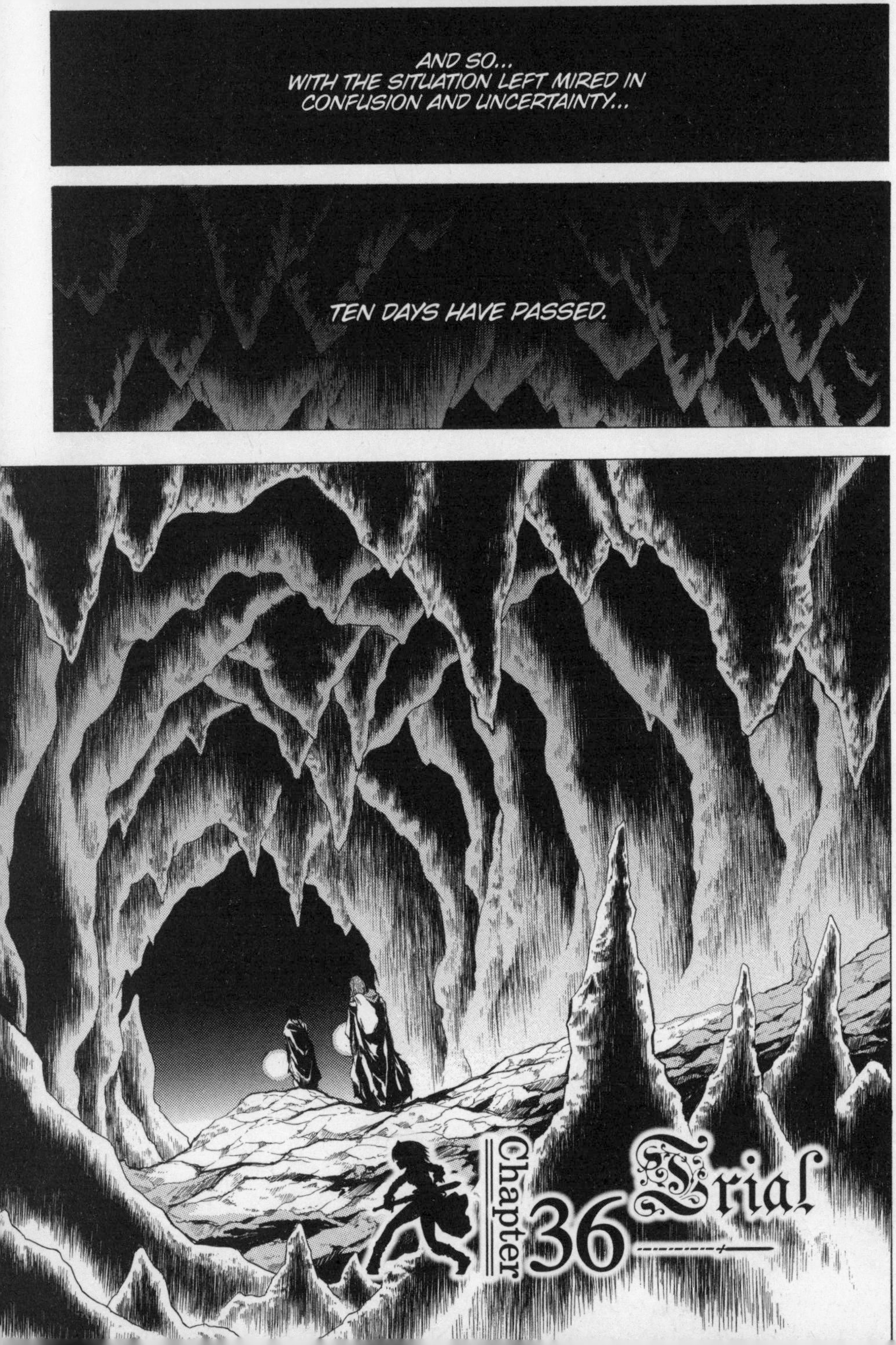
AND SO...
WITH THE SITUATION LEFT MIRED IN CONFUSION AND UNCERTAINTY...
TEN DAYS HAVE PASSED.
Chapter 36 Trial

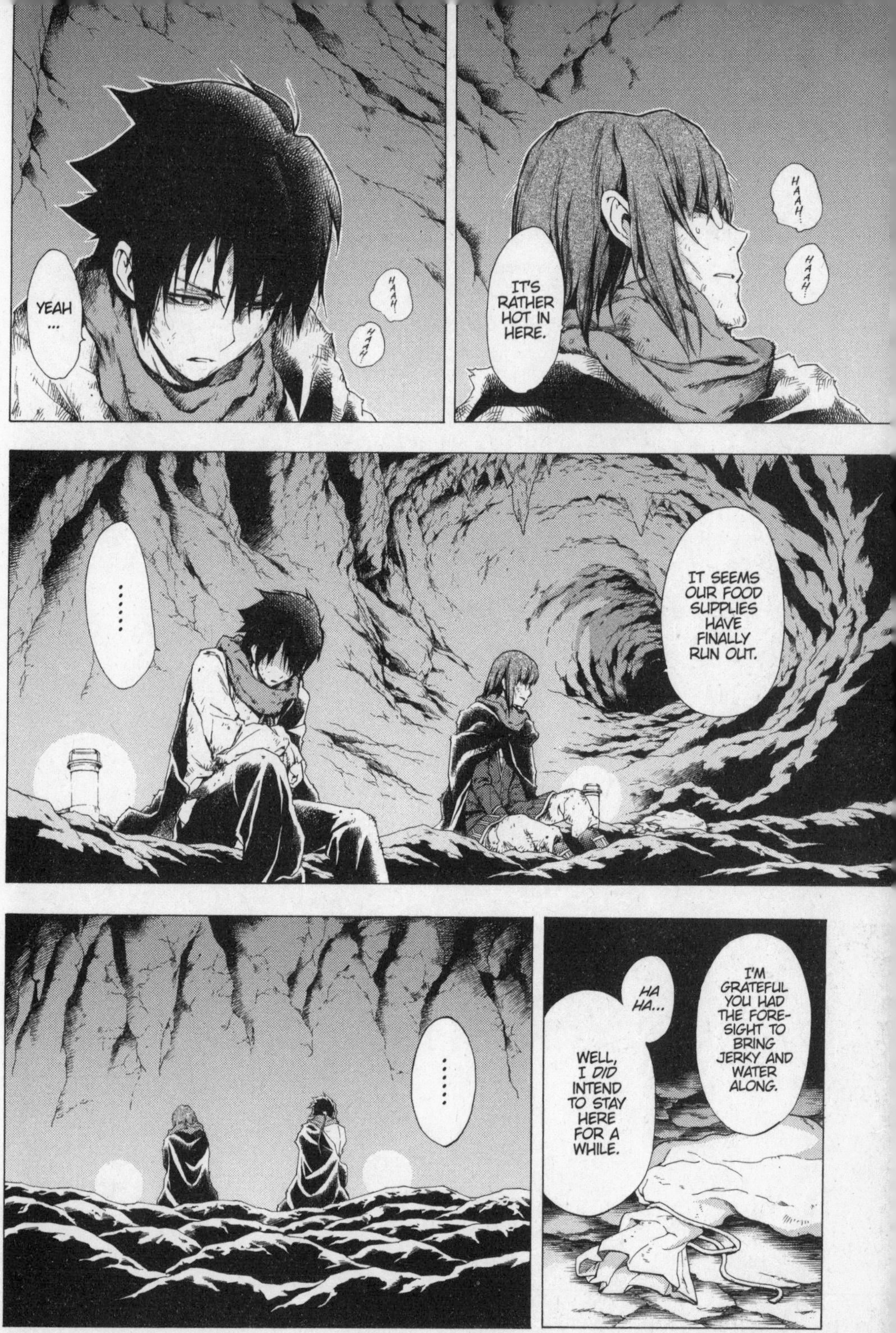
HAAH...
HAAH...
IT'S RATHER HOT IN HERE.
HAAH...
HAAH...
YEAH...
IT SEEMS OUR FOOD SUPPLIES HAVE FINALLY RUN OUT.
......
I'M GRATEFUL YOU HAD THE FORE-SIGHT TO BRING JERKY AND WATER ALONG.
HA HA...
WELL, I *DID* INTEND TO STAY HERE FOR A WHILE.
......

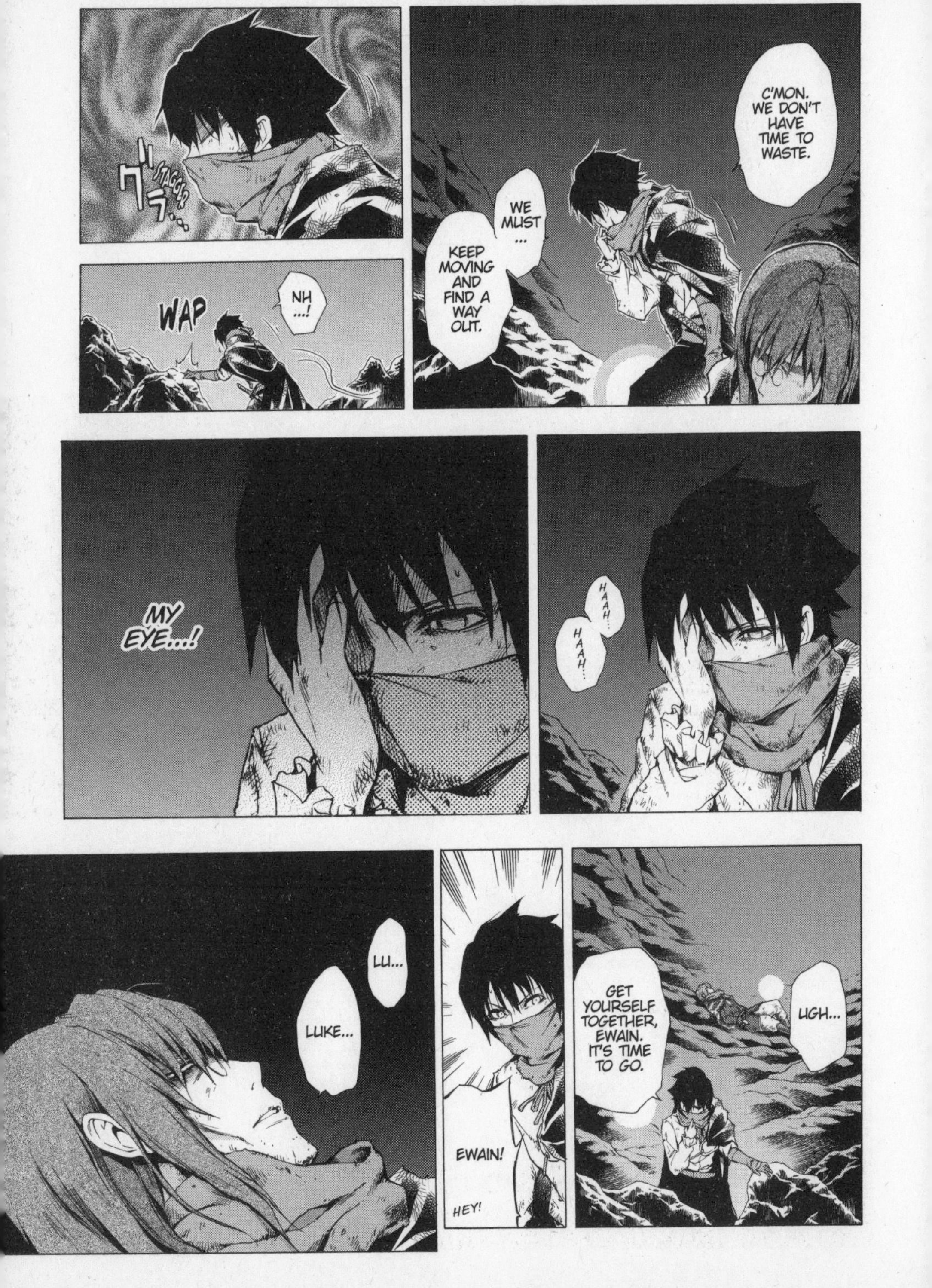
C'MON. WE DON'T HAVE TIME TO WASTE.
WE MUST ...
KEEP MOVING AND FIND A WAY OUT.
グラ
STAGGER...
NH ...!
WAP
HAAH...
HAAH...
MY EYE...!
UGH...
GET YOURSELF TOGETHER, EWAIN. IT'S TIME TO GO.
EWAIN!
HEY!
LU...
LUKE...

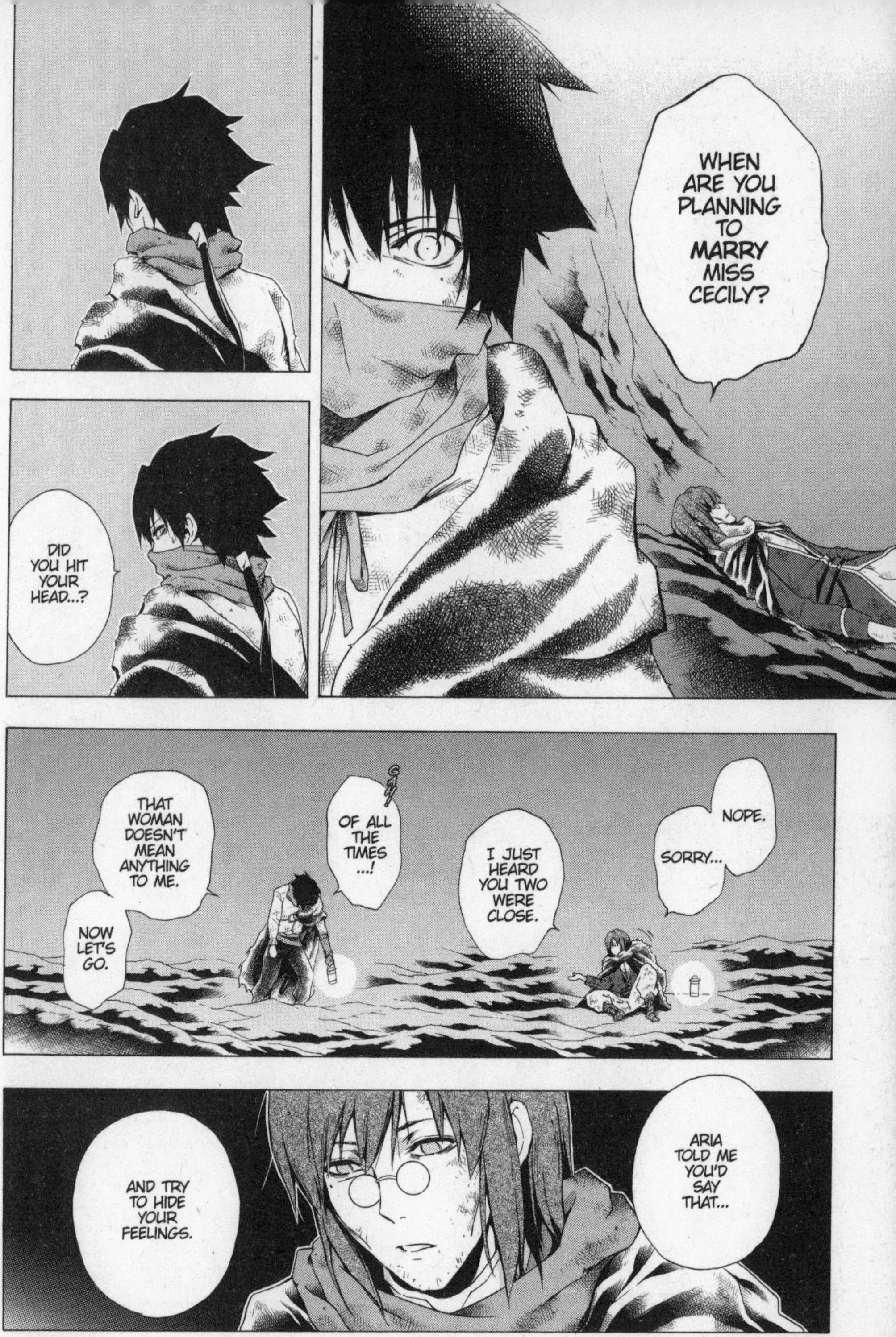
WHEN ARE YOU PLANNING TO MARRY MISS CECILY?
DID YOU HIT YOUR HEAD...?
NOPE.
SORRY...
I JUST HEARD YOU TWO WERE CLOSE.
GAH!
OF ALL THE TIMES ...!
THAT WOMAN DOESN'T MEAN ANYTHING TO ME.
NOW LET'S GO.
ARIA TOLD ME YOU'D SAY THAT...
AND TRY TO HIDE YOUR FEELINGS.

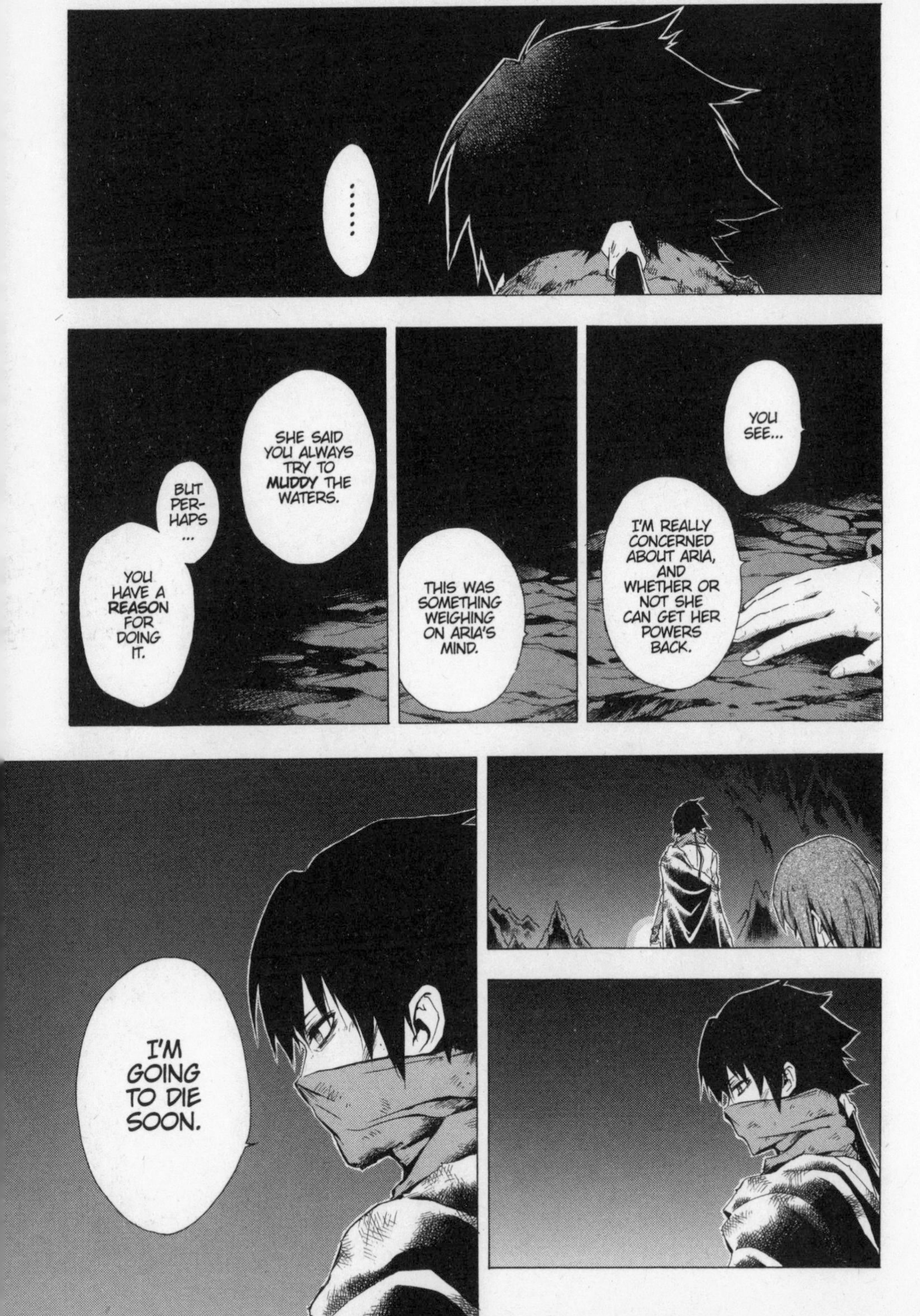
......
YOU SEE...
I'M REALLY CONCERNED ABOUT ARIA, AND WHETHER OR NOT SHE CAN GET HER POWERS BACK.
THIS WAS SOMETHING WEIGHING ON ARIA'S MIND.
SHE SAID YOU ALWAYS TRY TO **MUDDY** THE WATERS.
BUT PER-HAPS...
YOU HAVE A **REASON** FOR DOING IT.
I'M GOING TO DIE SOON.

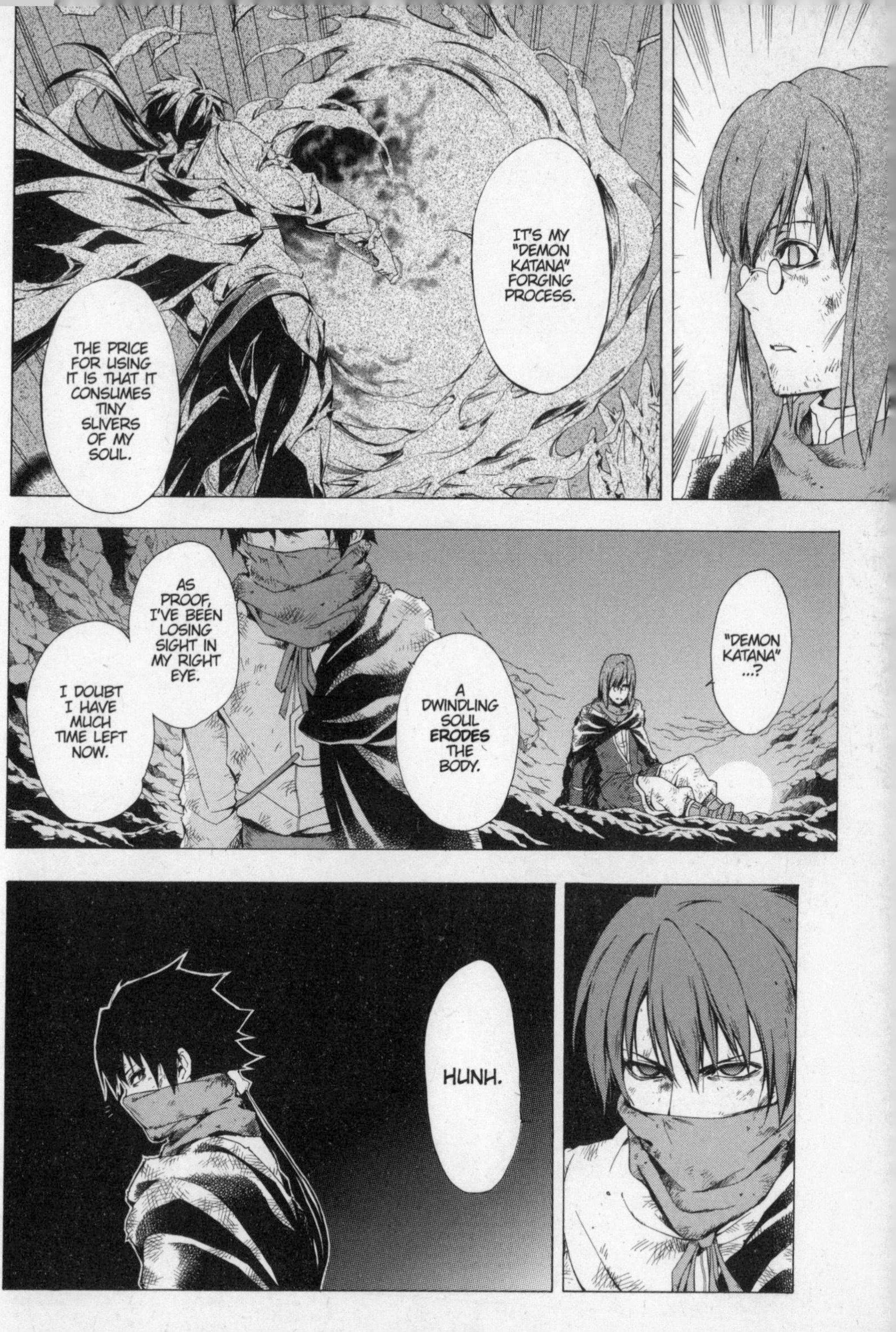
IT'S MY "DEMON KATANA" FORGING PROCESS.
THE PRICE FOR USING IT IS THAT IT CONSUMES TINY SLIVERS OF MY SOUL.
"DEMON KATANA" ...?
A DWINDLING SOUL ERODES THE BODY.
AS PROOF, I'VE BEEN LOSING SIGHT IN MY RIGHT EYE.
I DOUBT I HAVE MUCH TIME LEFT NOW.
HUNH.

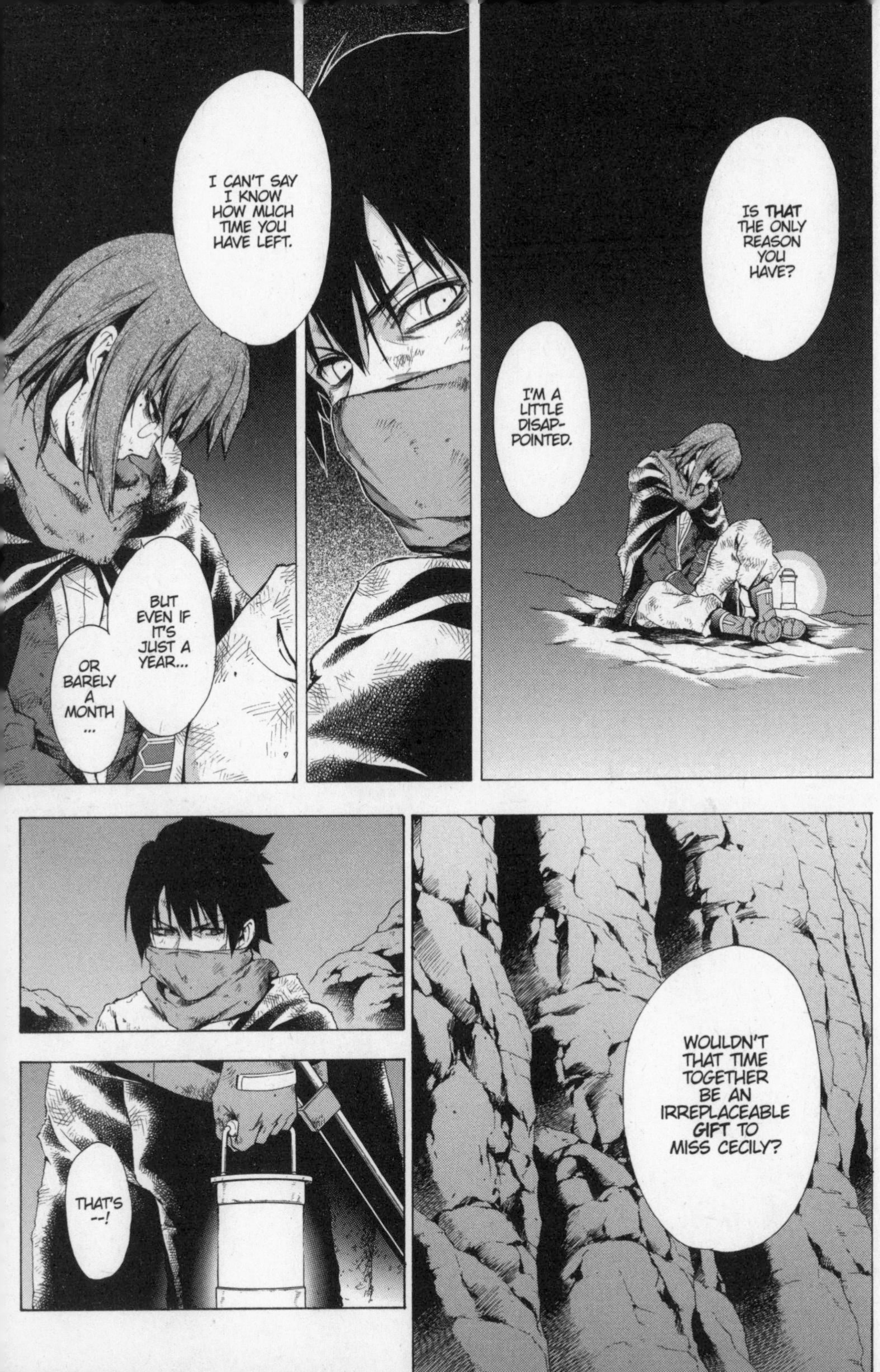
IS THAT THE ONLY REASON YOU HAVE?
I'M A LITTLE DISAP-POINTED.
I CAN'T SAY I KNOW HOW MUCH TIME YOU HAVE LEFT.
BUT EVEN IF IT'S JUST A YEAR...
OR BARELY A MONTH ...
WOULDN'T THAT TIME TOGETHER BE AN IRREPLACEABLE GIFT TO MISS CECILY?
THAT'S --!

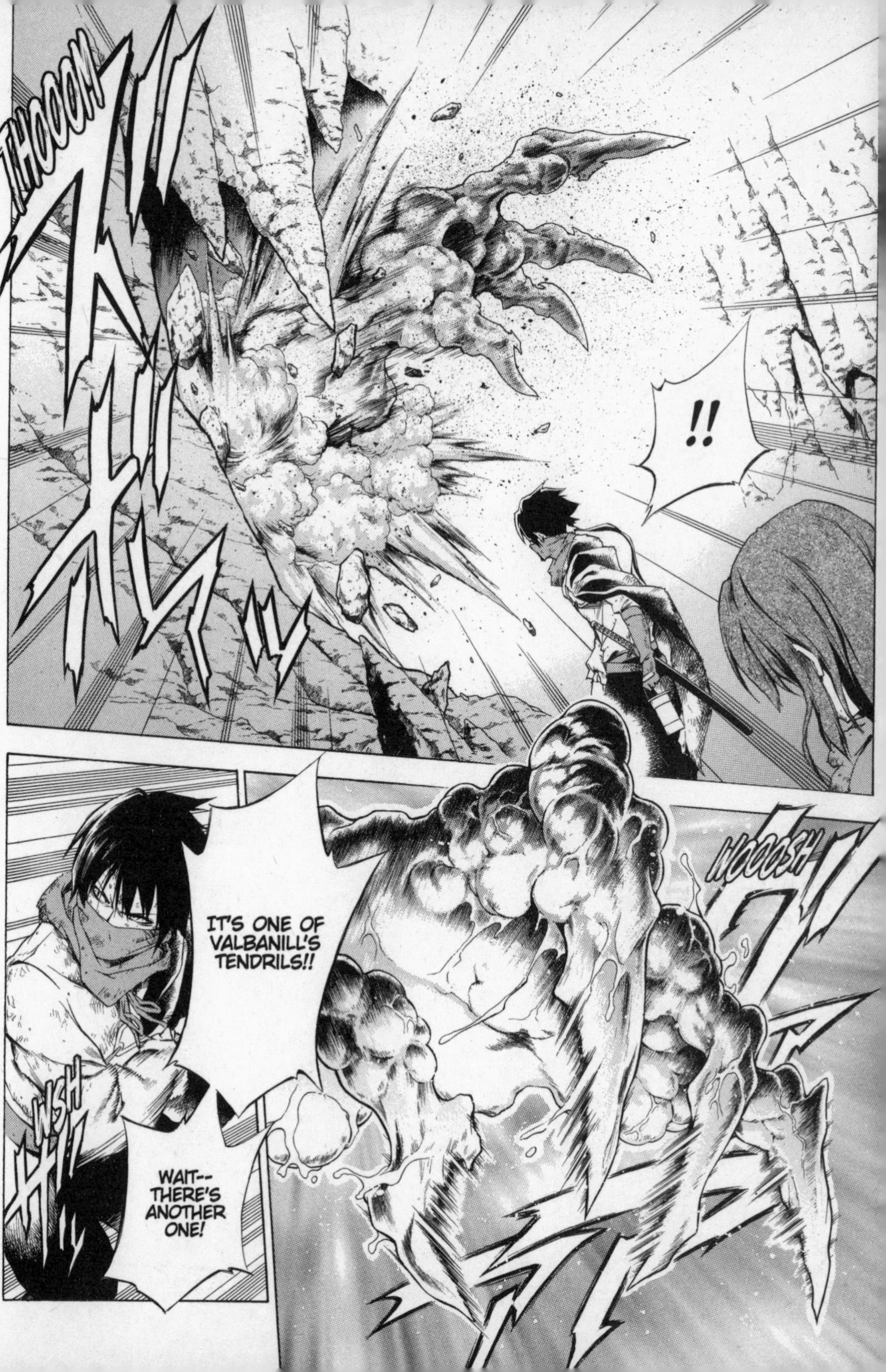
THOOOM
!!
WHOOSH
IT'S ONE OF VALBANILL'S TENDRILS!!
WSH
WAIT-- THERE'S ANOTHER ONE!

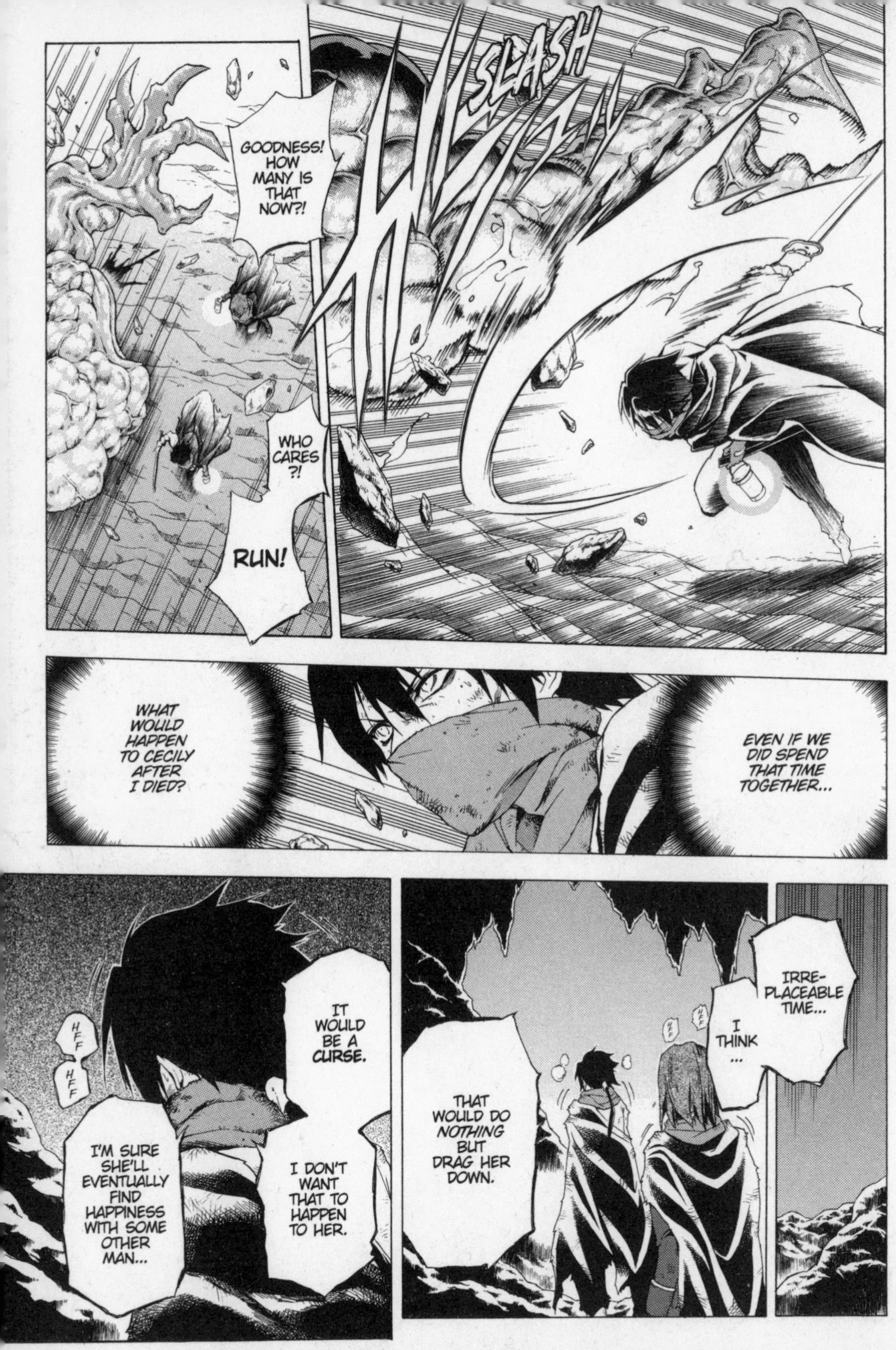
SLASH
GOODNESS! HOW MANY IS THAT NOW?!
WHO CARES?!
RUN!
EVEN IF WE DID SPEND THAT TIME TOGETHER...
WHAT WOULD HAPPEN TO CECILY AFTER I DIED?
IRRE-PLACEABLE TIME...
HFF
HFF
I THINK ...
THAT WOULD DO NOTHING BUT DRAG HER DOWN.
IT WOULD BE A CURSE.
HFF
HFF
I DON'T WANT THAT TO HAPPEN TO HER.
I'M SURE SHE'LL EVENTUALLY FIND HAPPINESS WITH SOME OTHER MAN...

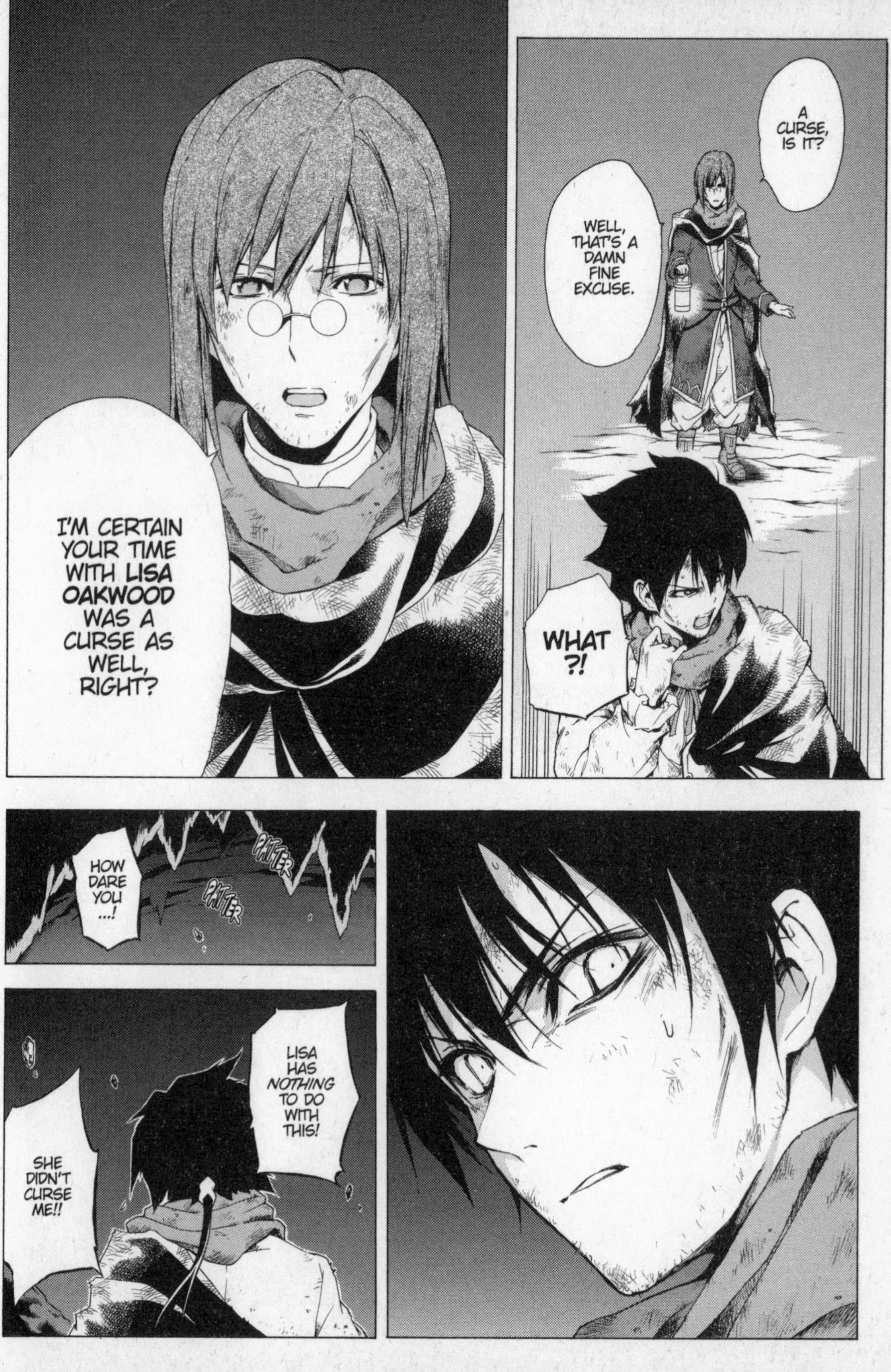
A CURSE, IS IT?
WELL, THAT'S A DAMN FINE EXCUSE.
WHAT ?!
I'M CERTAIN YOUR TIME WITH LISA OAKWOOD WAS A CURSE AS WELL, RIGHT?
HOW DARE YOU ...!
PATTER
PATTER
LISA HAS *NOTHING* TO DO WITH THIS!
SHE DIDN'T CURSE ME!!

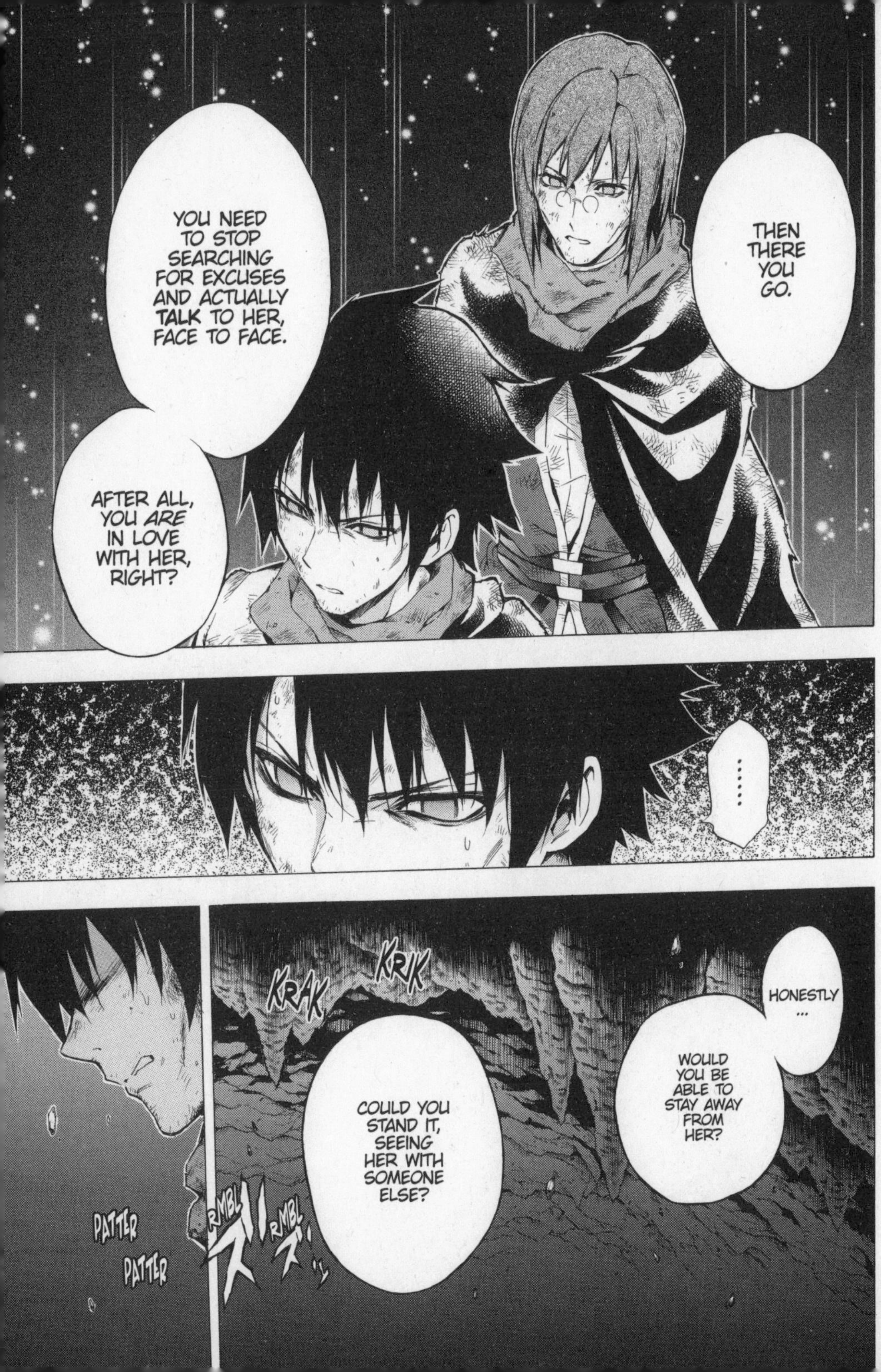
THEN THERE YOU GO.
YOU NEED TO STOP SEARCHING FOR EXCUSES AND ACTUALLY TALK TO HER, FACE TO FACE.
AFTER ALL, YOU ARE IN LOVE WITH HER, RIGHT?
......
HONESTLY...
WOULD YOU BE ABLE TO STAY AWAY FROM HER?
KRIK
KRAK
COULD YOU STAND IT, SEEING HER WITH SOMEONE ELSE?
RMBL
RMBL
PATTER
PATTER

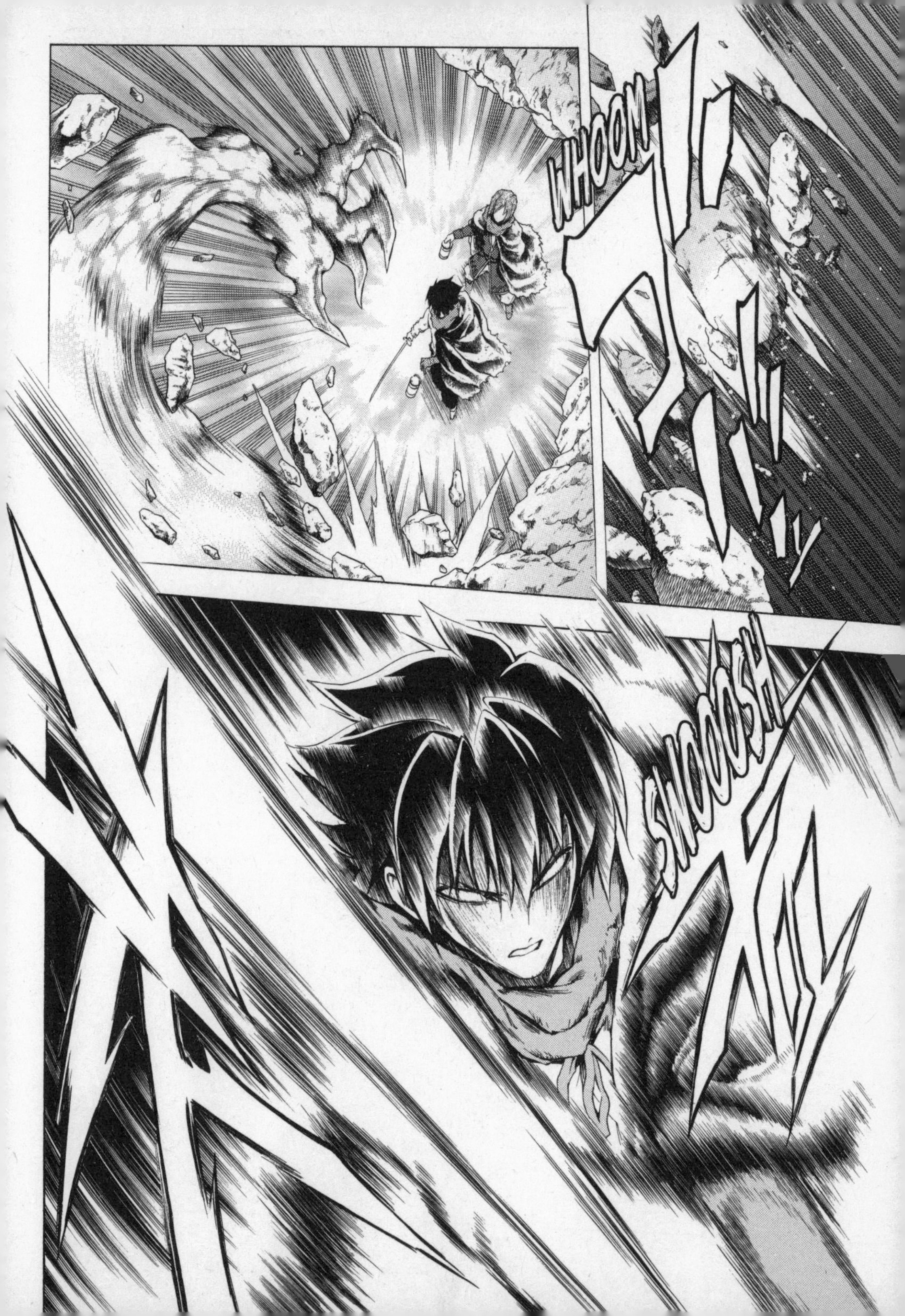
WHOOM
SWOOSH

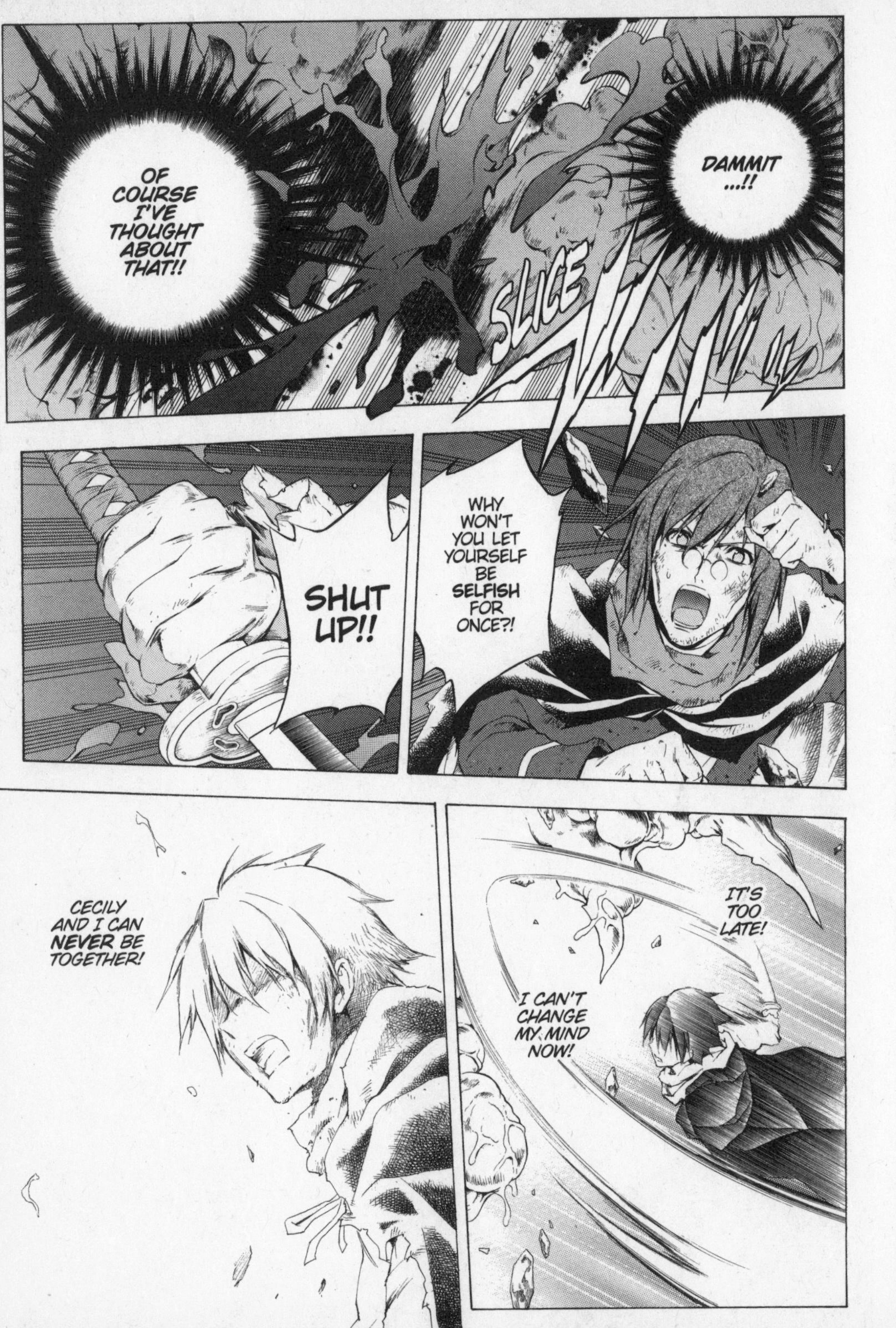
DAMMIT ...!!
OF COURSE I'VE THOUGHT ABOUT THAT!!
SLICE
WHY WON'T YOU LET YOURSELF BE SELFISH FOR ONCE?!
SHUT UP!!
IT'S TOO LATE!
I CAN'T CHANGE MY MIND NOW!
CECILY AND I CAN NEVER BE TOGETHER!

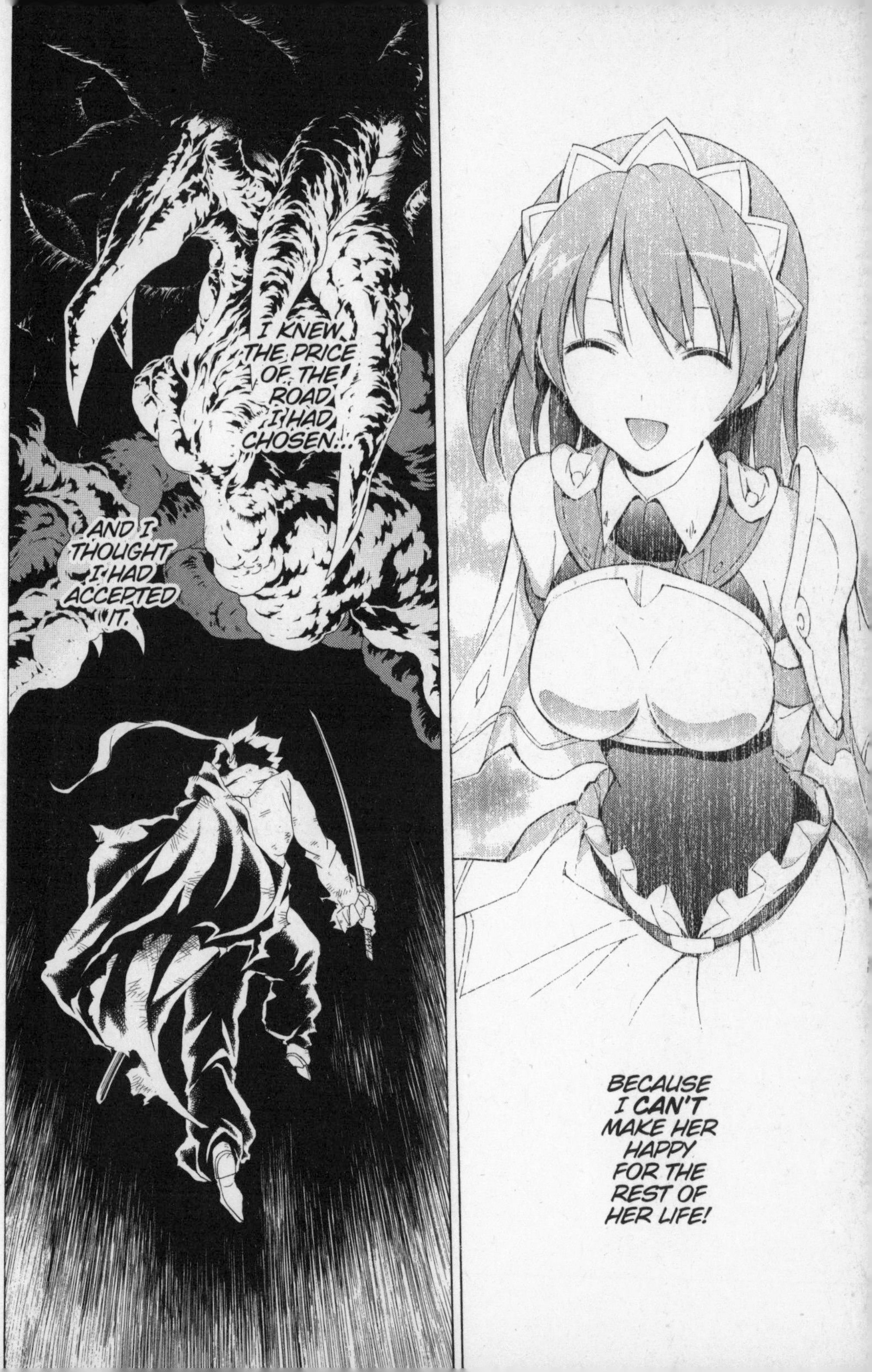
BECAUSE I CAN'T MAKE HER HAPPY FOR THE REST OF HER LIFE!
I KNEW THE PRICE OF THE ROAD I HAD CHOSEN...
AND I THOUGHT I HAD ACCEPTED IT.

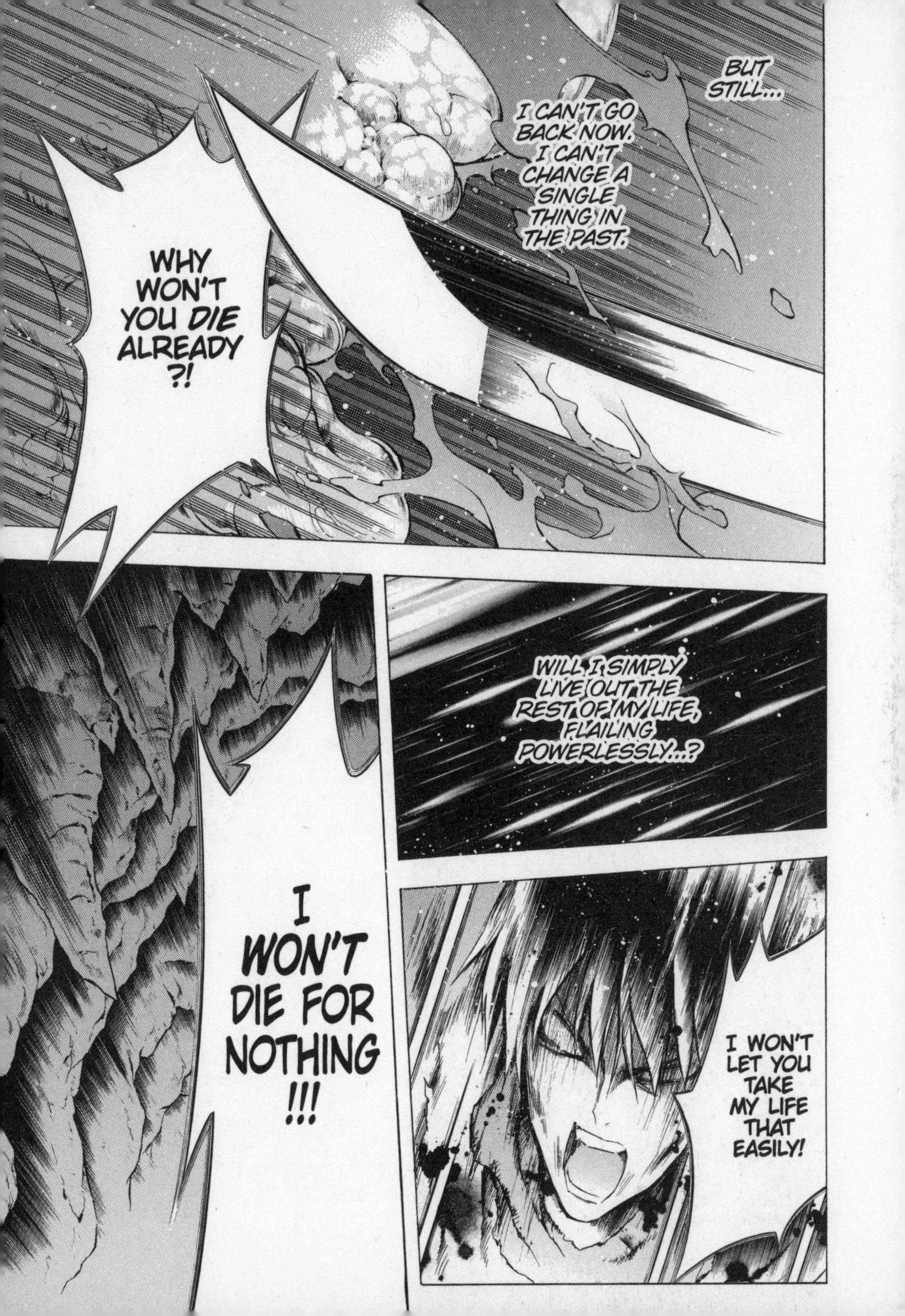
BUT STILL...
I CAN'T GO BACK NOW. I CAN'T CHANGE A SINGLE THING IN THE PAST.
WHY WON'T YOU DIE ALREADY?!
WILL I SIMPLY LIVE OUT THE REST OF MY LIFE, FLAILING POWERLESSLY...?
I WON'T LET YOU TAKE MY LIFE THAT EASILY!
I WON'T DIE FOR NOTHING!!!

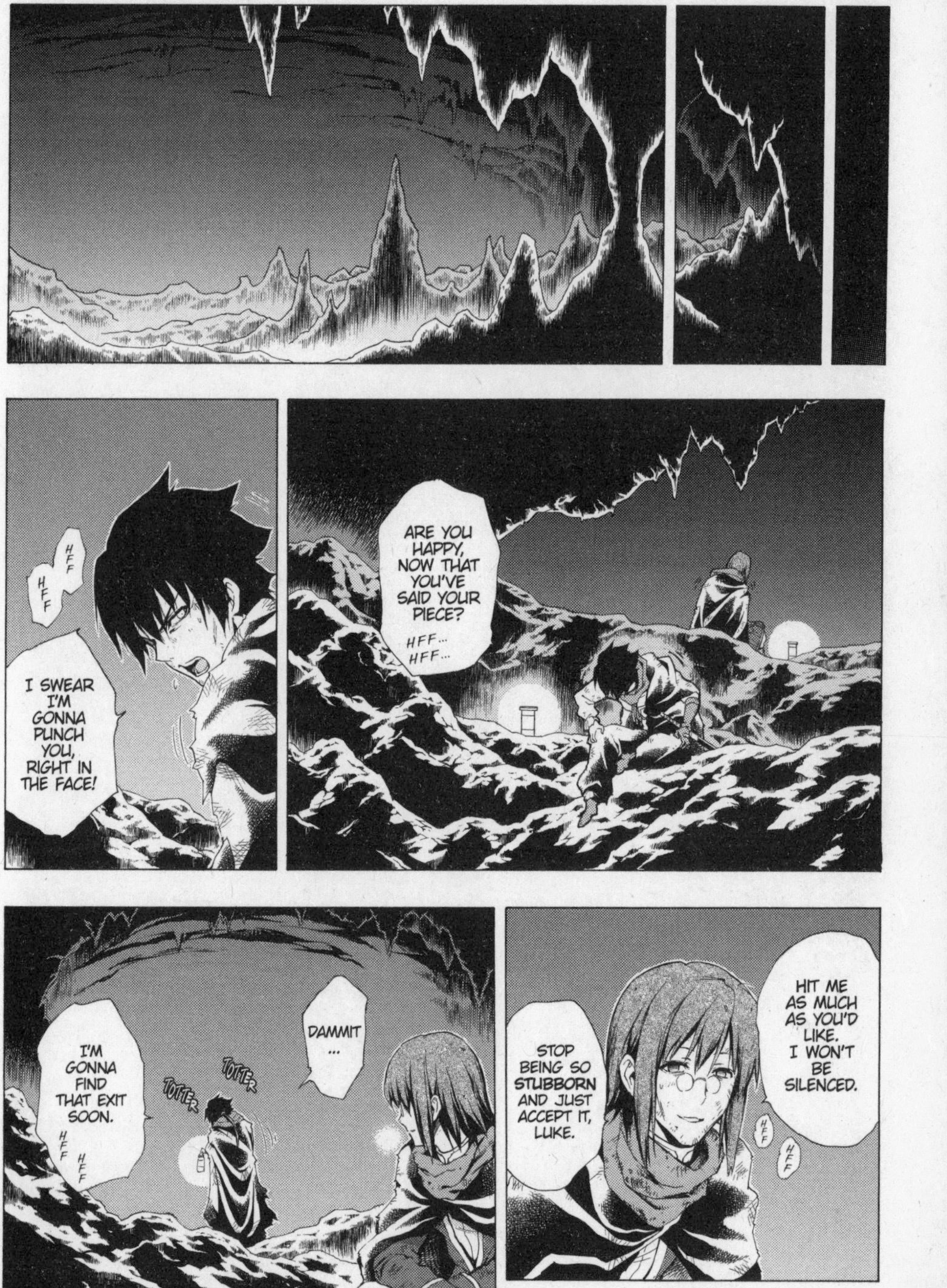
ARE YOU HAPPY, NOW THAT YOU'VE SAID YOUR PIECE?
HFF... HFF...
HFF HFF
I SWEAR I'M GONNA PUNCH YOU, RIGHT IN THE FACE!
HIT ME AS MUCH AS YOU'D LIKE. I WON'T BE SILENCED.
STOP BEING SO STUBBORN AND JUST ACCEPT IT, LUKE.
HFF HFF
DAMMIT ...
TOTTER TOTTER
I'M GONNA FIND THAT EXIT SOON.
HFF HFF

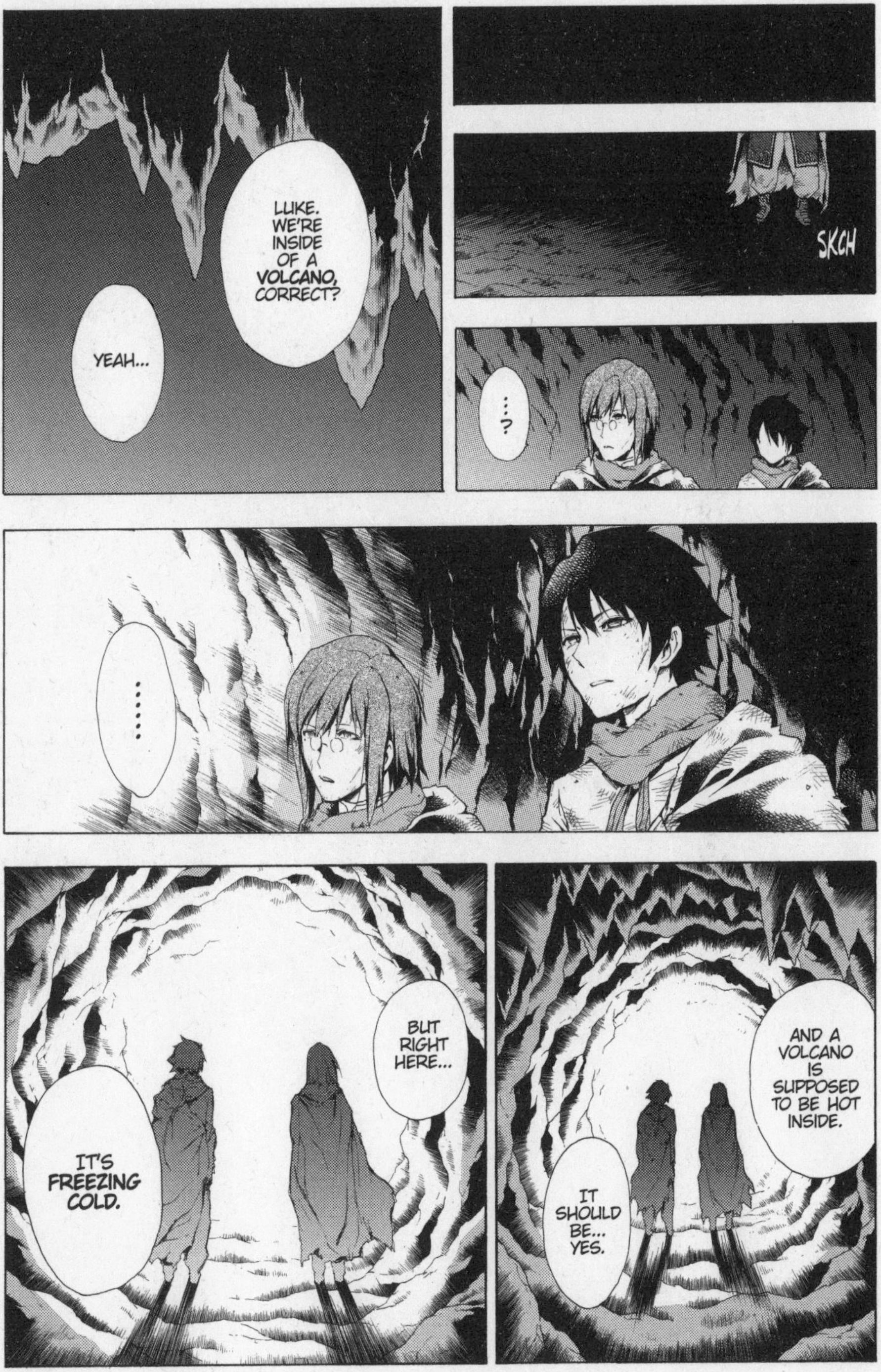
SKCH
...?
LUKE. WE'RE INSIDE OF A VOLCANO, CORRECT?
YEAH...
......
AND A VOLCANO IS SUPPOSED TO BE HOT INSIDE.
IT SHOULD BE... YES.
BUT RIGHT HERE...
IT'S FREEZING COLD.

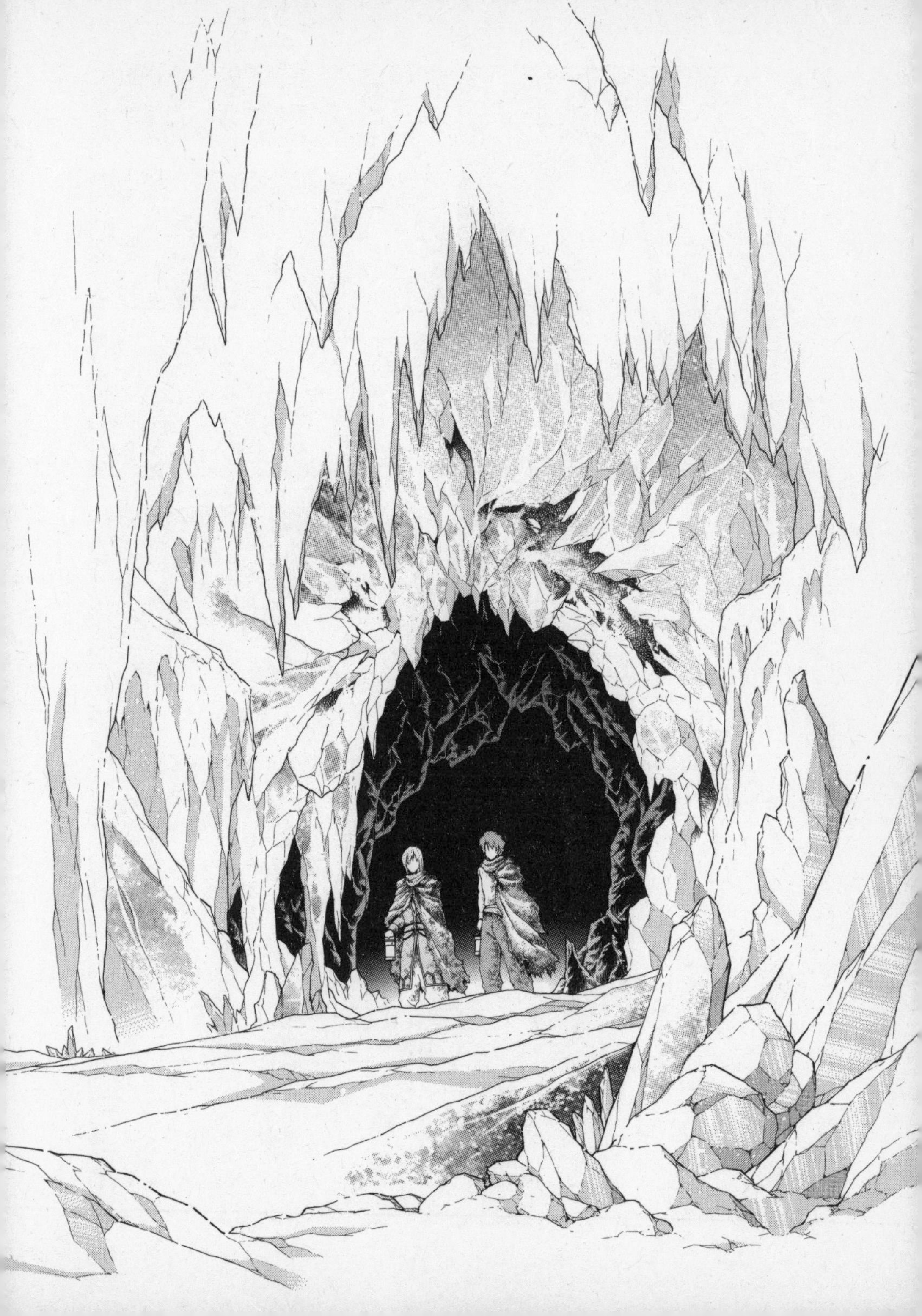

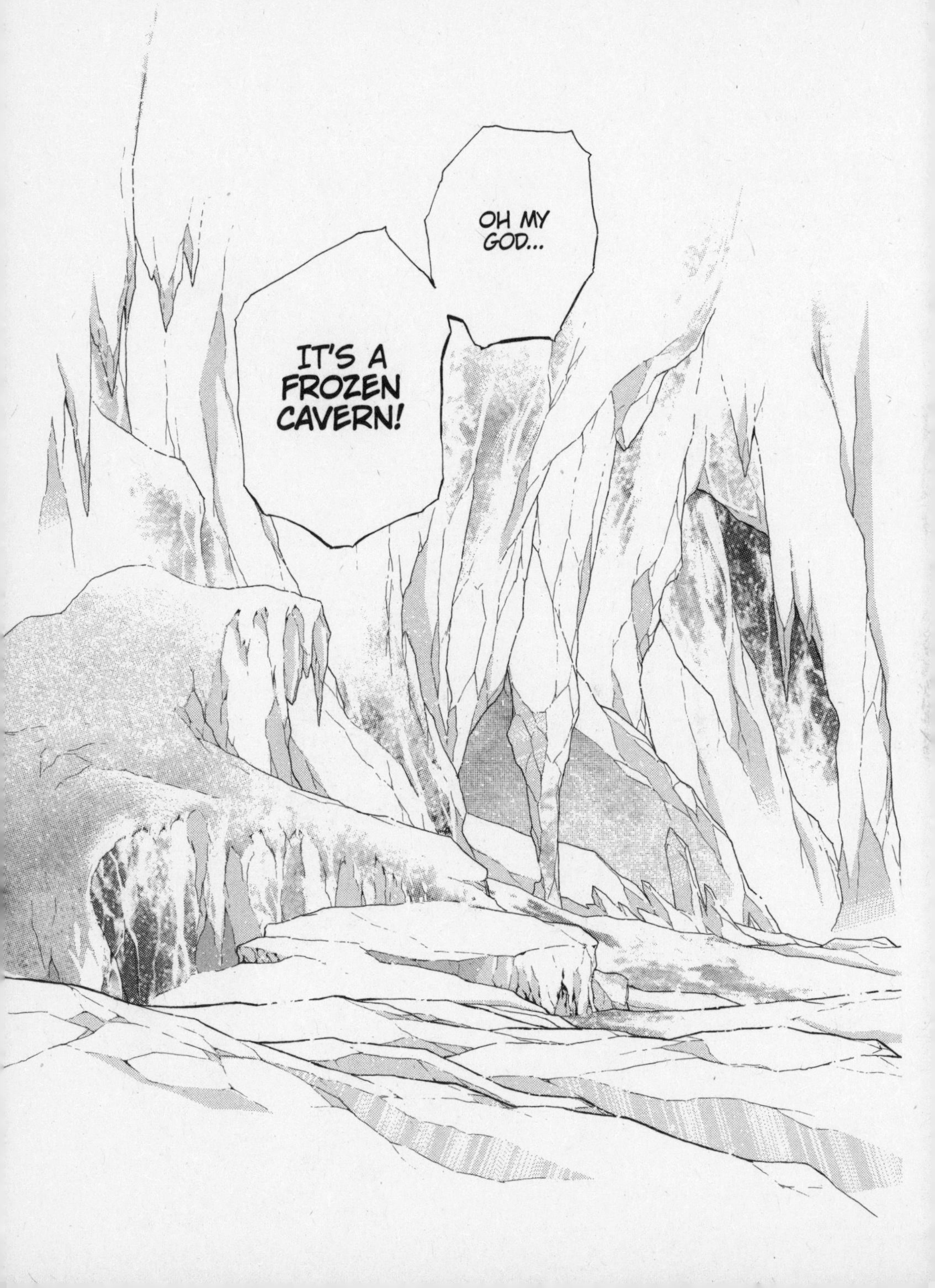
OH MY GOD...
IT'S A FROZEN CAVERN!

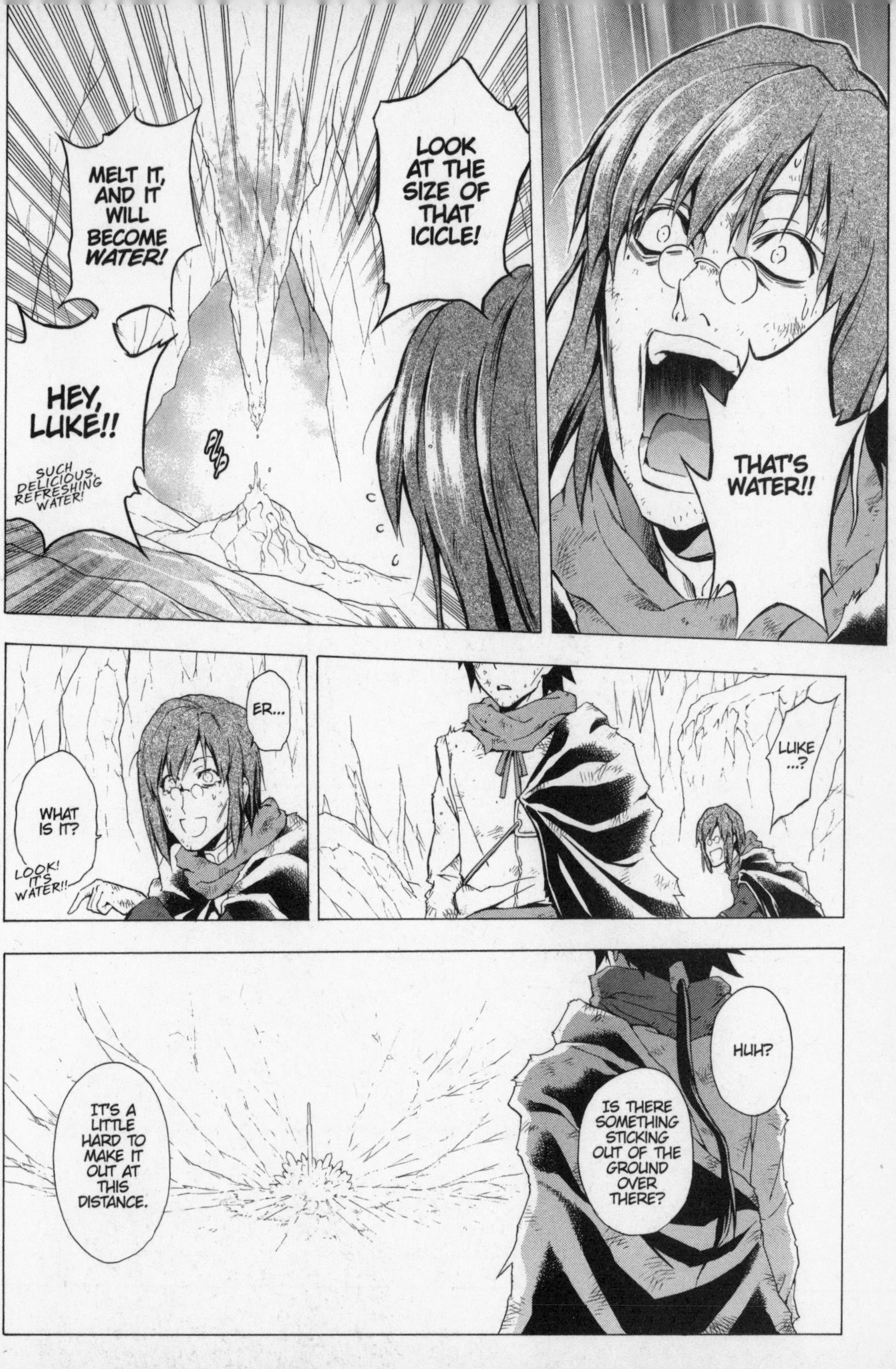
THAT'S WATER!!
LOOK AT THE SIZE OF THAT ICICLE!
MELT IT, AND IT WILL BECOME WATER!
HEY, LUKE!!
SUCH DELICIOUS, REFRESHING WATER!
LUKE ...?
ER...
WHAT IS IT?
LOOK! IT'S WATER!!
HUH?
IS THERE SOMETHING STICKING OUT OF THE GROUND OVER THERE?
IT'S A LITTLE HARD TO MAKE IT OUT AT THIS DISTANCE.

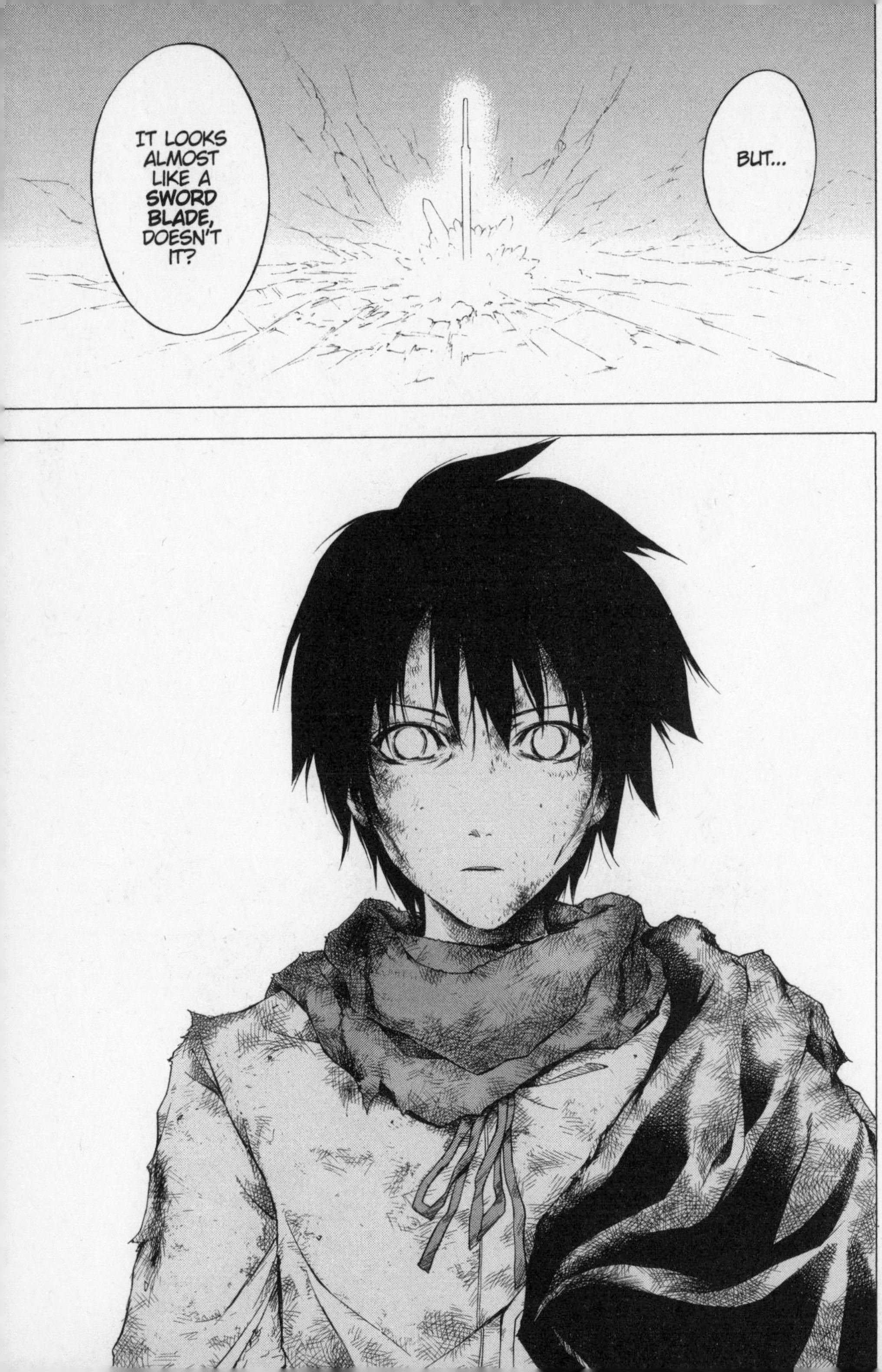
BUT...
IT LOOKS ALMOST LIKE A SWORD BLADE, DOESN'T IT?

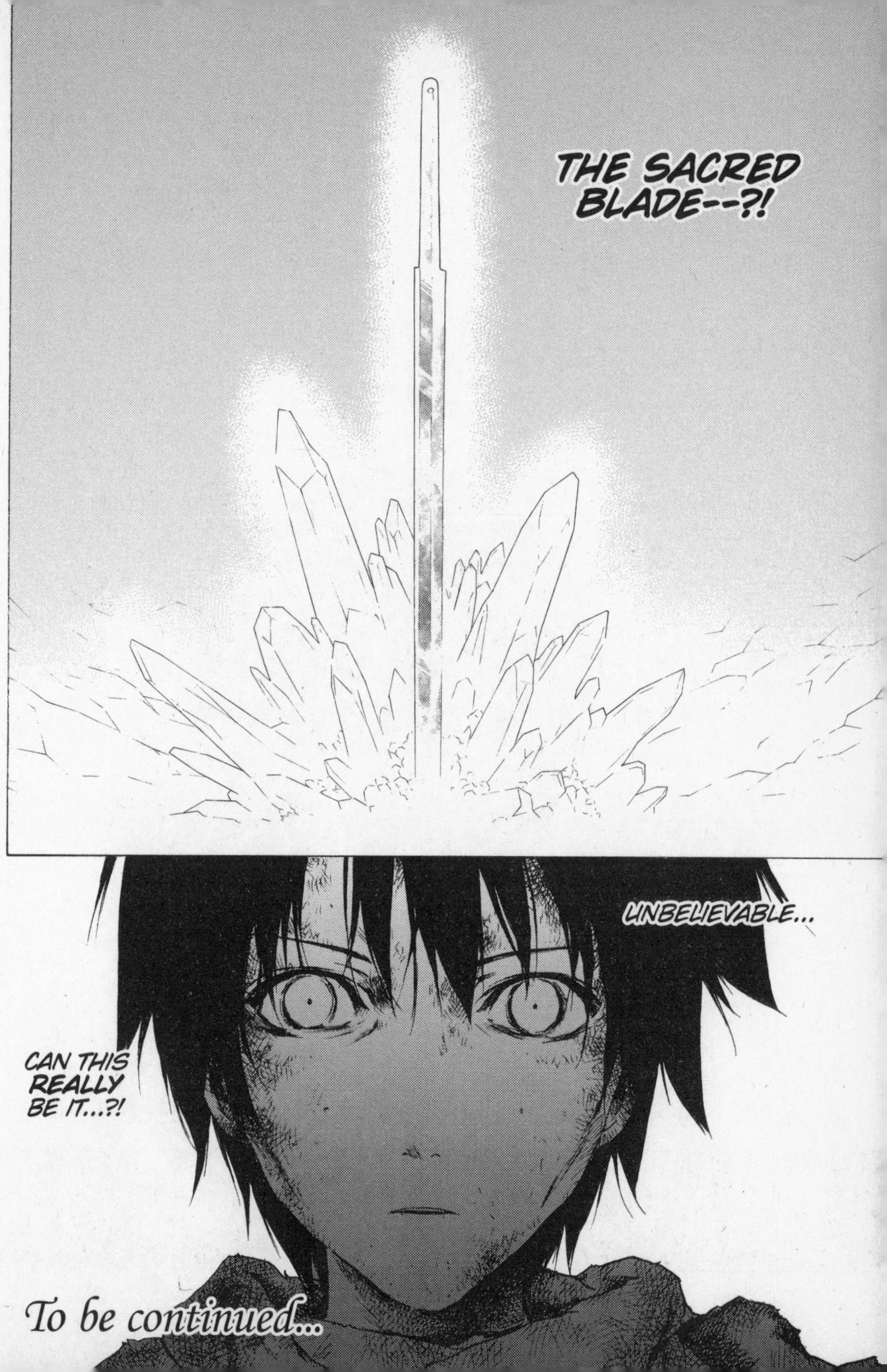
THE SACRED BLADE--?!
UNBELIEVABLE...
CAN THIS REALLY BE IT...?!
To be continued...

The Sacred Blacksmith

聖剣の刀鍛冶

アトリエ 工房リーザ atelier Liza BRANCH OFFICE EXTRA LARGE ED.

Due to high demand, this volume will bring you an extra large edition of Atelier Liza. Take a look at everyone's enthusiasm!

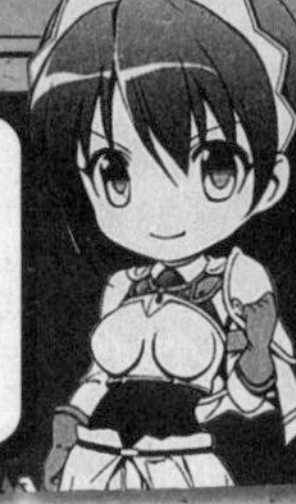

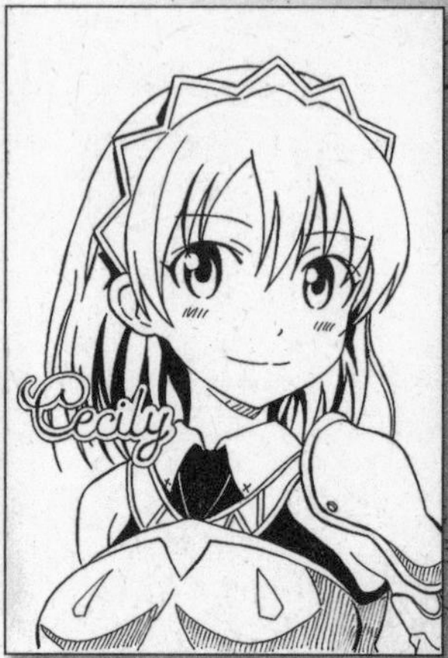

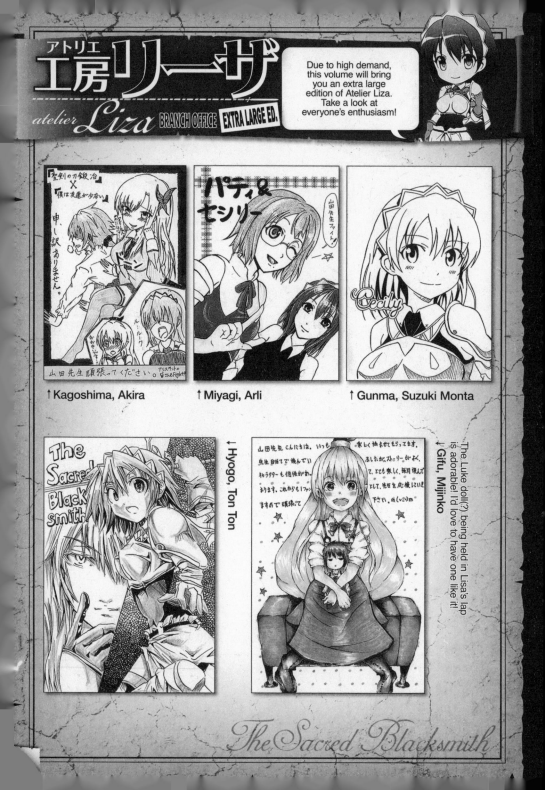

Cecily

↑ Gunma, Suzuki Monta

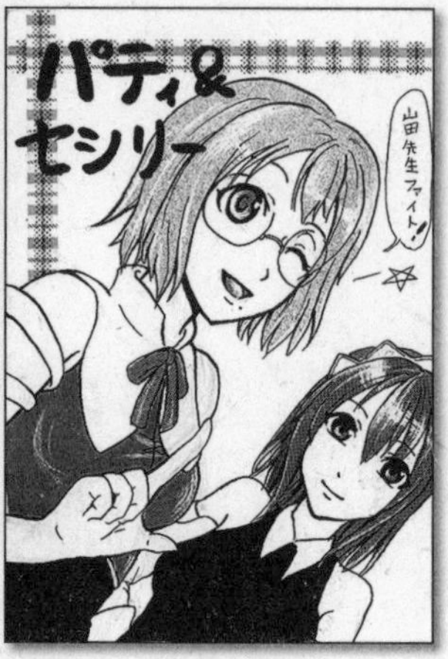

パティ＆セシリー
山田先生ファイト！

↑ Miyagi, Arli

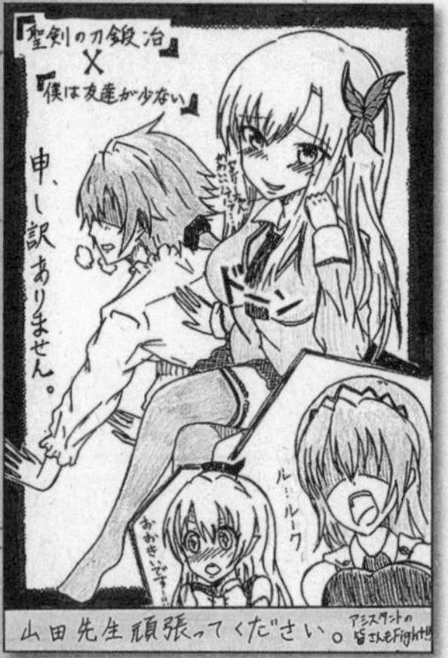

『聖剣の刀鍛冶』
X
『僕は友達が少ない』
申し訳ありません。
山田先生頑張ってください。
アシスタントの皆さんもFight!!

↑ Kagoshima, Akira

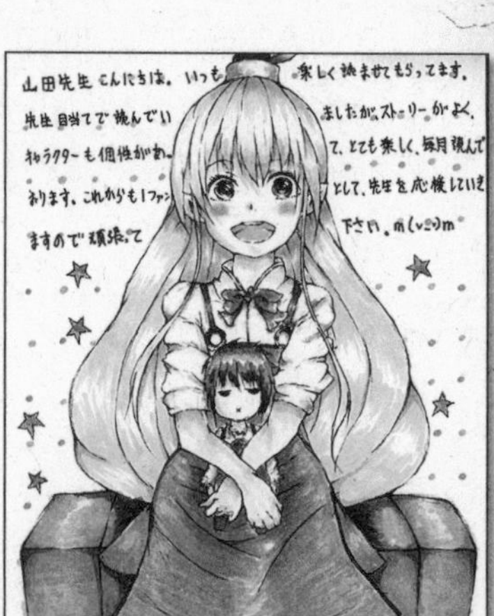

山田先生こんにちは。いつも楽しく読ませてもらってます。先生目当てで読んでいましたが、ストーリーがよく、キャラクターも個性があって、とても楽しく、毎月読んでおります。これからも1ファンとして、先生を応援していきますので頑張って下さい。m(_ _)m

← Gifu, Mijinko
The Luke doll(?) being held in Lisa's lap is adorable! I'd love to have one like it!

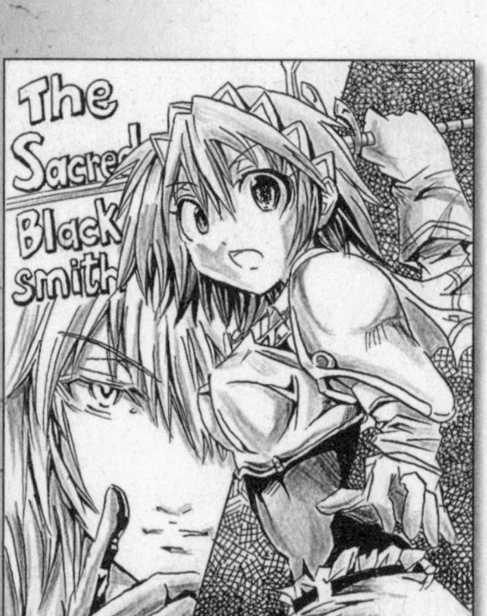

The Sacred Black smith

← Hyogo, Ton Ton

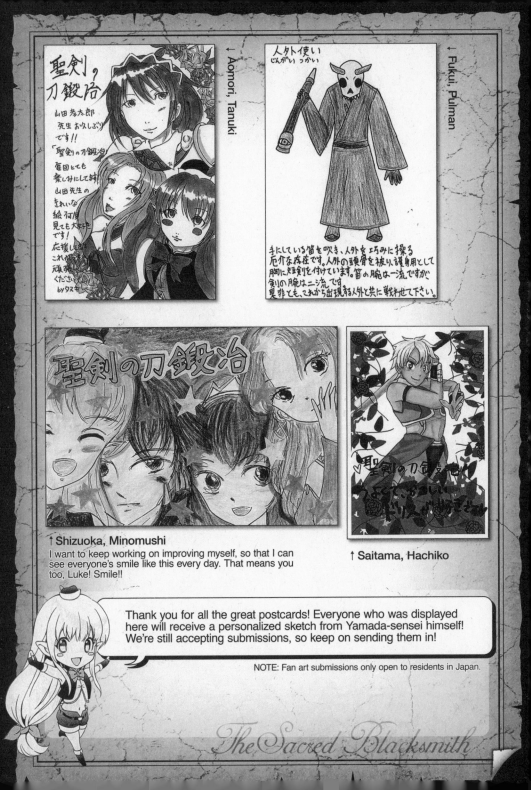

← Fukui, Pulman

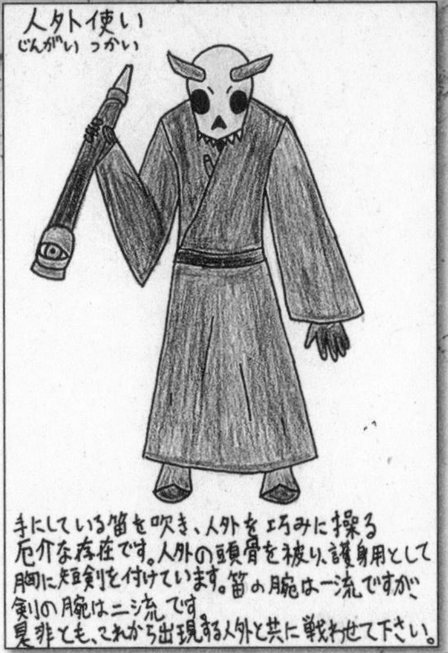
人外使い
じんがいつかい
手にしている笛を吹き、人外を巧みに操る
厄介な存在です。人外の頭骨を被り、護身用として
胸に短剣を付けています。笛の腕は一流ですが、
剣の腕は二流です
是非とも、これから出現する人外と共に戦わせて下さい。

← Aomori, Tanuki

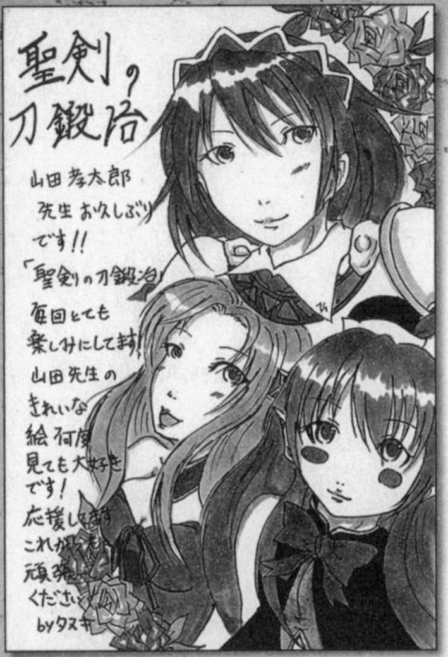
聖剣の刀鍛冶
山田孝太郎
先生お久しぶりです!!
「聖剣の刀鍛冶
毎回とても楽しみにしてます!
山田先生のきれいな絵何度見ても大好きです!

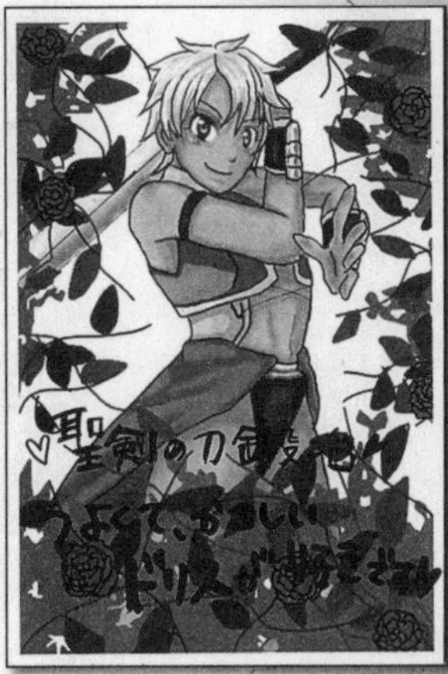
聖剣の刀鍛冶

↑ Saitama, Hachiko

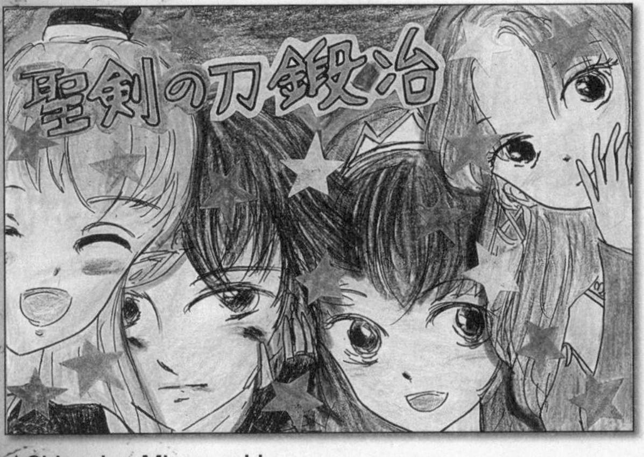
聖剣の刀鍛冶

↑ **Shizuoka, Minomushi**

I want to keep working on improving myself, so that I can see everyone's smile like this every day. That means you too, Luke! Smile!!

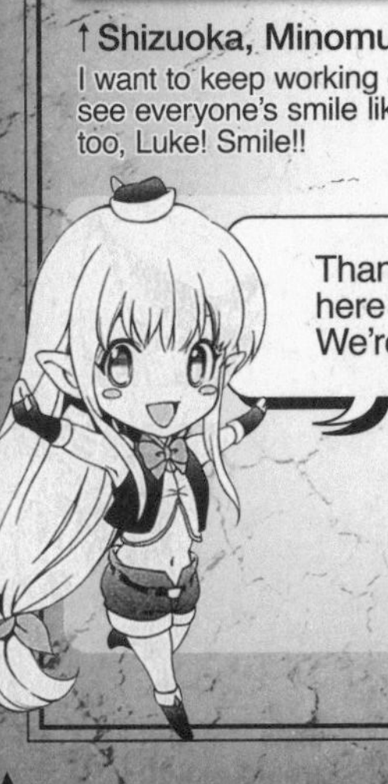

Thank you for all the great postcards! Everyone who was displayed here will receive a personalized sketch from Yamada-sensei himself! We're still accepting submissions, so keep on sending them in!

NOTE: Fan art submissions only open to residents in Japan.

The Sacred Blacksmith

Lisa's

Let's Learn Blacksmithing Corner!

Hi, everyone! It's been a while. I'm Lisa!

With the convening of the "Valbanill Meeting" and the introduction of all the VIPs from across the continent, the world that Cecily, Luke and the others live in just got a little bit bigger, didn't it? In order to make the upcoming story even more interesting, let me tell you some more about the world of *The Sacred Blacksmith!*

Class #6: The World of *The Sacred Blacksmith* ~The World~

Trapped in the clutches of an inescapable fate--
Curse the king or use him, the world must still live by him.

That strange inhuman with swords sprouting from its back charged straight towards its "king." Aria, a Demon Blade, also feels an odd sense of hatred swelling up inside of her at the mention of Valbanill.

The Imperial Crowd Power (formerly the Empire and the Crowd Powers), along with the Militant Nation, use Demon Pacts--fragments of Valbanill's power--as deterrents to prevent a continental war. This is a land that lives by spirit essence, the invisible substance exuded by Valbanill.

To the City, he is "God." To the Empire, he is "Emperor." To the Militant Nation, he is the "Beast." To the Crowd Powers, he is "Machina." Known by many names, the legendary inhuman even gave his name as a pseudonym for what was formally dubbed "The War of the Pacts." Valbanill is at the center of everything in our world.

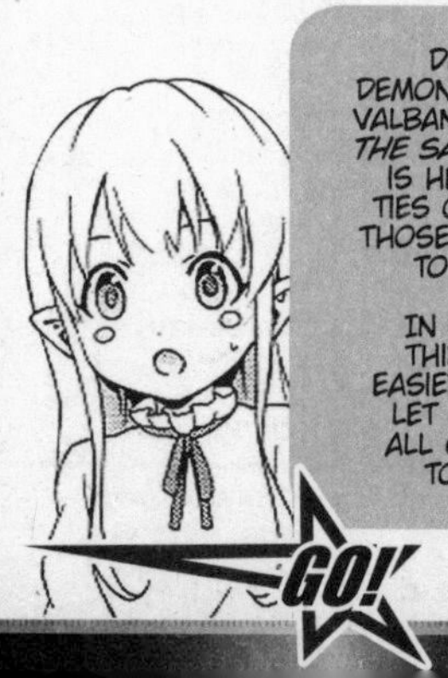
GO!

DEMON BLADES. DEMONS. SPIRIT ESSENCE. VALBANILL. THE WORLD OF *THE SACRED BLACKSMITH* IS HELD TOGETHER BY TIES OF FATE THAT BIND THOSE DISPARATE THINGS TO ONE ANOTHER.

IN ORDER TO MAKE THINGS THAT MUCH EASIER TO UNDERSTAND, LET ME EXPLAIN HOW ALL OF THESE RELATE TO EACH OTHER!

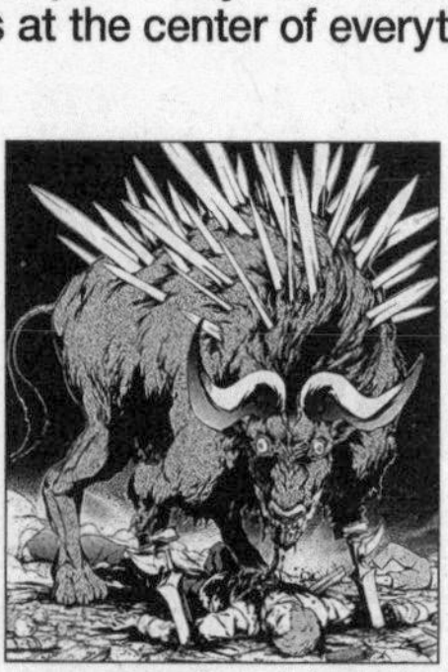

What is it that connects all of these things together? Once we discover what that is, it will make the story of *The Sacred Blacksmith* that much more intriguing!

Comprehensive Overview!

The World of The Sacred Blacksmith: WORLD SYSTEM DIAGRAM

There have been a few explanations in the main storyline already, but I have collected them all right here in one convenient location for you to read!

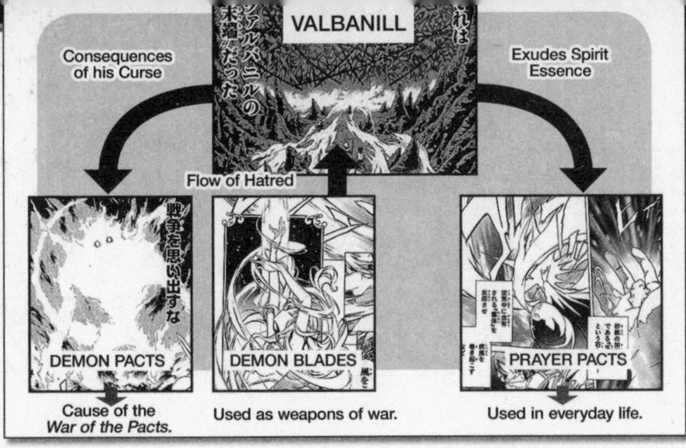

VALBANILL
ヴァルバニルの末端だった
Consequences of his Curse
Exudes Spirit Essence
Flow of Hatred
戦争を思い出すな
DEMON PACTS
DEMON BLADES
PRAYER PACTS
Cause of the *War of the Pacts.*
Used as weapons of war.
Used in everyday life.

SPIRIT ESSENCE

Spirit Essence is an invisible substance, present in the air. Prayer Pacts require it to work. Demons absorb it as a source of nutrition. The source of Spirit Essence is Valbanill itself, who naturally exudes it from its prison in Blair Volcano.

IN THE WORLD OF *THE SACRED BLACKSMITH*, THERE ARE LOTS OF OTHER CREATURES BESIDES HUMANS. LET'S GO OVER SOME OF THE ONES THAT HAVE APPEARED IN THE STORY SO FAR.

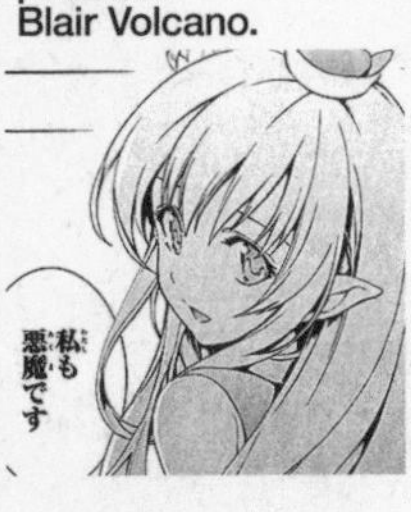

私も悪魔です

DEMON PACTS

A Demon Pact is triggered when a person chants a "Death Phrase" and makes a deal to offer a piece of their flesh to the spirits in the air. The spirits devour this flesh and initiate the person's transformation into a demon. These demons were frequently used as weapons during the War of the Pacts, but current continental law forbids their use. Death Phrases are said to be carved onto the hearts of every individual living on the continent by the same invisible spirits that are involved in the formation of Demon Pacts. In the heat of battle, priests would chant Prayer Pacts to anesthetize their victim, open their chest cavity and read the Death Phrase written on their heart. Then they would force the victim to recite it and make a Demon Pact.

DEMONS

Demons are the creatures birthed from Demon Pacts. They can take a wide variety of forms, from inanimate swords to human bodies. Both Lisa and Aria are demons. However, many mysteries still surround them.

PRAYER PACTS

A Prayer Pact occurs when a type of ore called "jewel steel" is made to resonate with the spirits in the air, causing various miraculous effects. A procedure developed by the first Housman, Prayer Pacts have a variety of uses, from powering streetlights to purifying wells to healing injuries. Given how integral Prayer Pacts are to their livelihoods, many people revere Blair Volcano--and thus, Valbanill--as a god.

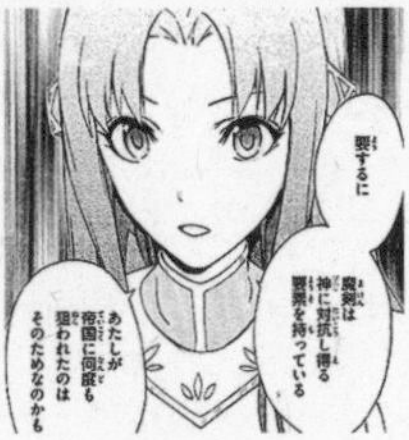

要するに
魔剣は神に対抗し得る要素を持っている
あたしが帝国に何度も狙われたのはそのためなのかも

DEMON BLADES

Demon Blades are weapons with special powers, created by Demon Pacts. For these weapons to have the ability to transform into humans--such as Aria and Evadne--the instigator of the Demon Pact must have a deep-seated hatred towards "God." Since most equate "God" with Valbanill, these Demon Blades have the power to fight against and even damage the creature. Accordingly, the Empire puts great effort into tracking down and collecting Demon Blades.

INHUMANS

Any creature not human is considered an "inhuman." It's a very broad identifier, where any non-human creature, from simple stray dogs up to tentacle beasts, carnivorous plants and even demons fall into this category.

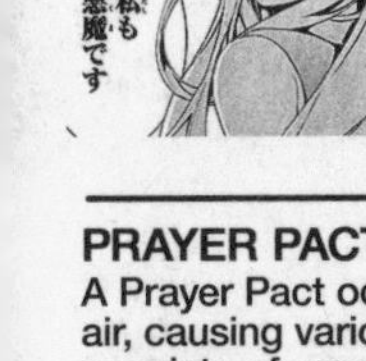

WE KEEP FINDING OUT MORE AND MORE ABOUT THE WORLD OF *THE SACRED BLACKSMITH!* THERE'S SO MUCH GOING ON... WHAT'S GOING TO HAPPEN NEXT? WE HAVEN'T EVEN SETTLED THE SCORE WITH SIEGFRIED YET! I CAN'T WAIT TO SEE WHAT'S COMING!!

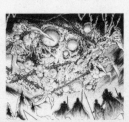

VALBANILL

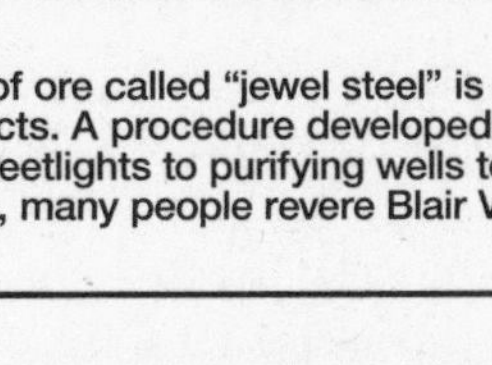

A legendary inhuman, Valbanill's name has even been used as a nickname for the War of the Pacts. The stories say that centuries ago, he would rage across the continent, flattening mountains, cleaving the earth and drinking the ocean dry. He was eventually sealed inside Blair Volcano with a special sword. In the present day, it is said that the seal holding him won't last for much longer, perhaps only a year...

See You Next Time!

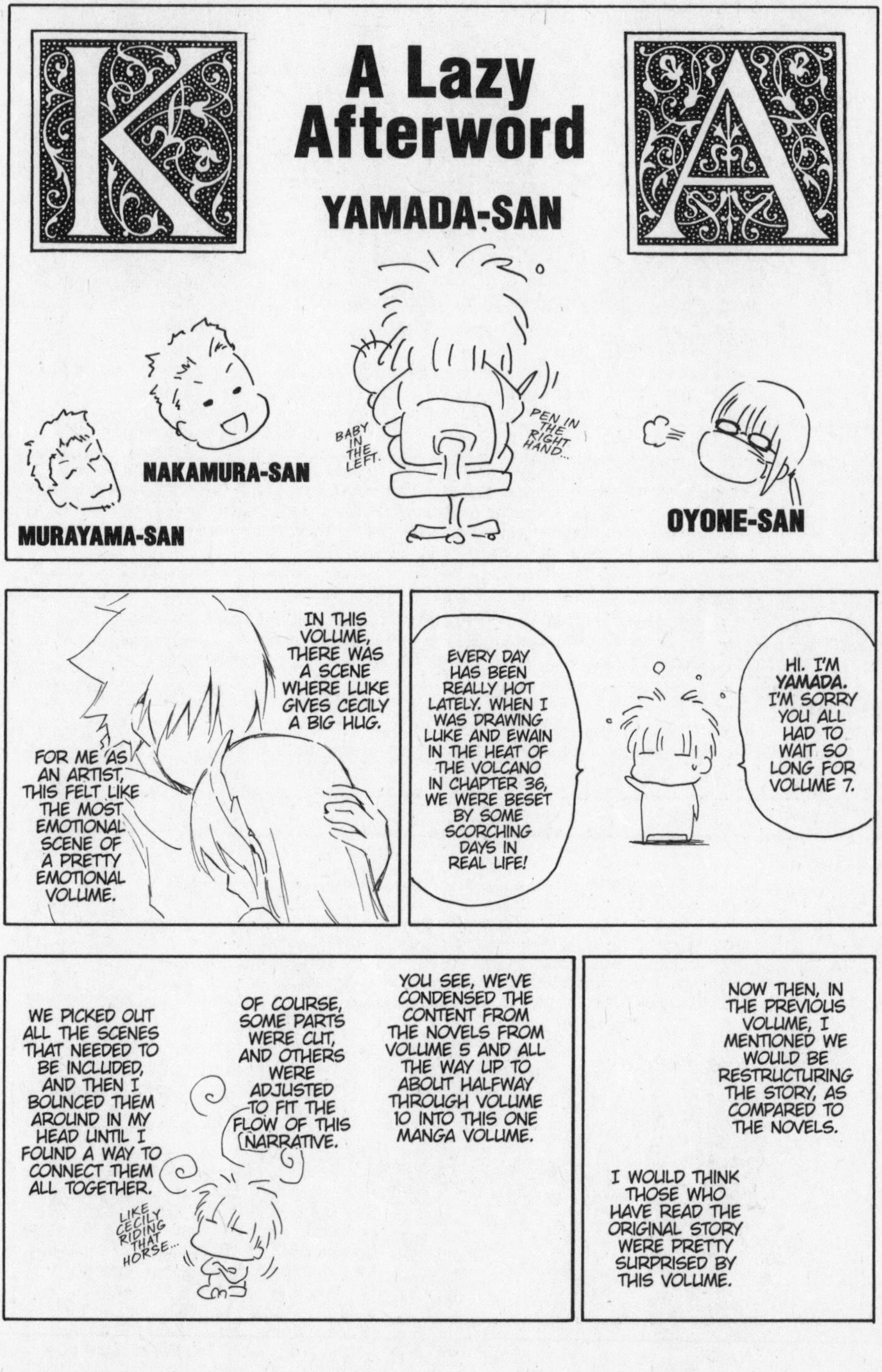
K
A Lazy Afterword
A
YAMADA-SAN
OYONE-SAN
PEN IN THE RIGHT HAND...
BABY IN THE LEFT.
NAKAMURA-SAN
MURAYAMA-SAN
HI. I'M YAMADA. I'M SORRY YOU ALL HAD TO WAIT SO LONG FOR VOLUME 7.
EVERY DAY HAS BEEN REALLY HOT LATELY. WHEN I WAS DRAWING LUKE AND EWAIN IN THE HEAT OF THE VOLCANO IN CHAPTER 36, WE WERE BESET BY SOME SCORCHING DAYS IN REAL LIFE!
IN THIS VOLUME, THERE WAS A SCENE WHERE LUKE GIVES CECILY A BIG HUG.
FOR ME AS AN ARTIST, THIS FELT LIKE THE MOST EMOTIONAL SCENE OF A PRETTY EMOTIONAL VOLUME.
NOW THEN, IN THE PREVIOUS VOLUME, I MENTIONED WE WOULD BE RESTRUCTURING THE STORY, AS COMPARED TO THE NOVELS.
I WOULD THINK THOSE WHO HAVE READ THE ORIGINAL STORY WERE PRETTY SURPRISED BY THIS VOLUME.
YOU SEE, WE'VE CONDENSED THE CONTENT FROM THE NOVELS FROM VOLUME 5 AND ALL THE WAY UP TO ABOUT HALFWAY THROUGH VOLUME 10 INTO THIS ONE MANGA VOLUME.
OF COURSE, SOME PARTS WERE CUT, AND OTHERS WERE ADJUSTED TO FIT THE FLOW OF THIS NARRATIVE.
WE PICKED OUT ALL THE SCENES THAT NEEDED TO BE INCLUDED, AND THEN I BOUNCED THEM AROUND IN MY HEAD UNTIL I FOUND A WAY TO CONNECT THEM ALL TOGETHER.
LIKE CECILY RIDING THAT HORSE...

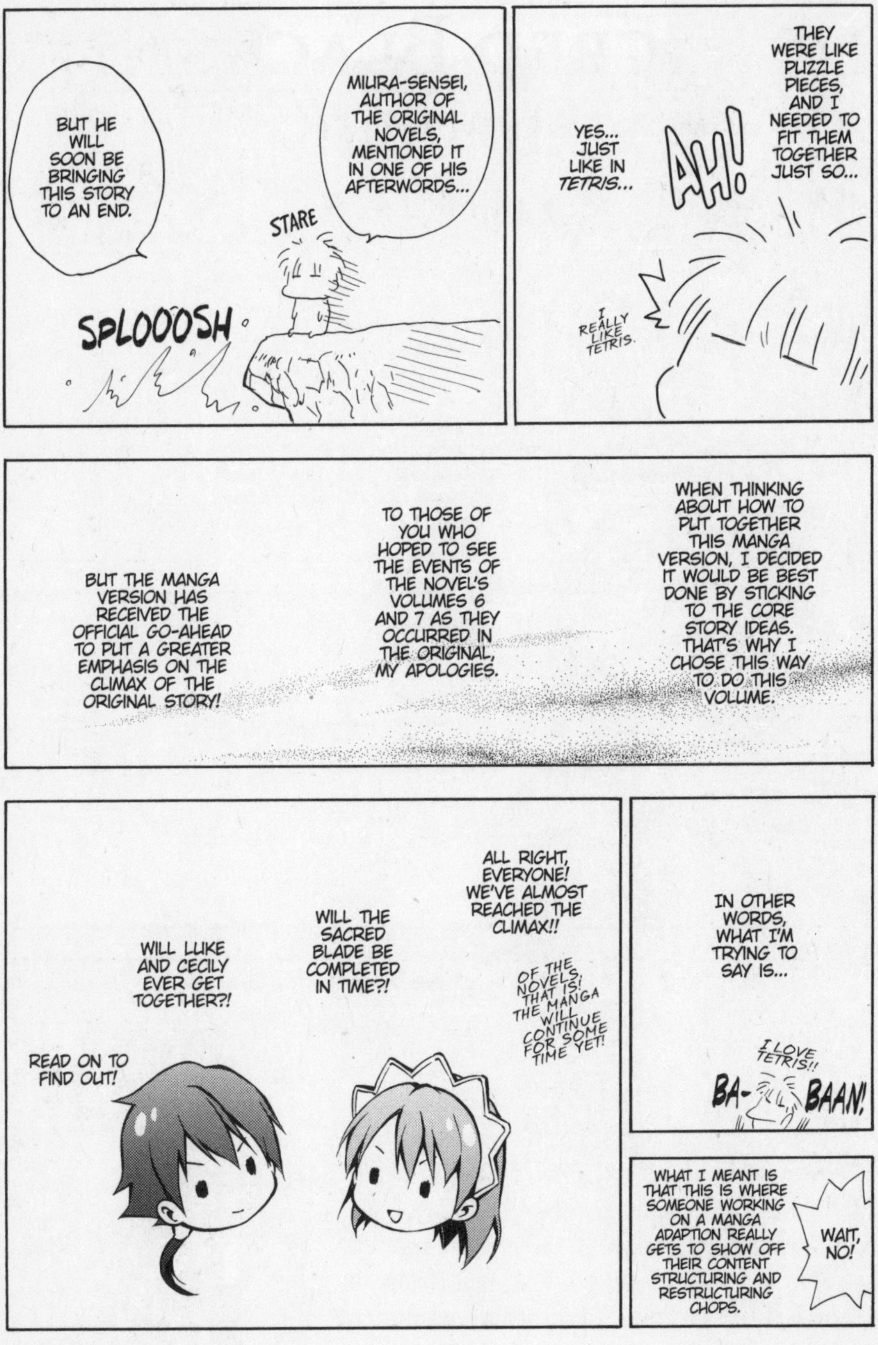
THEY WERE LIKE PUZZLE PIECES, AND I NEEDED TO FIT THEM TOGETHER JUST SO...
AH!
YES... JUST LIKE IN TETRIS...
I REALLY LIKE TETRIS.
MIURA-SENSEI, AUTHOR OF THE ORIGINAL NOVELS, MENTIONED IT IN ONE OF HIS AFTERWORDS...
STARE
BUT HE WILL SOON BE BRINGING THIS STORY TO AN END.
SPLOOOSH
WHEN THINKING ABOUT HOW TO PUT TOGETHER THIS MANGA VERSION, I DECIDED IT WOULD BE BEST DONE BY STICKING TO THE CORE STORY IDEAS. THAT'S WHY I CHOSE THIS WAY TO DO THIS VOLUME.
TO THOSE OF YOU WHO HOPED TO SEE THE EVENTS OF THE NOVEL'S VOLUMES 6 AND 7 AS THEY OCCURRED IN THE ORIGINAL, MY APOLOGIES.
BUT THE MANGA VERSION HAS RECEIVED THE OFFICIAL GO-AHEAD TO PUT A GREATER EMPHASIS ON THE CLIMAX OF THE ORIGINAL STORY!
IN OTHER WORDS, WHAT I'M TRYING TO SAY IS...
I LOVE TETRIS!!
BA-BAAN!
WAIT, NO!
WHAT I MEANT IS THAT THIS IS WHERE SOMEONE WORKING ON A MANGA ADAPTION REALLY GETS TO SHOW OFF THEIR CONTENT STRUCTURING AND RESTRUCTURING CHOPS.
ALL RIGHT, EVERYONE! WE'VE ALMOST REACHED THE CLIMAX!!
OF THE NOVELS, THAT IS! THE MANGA WILL CONTINUE FOR SOME TIME YET!
WILL THE SACRED BLADE BE COMPLETED IN TIME?!
WILL LUKE AND CECILY EVER GET TOGETHER?!
READ ON TO FIND OUT!

SEVEN SEAS ENTERTAINMENT PRESENTS

THE SACRED BLACKSMITH

art by **KOTARO YAMADA** / story by **ISAO MIURA**

Original Character Designs by **LUNA**

VOLUME 7

TRANSLATION
Adrienne Beck

ADAPTATION
Janet Houck

LETTERING
Roland Amago

LAYOUT
Bambi Eloriaga-Amago

COVER DESIGN
Nicky Lim

PROOFREADER
Shanti Whitesides

MANAGING EDITOR
Adam Arnold

PUBLISHER
Jason DeAngelis

THE SACRED BLACKSMITH VOL. 7
©2012 Kotaro Yamada, ©2012 Isao Miura
Edited by MEDIA FACTORY.
First published in Japan in 2012 by KADOKAWA CORPORATION, Tokyo.
English translation rights reserved by Seven Seas Entertainment, LLC.
under the license from KADOKAWA CORPORATION, Tokyo.

Seven Seas books may be purchased in bulk for educational, business, or promotional use. For information on bulk purchases, please contact Macmillan Corporate & Premium Sales Department at 1-800-221-7945 (ext 5442) or write specialmarkets@macmillan.com.

Seven Seas and the Seven Seas logo are trademarks of Seven Seas Entertainment, LLC. All rights reserved.

ISBN: 978-1-626921-21-4

Printed in Canada

First Printing: March 2015

10 9 8 7 6 5 4 3 2 1

FOLLOW US ONLINE: *www.gomanga.com*

READING DIRECTIONS

This book reads from *right to left*, Japanese style. If this is your first time reading manga, you start reading from the top right panel on each page and take it from there... numbered diagram... first, but you'll ge...